Connecticut
REAL ESTATE
Practice & Law

TWELFTH EDITION

Katherine A. Pancak

Dearborn

A Kaplan Real Estate Education Company

President: Dr. Andrew Temte
Chief Learning Officer: Dr. Tim Smaby
Vice President, Real Estate Education: Asha Alsobrooks
Development Editor: Trude Irons

CONNECTICUT REAL ESTATE PRACTICE & LAW TWELFTH EDITION
© 2011 by Kaplan, Inc.
Published by DF Institute, Inc., d/b/a Dearborn Real Estate Education
332 Front St. S., Suite 501
La Crosse, WI 54601
www.dearbornRE.com

Printed in the United States of America
10   11   12   10   9   8   7   6   5   4   3   2   1
ISBN: 978-1-4277-2782-4 / 1-4277-2782-1
PPN: 1510-2712

Contents

Preface   x

Acknowledgments   xii

CHAPTER 1

Real Estate Brokerage and Agency   1

Overview   1

Licensing Law   2

Agency Law   5

Types of Agency Relationships   8

Broker Compensation   11

Record Retention   16

Web Links   16

Chapter 1 Quiz   23

CHAPTER 2

Listing and Buyer Agency Agreements   25

Overview   25

Agency Agreements   25

Content of Listing and Buyer Agency Agreements   27

Net Listings   28

Obligations Associated with Exclusive Agreements   28

Fair Housing   29

Disclosure   29

Advertising   30

Record Retention   31

Web Link   32

Chapter 2 Quiz   51

CHAPTER 3

Interest in Real Estate   53

Overview   53

Dower and Curtesy   53

Homestead Property   54

Deed Restrictions   54

Easements by Prescription   54

License   56

Water Rights   56

Web Links   57

Chapter 3 Quiz   58

CHAPTER 4

Forms of Real Estate Ownership   59

Overview   59

Co-Ownership   59

Partitions   60

Trusts   61

Ownership of Real Estate by Business Organizations   61

Common Interest Ownership Act   62

Web Links   66

Chapter 4 Quiz   67

CHAPTER 5

Legal Descriptions   68

Overview   68

Metes-and-Bounds Description   68

Land Surveyors   70

Government Survey System   70

Lost Boundary   70

Common Interest Ownership   70

Web Link   71

Chapter 5 Quiz   72

CHAPTER 6

Real Estate Taxes and Other Liens   73

Overview   73

Property Taxes   73

Capital Gains Tax   76

Conveyance Tax   77

Other Liens and Transfer Taxes   77

Web Links   78

Chapter 6 Quiz   79

CHAPTER 7

Real Estate Contracts   81

Overview   81

Broker's Authority to Prepare Documents   81

Standard Contractual Requirements   82

Real Estate Contracts   83

Residential Property Condition Disclosure   86

Disclosure of Off-Site Conditions   87

Web Links   87

Chapter 7 Quiz   104

C H A P T E R   8

Transfer of Title   105

Overview   105

Deeds of Conveyance   105

Real Estate Conveyance Taxes   106

Adverse Possession   109

Transfer of a Deceased Person's Property   110

Web Links   112

Chapter 8 Quiz   113

C H A P T E R   9

Title Records   115

Overview   115

The Necessity to Record   115

Evidence of Title   117

Marketable Record Title Act   120

Web Links   121

Chapter 9 Quiz   122

C H A P T E R   10

Real Estate License Law   123

Overview   123

Connecticut Real Estate Commission   123

Activities Requiring a License   124

Licensing Procedure   126

Maintaining a Real Estate License   131

Conduct of Licensees   132

Suspension or Revocation of a License   139

Real Estate Guaranty Fund   140

Other Licensing Laws   141

Web Links   142

Chapter 10 Quiz   143

CHAPTER 11

Real Estate Financing: Principles/Practice   147

Overview   147

Mortgage Deed and Note   147

Mortgage Brokerage   149

Predatory Lending   151

Mortgage Foreclosure   151

Sources of Mortgage Funds   155

Home Mortgage Disclosure Act   157

Web Links   158

Chapter 11 Quiz   159

CHAPTER 12

Leases   160

Overview   160

Lease   160

Leasehold Estates   161

Landlord and Tenant Act   161

Summary Process (Actual Eviction)   168

Fair Rent Commission   170

Nonresident Landlord Registration   170

Web Links   171

Chapter 12 Quiz   176

CHAPTER 13

Real Estate Appraisal   178

Overview   178

Connecticut Real Estate Appraisal Commission   178

Who Must Be Licensed   179

License Categories   179

Obtaining a License   180

Federal Registry   182

License Renewal   183

Appraisal Standards   183

Appraisers Licensed in Another State   183

Appraisal Management Companies   185

Web Links   186

Chapter 13 Quiz   187

C H A P T E R   14

Land-Use Controls and Property Development 188

Overview 188

Planning and Zoning 188

New Home Construction 195

Home Improvement Contractors 196

Commercial/Industrial Construction 197

Private Land-Use Control 197

Building Accessibility 197

Connecticut Interstate Land Sales 198

Eminent Domain 199

Web Links 199

Chapter 14 Quiz 200

C H A P T E R   15

Fair Housing 202

Overview 202

Understanding Fair Housing Laws 203

Protected Classes in Connecticut 203

Discriminatory Housing Practices 204

Administrative Enforcement 207

Nonmaterial Fact 209

Accessibility Requirements 209

Public Accommodations Law 209

Implications for Connecticut Real Estate Brokers and Salespeople 210

Web Links 210

Chapter 15 Quiz 211

C H A P T E R   16

Closing the Real Estate Transaction 213

Overview 213

Closing Process 213

At the Closing 215

Chapter 16 Quiz 217

C H A P T E R   17

Environmental Issues and the Real Estate Transaction 218

Overview 218

Asbestos 218

Lead-Based Paint 219

Radon 219

Mold 220

Foam and Drywall   220

Water Wells and Groundwater Contamination   220

Water Diversion   221

Underground Storage Tanks   221

Hazardous Waste and Other Contamination   221

Waste Disposal Sites   222

Web Links   223

Chapter 17 Quiz   225

APPENDIX A
Real Estate Securities   227

Overview   227

Types of Real Estate Securities   227

Connecticut Regulations on the Sale of Real Estate Securities   228

Real Property Securities   229

Real Estate Syndicate Securities   232

Web Links   234

Appendix A Quiz   235

APPENDIX B
State Sources of Information   236

APPENDIX C
Connecticut Transaction Documentation   241

APPENDIX D
Connecticut Specific Real Estate Math Applications   242

Percentages   242

Prorations (Chapter 16)   245

APPENDIX E
Electronic Signatures and Contracts   248

Introduction   248

Connecticut Law and "Wet" Signatures   248

Enter Congress   249

Electronic Records and Signature in Commerce Act   249

Protection for Consumers   250

Enter the Connecticut Legislature   250

Advice for REALTORS®   252

Summary   252

Answer Key   254

Practice Exam   265

Practice Exam Answers   277

Index   282

Preface

Connecticut Real Estate: Practice & Law is a key component of Dearborn Real Estate Education's complete principles learning system. This system offers students and educators a complete turnkey package for prelicense real estate courses, continuing education, and professional enrichment. As the demographics and structure of the real estate industry change, Dearborn Real Estate Education is helping students, instructors, and practitioners adapt to this new environment by providing more accessible and versatile educational tools.

This book can be used with equal effectiveness with *any* of our principles books or software:

- *Modern Real Estate Practice*
- *Mastering Real Estate Principles*
- *Real Estate Fundamentals*
- *National Real Estate Principles*

Connecticut Real Estate: Practice & Law also offers current real estate professionals a practical handbook of Connecticut's real estate law and rules, along with the most current developments. Every effort has been made to ensure that the information contained in this book is both relevant and current. There are also numerous references to Connecticut statutes and the Real Estate Commission's Rules and Regulations, so readers can look up the law themselves online.

Connecticut Real Estate: Practice & Law will help readers prepare for the state portion of the real estate licensing examination; the book does not address the general or national topics of the real estate examination. Students are advised to first read the relevant material in one of the main principles books or software, then turn to *Connecticut Real Estate: Practice & Law* for a focus on Connecticut's particular laws and practices as they relate to that subject. *This book is designed to discuss the statutes, rules, and practical real estate issues that arise in the state of Connecticut.*

■ HOW TO USE THIS BOOK

The conversion table on the next page provides a quick and easy reference for using *Connecticut Real Estate: Practice & Law* in conjunction with various principles books. For instance, *Connecticut Real Estate: Practice & Law*'s Chapter 16, "Closing the Real Estate Transaction," may be read in conjunction with Chapter 22 in *Modern Real Estate Practice*, 18th Edition; Chapter 17 in *Real Estate Fundamentals*, 7th Edition; Chapter 12 in *Mastering Real Estate Principles*, 4th Edition; and Unit 22 in *National Real Estate Principles* software. The chart also provides students with a useful reference to the *Guide to Passing the PSI Real Estate Exam*, 5th Edition, by Lawrence Sager.

Chapter Conversion Table

Connecticut Real Estate Practice & Law, 12th Edition	Modern Real Estate Practice, 18th Edition	Real Estate Fundamentals, 7th Edition Update	Mastering Real Estate Principles, 5th Edition	Modern Real Estate Principles	Guide to Passing The PSI Real Estate Exam, 6th Edition Update
1. Real Estate Brokerage and Agency	4, 5	7	13	4, 5	7, 14
2. Listing Agreements and Buyer Agency Agreements	6	7, 8	15	6	9
3. Interests in Real Estate	7	3	4, 7	7	3
4. Forms of Real Estate Ownership	8	5	9	8	3
5. Legal Descriptions	9	2	6	9	3
6. Real Estate Taxes and Other Liens	10	10	5, 25	10	10
7. Real Estate Contracts	11	8	14	11	9
8. Transfer of Title	12	4	10	12	10
9. Title Records	13	6	11	13	10
10. Real Estate License Laws	—	—	16	—	—
11. Real Estate Financing: Principles/Practice	14, 15	12, 13	Unit VII	14, 15	6, 14
12. Leases	16	9	8	16	13
13. Real Estate Appraisal	18	11	Unit VI	18	5
14. Land-Use Controls and Property Development	19	14	3	19	4
15. Fair Housing and Ethical Practices	20	15	17	20	11
16. Closing the Real Estate Transaction	22	17	12	22	10
17. Environmental Issues and the Real Estate Transaction	21	16	3	—	4

Acknowledgments

The publisher and author would like to thank reviewers Teresa Sirico and Judith Johannsen, who both provided professional guidance and expertise on changes needed for this new edition.

Recognition and thanks are given to Teresa Sirico for writing the final exam questions and to Eugene Marconi for contributing Appendix E.

Thanks also go to the Connecticut Association of REALTORS®, Inc., and Bridgeport Board of REALTORS®, Inc., for permission to reprint forms and documents in this edition.

■ ABOUT THE AUTHOR

Katherine A. Pancak is Professor in Residence of Finance and Real Estate at the University of Connecticut School of Business. She is also a member of the faculty in the University's Center for Real Estate and Urban Economic Studies, an internationally recognized academic institute for real estate teaching, research, and service. Prior to joining the University, she was a practicing attorney specializing in the area of real estate.

The author has again dedicated this edition to her parents, Ellen and John Stadtmueller, for all their love and support and for instilling in her a passion for both real estate and education.

CHAPTER

1

Real Estate Brokerage and Agency

■ OVERVIEW

Real estate *brokerage* is the business of bringing parties together in a real estate transaction. Connecticut law requires that people and entities working in brokerage have a *real estate license*. There are two categories of license: broker and salesperson. A broker is defined as a person who or an entity that is paid a fee to act for another person in the purchase, sale, rental, or exchange of real estate. A *salesperson* must be affiliated with and supervised by a real estate broker, and acts on behalf of the broker.

Real estate *agency* is the legal representational relationship that a broker has with a client. A real estate broker can work with a person involved in a real estate transaction in one of two ways: either representing the person or not representing the person. When a broker *represents* a person, an *agency relationship* is created; the broker is the agent, and the person represented is the client (also referred to as *principal*). An agent owes fiduciary duties to a client, legally requiring that the agent look out for the client's best interest.

When a broker is working with a person but does not represent that person, no agency relationship is created. In this situation, the person is referred to as a *customer*. The broker does not owe the customer fiduciary duties but must still deal with the customer in an honest and fair manner.

In Connecticut, only a broker can enter into an agency relationship with a client. In other words, agency runs from the broker to the client. All salespersons working for the broker are automatically agents of the broker's clients and owe those clients fiduciary duties. A salesperson cannot enter into an agency relationship with a person on his or her own.

Connecticut law allows a broker to be the agent of a seller, buyer, landlord, or tenant. While an agency relationship can be created by action or verbal agreement, a *written agency agreement* is required by law if the broker wishes to collect payment for services provided.

Connecticut law does permit a broker to represent two clients involved in the same transaction (such as both the seller and the buyer, or the landlord and the tenant). This is referred to as *dual agency* and is allowed only if both clients give their written informed consent. In a dual agency situation, all salespersons working for the broker are also dual agents. However, the broker has the option of designating one salesperson to specifically represent only one client and another salesperson to specifically represent only the other client. While the broker would still be a dual agent, the two designated salespeople would not be. This is called *designated agency*, and again it is only allowed if both clients give their written informed consent.

A broker or salesperson, working with an unrepresented customer, must clearly *disclose* to the unrepresented customer that the broker or salesperson does not represent the customer but rather represents whoever the broker's client is in the transaction. This disclosure is provided through a state-mandated form called Real Estate Agency Disclosure Notice Given to Unrepresented Persons.

■ LICENSING LAW

Connecticut requires that people and entities engaging in the real estate brokerage business be licensed. Licenses are obtained through the *Connecticut Real Estate Commission*, which is part of the Connecticut Department of Consumer Protection. The *state law* requiring licenses, and overseeing the activities of licensees, can be found at Chapter 392 of the Connecticut General Statutes (entitled Real Estate Brokers and Salespersons). The Real Estate Commission has also enacted *regulations* regarding the conduct of real estate licensees. The Connecticut state law and regulations are discussed in detail in Chapter 10.

There are two categories of real estate licenses: brokers and salespersons. The two categories are sometimes generically referred to as "licensees" or "agents" but are quite different. A broker actually enters into brokerage relationships with clients. A salesperson works on behalf of a broker and must be affiliated with and supervised by that broker.

Once licensed, brokers and salespeople are authorized to perform real estate brokerage activities within the scope of their licenses. However, they must recognize that there are limitations to their authority and that there are real estate–related activities that require additional licensure. For example, real estate licensees are not authorized to give legal advice; a person must be an attorney to do that. Mortgage brokerage, appraisal, home inspection, and insurance counseling all require separate licenses and are outside the scope of a real estate license. Additionally, when asked to provide a referral, a real estate licensee should provide a minimum of two to three names of real estate professionals whom the licensee knows to be qualified.

Broker

A *real estate broker* is an individual or entity that *performs, offers, or attempts to negotiate* any of the following activities related to real estate *for another person and for compensation*:

- Lists for sale
- Sells
- Buys
- Exchanges
- Rents or collects rent for the use of
- Resells a mobile home

State licensing law prohibits a person or entity from doing any of the above real estate brokerage activities without first obtaining a broker's license. Once licensed, a broker then has the authority to be hired to perform any of these activities.

Corporations, partnerships, and other legal entities involved in the real estate brokerage business must be licensed as a broker. All persons that have an ownership interest in a legal entity that is licensed as a broker must hold either a broker or salesperson license, with licensed brokers owning at least 51 percent of the entity. For example, assume Broker A and Salespersons B and C form a limited liability company named Action Realty, LLC. The entity, Action Realty must obtain a real estate broker's license. In addition, all three owners of Action Realty must be individually licensed, and Broker A would have to own a minimum of 51 percent of the company (given that Broker A was the only one of the three licensed as a broker). Note that unlicensed or improperly licensed entities are subject to fines and may also be precluded from bringing actions to recover commissions and other compensation.

Salesperson

A *real estate salesperson* is defined as a person affiliated with a real estate broker to carry out the legally authorized activities of the broker (listed above). A salesperson can only perform real estate brokerage activities on behalf of a broker. Under no circumstances can a salesperson enter into an agency relationship or perform any brokerage activities on his or her own, independent of the broker.

The Broker-Salesperson Relationship

The broker that the salesperson is affiliated with is referred to as the salesperson's *"designated"* or "sponsoring" broker. When filling out an application for a salesperson's license, an applicant must specify who his or her designated broker will be. The designated broker is responsible for liability incurred by the salesperson while performing real estate brokerage activities.

A real estate salesperson in Connecticut is usually considered an *independent contractor* rather than an employee of his or her designated broker. For purposes of workers' compensation, brokers and salespeople are not considered employees if all or most of the remuneration for services performed is directly related to sales rather than to number of hours worked. However, in any action brought by a third party against a real estate salesperson affiliated with a real estate broker as an independent contractor, the broker is liable to the same extent as if the salesperson were an employee.

A salesperson can only work for another broker with the express knowledge and consent of the salesperson's designated broker. A salesperson can transfer broker affiliation by registering the change with the Real Estate Commission and paying a fee. If a salesperson changes broker affiliation, the salesperson is required to return all records and information acquired during the first broker affiliation to the first broker.

Unlicensed Personnel

People working in a real estate brokerage office in primarily custodial (i.e., on-site residential superintendents) or clerical capacities are not considered to be engaging in the real estate business and are not required to be licensed. Because they are not licensed, however, these types of employees are not authorized to perform any real estate brokerage activities.

Assistants

Brokers and salespersons often use unlicensed persons, such as administrative assistants, personal assistants, clerical support staff, and closing secretaries, to assist them in performing various tasks related to their real estate brokerage business. Unlicensed persons are prohibited from negotiating, listing, selling, or buying real estate for a client or customer. The Connecticut Real Estate Commission has adopted a policy on the Use of Unlicensed Persons by Licensees. Figure 1.1 outlines permitted and prohibited activities. Designated brokers are responsible for ensuring that unlicensed assistants, either directly employed or contracted by the broker or a salesperson under the broker's supervision, are not acting improperly.

Nonresident Licensing

Connecticut does not have blanket reciprocal licensing arrangements with other states; therefore, having a real estate broker's license from another state does not entitle a person to perform real estate brokerage activities in Connecticut. A licensed broker from another state who enters into an agency contract for the sale of real property in Connecticut is considered to be unlicensed and would not be able to collect commission or compensation. Other nonresident licensing issues are discussed in Chapter 10.

The Connecticut Real Estate Commission does maintain *reciprocal agreements* with the following states that adhere to substantially equivalent licensing requirements: Alabama, Colorado, Florida, Georgia, Illinois, Indiana, Massachusetts,

FIGURE 1.1

Unlicensed Assistant Activities

Permitted Activities	Prohibited Activities
■ Answer phone and forward calls to licensee.	■ Host open houses, kiosks, home show booths or fairs, or hand out materials at such functions.
■ Transmit listings and changes to multiple listing services (MLSs).	■ Show property.
■ Follow up on loan commitments after a contract has been negotiated.	■ Answer any questions from consumers on listings, title, financing, closing, etc.
■ Assemble documents for closing.	■ Contact cooperating brokers, in person or otherwise, regarding any negotiations or open transactions.
■ Secure public documents from city hall, courthouse, sewer/water districts, tax assessor, etc.	■ Discuss or explain a contract, purchase offer, agreement, listing, or other real estate document with anyone outside of the firm.
■ Have keys made for company listings.	
■ Write and prepare ads, flyers, and promotional materials and place such advertising (which must be reviewed by licensee).	■ Be paid on the basis of commission, or any amount based on listings, sales, etc.
■ Record/deposit earnest money and other trust funds.	■ Negotiate or agree to any commission, commission split, or referral fee on behalf of a licensee.
■ Type contract forms under direction of licensee.	■ Place calls requiring a license—cold calling, soliciting listings, contacting "For Sale by Owners" or expired listings, extending invitations to open houses, etc.
■ Monitor licenses and personnel files.	
■ Compute commission checks.	
■ Place signs on property.	■ Attend inspections or preclosing walk-throughs unless accompanied by licensee.
■ Order items of routine repair as directed by licensee and/or supervising broker.	
■ Act as a courier to transport documents, keys, etc.	■ The unlicensed assistant must not act as a decision maker; rather, he or she shall take all directions from a supervising licensee.
■ Schedule appointments for licensees to show property.	
■ Measure property.	

Mississippi, Nebraska, New York, North Carolina, Ohio, Oklahoma, Rhode Island, and Tennessee. (Note that this list does change periodically; a current list can be obtained at the Connecticut Department of Consumer Protection Web site.) Connecticut's reciprocal arrangements do not eliminate the necessity of obtaining a Connecticut license—they merely waive some of the examination and application requirements.

AGENCY LAW

Agency is the legal representational relationship between a broker and a client. Connecticut agency law comes from state real estate licensing laws and regulations, state common law concepts of agency, and Connecticut Real Estate Commission policies regarding agency.

A real estate broker can work with a person involved in a real estate transaction in one of two ways: either representing the person or not representing the person. When a broker *represents* a person, an *agency relationship* is created; the broker is the *agent* and the person represented is the *client* (also referred to as *principal*). An agent owes fiduciary duties to a client, legally requiring that the agent look out for the client's best interest.

When a broker is working with a person but does not represent that person, no agency relationship is created. In this situation; the person is referred to as a *customer*. The broker does not owe the customer fiduciary duties but must still deal with the customer in an honest manner.

As an example of the above two relationships, assume a broker enters into an agreement to represent a seller in the sale of the seller's house. The representation agreement would create an agency relationship, and the broker would be the agent of the seller-client. If a potential buyer contacts the broker about the seller's house but has not entered into any type of representation agreement with the licensee, the buyer would be a customer. In this situation, the broker represents the seller as an agent. The broker does not represent the buyer but can certainly work with the buyer in an effort to sell the seller's house.

Creation of Agency Relationship

Connecticut law allows a broker to be the agent of a seller, buyer, landlord, or tenant. While an agency relationship can be created by action or verbal agreement, a *written agency agreement* is required by law if the broker wishes to collect payment for services provided. Agency agreements with a seller are called *listing agreements*; agency agreements with a buyer are called *buyer agency agreements*. Agency agreements are discussed briefly below and will be discussed in detail in Chapter 2. A licensee should keep in mind that agency agreements are actually a *contract* with the client.

Under a standard agency agreement with a seller, a broker does not have the right to convey the seller client's property—he or she has only limited authority to act as a *special agent* to locate a buyer and obtain an offer to purchase the seller's property. Thus, the agency agreement is an agency contract of employment in which a broker is provided with limited power and authority to act on behalf of his or her principal. Even though brokers are commonly said to "sell" real estate, "sell" in this sense is not equivalent to "convey." Unless the broker has definite authority, such as power of attorney, he or she really does not "sell" at all but simply brings together buyers and sellers in the marketplace. Hence, the broker is hired to "market" the property for sale, lease, or exchange. The same holds true in the case of buyer agency contracts; a broker is not employed to actually "buy" property but to conduct research on behalf of a buyer, introduce the buyer to properties, and help the buyer negotiate a purchase.

Agency runs to broker, not individual salespeople. Agency relationships are entered into between a client and a brokerage firm's designated broker. Because salespersons work for a designated broker, all clients of the designated broker are also clients of all the broker's salespersons. (See Figure 1.2 depicting this *agency umbrella* concept.) This means that if the designated broker has entered into an agency agreement with a seller, then all of the brokers and salespersons in that designated broker's firm are agents of that seller, represent that seller, and owe fiduciary duties to that seller. Likewise, if the designated broker enters into a buyer agency agreement with a buyer, then all of the brokers and salespersons in that designated broker's firm are the agents of the buyer, represent that buyer, and owe fiduciary duties to that buyer. Therefore, one salesperson in a firm cannot say that

FIGURE 1.2

Agency Umbrella

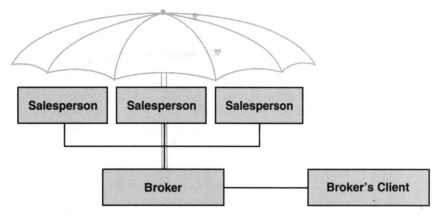

Designated broker in firm enters into agency relationship with client; agency umbrella means that all salespersons who work for that broker are then also agents of that client.

a buyer-client working with another salesperson in the same firm "is not my client." To the contrary, that buyer is the client of each and every salesperson in the firm, and each and every salesperson in the firm must watch out for that buyer's best interests. (The only exception to this is in the case of appointment of designated agents, which will be discussed later.)

Dispute over an agency relationship.   It is the duty of the party who claims existence of the agency to submit strong evidence to support that allegation. This fact is a key reason why brokers are required to have written agency agreements. Although there may be instances in which brokers are paid commissions without a written listing agreement, the law does not support a broker's right to sue for compensation under these circumstances. Therefore, it is important that a broker enter into a written agency agreement with one of the parties to a transaction.

Fiduciary Responsibilities

An agent owes common law *fiduciary duties* to a client, meaning a broker or salesperson who represents a client owes the client the duties of care, obedience, loyalty, disclosure, accounting, and confidentiality. Basically, an agent must watch out for a client's best interests at all times. In Connecticut, this includes presenting all offers received without altering or omitting pertinent details likely to influence any of the parties to the transaction, as well as making sure that offers written up include all essential terms and conditions.

While fiduciary duties are not owed to customers, brokers and salespersons are still required to deal honestly with persons that they do not represent. In particular, licensees must avoid making misleading or false statements concerning properties they are selling. Brokers or salespeople found guilty of misrepresenting material facts or violating the agency agreement may be denied the right to collect a commission and are subject to both fines and possible suspension and revocation of their licenses.

Confidential information.   A real estate licensee may not reveal confidential information about a client at any time during or after an agency relationship.

Further, the licensee may not use confidential information about the person that he or she represented to that person's disadvantage or to the advantage of another. *Confidential information* means facts concerning a person's assets; liabilities; income; expenses; motivations to purchase, rent, or sell; and previous offers received or made that are not a matter of public record.

Conduct of Brokers and Salespersons

In addition to fiduciary duties, the state real estate licensing regulations impose specific requirements on brokers and salespersons. Among other things, these regulations discuss the duties that brokers and salespersons have to the parties in a real estate transaction; the handling of deposits and escrow monies, compensation, referral fees; and interference with other licensees' agency relationships. See Chapter 10 for a detailed discussion of these regulations.

■ TYPES OF AGENCY RELATIONSHIPS

Single Agency

Connecticut law allows a broker to be the agent of a seller, buyer, landlord, or tenant. If a broker represents only one party in a transaction, the broker is considered a single agent. Often, one broker will represent a seller in a transaction and another broker will represent the buyer in the same transaction. If this is the case, both brokers are single agents and owe fiduciary duties only to their respective clients. From an agency perspective, this is perhaps an ideal situation because both clients have an agent watching out for their individual best interests without a conflict.

Dual Agency

When one broker (or brokerage firm) represents both the buyer and the seller (or landlord and tenant) in the same transaction, dual agency exists. Dual agency with *informed consent* is permitted in Connecticut. It is, however, not considered an ideal situation from an agency perspective, given that attempting to represent both the buyer's and seller's best interests in the same transaction creates an inherent conflict of interests.

Connecticut has provided that a client can give informed consent to dual agency by signing a statutorily prescribed *Dual Agency Consent Agreement* prior to executing a purchase, sale, or lease contract. Such agreement is shown in Figure 1.7. The Consent Agreement form specifies what disclosures can and cannot be made to the dual parties.

Timing of dual agency documentation.   In a dual agency situation, the Dual Agency Consent Agreement form must be signed by both the buyer and seller *before* the buyer makes an offer on the seller's property.

Many brokers have clients sign the Dual Agency Consent Agreement at the time an agency agreement is entered into. This is permitted as a way of introducing the client to the concept of dual agency but does not meet the statutory informed consent requirement if a specific buyer has not yet been matched with a specific seller's property.

The Real Estate Commission provides us with the following policy guidance. The Dual Agency Consent Agreement may be generically signed by the seller at the time a listing agreement is entered into, identifying the buyer as "all buyers that the licensee now represents or may represent in the future." Likewise, the Dual Agency Consent Form may be generically signed by the buyer at the time the buyer agency agreement is entered into, identifying the seller as "all sellers that the licensee now represents or may represent in the future" and the property as "all property currently listed with the licensee or listed with the licensee in the future." Additionally, however, before a specific buyer-client makes an offer on a specific seller-client's property, both the buyer and seller must execute a specific Dual Agency Consent Form, listing the proper parties and property.

Any possibility of dual agency must be stated in agency agreements. If a brokerage firm represents both buyers and sellers (or landlords and tenants), the *firm's agency agreements must contain a statement that the potential exists for the firm to be a dual agent.*

Designated Agency

When a real estate broker (or brokerage firm) represents both the buyer and seller (or landlord and tenant) in the same transaction, which amounts to dual agency, the designated broker may appoint a separate seller agent and separate buyer agent to represent the parties, if the parties agree. This type of agency is referred to as *designated agency*, and the appointed agents would be designated agents. Designated agents are not dual agents, although the brokerage firm and all nondesignated licensees would be dual agents.

If a firm is going to designate agents in a dual agency situation, the Dual Agency Consent Form is not used. Instead, to disclose the dual/designated agency situation and to obtain all parties' informed consent to the dual/designated agency, the *Dual Agency/Designated Agency Notice and Consent Agreement* is to be used (see Figure 1.8). Before a buyer makes a written offer, the buyer, seller, and firm's broker must sign the form with the names of the designated agents inserted. As with the Dual Agency Consent Form, the Dual Agency/Designated Agency Notice and Consent Agreement may be generically signed at the time an agency agreement is entered into, but it must be re-executed at the appropriate time with the appropriate information included.

Designated agency is not available to only one party in a transaction. For example, a brokerage firm cannot designate a designated agent solely to represent a buyer without also designating an agent for the seller.

Disclosure of Agency to Unrepresented Persons

Connecticut real estate licensing law requires *mandatory written disclosure of agency representation* to unrepresented prospective purchasers, sellers, landlords, or tenants. Figure 1.3 visually illustrates how this disclosure works. Disclosure is required to be made by the licensed broker or salesperson representing a seller, purchaser, seller and purchaser (dual agency), landlord, or tenant only when the agent is also working with *another party who is not represented by the agent's firm OR another firm*. The required notice form is called the Real Estate Agency Disclosure Notice Given to Unrepresented Persons and is seen in Figure 1.6. Disclosure must be given in residential and commercial purchase and sale transactions, as well as in leasing transactions.

This disclosure must be given at the beginning of the first personal meeting concerning the unrepresented party's needs. It is then required to be attached to any offer, binder, option, or agreement to purchase or lease.

If a person required to sign the disclosure refuses to do so, the agent should note this refusal on the line indicated for the person's signature and attach that disclosure.

The required disclosure need not be given to prospective buyers or lessees at an open house, provided there is a sign or pamphlet disclosing the licensee's agency relationship and the specific real estate needs of the prospective buyer or lessee are not discussed.

Note that the above discussion on agency disclosure details the state law requirements. Members of professional associations, such as the National Association of REALTORS® (NAR), may be held to stricter requirements.

Subagency

Often real estate brokers who represent a seller will allow other brokers to introduce buyers to the seller's property. When brokers have this type of working relationship, it is referred to as *co-brokerage*. Traditionally, co-brokers were considered subagents of the seller. In Connecticut, subagency is not permitted in a co-brokered transaction without the written consent of the person being represented. Such

FIGURE 1.3

Agency Disclosure

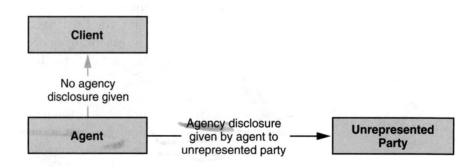

consent must include the name and license number of all real estate licensees to be appointed as subagents as well as a statement that the person being represented may be vicariously liable for the acts of the subagent. Although subagency is legal in Connecticut, it is rarely used in residential real estate transactions.

This limitation on subagency does not apply to leasing transactions. In a lease transaction (but not a lease-purchase-option transaction), licensees working with a tenant may be a subagent of the landlord without obtaining the landlord's consent. The limitation on subagency does apply to commercial purchase and sale transactions.

Agency Relationships in Practice

The Connecticut Real Estate Commission has provided policy guidance on (1) the various agency documents required to be entered into with or given to buyers and sellers (see Figure 1.4) and (2) an outline of issues to consider regarding the practical application of agency relationships (see Figure 1.5).

■ BROKER COMPENSATION

The amount of compensation is an integral part of the contract between a broker and a client. Typically, broker compensation is calculated as a percentage of a property's sales price, referred to as a *commission*, but it may also be a flat fee or calculated in another manner. The only type of compensation not allowed in Connecticut is a net amount, whereby the broker retains all funds above a certain net-to-the-seller figure as compensation.

A broker may negotiate for any compensation he or she feels is commensurate with the duties expected of him or her under the listing or buyer agency agreement. Compensation can be paid by either the seller or buyer. Commissions and compensation, unlike interest rates, are not subject to usury law (maximum interest rates allowed by statute).

Written agency agreements must state (in boldface type or in another prominent manner) that compensation may be *negotiable* (see Chapter 10 for more details). The following language is legally required to be inserted in agency agreements immediately preceding any provision relating to compensation:

NOTICE: THE AMOUNT OR RATE OF REAL ESTATE BROKER COMPENSATION IS NOT FIXED BY LAW. IT IS SET BY EACH BROKER INDIVIDUALLY AND MAY BE NEGOTIABLE BETWEEN YOU AND THE BROKER.

A broker in Connecticut is not entitled to compensation unless **reasonable cause for payment exists.** In the case of a listing agreement, if an offer meets all the terms and conditions agreed to under the contract, the broker is deemed to have produced a ready, willing, and able buyer, and reasonable cause exists to award him or her a commission. Furthermore, when a broker procures a buyer who is ready, willing, and able to purchase on terms other than those on the listing agreement but that are acceptable to the seller, the broker is entitled to a commission once

FIGURE 1.4

Required Connecticut Agency Documents

	Agency Representation Agreement	Agency Disclosure Notice	Dual Agency/Designated Agency Notice & Consent Agreement
Cooperating Sale			
Broker represents Seller	Listing Agreement	Give to unrepresented potential Buyer at time of first personal meeting concerning Buyer's need (not required if Buyer represented by another agent)	N/A
Broker represents Buyer	Buyer Agency Agreement	Give to unrepresented potential Seller at time of first personal meeting with Seller (not required if Seller represented by another agent)	N/A
Broker working with Buyer, subagent of Seller	Seller Consent to Subagency	Give to unrepresented potential Buyer at time of first personal meeting concerning Buyer's needs	N/A
In-House Sale			
Broker represents both Seller and Buyer, no Designated Agents	Listing Agreement and Buyer Agency Agreement (must contain statement about possibility of dual agency)	N/A	Before Buyer makes a written offer: both Buyer and Seller must sign "Dual Agency Consent Agreement"
Broker represents both Seller and Buyer, Designated Agents have been appointed	Listing Agreement and Buyer Agency Agreement (must contain statement about possibility of dual agency)	N/A	Before Buyer makes a written offer: Buyer, Seller, and Broker must sign "Dual Agency/ Designated Agency Disclosure Notice and Consent Agreement" with names of Designated Agents inserted
Broker represents only Seller, working with Buyer	Listing Agreement	Give to unrepresented potential Buyer at time of first personal meeting concerning Buyer's needs (not required if Buyer represented by another agent)	N/A

From the Connecticut Real Estate Commission Policy on Agency, adopted January 6, 2000.

F I G U R E   **1.5**

Connecticut Real Estate Agency Relationships in Practice

Brokerage Firm Represents Seller	Brokerage Firm Represents Buyer	Brokerage Firm Working with Buyer as Customer
STEP A1. Enter into written Listing Agreement. Go to STEP A2. **STEP A2.** Before Seller's property is shown to each potential Buyer, determine whether Buyer is represented by a brokerage firm. (i) If Buyer is not represented but would like to be represented by your firm, go to STEP B1. (ii) If Buyer is not represented and does not wish to be represented, go to STEP A3. (iii) If Buyer is represented by another firm, go to STEP A4. (iv) If Buyer is represented by your firm, go to STEP A5. **STEP A3.** Give Agency Disclosure Notice to unrepresented Buyer at time of first personal meeting concerning Buyer's needs. Go to STEP A4. **STEP A4.** Proceed as Seller's Agent. **STEP A5.** Have both Buyer and Seller given their informed consent to dual agency? (i) If yes, both Buyer and Seller must sign either Dual Agency Consent Agreement (if not designating agents) or Dual Agency/ Designated Agency Disclosure Notice and Consent Agreement (if also designating agent). Go to STEP A6. (ii) If no, Stop. Cannot represent both parties in the same transaction without obtaining their informed consent. **STEP A6.** Have Brokerage Firm and both Buyer and Seller agreed to the appointment of Designated Agents? (i) If yes, Buyer, Seller, and Broker sign Dual Agency/Designated Agency Disclosure Notice and Consent Agreement and Broker must appoint designated agents in that Agreement. Designated agents proceed as such; rest of office proceeds as Dual Agent. (ii) If no, proceed as Dual Agent, with no designated agency.	**STEP B1.** Enter into written Buyer Agency Agreement. Go to STEP B2. **STEP B2.** Before Buyer is shown a property, determine whether the Seller of that property is represented by a brokerage firm. (i) If Seller is not represented, go to STEP B3. (ii) If Seller is represented by another firm, go to STEP B4. (iii) If Seller is represented by your firm, go to STEP A5. **STEP B3.** Give Agency Disclosure Notice to unrepresented Seller at time of first personal meeting with Seller. Go to STEP B4. **STEP B4.** Proceed as Buyer's Agent.	**STEP C1.** Determine whether Buyer seeks representation. (i) If yes, go to STEP B1. (ii) If no, go to STEP C2. **STEP C2.** This is a difficult way to go, although it is allowed by the law. Procedure depends upon whether Buyer is going to be shown an in-house listing or another firm's listing. (i) For in-house listings, go to STEP C3. (ii) For another firm's listings, go to STEP C4. **STEP C3.** Broker may work with Buyer as the Seller's Agent. Go to STEP A3. **STEP C4.** Does Seller agree to Broker being Seller's subagent? (i) If yes, Broker must obtain Seller's written consent to subagency, containing subagent Broker's name and licensee number and containing a statement that the law imposes vicarious liability on the Seller for the acts of the subagent. Go to STEP A3. (ii) If no, Stop. Cannot proceed in this transaction and be legally entitled to compensation.

Note: These are the most common scenarios that a Broker may encounter, although this outline is not all encompassing. Refer to the Connecticut General Statutes for further detail and clarification on Connecticut agency relationships.

From the Connecticut Real Estate Commission Policy on Agency, adopted January 6, 2000.

Brokers Compensation

the seller has formally accepted the offer of the prospective buyer and all the conditions prescribed by the offer have been met. The fact that a sale may not actually take place does not change the right of a licensed broker to recover a commission from the principal. If the seller defaults on the sales contract, the broker is still entitled to a commission. If the buyer procured by the broker defaults, however, the broker has no recourse against the seller for collecting a commission but may sue the buyer to recover damages.

In the case of a buyer agency contract, if the broker meets the requirements of the contract, the broker will be owed the agreed-on compensation. A broker entering into a buyer brokerage agreement with a buyer is required to accurately explain the provisions of the agreement that detail the compensation arrangement. If a buyer brokerage agreement calls for zero (or blank) compensation, the buyer's broker cannot look to the buyer for compensation even if the seller's agent does not agree to compensate the buyer's broker. A broker cannot advertise or state that buyers can be represented with no liability to pay a fee or commission, unless in fact the buyer has no obligation to pay compensation in any circumstances under the agreement. (Note that a buyer brokerage agreement where the buyer has no obligation to pay the broker may be legally unenforceable for lack of consideration.)

Brokers may be denied the right to collect compensation under a variety of circumstances, ranging from fraud and misrepresentation to criminal intent and operating without a license. Commissions may be denied by virtue of an aggrieved party's substantiated complaint (through the Real Estate Commission) or by court action. Any actions by a broker that violate his or her agency relationship or the laws governing licensing and conduct may be sufficient cause for denial of compensation.

Broker's Lien

A broker who has performed services relating to *residential* or *commercial* real estate has the right to place a *lien on the real estate* to secure payment of compensation pursuant to Section 20-325a of the Connecticut General Statutes. The lien does not attach until it is recorded in the land records in the town where the property is located. At the time of recording, the broker must be entitled to compensation, without any contingencies (except the transfer of title), under terms set forth in a written contract.

For services relating to a seller, the claim of lien must be recorded prior to conveyance. Where the broker represents a landlord in a lease transaction, the claim must be recorded within 30 days after the tenant takes possession, unless the broker receives notice of the lease signing date in advance, in which case the lien must be recorded prior to the lease signing. If compensation is due in installments, any claim for lien for amounts owing after a conveyance or lease must be recorded subsequent to the transaction. In the case of a broker representing a buyer or a tenant, the claim of lien must be filed within 30 days of the conveyance or lease signing.

[Handwritten margin notes: "What a Hackel / Has to have / Recorded"] [and] ["has to be / signed w/in 30days / w/in"]

The claim for lien must include the following:

- The name of the property owner
- The commission amount that is being claimed in the lien
- The name of the broker
- The broker's real estate license number
- A description of the real estate on which the lien is being claimed
- A statement sworn to and signed by the broker stating that the information contained in the notice is true and accurate to his or her knowledge (an authorized agent of the broker can sign on behalf of the broker)

The broker's lien law goes into detail about what types of notices must be served and procedures followed to claim and enforce the lien, including a notice of intent to lien. Enforcing the lien requires filing an action in superior court and is very much like foreclosing on a mortgage. See Figure 1.9 for examples of a broker's lien notice and filing. *If a broker does not file a suit to enforce the lien within one year of filing it, the lien is extinguished.* The owner of the property can demand that the broker commence an action sooner, in which case the suit must be filed within 45 days of the demand or the lien is extinguished.

A closing or leasing cannot be prevented solely on the basis of a recorded broker's lien. If a recorded lien creates a problem in the transaction, the law requires that an escrow account for the amount of the disputed compensation be established from the proceeds of the transaction. The broker is then required to release the claim for lien. The escrow is released to the appropriate party when the dispute is resolved.

Notice of Commercial Lease Commission Rights

A broker who is entitled to a future commission for a commercial lease transaction can protect his or her right to receive that commission in the event the landlord sells the property. To do so, the broker must record a Notice of Commission Rights in the municipal land records in the municipality where the leased property is located. This notice must be recorded within 30 days of execution of the lease or when the tenant takes occupancy of the leased property, whichever is later. Section 20-325k of the Connecticut General Statutes dictates the form of notice and provisions for release. If the notice requirements are followed properly, future owners of the leased property will be bound to pay the future commission owed. See Figure 1.10 for the required notice form.

Referral Fees

A real estate broker or salesperson may receive a referral fee from other brokers licensed in Connecticut and other states. However, a broker or salesperson cannot receive any type of referral fee for the *referral* of any buyer to an attorney or mortgage broker or lender. Likewise, no attorney or mortgage lender may receive a referral fee for the referral of a person to a real estate broker or salesperson (unless the attorney or mortgage lender holds a real estate license).

Mortgage Brokerage Service Fees

It is not unusual for a real estate broker to act as a *mortgage broker* for the buyer. The broker's fee must be for negotiating or arranging for a mortgage loan for the buyer and *not for the referral* of the buyer to a mortgage lender. A real estate broker acting as a mortgage broker for a buyer should be familiar with the laws governing the licensure of first and second mortgage brokerage, which are described in Chapter 11.

When a real estate broker or salesperson receives a commission for the sale of the property, an additional fee for placing the mortgage loan can be received *only with full disclosure* using the mortgage brokerage disclosure statement set out in Figure 1.11, printed in at least 10-point boldface capital letters.

■ RECORD RETENTION

Real estate brokers are required to retain certain real estate brokerage records for seven years. The following documents must be kept:

- ■ Offers and counteroffers drafted by the broker's office
- ■ Contracts
- ■ Leases
- ■ Agency agreements and disclosures
- ■ Escrow and trust account checks and bank statements

The documents must be kept regardless of whether the transaction actually closed or not. The seven years starts running from the time when a transaction closes or funds held in escrow are disbursed, or in the case of a transaction that does not close, when the agency agreement expires. Retention can be in electronic form, as long as a paper copy can be made.

■ WEB LINKS

Connecticut General Statutes: *www.cga.ct.gov*
Chapter 392 of Connecticut General Statutes, Real Estate Brokers and
     Salespersons: *www.cga.ct.gov/2009/pub/Chap392.htm*
Connecticut Department of Consumer Protection: *www.ct.gov/dcp*
Connecticut Association of REALTORS®, Inc.:   *www.ctrealtor.com*

F I G U R E 1.6

Real Estate Agency Disclosure Notice Given to Unrepresented Persons

REAL ESTATE AGENCY DISCLOSURE NOTICE
GIVEN TO **UNREPRESENTED PERSONS**

This is not a contract. Connecticut law requires that you be given this notice disclosing whom the real estate licensee represents. The purpose of such disclosure is to enable you to make informed choices about your relationship with real estate licensees.

GIVEN TO:_____
(UNREPRESENTED PERSON/PERSONS)

ON _____ (DATE)

OUR FIRM _____ REPRESENTS

❑ SELLER   ❑ LANDLORD   ❑ BUYER   ❑ TENANT

UNREPRESENTED PERSON(S)'S RIGHTS AND RESPONSIBILITIES

1. The broker and salespersons (referred to as agents or licensees) in this transaction owes the other party to this transaction undivided fiduciary obligations, such as: loyalty, reasonable care, disclosure, and obedience to lawful instruction, confidentiality and accountability. The agent(s) must put the other party's interest first and negotiate for the best terms and conditions for them, not for you.

2. All real estate agents, whether representing you or not, are obligated by law to treat all parties to a real estate transaction honestly and fairly.

3. You have the responsibility to protect your own interests. Carefully read all agreements to make sure they accurately reflect your understanding. If you need additional advice for legal, tax, insurance or other such matters, it is your responsibility to consult a professional in those areas.

4. Whether you are a buyer, seller, tenant, or landlord, you can choose to have the advice, assistance and representation of your own real estate brokerage firm and its agents. Do not assume that a real estate brokerage firm or its agents are representing you or are acting on your behalf unless you have contracted in writing with that real estate brokerage firm.

ACKNOWLEDGMENT   **ACKNOWLEDGEMENT OF AGENT**
OF UNREPRESENTED PERSON(S)*

_____   _____
Signature(s)   *Signature*

_____   _____
Print Name(s)   *Print Name*

_____   _____
Date   *Date*
                                                 *To be signed by the buyer/tenant when the agent represents the seller/landlord, or
                                                 To be signed by the seller/landlord when the agent represents the buyer/tenant*

Connecticut Department of Consumer Protection form issued June, 2002

Dual Agency Consent Agreement

DUAL AGENCY CONSENT AGREEMENT
Pursuant to Public Act 96-159

Property Address: _____

Seller(s) or Landlord(s): _____

Buyer(s) or Tenant(s): _____

(1) This Dual Agency Consent Agreement is an addendum to and made part of (check all that apply):

❏ Listing Agreement dated _____ between brokerage firm and seller or landlord.

❏ Buyer or tenant agency agreement dated _____ between brokerage firm and buyer or tenant.

(2) Seller and buyer (or landlord and tenant, as the case may be) hereby acknowledge and agree that _____ _____ (name of brokerage firm) is representing both buyer and seller (or landlord and tenant, as the case may be) in the purchase and sale (or lease) of the above referenced property and that brokerage firm has been and is now the agent of both seller and buyer (or landlord and tenant, as the case may be). Seller and buyer (or landlord and tenant, as the case may be) have both consented to and hereby confirm their consent to this dual representation.

(3) Seller and buyer (or landlord and tenant, as the case may be) agree:

(A) The brokerage firm shall not be required to and shall not disclose to either buyer or seller (or landlord or tenant, as the case may be) any personal, financial or other confidential information to such other party without the express written consent of the party whose information is disclosed, other than information related to material property defects which are known to the brokerage firm and other information the brokerage firm is required to disclose by law.

(B) The brokerage firm may not disclose: (i) To the buyer that the seller (landlord) will accept less than the asking or listed price, unless otherwise instructed to do so in writing by the seller (landlord); (ii) to the seller (landlord) that the buyer (tenant) can or will pay a price greater than the price submitted in a written offer to the seller (landlord), unless otherwise instructed to do so in writing by the buyer (tenant); (iii) the motivation of the seller or buyer (or landlord or tenant, as the case may be) for selling, buying or leasing property, unless otherwise instructed in writing by the respective party; or (iv) that a seller or buyer will agree to financing terms other than those offered, unless instructed in writing by the respective party.

(4) Property information available through the multiple listing service or otherwise, including listed and sold properties, which has been requested by either the seller or the buyer (or landlord or tenant, as the case may be) shall be disclosed to both seller and buyer (or landlord and tenant, as the case may be).

(5) Both parties are advised to seek competent legal and tax advice with regard to this transaction, and with regard to all documents executed in connection with this transaction, including this Dual Agency Consent Agreement.

I have read and understand the above agreement.

Buyer (Tenant)	**Seller (Landlord)**	**Brokerage Firm**
_____	_____	_____
		Company Name
_____	_____	_____
		Authorized Signature
Date:_____	Date:_____	Date:_____

FIGURE 1.8

Dual Agency/Designated Agency Notice and Consent Agreement

Dual Agency/Designated Agency
Disclosure Notice and Consent Agreement
Given to Persons Represented by the Same
Brokerage Firm

Brokerage Firm: _____

Property Address: _____

Buyer (Tenant): _____

Seller (Landlord): _____

The Brokerage Firm has entered into a written agency relationship with both Buyer and Seller (or Tenant and Landlord). Buyer (Tenant) is now interested in buying (leasing) Seller's (Landlord's) Property. If this transaction proceeds, Brokerage Firm will be a dual agent, since Brokerage Firm represents both parties. Connecticut law allows Brokerage Firm to be a dual agent, but only after both Buyer and Seller (or Tenant and Landlord) understand what dual agency is and consent to it.

Connecticut law also allows Brokerage Firms that are dual agents to appoint individual designated agents within their firm to solely represent Buyer and Seller (or Tenant and Landlord); again, this designation can only be made after both Buyer and Seller (or Tenant and Landlord) understand what designated agency is and consent to it.

Both Buyer and Seller (or Tenant and Landlord) are free to seek legal and tax advice with regard to this <u>transaction, and with regard to all documents signed in connection with this transaction.</u>

Understanding Dual Agency

Dual Agency means that the Brokerage Firm, and all the brokers and salespersons for the firm (unless designated agency is chosen) act in a fiduciary capacity for both Buyer and Seller (or Tenant and Landlord). In Dual Agency, the Brokerage Firm does not represent either the Buyer or Seller (or Tenant or Landlord) exclusively, and the parties can not expect the Brokerage Firm's undivided loyalty.

The Brokerage Firm may not disclose to either the Buyer or Seller (or Tenant or Landlord) any personal, financial, or confidential information to the other party except as authorized by either party or required by law. The Brokerage Firm may not disclose, unless otherwise instructed by the respective party:
–   to Buyer (Tenant) that Seller (Landlord) will accept less than the asking or listed price
–   to the Seller (Landlord) that the Buyer (Tenant) can pay a price greater than otherwise instructed to do so in writing by the Buyer (Tenant);
–   the motivation of either Buyer or Seller (or Tenant or Landlord) for selling, buying, leasing the Property; and that
–   that Buyer or Seller will agree to financing terms other than those offered.

Dual Agency Consent

Buyer and Seller (or Landlord and Tenant) understand dual agency and consent to Brokerage Firm acting as a dual agent in this transaction.

FIGURE 1.8 (continued)

Dual Agency/Designated Agency Notice and Consent Agreement

Understanding Designated Agency

Designated Agency means the appointment by the Brokerage Firm of one broker or salesperson (referred to as agent) affiliated with or employed by the Brokerage Firm to solely represent Buyer (Tenant) as a Designated Buyer's Agent and appoint another to solely represent Seller (Landlord) as a Designated Seller's Agent in this transaction.

A Designated Buyer's Agent and Designated Seller's Agent owe the party for whom they have been appointed undivided fiduciary obligations, such as loyalty, reasonable care, disclosure, obedience to lawful instruction, confidentiality and accountability. The Designated Agent is not deemed to be a Dual Agent, and thus does not owe fiduciary duties to the other party. A designated agent may use confidential information obtained about the other party while a designated agent for the benefit of the party for whom they have been appointed, however, information obtained before the designation is still confidential. In the case of Designated Agency, Brokerage Firm is still considered a Dual Agent.

Appointment of Designated Agents

Buyer and Seller (or Landlord and Tenant) understand designated agency and have agreed to the appointment of designated agents.

If designated agency has been agreed to, the following designated agents have been appointed:

_____ has been designated to solely represent Buyer (Tenant) as a Designated Buyer Agent.

_____ has been designated to solely represent Seller (Landlord) as a Designated Seller Agent.

Appointing broker/authorized agent: _____

Date: _____

Acknowledgment of Buyer (Tenant)   Acknowledgement of Seller (Landlord)

_____   _____

Signature(s)   *Date*   *Signature(s)*   *Date*

_____   _____

Print Name(s)   Print Name(s)

FIGURE 1.9

Brokers Lien Notice and Filing

BROKER'S LIEN

This is to certify that [*Broker Name and Address*], Connecticut in accordance with a certain listing contract/buyer representation agreement [*specify type of agreement*] with [*Name and address of Property Owner or Person executing agreement*], for the sale/ purchase [*specify which*] of real property located at [Property Address] in the Town of _____, County of _____, and State of Connecticut has a lien under P. A. 95-186 on the following described premises owned by [*Name of Property Owner (or Buyer, if buyer representation agreement)*] in the amount of [*Amount of Commission Claimed*] which amount is justly due.

The subject premises are bounded and described as follows: {Attach legal description of property}

SEE SCHEDULE A ATTACHED HERETO AND MADE A PART HEREOF

IN WITNESS WHEREOF, I have hereunto set my hand and seal this _____ day of _____, 20____.

By: _____   License Number:

STATE OF CONNECTICUT   )
)   SS:
COUNTY OF   )

Personally appeared _____, signer and sealer of the foregoing instrument, who acknowledged the same to be his free act and deed, before me.

_____   Notary Public
                                         Commissioner of Superior
                                         Court

NOTICE OF INTENT TO CLAIM BROKER'S LIEN

THIS NOTICE IS GIVEN TO

Seller Name and Address   Buyer Name and Address

[*Name and Address of Real Estate Broker*], Connecticut, real estate broker, hereby gives you notice pursuant to P. A. 95-186 that said real estate broker claims a lien on certain real property located at [Property Address], Connecticut, owned by [*Name and address of Property Owner or Person executing agreement*] on account of services performed under a certain listing contract/buyer agency agreement [*Specify type of agreement*] and that said real estate broker intends to claim a lien therefore on said premises to the amount of [*Amount of Commission Claimed*].

The said premises are situated in the Town of _____, County of _____ and State of Connecticut, recorded in the name of _____ in volume _____ at page _____ of the Town of _____ land records and bounded and described as more fully appears on schedule A attached hereto.

Dated at _____, Connecticut, this _____ day of _____, 20____.

By: _____   License Number:

F I G U R E 1.10

Notice of Commissions Rights

NOTICE OF COMMISSION RIGHTS

The undersigned licensed Connecticut real estate broker does hereby publish this NOTICE OF COMMISSION RIGHTS to establish that the lease referenced below was procured by a real estate broker pursuant to a written brokerage commission agreement providing for the payment or promise of payment of compensation for brokerage services.

Owner: _____

Landlord: _____

Tenant: _____

Lease date: _____

Lease term: _____

Project or building name (if any):

Real estate broker name _____

Address _____

Telephone number _____

Real estate license number _____

F I G U R E 1.11

Mortgage Brokerage Disclosure

I UNDERSTAND THAT THE REAL ESTATE BROKER OR SALESPERSON IN THIS TRANSACTION HAS OFFERED TO ASSIST ME IN FINDING A MORTGAGE LOAN. ADDITIONALLY, I UNDERSTAND THAT THIS REAL ESTATE BROKER OR SALESPERSON DOES NOT REPRESENT ANY PARTICULAR MORTGAGE LENDER AND WILL ATTEMPT TO OBTAIN THE BEST TERMS AVAILABLE WITHIN THE MORTGAGE LOAN MARKET FOR MY SPECIFIC HOME FINANCING NEEDS. IF THE REAL ESTATE BROKER OR SALESPERSON DOES NOT FULFILL HIS OR HER FIDUCIARY OBLIGATION I MAY FILE A COMPLAINT WITH THE DEPARTMENT OF BANKING. I ALSO UNDERSTAND THAT I MAY ATTEMPT TO FIND A MORTGAGE LOAN TO FINANCE THE PURCHASE OF MY HOME WITHOUT THE ASSISTANCE OF THE REAL ESTATE BROKER OR SALESPERSON IN WHICH CASE I WILL NOT BE OBLIGATED TO PAY A FEE TO THE REAL ESTATE BROKER OR SALESPERSON.

CHAPTER 1 QUIZ

1. A person engaging in real estate activities for another and for a fee must hold a valid
   a. agent's license.
   b. broker's license.
   c. salesperson's license.
   d. broker's or salesperson's license.

2. A licensed real estate salesperson must be
   a. affiliated with a licensed real estate broker.
   b. an employee of a licensed real estate broker.
   c. an independent contractor.
   d. willing to enter into agency relationships with clients.

3. A real estate broker's license allows a broker to do all of the following EXCEPT
   a. sell real estate.
   b. resell a mobile home.
   c. collect rent on behalf of a landlord.
   d. appraise real estate.

4. Under Connecticut licensing law, a limited liability corporation (LLC) will be granted a broker's license only if
   a. the LLC is owned exclusively by licensed brokers.
   b. all owners of the LLC have either a broker or salesperson license, and a majority of the entity is owned by brokers.
   c. the LLC passes a state exam.
   d. Connecticut law is changed; currently a legal entity cannot be licensed as a broker.

5. A broker entered into a listing agreement with the seller. Through the multiple listing service, a broker from a different office had been working with the buyer, who is interested in making an offer on the seller's property. Typically, in this kind of transaction, the broker working with the buyer would enter into a written representation contract with
   a. the seller as a subagent.
   b. the buyer as an agent.
   c. the buyer as a subagent.
   d. neither the buyer nor the seller.

6. In the previous question, if the broker wished to represent the buyer, Connecticut licensing law requires that the broker enter into a(n)
   a. oral agency agreement.
   b. co-brokerage agreement.
   c. dual agency agreement.
   d. written agency agreement.

7. When a broker represents the seller of real estate, an agency disclosure must be given to
   a. any potential unrepresented purchaser, at the beginning of the first personal meeting with the purchaser.
   b. all potential purchasers, at the beginning of the first personal meeting with the purchaser.
   c. the purchaser, before the purchase and sale contract is signed.
   d. the seller, at the time the listing agreement is signed.

8. A realty has entered into agency agreements with both the seller and the buyer. The buyer is interested in making an offer on the seller's property. Can this occur?
   a. No, because the realty would then be a dual agent.
   b. Yes, as long as written agency agreements have been entered into with both parties.
   c. Yes, if both the buyer and the seller give their consent to dual agency.
   d. Yes, but only if the realty designated separate agents to represent each party.

9. A realty has entered into agency agreements with both the seller and the buyer. The seller and the buyer agreed to dual agency but not designated agency. A salesperson with the same realty has been working with the buyer. Legally, the salesperson is not allowed to do any of the following *EXCEPT*

a. provide comparable market data to the seller after the buyer requests and receives such data from the REALTOR®.
b. disclose the buyer's financial qualifications to the seller.
c. disclose to the buyer that the seller will accept less than the listing price.
d. disclose to the seller that the buyer will pay more than the offering price.

10. Sal's listing agreement with the seller has terminated. The seller now enters into a listing agreement with another brokerage firm. When Sal finds a buyer interested in the seller's property, Sal cannot

a. become a dual agent.
b. disclose to the buyer offers received on the seller's property while it was listed with him.
c. disclose to the buyer information about the physical condition of the property.
d. represent the buyer.

11. Buona Vista Realty has entered into agency agreements with both the seller and the buyer. Angela, a salesperson with Buona Vista, has been designated to represent the seller, and Bao, another salesperson, has been designated to represent the buyer. In this situation

a. Angela and Bao are dual agents.
b. all the other salespersons that work for Buona Vista are dual agents, but not Angela and Bao.
c. Buona Vista Realty has violated the licensing laws.
d. Angela and Bao may reveal confidential information about their clients to each other.

12. An unlicensed personal assistant working for a real estate licensee is *NOT* allowed to

a. host an open house.
b. answer the phone and discuss questions about the licensee's listings.
c. write and prepare promotional material.
d. show property listed with the licensee.

13. A real estate broker has been working with buyers. After the broker helps them negotiate for their home, the buyers ask whether the broker can help them obtain a mortgage. A bank offers to pay the broker a fee for referring purchasers. This is

a. not allowed.
b. allowed if the seller and the broker have entered into a written buyer agency agreement.
c. allowed if the broker discloses the referral fee to the buyers.
d. allowed if the bank offers the best interest rates and terms available in the market.

14. To secure payment of compensation for her services, a broker may place a lien on a(n)

a. condominium unit.
b. four-family apartment building.
c. office building.
d. all of these.

CHAPTER 2

Listing and Buyer Agency Agreements

■ OVERVIEW

Connecticut law allows a real estate broker to enter into an agency relationship with a seller, landlord, buyer, or tenant. Agency agreements with sellers and landlords are referred to as *listing agreements*. Agency agreements with buyers are referred to as *buyer agency agreements*. Agency agreements are contracts between a broker and client. They must be in writing and contain certain provisions required by the licensing law in order for the agreement to be enforceable and for a broker to collect compensation.

Electronic agency contracts (including e-mails and faxes) must meet federal and state guidelines for electronic documents and signatures. See Appendix E for a discussion of the electronic agency contract requirements.

■ AGENCY AGREEMENTS

Listing Agreements

To represent a seller or landlord, a written listing agreement must be entered into. The agreement must be entered into before a broker or salesperson attempts to negotiate on behalf of the seller or landlord. The following three basic types of listing agreements are recognized in Connecticut:

1. Exclusive right to sell (exclusive agreement with one broker; seller pays broker regardless of who sells property)

2. Exclusive agency (exclusive agreement with one broker; seller retains right to sell without owing compensation to broker)
3. Open listing (nonexclusive agreement multiple broker; only selling broker is compensated)

Examples of these types of listing contracts can be found in Figures 2.1, 2.2, and 2.3, respectively.

Buyer Agency Agreements

To represent a buyer, a written buyer agency agreement must be entered into. Written buyer agency agreements may be requested by a seller broker at the closing if the seller broker is providing compensation to the buyer broker. There are three basic types of buyer agency agreements:

1. Exclusive right to represent buyer (exclusive agreement with one broker; broker is entitled to compensation regardless of who located property). While allowed, this type of agency agreement is not typically used in Connecticut. An example of this type of agency agreement can be found in Figure 2.4.
2. Exclusive agency right to represent buyer (exclusive agreement with one broker; broker is only entitled to compensation if broker locates property). An example of this type of agency agreement can be found in Figure 2.5
3. Open right to represent buyer (nonexclusive agreement with multiple brokers; only broker that locates the property is compensated). An example of this type of agency agreement can be found in Figure 2.6.

The buyer agency agreement must be entered into before a broker or salesperson attempts to *negotiate* on behalf of a prospective buyer or tenant. *Negotiate* has been defined to include the following: showing the buyer any property, discussing an offer with the buyer, engaging in negotiation on behalf of the buyer, *or* giving advice to the buyer about particular real estate.

Preliminary activities for buyer.   A licensee may conduct preliminary activities for a buyer before a written buyer representation agreement is entered into, given that the following Real Estate Commission policy guidelines are met.

Before a licensee works with a buyer, the licensee should take three steps:

1. Ask whether the buyer is currently being represented by another firm
2. Explain the real estate firm's office policy on the various agency and customer relationships that the licensee could potentially have with the buyer
3. Specifically tell the buyer not to provide confidential information unless and until the buyer and licensee have entered into an agency relationship

A licensee can do the following for a buyer without entering into a written buyer agency agreement:

■   Give the buyer property information
■   Give the buyer information on the licensee's firm
■   Give the buyer information on mortgage rates and lending institutions

A licensee *cannot* do the following six things for a buyer *unless either* a written buyer agency agreement is entered into, *or* the licensee is going to represent the seller and has presented the buyer with an Agency Disclosure Notice stating that the licensee represents the seller (and for cooperating sales, obtains the seller's consent to subagency):

1. Ask the buyer to disclose confidential information (including information about the buyer's financial status, reasons for purchasing, etc.)
2. Express an opinion or give advice about particular real estate (note that a licensee representing the seller should be cautious expressing an opinion or giving advice)
3. Physically show the buyer in-house listings
4. Physically show the buyer property listed with another firm
5. Discuss an offer with the buyer
6. Engage in any verbal or written negotiations concerning purchase price, terms, or conditions

■ CONTENT OF LISTING AND BUYER AGENCY AGREEMENTS

The license laws require that *agency agreements* must be *in writing* and contain the following information:

■ The name and address of broker performing the services and the name of the person or persons for whom the acts were done or services rendered

■ All the terms and conditions to the contract

■ The date on which the agreement is entered into

■ The expiration date of the agreement

■ The type of listing agreement

■ The signature of the real estate broker or the broker's authorized agent

■ The signature(s) of the person(s) for whom the services will be rendered or an agent authorized to act on behalf of such person(s) (except that listing contracts for one- to four-family residences must be signed by the owner(s) of the property or an agent authorized to act pursuant to a written agreement)

■ If a brokerage firm represents both buyers and sellers (or landlords and tenants), a statement that the potential exists for a broker to be a dual agent

■ An identification of the compensation to be paid and, in boldface type immediately preceding the provision relating to compensation, the following statement:

NOTICE: THE AMOUNT OR RATE OF REAL ESTATE BROKER COMPENSATION IS NOT FIXED BY LAW. IT IS SET BY EACH BROKER INDIVIDUALLY AND MAY BE NEGOTIABLE BETWEEN YOU AND THE BROKER.

■ A statement acknowledging adherence to the Connecticut statutes pertaining to fair housing:

This agreement is subject to the Connecticut general statutes prohibiting discrimination in commercial and residential real estate transactions (CGS Title 46a, Chapter 814c).

■ The following statement regarding broker's lien rights:

THE REAL ESTATE BROKER MAY BE ENTITLED TO CERTAIN LIEN RIGHTS PURSUANT TO SECTION 20-325A OF THE CONNECTICUT GENERAL STATUTES.

Additional Requirements for Listing Contracts

The licensing regulations additionally require that listing agreements contain the following:

- A proper identification of the property must be provided.
- If the broker or agent has a present or contemplated interest in the property, the listing agreement must contain a disclosure of the interest.
- If the broker is going to allow unaffiliated brokers to advertise the listing, the listing agreement must contain a disclosure as to who will be allowed to advertise the property, exceptions to the advertising, and an authorization by the seller/landlord for such advertising.

While local practice or individual preference may dictate the additional provisions, the law requires only what is listed above. Licensees are required to immediately deliver a copy of an executed listing or buyer agency agreement to any party or parties who have executed it.

Agreements Other Than Listing Agreements or Buyer Agency Contracts

For all contractual commitments other than listing or buyer agency agreements, licensees are required to use their best efforts to ensure that the agreements are in writing, dated, and express the agreement of the parties involved. The licensee is responsible for immediately delivering a copy of such agreement to the party or parties executing it.

■ NET LISTINGS

Connecticut law imposes relatively few limitations on listing arrangements; the only strict prohibition concerns *net listings*. A *net listing* is defined as a listing contract in which the broker receives as a commission all excess monies above a minimum sales price agreed on by the broker and seller. Connecticut license law regulations provide that a licensed broker may not accept a listing that is based on a "net" price.

■ OBLIGATIONS ASSOCIATED WITH EXCLUSIVE AGREEMENTS

When an exclusive listing agreement is drawn up between an owner and a broker (or brokerage agency), this fact must be clearly indicated in the wording of the agency contract. A broker who enters into an exclusive listing with a seller or lessor must make a *diligent effort* to sell or lease the property involved because an exclusive-agency contract severely limits the number of persons who may market the property.

A broker that enters into an exclusive buyer agency agreement with a prospective buyer or lessee must make a *diligent effort* to find a property within the prospective buyer's or lessee's specifications.

■ FAIR HOUSING

Connecticut statutes pertaining to fair housing prohibit discrimination (on the basis of Connecticut's protected classes) with respect to rental housing, commercial property, the sale of building lots, and other real property interests. Connecticut licensing regulations require that all listing agreements and buyer agency agreements clearly state their adherence to the Connecticut Statutes pertaining to *fair housing* with *language* to the following effect:

> *"This agreement is subject to the Connecticut General Statutes prohibiting discrimination in commercial and residential real estate transactions (CGS Title 46a, Chapter 814c)."*

License law regulations also prohibit licensees from participating in activities that constitute blockbusting, steering, or redlining. Fair housing laws are discussed in more detail in Chapter 15.

■ DISCLOSURE

A licensee owes certain duties to parties above and beyond the fiduciary duties owed to clients under agency law.

Interest in Property

Licensees who have a present or contemplated interest in a property listed with them must disclose that interest to all parties concerned. Licensees must also disclose to the buyer or seller any relationship that exists to the seller or buyer, such as immediate family member or member of the same real estate firm.

Material Facts

A licensee has a duty to *disclose material facts* about a property or transaction and cannot misrepresent or conceal a material fact. This duty applies even when the licensee does not represent a party. For example, if a licensee represented a seller in the sale of real estate, the licensee has a duty to disclose material facts about the property to potential buyers.

A material fact is generally characterized as an important fact about real estate or the transaction involving the real estate which, if known, may persuade a buyer or seller of the real estate to make a different decision as to whether to purchase or sell the real estate and at what price. In other words, a material fact is a fact that might change a reasonable person's mind about buying the property or the price offered.

Nonmaterial Facts

By law, a fact related to whether a property occupant has or had a *disease* listed by the Public Health Commissioner, or the fact that there was a *death or felony* on the property, is *not considered material*. Therefore, sellers, landlords, and licensees are not liable for failure to disclose these issues. However, if a purchaser or tenant advises the owner or licensee in writing that this information is important to their decision, then the owner or licensee does have a duty to disclose in writing any knowledge about whether a suicide, murder, or other felony occurred on the property (but not disease status of persons that lived on the property).

Sales Price

Licensees are required to accurately represent the sales price of a property. In other words, in any documentation required to be submitted to a lender, government office, or other person or entity, the licensee must state the actual selling price of the property and not a lower or higher number.

Property Condition Disclosure

Sellers are required to provide prospective buyers with a *property condition report* in all residential real estate transactions (with few exceptions). Real estate licensees should advise a seller-client of the seller's responsibility. The state form and more information about this disclosure are presented in Chapter 7.

Off-site Conditions

Sellers and agents are potentially liable to a buyer for failure to disclose off-site hazardous waste conditions and properties on which hunting and shooting take place. Connecticut law excuses both the seller and the seller's agent of any such liability if the seller provides a written notice to potential purchasers of the availability of Connecticut Department of Environmental Protection lists and the list of properties used for hunting or shooting sports at the office of the town clerk. The notice needs to be given either before or at the time the purchase contract is signed; in practice it is often contained as a provision in the purchase contract. More detail about this and other environmental disclosures is provided in Chapter 17.

Agency Disclosure

A licensee representing a seller, buyer, landlord, or lessee is required to make a written disclosure of whom he or she represents in the transaction to any *unrepresented party* in the transaction. The state mandates the form to be used; see Figure 1.6 and refer to Chapter 1 for a complete discussion of this agency disclosure requirement.

■ ADVERTISING

For purposes of the licensing law, *advertising* is defined as "all forms of identification, representation, promotion, and solicitation disseminated in any manner and by any means of communication to the public for any purposes related to real estate activity."

The license law and regulations prohibit brokers and salespersons from advertising in a manner that misrepresents material facts or makes false promises. In addition, the following rules apply to ads:

■ Salespersons cannot advertise listed property in their own name. All advertisements placed by a salesperson must be made in the name of the broker (or brokerage agency) under whom the salesperson is licensed.

■ A broker must identify himself or herself or the brokerage agency in ads. A broker cannot imply in an ad that a non–real estate person is offering property. Ads containing only a post office box number, telephone number, or street address and no other identifying information are known as blind ads, and *blind ads* are illegal.

■ A broker must get permission to advertise real estate listed with another broker (in turn, that listing broker was required to get seller authorization to allow others to advertise the property) and also permission to modify any of the other broker's listing information. Advertising of real estate listed with another broker must specifically state that the real estate is not listed with the advertising broker and must be updated at least once every 72 hours.

Internet Advertising

All requirements outlined in the above section apply to advertising on the Internet. In addition, all Internet advertising by a broker or salesperson must include the following four items *on every page* of the Internet site:

1. Licensee's name and office address
2. Name of real estate broker that the licensee is affiliated with
3. All states where the licensee is licensed
4. Last date that property information was updated

Any electronic communication of advertising or marketing material must contain the first three items above on the first or last page of the communication. Electronic communication includes e-mail, e-mail discussion group postings, and bulletin board postings.

Signs

Brokers are not permitted to place For Sale or For Rent signs on the property of another without the consent of the owner and without a valid listing contract that authorizes use of the sign.

■ RECORD RETENTION

Real estate brokers are required to retain certain real estate brokerage records for *seven years*. The following documents must be kept:

■ Offers and counteroffers drafted by the broker's office
■ Contracts
■ Leases
■ Agency agreements and disclosures
■ Escrow and trust account checks and bank statements

The documents must be kept regardless of whether the transaction actually closed. The seven years starts running from the time when a transaction closes or funds held in escrow are disbursed, or in the case of a transaction that does not close, when the agency agreement expires. Retention can be in electronic form, as long as a paper copy can be made.

■ WEB LINK

Chapter 392 of Connecticut General Statutes, Real Estate Brokers and Salespersons: *www.cga.ct.gov/2009/pub/Chap392.htm*

FIGURE 2.1

Exclusive-Right-to-Sell Listing Contract

Exclusive Right to Sell Agreement

Date of this Agreement: _____ / _____ / _____

Address of Property: _____

Owner(s): _____

_____

List Price: _____

Present Encumbrances: ☐ first mortgage   ☐ second mortgage   ☐ right of way/easement
                        ☐ tax lien   ☐ other _____

Terms of Sale: _____

_____

Listing Beginning Date: _____ / _____ / _____   Listing Ending Date: _____ / _____ / _____

Fees: _____

Procuring Cause Protection Period: _____

Special Showing Instructions, including exceptions to Internet display: _____

_____

ENVIRONMENTALLY HAZARDOUS CONDITIONS AND MATERIALS

	Is Present	Is Not Present	Was Removed	No Knowledge of its presence
Lead Paint	☐	☐	☐	☐
Asbestos	☐	☐	☐	☐
Mold	☐	☐	☐	☐
Underground Storage Tank	☐	☐	☐	☐
Hazardous Waste	☐	☐	☐	☐
Radon	☐	☐	☐	☐

AGREEMENT

1. **Fees:** The Owner(s) agrees to pay the Broker the service fee specified above (a) if the Broker or its agent(s) produces a purchaser who is ready, willing and able to purchase the Property at the List Price and on the Terms stated, or at such other price or such other terms as may be acceptable to Owner(s), or (b) if a sale or exchange of said Property is made by the Owner(s) or any other person during the term of this Exclusive Right to Sell or any Procuring Cause Protection period set forth above. If fee is to be computed with reference to the sale or purchase price, the sale or purchase price shall be the greater of the amount shown as purchase or sale price on the purchase and sale contract between seller and buyer without reference to any credits or pro-rations, or the amount on which the conveyance tax due the Commissioner of Revenue Services is calculated, whichever is greater.

2. **Procuring Cause Protection Period:** The Owner(s) agrees to pay the service fee to the Broker should a sale be made directly or indirectly within the Procuring Cause Protection Period to parties the Broker or its agent(s) has submitted the Property to during the term of this Exclusive Right To Sell Agreement and Broker notifies Owner(s) in writing of the submissions during the Term of this Exclusive Right To Sell Agreement. This paragraph shall not apply if the Owner(s) subsequently executes a valid exclusive listing with any other real estate broker.

3. **Marketing:** The Broker agrees to market the Property for sale and to make a diligent effort to sell at the List Price and on the Terms stated herein until there is an enforceable contract for the sale of the Property or this Exclusive Right To Sell Agreement expires, whichever occurs first.

4. **Signs and Keys:** The Owner(s) gives the Broker the right to place a "For Sale" sign on the Property and to remove all other "For Sale" signs during continuance of this Exclusive Right To Sell Agreement. The Owner(s) agrees to furnish the Broker with a key to the Property and to permit the Broker to place a keybox on the door.

©2002-2007 Connecticut Association of REALTORS®, Inc.   1
May 23, 2002; Revised July 16, 2002; August 31, 2004; April 2, 2007, January 15, 2010

F I G U R E 2.1 (continued)

Exclusive-Right-to-Sell Listing Contract

5. **Entry and Control:** The Broker or any of its agent(s) may enter the Property at reasonable times for the purpose of showing it to prospective purchasers in accordance with any Special Showing Instructions as noted above. Owner(s) acknowledges that the Broker has a duty under state regulations and the Code of Ethics to cooperate with other brokers to show the Property. Owner(s) and Broker agree that Owner(s) shall at all times have control over the Property, its maintenance and preparation for showing to prospective purchasers. Owner agrees to indemnify and hold Broker, its successors and assigns, harmless from all suits, claims, demands or damages related to or arising from the physical condition of the Property.

6. **Owner(s)' Agreements:**
   a. Owner(s) agrees to complete and keep updated a Connecticut Residential Property Condition Disclosure Report and Title X Lead-based paint disclosure (if applicable) and authorizes the Broker to disclose the information contained therein.
   b. Owner(s) is either the Owner(s) of the Listed Property or has full authority to enter into this Agreement.
   c. Owner(s) has received a copy of this Agreement.
   d. Owner(s) represents that there are no other listings or agreements in effect concerning this Property, including open listings.
   e. Owner(s) understands that names of attorneys, contractors, and other professionals are furnished as an accommodation to Owner(s) and do not constitute an endorsement or guaranty of such professional or the professional's work product.
   f. Owner(s) agrees to pay reasonable attorney's fees that Broker may incur to collect monies due under this Agreement.
   g. Broker reserves the right to terminate this Contract by written notice to the Owner(s) if the Broker has reasonable cause to believe the Owner(s) may be unable to consummate a sale of the Listed Property for the List Price set forth above by reason of liens, encumbrances, title disputes or other matters affecting title to the Property.
   h. Owner(s) agrees to refer to Broker all requests for information about showings or offers for the Property, and to advise said Broker of any contacts made by any prospective buyer, tenant, or other broker.

7. **Property Information:** Owner(s) has reviewed the information contained on this Exclusive Right To Sell Agreement, the property data sheet, and any other disclosure of information forms where Owner(s) supplies information. To the best of Owner's knowledge and belief, Owner(s) represents that any material defects regarding the Listed Property have been disclosed to Broker and the information contained in such information forms are complete and accurate. Owner(s) agrees to indemnify and hold the Broker or its agent(s) harmless from any claim, action, damage or cost, including attorney fees, that Broker or its agent(s) may incur resulting from an incorrect or inaccurate representation, a misrepresentation or lack of representation of any of the information contained in such forms. Any representations made by Owner(s) are not warranties of any kind and may not be a substitute for an inspection or warranties that a prospective buyer may obtain. Owner(s) authorizes Broker as Owner's agent to disclose any information that Owner(s) provides to Broker concerning the Property.

8. **Multiple Listing Service and Internet Display:** Owner (s) acknowledges and agrees that all images, graphics, video recordings, virtual tours, written descriptions, remarks, narratives, pricing information, and other elements relating to the Property provided by Owner (s) to Broker or Broker's agent (the "Owner Listing Content"), or otherwise obtained or produced by Broker or Broker's agent in connection with this Agreement (the "Broker Listing Content"), and any changes to such Content may be included in compilations of listings, and otherwise distributed, displayed and reproduced to the Multiple Listing Service noted above for publication to and use by its participants. Unless otherwise indicated under "special showing instructions" above, Owner(s) agrees to permit other Brokers licensed in Connecticut to display Owner Listing Content on their web site(s) as part of the Internet Listing Display or similar program offered by the MLS or otherwise or with other media, at Broker's option. Broker may display the Property on its web sites. Owner(s) agrees that neither the provider of the MLS nor Broker are responsible for errors or omissions appearing in the MLS. The Owner(s) authorizes Broker to provide timely notice of status changes of this Exclusive Right to Sell Agreement and to provide sales information including selling price upon sale of the Property to any agreed upon Multiple Listing Service(s).

Owner hereby grants to Broker for the term of this listing, as may be extended from time-to-time, a non-exclusive, irrevocable, worldwide, royalty free license to use, sublicense through multiple tiers, publish, display, compile with other content and reproduce the Owner Listing Content, to prepare derivative works of the Owner Listing Content, and to distribute the Owner Listing Content or any derivative works of it. Owner acknowledges and agrees that as between Owner and Broker, all Broker Listing Content is owned exclusively by Broker, and Owner has no right, title or interest in or to any Broker Listing Content.

EQUAL HOUSING OPPORTUNITY   REALTOR®

F I G U R E 2.1 (continued)

Exclusive-Right-to-Sell Listing Contract

9. **Statements Required By Law or the REALTOR® Code of Ethics:**
   (a) This Agreement is subject to the Connecticut General Statutes prohibiting discrimination in commercial and residential real estate transactions (Connecticut General Statute Title 46a, Chapter 814c).
   (b) THE REAL ESTATE BROKER MAY BE ENTITLED TO CERTAIN LIEN RIGHTS PURSUANT TO SUBSECTION (d) OF SECTION 20-325a OF THE CONNECTICUT GENERAL STATUTES.
   (c) **NOTICE: THE AMOUNT OR RATE OF REAL ESTATE BROKER COMPENSATION IS NOT FIXED BY LAW. IT IS SET BY EACH BROKER INDIVIDUALLY AND MAY BE NEGOTIABLE BETWEEN YOU AND THE BROKER.**
   (d) Federal law requires the Owner(s) of "target property," which is generally property built prior to 1978, to disclose the presence of lead-based paint or lead-based paint hazards and to furnish any records, reports, inspections, or other documents in the Owner's possession concerning these items.
   (e) Agency Relationships: While Broker shall generally act as the agent for Owner(s), it may be necessary or appropriate for Broker to act as agent of both Owner(s) and buyer(s), exchange party, or one or more additional parties. Owner(s) understands that Broker may have or obtain listings on other properties and that potential buyers may consider, make offers on, or purchase other property through use of Broker's services.

10. **Electronic Signatures**: Broker and Owner(s) agree that they may use an electronic record, including fax or e-mail, to make and keep this Agreement. Either Broker or Owner(s) has the right to withdraw consent to have a record of this Agreement provided or made available to them in electronic form, but that does not permit that party to withdraw consent to the Agreement itself once it has been signed. Broker's and Owner's agreement to use electronic records applies only to this particular real estate transaction and not to all real estate transactions.

    For access to and retention of faxed records, there are no special hardware or software requirements beyond access to a fax machine or fax modem and accompanying software connected to a personal or laptop computer. For access to and retention of e-mail records, Owner(s) will need a personal or laptop computer, Internet account and e-mail software.

    Owner(s) has the following electronic addresses: Fax number is:_____

    E-mail address is:_____

    Each party will promptly inform the other of any change in e-mail address or fax number in writing or electronically.

11. The Owner(s) and Broker acknowledge, agree and understand that although this form has been furnished by the Connecticut Association of REALTORS®, Inc., the Association assumes no responsibility for its content and is not a party to this Agreement. **This Contract is binding and legal.**

OWNER	DATE	BROKER/AGENCY NAME

STREET	STREET

CITY/STATE/ZIP	CITY/STATE/ZIP

OWNER	DATE	AUTHORIZED AGENT

STREET	E-MAIL ADDRESS

CITY/STATE/ZIP

©2002-2007 Connecticut Association of REALTORS®, Inc.   3
May 23, 2002; Revised July 16, 2002; August 31, 2004; April 2, 2007, January 15, 2010

FIGURE 2.2

Exclusive-Agency Right to Sell

Exclusive Agency Right to Sell Agreement

Date of this Agreement: _____ / _____ / _____

Address of Property: _____

Owner(s): _____

_____

List Price: _____

Present Encumbrances: ☐ first mortgage   ☐ second mortgage   ☐ right of way/easement
                ☐ tax lien   ☐ Other_____

Terms of Sale: _____

_____

Listing Beginning Date : _____ / _____ / _____   Listing Ending Date: _____ / _____ / _____

Service Fee: _____

Procuring Cause Protection Period: _____

Special Showing Instructions, including exceptions to Internet display: _____

_____

ENVIRONMENTALLY HAZARDOUS CONDITIONS AND MATERIALS			
	Is Present	Is Not Present	Was Removed	No Knowledge of its presence
Lead Paint	☐	☐	☐	☐
Asbestos	☐	☐	☐	☐
Mold	☐	☐	☐	☐
Underground Storage Tank	☐	☐	☐	☐
Hazardous Waste	☐	☐	☐	☐
Radon	☐	☐	☐	☐

AGREEMENT

1. **Fees:** The Owner(s) agrees to pay the Broker the service fee specified above (a) if the Broker or its agent(s) produces a buyer who is ready, willing and able to purchase the Property at the List Price and on the Terms stated, or at such other price or such other terms as may be acceptable to Owner(s) or (b) if a sale or exchange of said Property is made by the Owner(s) to any person who became interested in the Property through or on account of Broker's efforts or any other real estate broker or salesperson's efforts during the term of this Exclusive Agency Right to Sell or any Procuring Cause Protection period set forth above. If fee is to be computed with reference to the sale or purchase price, the sale or purchase price shall be the greater of the amount shown as purchase or sale price on the purchase and sale contract between seller and buyer without reference to any credits or pro-rations, or the amount on which the conveyance tax due the Commissioner of Revenue Services is calculated, whichever is greater.

2. **Procuring Cause Protection Period:** The Owner(s) agrees to pay the service fee to the Broker should a sale be made directly or indirectly within the Procuring Cause Protection Period to parties the Broker has submitted the Property to during the term of this Exclusive Agency Right To Sell Agreement and Broker notifies Owner(s) in writing of the submissions during the Term of this Exclusive Agency Right To Sell Agreement. This paragraph shall not apply if the Owner(s) subsequently executes a valid exclusive listing with any other real estate broker.

3. **Marketing:** The Broker agrees to market the Property for sale and to make a diligent effort to sell at the List Price and on the Terms stated herein until there is an enforceable contract for the sale of the Property or this Exclusive Agency Right to Sell Agreement expires, whichever occurs first.

FIGURE 2.2 (continued)

Exclusive-Agency Right to Sell

4. **Signs and Keys:** The Owner(s) gives the Broker the right to place a "For Sale" sign on the Property and to remove all other "For Sale" signs during continuance of this Exclusive Agency Right To Sell Agreement. The Owner(s) agrees to furnish the Broker a key to the Property and permit the Broker to place a keybox on the door.

5. **Entry and Control:** The Broker or any of its agent(s) may enter the Property at reasonable times for the purpose of showing it to prospective purchasers in accordance with any Special Showing Instructions as noted above. Owner(s) acknowledges that the Broker has a duty under state regulations and the Code of Ethics to cooperate with other brokers to show the Property. Owner(s) and Broker agree that Owner(s) shall at all times have control over the Property, its maintenance and preparation for showing to prospective purchasers. Owner agrees to indemnify and hold Broker, its successors and assigns, harmless from all suits, claims, demands or damages related to or arising from the physical condition of the Property.

6. **Owner(s)'s Agreements:**
   (a) Owner(s) agrees to complete and keep updated a Connecticut Residential Property Condition Disclosure Report and authorizes the Broker to disclose the information contained therein.
   (b) Owner(s) is either the Owner(s) of the listed property or has full authority to enter into this Agreement.
   (c) Owner(s) has received a copy of this Agreement.
   (d) Owner(s) represents that there are no other listings or agreements in effect concerning this Property, including open listings.
   (e) Owner(s) understands that names of attorneys, contractors, and other professionals are furnished as an accommodation to Owner(s) and do not constitute an endorsement or guaranty of such professional or the professional's work product.
   (f) Owner(s) agrees to pay reasonable attorney's fees that Broker may incur to collect monies due under this Agreement.
   (g) Broker reserves the right to terminate this Contract by written notice to the Owner(s) if the Broker has reasonable cause to believe the Owner(s) may be unable to consummate a sale of the listed property for the List Price set forth above by reason of liens, encumbrances, title disputes or other matters affecting title to the Property.

7. **Property Information:** Owner(s) has reviewed the information contained on this Exclusive Agency Right To Sell Agreement and the property data sheet and any other disclosure of information forms where Owner(s) supplies information. To the best of Owner's knowledge and belief, Owner(s) represents that any material defects regarding the Listed Property have been disclosed to Broker and the information contained in such information forms are complete and accurate. Owner(s) agrees to indemnify and hold the Broker or its agent(s) harmless from any claim, action, damage or cost, including attorney fees that Broker or its agent(s) may incur resulting from an incorrect or inaccurate representation, a misrepresentation, or lack of representation of any of the information contained in such forms. Any representations made by Owner(s) are not warranties of any kind and may not be a substitute for an inspection or warranties that a prospective buyer may obtain. Owner(s) authorizes Broker as Owner's agent to disclose any information that Owner(s) provides to Broker concerning the Property.

8. **Multiple Listing Service:** Owner acknowledges and agrees that all images, graphics, video recordings, virtual tours, written descriptions, remarks, narratives, pricing information, and other elements relating to the Property provided by Owner(s) to Broker or Broker's agent (the "Owner Listing Content"), or otherwise obtained or produced by Broker or Broker's agent in connection with this Agreement (the "Broker Listing Content"), and any changes to such Content may be included in compilations of listings, and otherwise distributed, displayed and reproduced to the Multiple Listing Service noted above for publication to and use by its participants. Unless otherwise indicated under "special showing instructions" above, Owner(s) agrees to permit other Brokers licensed in Connecticut to display Owner Listing Content on their web site(s) as part of the Internet Listing Display or similar program offered by the MLS or otherwise or with other media, at Broker's option. Broker may display the Property on its web sites. Owner(s) agrees that neither the provider of the MLS nor Broker are responsible for errors or omissions appearing in the MLS. The Owner(s) authorizes Broker to provide timely notice of status changes of this Exclusive Agency Right to Sell Agreement and to provide sales information including selling price upon sale of the Property to any agreed upon Multiple Listing Service(s).

Owner hereby grants to Broker for the term of this listing, as may be extended from time-to-time, a non-exclusive, irrevocable, worldwide, royalty free license to use, sublicense through multiple tiers, publish, display, compile with other content and reproduce the Owner Listing Content, to prepare derivative works of the Owner Listing Content, and to distribute the Owner Listing Content or any derivative works of it. Owner acknowledges and agrees that as between Owner and Broker, all Broker Listing Content is owned exclusively by Broker, and Owner has no right, title or interest in or to any Broker Listing Content.

F I G U R E   2.2 (continued)

Exclusive-Agency Right to Sell

9. **Statements Required By Law or the REALTOR® Code of Ethics:**

   (a) This Agreement is subject to the Connecticut General Statutes prohibiting discrimination in commercial and residential real estate transactions (Connecticut General Statute Title 46a, Chapter 814c).

   (b) THE REAL ESTATE BROKER MAY BE ENTITLED TO CERTAIN LIEN RIGHTS PURSUANT TO SUBSECTION (d) OF SECTION 20-325a OF THE CONNECTICUT GENERAL STATUTES.

   (c) **NOTICE: THE AMOUNT OR RATE OF REAL ESTATE BROKER COMPENSATION IS NOT FIXED BY LAW. IT IS SET BY EACH BROKER INDIVIDUALLY AND MAY BE NEGOTIABLE BETWEEN YOU AND THE BROKER.**

   (d) Federal law requires the Owner(s) of "target property," which is generally property built prior to 1978, to disclose the presence of lead-based paint or lead-based paint hazards and to furnish any records, reports, inspections, or other documents in the Owner's possession concerning these items.

   (e) **Agency Relationships:** While Broker shall generally act as the agent for Owner(s), it may be necessary or appropriate for Broker to act as agent of both Owner(s) and buyer(s), exchange party, or one or more additional parties. Broker shall provide agency disclosure as required by law. Owner(s) understands that Broker may have or obtain listings on other properties and that potential buyers may consider, make offers on, or purchase other property through use of Broker's services.

10. **Electronic Signatures:** Broker and Owner(s) agree that they may use an electronic record, including fax or e-mail, to make and keep this Agreement. Either Broker or Owner(s) has the right to withdraw consent to have a record of this Agreement provided or made available to them in electronic form, but that does not permit that party to withdraw consent to the Agreement itself once it has been signed. Broker's and Owner's agreement to use an electronic record applies only to this particular real estate transaction and not to all real estate transactions.

   For access to and retention of faxed records, there are no special hardware or software requirements beyond access to a fax machine or fax modem and accompanying software connected to a personal or laptop computer. For access to and retention of e-mail records, Owner(s) will need a personal or laptop computer, Internet account and e-mail software.

   Owner(s) electronic addresses: Fax number is: _____

   E-mail address is: _____

   Each party will promptly inform the other of any change in e-mail address or fax number in writing or electronically.

11. The Owner(s) and Broker acknowledge, agree and understand that although this form has been furnished by the Connecticut Association of REALTORS®, Inc., the Association assumes no responsibility for its content and is not a party to this Agreement. **This Contract is binding and legal.**

_____	_____	_____
OWNER	DATE	BROKER/AGENCY NAME
_____		_____
STREET		STREET
_____		_____
CITY/STATE/ZIP		CITY/STATE/ZIP
_____	_____	_____
OWNER	DATE	AUTHORIZED AGENT
_____		_____
STREET		E-MAIL ADDRESS
_____		
CITY/STATE/ZIP		

F I G U R E 2.3

Open Listing Agreement

Open Listing Agreement

PARTIES AND PROPERTY:

I/We _____ , Owner(s), give You, __
_____ , Realtor® the right to list for sale
my/our real property on a non-exclusive basis at:
_____ , in _____ , CT.

SELLING TERMS:

The Listed Price shall be $_____ .

TERM OF THIS LISTING:

This Listing Agreement will take effect on _____ , 20____, and will remain in
effect through and including _____ , 20____, provided however that this Listing
Agreement shall terminate sooner if I/We notify You that I/We have entered into an Exclusive Agency or an
Exclusive Right to Sell Listing Agreement for the Listed Property and You have not yet earned a
commission as provided in this Agreement. Upon full execution of an agreement for the sale of the Listed
Property, all rights and obligations under this Listing Agreement will automatically extend through the date of
the actual closing of the Listed Property and may not be revoked or canceled once You have executed a
purchase contract for the sale of the Property to a buyer we found.

PAYMENT OF SERVICE OR FEE:

If during the term of this Listing Agreement You find a buyer ready, willing and able to buy the Listed
Property, either on the terms specified in this Listing Agreement or on any other terms acceptable to me/us,
I/We will pay You a service fee of: (check one)

☐ _____% (percent) of the sale price reported for conveyance tax purposes without
adjustment for any credits or pro-rations.
☐ a retainer of $_____ .
☐ a flat fee of $_____ .
☐ an hourly rate of $_____ per hour.
☐ Other _____

OWNER'S AND REALTOR'S® AGREEMENTS:

1. This is NOT an Exclusive Agency or Exclusive Right to Sell Listing Agreement. I/We understand that the
   Listed Property will not be placed in any multiple listing service. I/We may sell the Listed Property
   myself/ourselves or through another broker or agent.
2. If this is a 1-4 family residential property, I/We represent that I/We have good title to the Listed Property and
   that I/We have the right to sell the Listed Property.
3. I/We have received a copy of this Listing Agreement.
   I/We agree to pay any costs and attorney's fees which You may incur to collect any monies due to You
   under this Listing Agreement.
4. I/We authorize You, as my/our agent, to disclose any information that I/We provide You concerning the
   Listed Property. You may market this Property on the Internet or World Wide Web. You are not responsible
   for the accuracy of the information supplied to You by me/us.
5. You are not responsible for the management, maintenance or upkeep of, or for any physical damage to, the
   Listed Property or its contents.
6. This Listing Agreement is binding upon me/us, or against my/our heirs, administrators, executors,
   successors and assigns, and your successors and assigns.
7. The real estate broker may be entitled to certain lien rights pursuant to Section 20-325a of the Connecticut
   General Statutes.

Open Listing Agreement

8.   Other terms:

_____

_____

_____

_____

ENTRY AND CONTROL

You or any of your agent(s) may enter the Property at reasonable times for the purpose of showing it to prospective purchasers. I/We acknowledge that You have a duty under state regulations and the Code of Ethics to cooperate with other brokers to show the Property. I/We and You agree that I/We shall at all times have control over the Property, its maintenance and preparation for showing to prospective purchasers. I/We agree to indemnify and hold You, your successors and assigns, harmless from all suits, claims, demands or damages related to or arising from the physical condition of the Property.

ELECTRONIC SIGNATURE:

A.   I/We agree that You may use an electronic record, including fax or e-mail, to make and keep this Agreement.

B.   I/We need not agree to use an electronic record. By a written notice to You, I/We have the right to withdraw consent to have a record of this Agreement provided or made available to Me/Us in electronic form, but that does not permit Me/Us to withdraw consent to the Agreement itself once it has been signed. You will provide Me/Us with a paper copy of this Agreement should I/We request one in writing to the address, e-mail or fax number listed below. My/Our agreement to use an electronic record applies only to this particular real estate transaction and not to all real estate transactions in which I/We are a party.

C.   For access to and retention of faxed records, there is no special hardware or software requirements beyond access to a fax machine or fax modem and accompanying software connected to a personal or laptop computer. For access to and retention of e-mail records, I/We will need a personal or laptop computer, Internet account and e-mail software or web browser.

My/Our electronic addresses are: fax number is:_____

e-mail address is:_____

All electronic records will be sent to the fax number or e-mail address noted above unless I/We inform You of any change in My/Our e-mail address or fax number in writing to You at the Brokerage Firm address, e-mail or fax number set forth.

STATEMENTS REQUIRED BY LAW:

- THIS AGREEMENT IS SUBJECT TO CHAPTER 814c OF TITLE 64a OF THE GENERAL STATUTES AS AMENDED (HUMAN RIGHTS AND OPPORTUNITIES). IT IS UNLAWFUL UNDER FEDERAL AND STATE LAW TO DISCRIMINATE ON THE BASIS OF RACE, COLOR, RELIGION, NATIONAL ORIGIN, SEX, MARITAL STATUS, FAMILIES WITH CHILDREN AND/OR PHYSICAL HANDICAP IN THE ACQUISITION OR DISPOSITION OF REAL PROPERTY.

- **NOTICE: THE AMOUNT OR RATE OF REAL ESTATE BROKER COMPENSATION IS NOT FIXED BY LAW. IT IS SET BY EACH BROKER INDIVIDUALLY AND MAY BE NEGOTIABLE BETWEEN YOU AND THE BROKER.**

- Federal law requires the seller of a dwelling which is considered to be "target housing" (meaning with some exceptions, housing built before 1978) to disclose the presence of lead-based paint and lead-based paint hazards, and to furnish any records or reports concerning lead-based paint or lead-based paint hazards to a buyer. A seller must permit a buyer a 10-day period (unless the parties mutually agree in writing to a different time period) to conduct a risk assessment or inspection of the property for the presence of lead-based paint and lead-based paint hazards before a buyer is obligated to proceed with any Agreement.

FIGURE 2.3 (continued)

Open Listing Agreement

- Agency Relationships: While Broker shall generally act as the agent for Owner(s), it may be necessary or appropriate for Broker to act as agent of both Owner(s) and buyer(s), exchange party, or one or more additional parties. Broker shall provide agency disclosure as required by law. Owner(s) understands that Broker may have or obtain listings on other properties and that potential buyers may consider, make offers on, or purchase other property through use of Broker's services.

The Owner(s) and Broker acknowledge, agree and understand that although this form has been furnished by the Connecticut Association of REALTORS®, Inc., the Association assumes no responsibility for its content and is not a party to this Agreement. **This Contract is binding and legal.**

REALTOR® Firm Name		Owner	Date
Authorized Representative	Date	Owner	Date
Street		Street	
City	State	Zip	City	State	Zip
Telephone		Telephone	

F I G U R E 2.4

Exclusive Right to Represent Buyer or Tenant Authorization

Exclusive Right to Represent Buyer and Tenant Authorization
(Connecticut law requires that the real estate broker furnish you with a written agreement should you wish to be represented.)

I. Exclusive Right Appointment.

You, _____ (Buyer/Tenant), appoint

Us, _____ (Firm/Broker) as your exclusive real estate

broker to assist You to locate and purchase, exchange or lease real property acceptable to You and generally described

as: _____

_____ (the "Property").

II. Geographical Area.

This Authorization is limited to the following areas of the State of Connecticut:_____

_____

_____

III. Term of Authorization.

This Authorization is in effect from _____ to _____, inclusive.

IV. Broker's Duties.

    A. We will keep information You provide Us concerning your assets, liabilities, income and expenses, motivations to buy or rent and previous offers made confidential unless you give permission for disclosure or disclosure is mandated by law.

    B. We will provide You with the benefit of our advice and experience.

    C. We will attempt to locate the Property.

    D. We will negotiate on your behalf for terms and conditions agreeable to You.

    E. We will assist You in the purchase, exchange or lease, as the case may be, of the Property.

    F. We will act in your interest regarding the location and purchase, exchange or lease of the Property.

    G. **Questions or information requests concerning the legal title to property, the residence of convicted persons, tax considerations, wood destroying pests, environmental conditions, property and building inspections, engineering, or the uses or planned uses of neighboring properties should be referred to your attorney, tax advisor, building inspector or appropriate governmental agency.**

V. Buyer's/Tenant's Duties.

    A. You will cooperate with Us and be reasonably available to examine real property.

    B. Upon request, You will give Us financial and personal information regarding your purchase abilities and needs.

    C. We are relying on your statement that You have not signed an Exclusive Right to Represent Buyer or Tenant Authorization or Exclusive Agency Right to Represent Buyer or Tenant Authorization with any other brokerage firm covering the same time period, the same Property or the same Geographical Areas as stated above. If this is not the case, please tell Us immediately.

    D. You understand that the names of attorneys, contractors, home inspectors and other professionals are furnished as an accommodation to You and do not constitute an endorsement or guaranty of such professionals or their work product.

VI. Other Terms and Conditions.

    A. You understand and agree that We may also become a seller's or landlord's agent for the Property. In that event, We would become dual agents, representing both You and the seller or landlord. If this situation should arise, We will promptly disclose all relevant information to You and discuss the appropriate course of action to take under the circumstances. We will also discuss a Dual Agency Consent Agreement with You and present a statutory form of such an agreement for your review and signature.

    B. You know that We represent other buyers or tenants who may be interested in purchasing or renting the same Property as You.

FIGURE 2.4 (continued)

Exclusive Right to Represent Buyer or Tenant Authorization

C. We may, with your permission, share and disclose financial and personal information regarding your purchase abilities and needs with other agents who offer real property to Us.

D. This Authorization is binding upon and shall inure to the benefit of You and Us, and each of our heirs, administrators, executors, successors and assigns. You may not assign this Authorization.

E. You agree to pay any costs and attorneys' fees which We may incur to collect any monies due Us under this Authorization.

F. This Authorization may be modified, waived or discharged only by a written agreement signed by the parties.

G. You are notified that the Department of Environmental Protection is required pursuant to Section 22a-134f of the Connecticut General Statutes to furnish lists of hazardous waste facilities located within the town to the Town Clerk's office. You should refer to these lists and the Department of Environmental Protection for information on environmental questions concerning any property in which You are interested in and the lands surrounding that property.

H. You are notified that a list of local properties upon which hunting or shooting sports regularly take place may be available at the Town Clerk's office.

I. You acknowledge receipt of a copy of this Authorization.

VII. Fees.

A. In consideration of the services to be provided, You agree to pay Us a Professional Service fee calculated as follows:

1. If You are purchasing real estate, our professional service fee will be calculated as follows: $_____ or _____ % of the purchase price of the Property purchased by You, or of the value of Property obtained by You in an exchange.

2. If You are leasing real estate, our professional service fee will be calculated as follows:
$_____ or _____ % of the yearly rental of the Property leased by You. You also agree to pay a commission in the amount noted above on any renewals, enlargements, exercise of lease options, or new leases between yourself and the landlord. Such commission shall be due and payable at the commencement of the new lease, enlargement, renewal, or option term.

3. We earn the professional service fee if You (a) enter into a contract for the purchase or exchange of real property during the term of this Authorization and all material conditions have been met or are subsequently met regardless of how you learn about the Property; (b) enter into a lease, whether oral or written, for the rental of real property during the term of this Authorization and all material conditions have been met or are subsequently met or a lease entered into during the term of this Authorization is renewed or enlarged, You or a landlord exercise a lease option or You enter into a new lease with the landlord even if such renewal, enlargement, new lease or exercise of option takes place after the expiration of this Authorization; or (iii) You are introduced or take occupancy to real property during the term of this Authorization and obtain title to such property within _____ (____) months after the expiration of this Authorization, provided, however, that no fee will be due and payable under this Section VII.A.1.c(c) if You sign an exclusive agreement or authorization with another real estate broker after the expiration of this Authorization.

4. _____ (Other)

C. Any professional service fee We earn under this Authorization is your obligation. However, if You purchase, lease or exchange property either listed with Us or listed on a multiple listing service on which We are a participant, then We will credit you with whatever amounts we receive from either or both of these sources. We will also assist you in negotiating payment of this fee from the seller of the Property and will credit you with any amounts seller actually pays. These credits may pay our fee in full.

D. We will tell You before showing You a Property if the Property is not eligible for this credit, and you may refuse to be shown such properties without incurring a fee. We may accept amounts the seller, landlord or listing broker pay Us in excess of the professional service fee stated upon disclosure to You.

E. You will pay us our professional service fee no later than the date on which title to the real property transfers to You or the date on which You occupy, renew, enlarge a lease or an option is exercised whichever date is applicable to the type of transaction.

F I G U R E 2.4 (continued)

Exclusive Right to Represent Buyer or Tenant Authorization

VIII. Statements Required by Law

    1. This agreement is subject to the Connecticut General Statutes prohibiting discrimination in commercial and residential real estate transactions (C.G.S. Title 46a, Chapter 814c);

    2. THE REALE STATE BOKER MAY BE ENTITLED TO CERTAIN LINE RIGHTS PUSUANT TO SECTION 20-325a OF THE CONNECTICUT GENERAL STATUTES;

    3. **NOTICE: THE AMOUNT OR RATE OF REAL ESTATE BROKER COMPENSATION IS NOT FIXED BY LAW. IT IS SET BY EACH BROKER INDIVIDUALLY AND MAY BE NEGOTIABLE BETWEEN YOU AND THE BROKER.**

IX. Use of Electronic Record.

    A. You agree that we may use an electronic record, including fax or e-mail, to make and keep this Agreement.

    B. You need not agree to use an electronic record. By a written notice to Us, You have the right to withdraw your consent to have a record of this Agreement provided or made available to You in electronic form, but that does not permit You to withdraw your consent to the Agreement itself once it has been signed. We will provide You with a paper copy of this Agreement should You request one in writing to us at the address, e-mail or fax number listed below. Your agreement to use an electronic record applies only to this particular real estate transaction and not to all real estate transactions in which You are a party.

    C. For access to and retention of faxed records, there is no special hardware or software requirements beyond access to a fax machine or fax modem and accompanying software connected to a personal or laptop computer. For access to and retention of e-mail records, you will need a personal or laptop computer, Internet account and e-mail software or web browser.

    My electronic addresses are: Fax number is:_____

                                       E-mail address is:_____

    All electronic records will be sent to the fax number or e-mail address noted above unless you inform us of any change in your e-mail address or fax number in writing to the Brokerage Firm address, e-mail or fax number set forth.

REALTOR® FIRM NAME

By Agent

Street

City, State, Zip

Telephone number and/or e-mail address

Date

BUYER/TENANT

BUYER/TENANT

Street

City, State, Zip

Telephone number

Date

F I G U R E 2.5

Exclusive Agency Right to Represent Buyer or Tenant Authorization

Exclusive Agency Right to Represent Buyer or Tenant Authorization
(Connecticut law requires that the real estate broker furnish you with a written agreement should you wish to be represented by an agent.)

I.   Exclusive Agency Right Appointment.

You, _____ (Buyer/Tenant), appoint
Us, _____ (Firm/Broker), as your exclusive real estate broker to assist You to locate and purchase, exchange or lease real property acceptable to You and generally described as: _____
_____ (the "Property").

II.   Geographical Area.

This Authorization is limited to the following areas of the State of Connecticut:

_____

_____

_____

III.   Term of Authorization.

This Authorization is in effect from _____ to _____, inclusive.

IV.   Broker's Duties.

    A. We will keep information You provide Us concerning your assets, liabilities, income and expenses, motivations to buy or rent and previous offers made confidential unless you give permission for disclosure or disclosure is mandated by law.

    B. We will provide You with the benefit of our advice and experience.

    C. We will attempt to locate the Property.

    D. We will negotiate on your behalf for terms and conditions agreeable to You.

    E. We will assist You in the purchase, exchange or lease, as the case may be, of the Property.

    F. We will act in your interest regarding the location and purchase, exchange or lease of the Property.

    G. **Questions or information requests concerning the legal title to property, the residence of convicted persons, tax considerations, wood destroying pests, environmental conditions, property and building inspections, engineering, or the uses or planned uses of neighboring properties should be referred to your attorney, tax advisor, building inspector or appropriate governmental agency.**

V.   Buyer's/Tenant's Duties.

    A. You will cooperate with Us and be reasonably available to examine real property.

    B. Upon request, You will give Us financial and personal information regarding your purchase abilities and needs.

    C. We are relying on your statement that You have not signed an Exclusive Right to Represent Buyer or Tenant Authorization or Exclusive Agency Right to Represent Buyer or Tenant Authorization with any other brokerage firm covering the same time period, the same Property or the same Geographical Areas as stated above. If this is not the case, please tell Us immediately.

    D. You understand that the names of attorneys, contractors, home inspectors and other professionals are furnished as an accommodation to You and do not constitute an endorsement or guaranty of such professionals or their work product.

VI.   Other Terms and Conditions.

    A. You understand and agree that We may also become a seller's or landlord's agent for the Property. In that event We would become dual agents, representing both You and the seller or landlord. If this situation should arise, We will promptly disclose all relevant information to You and discuss the appropriate course of action to take under the circumstances. We will also discuss a Dual Agency Consent Agreement with You and present a statutory form of such an agreement for your review and signature.

    B. You know that We represent other buyers or tenants who may be interested in purchasing or renting the same Property as You.

    C. We may, with your permission, share and disclose financial and personal information regarding your purchase abilities and needs with other agents who offer real property to Us.

Copyright© 1996-2008 Connecticut Association of REALTORS®, Inc.
Revised February 27, 1997; July 22, 2002; June 11, 2004; April 9, 2007, February 6, 2008, March 3, 2010

F I G U R E 2.5 (continued)

Exclusive Agency Right to Represent Buyer or Tenant Authorization

    D. This Authorization is binding upon and shall inure to the benefit of You and Us, and each of our heirs, administrators, executors, successors and assigns. You may not assign this Authorization.

    E. You agree to pay any costs and attorneys' fees which We may incur to collect any monies due Us under this Authorization.

    F. This Authorization may be modified, waived or discharged only by a written agreement signed by the parties.

    G. You are notified that the Department of Environmental Protection is required pursuant to Section 22a-134f of the Connecticut General Statutes to furnish lists of hazardous waste facilities located within the town to the Town Clerk's office. You should refer to these lists and the Department of Environmental Protection for information on environmental questions concerning any property in which You are interested in and the lands surrounding that property.

    H. You are notified that a list of local properties upon which hunting or shooting sports regularly take place may be available at the Town Clerk's office.

    I. You acknowledge receipt of a copy of this Authorization.

VII.   **Fees.**

    A. In consideration of the services to be provided, You agree to pay Us a Professional Service fee calculated as follows:

        1. If You are purchasing real estate, our professional service fee will be calculated as follows: $_____ or _____ % of the purchase price of the Property purchased by You, or of the value of Property obtained by You in an exchange.

        2. If You are leasing real estate, our professional service fee will be calculated as follows: $ _____ or _____ % of the yearly rental of the Property leased by You. You also agree to pay a commission in the amount noted above on any renewals, enlargements, exercise of lease options, or new leases between yourself and the landlord. Such commission shall be due and payable at the commencement of the new lease, enlargement, renewal, or option term.

        3. We earn the professional service fee if You (a) enter into a contract for the purchase or exchange of real property during the term of this Authorization and all material conditions have been met or are subsequently met; (b) enter into a lease, whether oral or written, for the rental of real property we have introduced you to during the term of this Authorization and all material conditions have been subsequently met or a lease entered into during the term of this Authorization is renewed or enlarged, You or a landlord exercise a lease option or You enter into a new lease with the landlord even if such renewal, enlargement, new lease or exercise of option takes place after the expiration of this Authorization; or (c) You are introduced by Us or take occupancy to real property we have introduced you to during the term of this Authorization and obtain title to such property within _____ (____) months after the expiration of this Authorization, provided, however, that no fee will be due and payable under this Section if You sign an exclusive agreement or authorization with another real estate broker after the expiration of this Authorization.

        4. _____ (Other)

    B. Any professional service fee We earn under this Authorization is your obligation. However, if You purchase, lease or exchange property either listed with Us or listed on a multiple listing service on which We are a participant, then We will credit you with whatever amounts we receive from either or both of these sources. We will also assist you in negotiating payment of this fee from the seller of the Property and will credit you with any amounts seller actually pays. These credits may pay our fee in full.

    C. We will tell You before showing You a Property if the Property is not eligible for this credit, and you may refuse to be shown such properties without incurring a fee. We may accept amounts the seller, landlord or listing broker pay Us in excess of the professional service fee stated upon disclosure to You.

    D. You will pay us our professional service fee no later than the date on which title to the real property transfers to You or the date on which You occupy, renew, enlarge a lease or an option is exercised whichever date is applicable to the type of transaction.

F I G U R E 2.5 (continued)

Exclusive Agency Right to Represent Buyer or Tenant Authorization

VIII.   **Statements Required by Law.**

A. This agreement is subject to the Connecticut General Statutes prohibiting discrimination in commercial and residential real estate transactions (C.G.S. Title 46a, Chapter 814c).

B. THE REAL ESTATE BROKER MAY BE ENTITLED TO CERTAIN LIEN RIGHTS PURSUANT TO SECTION 20-325a OF THE CONNECTICUT GENERAL STATUTES.

C. **NOTICE: THE AMOUNT OR RATE OF REAL ESTATE BROKER COMPENSATION IS NOT FIXED BY LAW. IT IS SET BY EACH BROKER INDIVIDUALLY AND MAY BE NEGOTIABLE BETWEEN YOU AND THE BROKER.**

IX.   **Use of Electronic Record.**

A. You agree that we may use an electronic record, including fax or e-mail, to make and keep this Agreement.

B. You need not agree to use an electronic record. By a written notice to Us, You have the right to withdraw your consent to have a record of this Agreement provided or made available to You in electronic form, but that does not permit You to withdraw your consent to the Agreement itself once it has been signed. We will provide You with a paper copy of this Agreement should You request one in writing to Us at the address, e-mail or fax number listed below. Your agreement to use an electronic record applies only to this particular real estate transaction and not to all real estate transactions in which You are a party.

C. For access to and retention of faxed records, there is no special hardware or software requirements beyond access to a fax machine or fax modem and accompanying software connected to a personal or laptop computer. For access to and retention of e-mail records, You will need a personal or laptop computer, Internet account and e-mail software or web browser.

Buyer/Tenant electronic addresses are: Fax number is:_____
                                            E-mail address is:_____

All electronic records will be sent to the fax number or e-mail address noted above unless You inform Us of any change in your e-mail address or fax number in writing to the Brokerage Firm address, e-mail or fax number set forth.

_____   _____
BROKER/ FIRM NAME   BUYER/TENANT

_____   _____
By Agent   BUYER/TENANT

_____   _____
Street   Street

_____   _____
City, State, Zip   City, State, Zip

_____   _____
Telephone number and/or e-mail address   Telephone number

_____   _____
Date   Date

FIGURE 2.6

Open Right to Represent Buyer Authorization

OPEN RIGHT TO REPRESENT BUYER OR TENANT AUTHORIZATION

(Connecticut law requires that the real estate broker furnish you with a written agreement should you wish to be represented.)

I.   Exclusive Right Appointment.

You, _____ (Buyer/Tenant). appoint

Us, _____ (Firm/Broker) as your exclusive real estate

broker to assist You to locate and purchase, exchange or lease real property acceptable to You and generally described

as: _____

_____ (the "Property").

II. Geographical Area.

This Authorization is limited to the following areas of the State of Connecticut:_____

_____

III. Term of Authorization.

This Authorization is in effect from _____ to _____, inclusive.

IV. Broker's Duties.

    A.   We will keep information You provide Us concerning your assets, liabilities, income and expenses, motivations to buy or rent and previous offers made confidential unless you give permission for disclosure or disclosure is mandated by law.

    B.   We will provide You with the benefit of our advice and experience.

    C.   We will attempt to locate the Property.

    D.   We will negotiate on your behalf for terms and conditions agreeable to You.

    E.   We will assist You in the purchase, exchange or lease, as the case may be, of the Property.

    F.   We will act in your interest regarding the location and purchase, exchange or lease of the Property.

    G.   **Questions or information requests concerning the legal title to property, the residence of convicted persons, tax considerations, wood destroying pests, environmental conditions, property and building inspections, engineering, or the uses or planned uses of neighboring properties should be referred to your attorney, tax advisor, building inspector or appropriate governmental agency.**

V. Buyer's/Tenant's Duties.

    A.   You will tell Us about all past and current contacts with any real property or any other real estate agents.

    B.   You will cooperate with Us and be reasonably available to examine real property.

    C.   Upon request, You will give Us financial and personal information regarding your purchase abilities and needs.

    D.   We are relying on your statement that You have not signed an Exclusive Right to Represent Buyer or Tenant Authorization or Exclusive Agency Right to Represent Buyer or Tenant Authorization with any other brokerage firm covering the same time period, the same Property or the same Geographical Areas as stated above. If this is not the case, please tell Us immediately.

    E.   You understand that the names of attorneys, contractors, home inspectors and other professionals are furnished as an accommodation to You and do not constitute an endorsement or guaranty of such professionals or their work product.

VI. Other Terms and Conditions.

    A.   You understand and agree that We may also become a seller's or landlord's agent for the Property. In that event We would become dual agents, representing both You and the seller or landlord. If this situation should arise, We will promptly disclose all relevant information to You and discuss the appropriate course of action to take under the circumstances. We will also discuss a Dual Agency Consent Agreement with You and present a statutory form of such an agreement for your review and signature.

    B.   You know that We represent other buyers or tenants who may be interested in purchasing or renting the same Property as You.

F I G U R E 2.6 (continued)

Open Right to Represent Buyer Authorization

C.   We may, with your permission, share and disclose financial and personal information regarding your purchase abilities and needs with other agents who offer real property to Us.

D.   This Authorization is binding upon and shall inure to the benefit of You and Us, and each of our heirs, administrators, executors, successors and assigns. You may not assign this Authorization.

E.   You agree to pay any costs and attorneys' fees which We may incur to collect any monies due Us under this Authorization.

F.   This Authorization may be modified, waived or discharged only by a written agreement signed by the parties.

G.   You are notified that the Department of Environmental Protection is required pursuant to Section 22a-134f of the Connecticut General Statutes to furnish lists of hazardous waste facilities located within the town to the Town Clerk's office. You should refer to these lists and the Department of Environmental Protection for information on environmental questions concerning any property in which You are interested in and the lands surrounding that property.

VII. Fees.

1. In consideration of the services to be provided, You agree to pay Us a Professional Service fee calculated as follows:

a.   If You are purchasing real estate, our professional service fee will be calculated as follows: \$_____ or _____ % of the purchase price of the Property purchased by You, or of the value of Property obtained by You in an exchange.

b.   If You are leasing real estate, our professional service fee will be calculated as follows: \$_____ or _____ % of the yearly rental of the Property leased by You. You also agree to pay a commission in the amount noted above on any renewals, enlargements, exercise of lease options, or new leases between yourself and the landlord. Such commission shall be due and payable at the commencement of the new lease, enlargement, renewal, or option term.

c.   We earn the professional service fee if You (i) enter into a contract for the purchase or exchange of real property during the term of this Authorization and all material conditions have been met or are subsequently met regardless of how you learn about the Property; (ii) enter into a lease, whether oral or written, for the rental of real property during the term of this Authorization and all material conditions have been met or are subsequently met or a lease entered into during the term of this Authorization is renewed or enlarged, You or a landlord exercise a lease option or You enter into a new lease with the landlord even if such renewal, enlargement, new lease or exercise of option takes place after the expiration of this Authorization; or (iii) You are introduced or take occupancy to real property during the term of this Authorization and obtain title to such property within _____ (_____) months after the expiration of this Authorization, provided, however, that no fee will be due and payable under this Section VII.A.1.c(iii) if You sign an exclusive agreement or authorization with another real estate broker after the expiration of this Authorization.

d.   _____ (Other)

2.   Any professional service fee We earn under this Authorization is your obligation. However, if You purchase, lease or exchange property either listed with Us or listed on a multiple listing service on which We are a participant, then We will credit you with whatever amounts we receive from either or both of these sources. We will also assist you in negotiating payment of this fee from the seller of the Property and will credit you with any amounts seller actually pays. These credits may pay our fee in full.

3.   We will tell You before showing You a Property if the Property is not eligible for this credit, and you may refuse to be shown such properties without incurring a fee. We may accept amounts the seller, landlord or listing broker pay Us in excess of the professional service fee stated upon disclosure to You.

4.   You will pay us our professional service fee no later than the date on which title to the real property transfers to You or the date on which You occupy, renew, enlarge a lease or an option is exercised whichever date is applicable to the type of transaction.

VIII.   Statements Required by Law

1.   This Authorization is subject to the Connecticut General Statutes prohibiting discrimination in commercial and residential real estate transactions (C.G.S. Title 46a, Chapter 814c);

2.   The real estate broker may be entitled to certain lien rights pursuant to Section 20-325a of the Connecticut General Statutes;

3.   **NOTICE: THE AMOUNT OR RATE OF REAL ESTATE BROKER COMPENSATION IS NOT FIXED BY LAW. IT IS SET BY EACH BROKER INDIVIDUALLY AND MAY BE NEGOTIABLE BETWEEN YOU AND THE BROKER.**

4.   **IT IS UNLAWFUL UNDER FEDERAL AND/OR STATE LAW TO DISCRIMINATE ON THE BASIS OF RACE, CREED, COLOR, NATIONAL ORIGIN, ANCESTRY, SEX, SEXUAL ORIENTATION, MARITAL**

F I G U R E 2.6 (continued)

Open Right to Represent Buyer Authorization

STATUS, AGE, LAWFUL SOURCE OF INCOME, LEARNING DISABILITY, MENTAL RETARDATION, FAMILIAL STATUS AND MENTAL OR PHYSICAL DISABILITY.

IX.   **Use of Electronic Record.**

A.   You agree that we may use an electronic record, including fax or e-mail, to make and keep this Agreement.

B.   You need not agree to use an electronic record. By a written notice to Us, You have the right to withdraw your consent to have a record of this Agreement provided or made available to You in electronic form, but that does not permit You to withdraw your consent to the Agreement itself once it has been signed. We will provide You with a paper copy of this Agreement should You request one in writing to us at the address, e-mail or fax number listed below. Your agreement to use an electronic record applies only to this particular real estate transaction and not to all real estate transactions in which You are a party.

C.   For access to and retention of faxed records, there is no special hardware or software requirements beyond access to a fax machine or fax modem and accompanying software connected to a personal or laptop computer. For access to and retention of e-mail records, you will need a personal or laptop computer, Internet account and e-mail software or web browser.

My electronic addresses are: My fax number is:_____
                                   My e-mail address is:_____

All electronic records will be sent to the fax number or e-mail address noted above unless you inform us of any change in your e-mail address or fax number in writing to the Brokerage Firm address, e-mail or fax number set forth.

Each party will promptly inform the other of any change in E-mail address or fax number in writing.

X.   **Copy.**

You acknowledge receipt of a copy of this Authorization.

_____   _____
REALTOR® FIRM NAME   BUYER/TENANT

_____   _____
By Agent   BUYER/TENANT

_____   _____
Street   Street

_____   _____
City, State, Zip   City, State, Zip

_____   _____
Telephone number and/or e-mail address   Telephone number

_____   _____
Date   Date

CHAPTER 2 QUIZ

1. Buyer-brokerage contracts in Connecticut
   a. must be in writing to be enforceable.
   b. must be on specific forms.
   c. are not regulated under the license laws.
   d. are illegal.

2. A broker enters into a listing agreement with a seller. The property does not sell, and the listing expires. For how long does the broker need to keep a copy of the listing agreement and related documents?
   a. Forever
   b. Seven years
   c. One year
   d. The broker does not need to keep records for transactions that do not close.

3. In Connecticut, real estate commission and compensation are
   a. set by law.
   b. set by the Real Estate Commission.
   c. determined by local groups of brokers.
   d. negotiable between the seller or the buyer and the broker.

4. In Connecticut, an exclusive-right-to-buy contract
   a. is illegal.
   b. is equivalent to a listing agreement.
   c. requires the signature of the principal only.
   d. must be indicated as such in the buyer agency agreement.

5. A broker who enters into an exclusive-agency listing contract
   a. is guaranteed a commission.
   b. must split his or her commission.
   c. must make a diligent attempt to sell or lease the property.
   d. has violated the law.

6. Betty Buyer contacts Hartfield Realty and is interested in potentially purchasing a home in the Hartfield area. Without entering into a buyer agency relationship with Betty, a salesperson from Hartfield Realty can do all of the following for her *EXCEPT*
   a. prequalify Betty for a mortgage.
   b. give Betty information on mortgage interest rates and terms.
   c. give Betty information on properties for sale in Hartfield.
   d. explain to Betty about buyer agency, seller agency, and dual agency.

7. Betty is interested in seeing a house listed with Hartfield Realty but does not wish to enter into a buyer agency agreement with Hartfield Realty. A salesperson from Hartfield Realty can show Betty an in-house listing if
   a. the salesperson obtains the seller's permission.
   b. Betty verbally agrees to buyer agency.
   c. the salesperson provides Betty with an Agency Disclosure Notice, stating that Hartfield Realty represents the seller.
   d. the salesperson provides Betty with a Dual Agency Consent Form.

8. In Connecticut a net listing is
   a. based on a set rate of commission.
   b. similar to an open listing.
   c. common.
   d. illegal

9. A broker who wishes to place a For Sale sign on a listed property must first
   a. obtain the consent of the owner of the property.
   b. sell the property.
   c. list the property.
   d. get Connecticut law changed to permit For Sale signs on properties.

10. Can a salesperson advertise property listed with his or her brokerage firm in his or her own name?

   a. Yes, the salesperson can, as long as it is that salesperson's listing.

   b. Yes, the salesperson can, as long as the salesperson is affiliated with the brokerage firm.

   c. No, a salesperson can never advertise listed property under his or her name.

   d. No, a salesperson cannot advertise.

11. Bob Broker has obtained permission from Sonjay Broker and Ken Broker to advertise Sonjay's and Ken's listings on his office Web site. Bob Broker now has an obligation to

   a. obtain the seller's permission for such advertising.

   b. advertise Sonjay's and Ken's listings on the first page of the Internet site.

   c. include Sonjay's and Ken's names and e-mail addresses under the listing information.

   d. update the listing information at least every 72 hours.

12. A salesperson sends out an e-mail to all the parents in her daughter's first-grade class, informing them that she is a real estate agent and providing them with pictures of houses that she has currently listed. In this e-mail, the salesperson is legally required to also include

   a. the name of the real estate broker she is affiliated with.

   b. listing prices of the properties.

   c. the last date when the property information was updated.

   d. none of the above because a simple e-mail such as this is not considered advertising.

CHAPTER 3

Interest in Real Estate

■ OVERVIEW

Although never officially recognized, many of the statutory and common-law concepts relating to real estate ownership and land title in Connecticut were developed from English common-law principles. In general, Connecticut laws recognize the various types and categories of estates discussed in the principles books (see the conversion table in the Preface for chapter references). However, there are several exceptions. Connecticut does not recognize curtesy and dower rights or the homestead exemption. Further, easements in Connecticut generally "run with the land."

■ DOWER AND CURTESY

Since 1877 neither dower nor curtesy has been recognized in Connecticut. The interest of a person in the property of his or her spouse is provided for via statutory survivorship rights under laws pertaining to the property rights of husband or wife or to a joint tenancy with survivorship rights (see Chapter 4).

Under the statutes relating to the property rights of a surviving spouse, the husband or wife would be entitled to a life estate equal in value to one-third of the deceased partner's property (real and personal). This interest attaches to the survivor on the death of his or her spouse, so it is not necessary for a nonowning spouse to sign any conveyances of an owning spouse's real estate to release these statutory survivorship rights while the owning spouse is alive. The statutory survivorship interest flows to the surviving spouse regardless of the terms of a will that might dispose of the estate to other parties. Such survivorship interest must be declared

in writing, signed by the surviving spouse, and lodged with the court of probate within a prescribed number of days of the appointment of the administrator of the estate. An estranged spouse has no right to such a declaration. (CGS Section 45a-436)

Should the deceased partner die without a will, or should a portion of the estate remain undisposed of after all dispositions have been made, the surviving spouse would inherit as prescribed by the intestate law of descent (see Chapter 8).

■ HOMESTEAD PROPERTY

Connecticut does not recognize a homestead exemption. It does provide, however, for a temporary application of homestead in its *probate court* procedures and for a homestead exemption in *debt collection* procedures. (CGS Section 45a-321)

Probate court procedure has stipulated that the family of a deceased property owner may occupy the property designated as the homestead during the period of estate settlement. Once the estate has been settled, however, the executor or administrator of the estate may require that the property be vacated. For the purposes of this statute, the word *family* refers to the collective group of blood relatives and relatives by marriage. To enforce homestead occupancy, the family members in question must have been members of the household at the time of the decedent's death. The probate judge's decision is final in all cases.

A homeowner subject to a debt collection procedure due to an involuntary lien or money judgment may exempt his or her homestead from the collection up to a value of $75,000 (value is defined as fair market value of the property less any consensual lien, so this value figure is more akin to equity in the home). This exemption is *not allowed* for collection of debt due to loans secured by a mortgage on the property, mechanics' liens, tax liens, and other liens consented to by the homeowner. (CGS Sections 52-352a and 52-352b)

■ DEED RESTRICTIONS

Conservation and preservation restrictions may be acquired by any governmental body, charitable corporation, or trust. Such restrictions can take the form of a deed restriction, easement, covenant, or condition in any deed. The purpose of a *conservation* restriction is to retain land or water areas in agricultural, farming, forest, or open space use. The purpose of a *preservation* restriction is to preserve historically significant structures or sites. (CGS Sections 47-42a–47-42d)

■ EASEMENTS BY PRESCRIPTION

Easements created in Connecticut generally "run with the land," which means they pass with the property ownership rights on conveyance. The manner in which easements may be created is essentially equivalent to the methods discussed in the principles books. The time required for acquisition of prescriptive easements is *15 years*. (CGS Sections 47-3–47-42d)

Extent of Right

[handwritten margin note: may not Extend Easement Like a Bigger truck]

When an easement in Connecticut is created by prescription, the very use that establishes the right also limits and qualifies the right. In other words, the user who acquires the easement may not expand his or her use to exceed the original use. For example, if a right-of-way is acquired across another's property for the purpose of hauling logs, the easement cannot be enlarged to encompass any other use, such as hauling cut lumber or finished wood products back across the land.

Location of Boundaries

The boundaries within which a right-of-way acquired through prescription will be exercised must be defined with reasonable explicitness to be valid. Once these boundaries have been established, the user cannot expand them to enlarge the right-of-way or to extend the uses possible under such right-of-way.

Burden of Proof

In nearly all instances, the burden of proof in matters concerning rights-of-way and other easements lies with the user. The owner of the servient tenement (the land over which the right-of-way passes) does not have to disprove the user's right to an easement; the user must establish his or her rights with adequate proof.

Question of Fact

In determining whether an easement has been acquired through prescription, the court must decide whether in fact all the requirements for this have been met. The burden of proof still lies on the person claiming the right to the easement.

Light and Air

Easement of light and air *cannot* be acquired by prescription if the creation of such an easement would make it unlawful for an adjoining landowner to erect a structure, even though all the requirements for the creation of an easement by prescription have been met. For example, the Connecticut courts have held that a person who has owned a building adjacent to a vacant lot for the prescribed 15 years cannot claim an easement for light and air that would deny the vacant lot owner the right to build a structure—even though that structure would intercept cool breezes and sunlight.

Abandonment

An easement by prescription may be extinguished if the owner of the property on which the easement has been made takes, obtains, or regains open and continuous control and possession of the property for the prescriptive period of 15 years.

[handwritten margin note: 15 yrs]

Preventing Acquisition by Prescription

When the owner of a property seeks to prevent another's acquisition of a right-of-way or easement, he or she must abide by the statutory procedures. Mere letters to, or verbal contact with, the persons claiming the right will not qualify as an interruption of use in most cases.

(handwritten margin note: Recorded w/ 3 months)

The owner must issue a written notice to the person claiming the right or privilege in the same manner as one would serve an original summons in a civil action (usually by a state marshal or other court-appointed process server). The notice must be signed and returned to the owner and recorded within three months of the date when the notice was served. If the claimant is not available, the notice may be served on his or her agent or guardian. If the claimant resides out of state, it may be served on the occupant of the claimant's estate. When neither the claimant nor an estate occupant can be located, the property owner can prevent the acquisition of an easement by posting a conspicuous notice on the property and serving notice on the person to whom the premises were last assessed for tax purposes and by recording this service within three months. Once notice is served, the owner has effectively disturbed the claimant's right and interrupted the claimant's use.

■ LICENSE

A license is permission to be on another person's land for a specific purpose. Unlike an easement or a lease, it is not considered an interest in real estate. It is a personal privilege and therefore can not be transferred by the licensee and can be revoked by the licensor.

■ WATER RIGHTS

Connecticut laws relating to riparian rights are generally the same as those described in the principles books. Under law, a riparian landowner may use the water while it runs over his or her land but cannot unreasonably contain, divert, or destroy it. This is explained in the Connecticut Supreme Court case of *Parker v. Griswold, 17 Conn. 388 (1845)*. In this case, two neighbors owned land on a stream. The upstream owner built a mill and dam on his property, and diverted the stream so that it no longer ran through the downstream owner's property. The court found that the upstream owner had no right to divert the stream.

The most critical factor in establishing the boundary of an upland owner is the determination of whether the body of water adjoining the owner's property is navigable. If it is navigable, upland owners own to the water's edge; if it is not navigable, they own to the center of the stream or water body. In Connecticut, the decision as to navigability is generally accorded to the state through its court procedures. No single state agency is charged with the responsibility of defining navigable waters. Such decisions are typically made on the basis of widely accepted court interpretations and the advisement of the U.S. Army Corps of Engineers in cases involving bodies of water located in more than one state.

■ WEB LINKS

Connecticut General Statutes: *www.cga.ct.gov*

Connecticut Probate Record Research Guide: *www.cslib.org/probintr.htm*

Preservation Easements, Connecticut Trust for Historic Preservation:
http://cttrust.org/index.cgi/1053

Conservation Easements, The Land Trust Alliance:
www.lta.org/conserve/index.html

CHAPTER 3 QUIZ

1. In Connecticut dower and curtesy are
   a. currently recognized.
   b. recognized voluntarily.
   c. recognized but not enforced.
   d. not recognized.

2. If a husband dies in Connecticut, his wife is entitled to
   a. a life estate in all property owned by the husband during his life.
   b. a life estate in all property owned by the husband at the time of his death.
   c. an election to take a life estate equal to one-third of the property owned by the husband at the time of his death.
   d. nothing.

3. A homeowner may exempt the following amount from debt owed a foreclosing mortgagee:
   a. $75,000.
   b. $150,000.
   c. the value of the home.
   d. nothing.

4. The burden of proof in acquiring an easement by prescription lies with the
   a. party claiming the easement.
   b. court in equity.
   c. party protesting the claim of right.
   d. owner of the land on which the easement is to be laid.

5. In Connecticut, the prescriptive period to acquire an easement is
   a. 100 months.
   b. 12 years.
   c. 15 years.
   d. 30 years.

6. To be extinguished by law, a right-of-way must have been abandoned for at least
   a. 100 months.
   b. 12 years.
   c. 15 years.
   d. 30 years.

7. The decision as to whether a claimant has met all the requirements for acquiring an easement by prescription is made by the
   a. attorney of the person claiming the right.
   b. court.
   c. owner's attorney.
   d. user of the right or privilege.

8. A man and a woman are neighboring property owners. The man has been crossing the woman's property to get to a state beach. The woman wishes to prevent the man from acquiring an easement to cross her land. To do so effectively, she can
   a. follow Connecticut's statutory procedures.
   b. write him a letter granting him permission to cross the property.
   c. write him a letter forbidding him to cross the property.
   d. put up a "no trespassing" sign.

9. A UConn student has been given a ticket (license) to enter Gampel Pavilion to watch the Huskies basketball team. UConn can revoke or cancel this license for all of the following reasons *EXCEPT*
   a. the student was throwing popcorn.
   b. the student attempted to jump onto the court.
   c. UConn decided to revoke all student tickets for no reason.
   d. the Pavilion had a power outage.

10. What is the most critical factor in establishing riparian rights?
    a. Determining whether the body of water adjoining the owner's property is navigable
    b. Determining the size of the body of water adjoining the owner's property
    c. Determining the number of states the body of water passes through
    d. Determining the depth of the waterway adjoining the owner's property

CHAPTER 4

Forms of Real Estate Ownership

■ OVERVIEW

In Connecticut, ownership rights or interests in land may be held in severalty, in co-ownership, or in trust. Connecticut recognizes two forms of co-ownership: tenancy in common and joint tenancy. For joint tenancy in Connecticut, property can be held in equal or unequal shares. Real estate may also be owned by trusts and by business entities such as partnerships and corporations. Connecticut allows for condominium and cooperative ownership under the Common Interest Ownership Act.

■ CO-OWNERSHIP

A conveyance by deed to two or more people is presumed to be as tenants in common, unless the conveyance includes specific language creating a right of survivorship. If there is language stating that the grant includes a right of survivorship, then a joint tenancy with right of survivorship is created. (CGS Sections 47-14a–47-14k)

Unlike other states that require that all tenants hold equal shares in a joint tenancy, in Connecticut property can be held in equal or unequal shares in a joint tenancy. That means, for example, that if two people own property together as joint tenants, one can own one-third of the property and the other two-thirds (or other such combination), and still have rights of survivorship.

Connecticut allows conveyance of a deed directly from a grantor to himself or herself and others as joint tenants without the use of a third party. Joint tenants may convey or encumber their interests, but a conveyance from fewer than all the joint tenants to a person other than another joint tenant would sever the joint tenancy as to that portion conveyed. A lien on a joint tenant's interest is still valid against that interest after death.

Ownership by Married Couples

Connecticut law does not recognize a tenancy by the entirety. Any conveyance to a husband and wife, without specific language indicating otherwise, would be treated in the same manner as a conveyance to two or more unrelated parties—as a tenancy in common. If the deed contains specific language indicating a joint tenancy, the law will recognize it as such. The joint tenancy with the right of survivorship is the most common form of property ownership between a husband and wife in Connecticut.

Under Connecticut statutes, property rights acquired by either husband or wife prior to marriage remain as separate interests. However, either spouse may acquire and hold property acquired after marriage as an individual in severalty or with persons other than his or her spouse. The interests of the surviving spouse in such property are discussed in Chapter 3. (CGS Sections 46b-3b)

When a husband and wife hold real estate as joint tenants (by themselves or with others) and subsequently file for and obtain a divorce, the divorce decree usually serves to extinguish the joint tenancy and convert it to a tenancy in common. Because property owned jointly by a husband and wife almost always falls under the provisions of a joint tenancy with survivorship rights, the concept of community property (as discussed in the principles texts) is of no particular importance and is not recognized as a form of ownership in Connecticut. (CGS Sections 47-14)

■ PARTITIONS

Partition is the physical division of co-owned real estate. Under all forms of concurrent ownership, the co-owners may voluntarily partition the real estate at any time. However, if one of the owners does not agree to a partition (i.e., the partition is involuntary), the other owner(s) must petition the courts for equitable relief. The court then appoints a committee to accomplish the partition. This is the most common partition in cases involving the dissolution of joint tenancies or other forms of co-ownership. (CGS Chapter 919)

Occasionally, it is physically impossible to fairly and equitably partition an interest in real estate. In the event of such a situation, the court may order the property sold and the proceeds distributed in proportion to each owner's undivided interest (if interest is not stated in the owner's deed, the property will be divided equally). Alternatively, if one or more of the owners has only a minimal interest, the court may decide to distribute the property to the majority owners and order just compensation to be paid to those owners with a minimal interest. All partitions (whether voluntary or involuntary) must be recorded in the land records.

■ TRUSTS

The types of trusts outlined in the principles books are equivalent to those recognized in Connecticut. The Fiduciary Powers Act specifically outlines a trustee's duties and the relationship between trustee and beneficiaries. (CGS Sections 45-100d –g)

■ OWNERSHIP OF REAL ESTATE BY BUSINESS ORGANIZATIONS

Connecticut law permits business organizations to own real estate. Types of organizations include general partnerships, limited partnerships, corporations, S corporations, and limited liability companies.

monetarily

Partnerships

General and limited partnerships may own real property. The partners' responsibilities and liabilities are spelled out in both the partnership agreement and the statutes pertaining to partnerships.

In Connecticut, the use of limited partnerships as a form of real property ownership is particularly important. Under a limited partnership, a property is divided (monetarily) into units, each of which can be purchased by a limited partner. The financial liability of each limited partner extends no further than his or her initial capital outlay unless the partnership agreement specifically provides for additional contributions of liability. Under a typical arrangement, one or more general partners will be selected to manage the partnership property and are responsible for reporting to the limited partners as required by the agreement. The general partner is empowered to carry out management and financing duties and retains unlimited liabilities unless specified otherwise. The principal attractions of limited partnerships (much like those of real estate investment trusts or syndicates) lie with their financial accessibility to the smaller investor and their freedom from management burdens.

The specific statutory provisions covering the setup and operation of both general and limited partnerships can be found under Title 34 of the Connecticut General Statutes: Chapter 611—Uniform Partnership Act and Chapter 610—Uniform Limited Partnership Act.

Corporations

Corporations and S corporations in Connecticut are equivalent to the descriptions discussed in the principles books. They are formed by making appropriate filings with the Connecticut Secretary of State.

Connecticut allows for the creation of a *limited liability company* (referred to as an LLC). An LLC, which is neither a corporation nor partnership, combines the tax status of partnerships with the limited liability of corporations. Unlike a limited partnership, there is no requirement that a general partner be generally liable. An

LLC is less restrictive than an S corporation because it does not limit the number of owners to 35 or restrict business entities or foreign investors from becoming partners. This form of entity has become popular for ownership of investment real estate.

The specific statutory provisions covering the setup and operation of both corporations and limited liability companies can be found under Title 33 of the Connecticut General Statutes.

■ COMMON INTEREST OWNERSHIP ACT

The Connecticut Common Interest Ownership Act regulates the development and operation of common interest ownership properties. This law covers condominiums, cooperatives, and all other forms of real property unit ownership including planned unit developments (PUDs). The Common Interest Ownership Act identifies these types of ownership as *"common interest communities,"* where *ownership of a unit requires financial contribution for the maintenance of common areas.*

The specific statutory provisions covering the setup and operation of both common interest ownership communities can be found under Title 47 of the Connecticut General Statutes.

Note that condominiums developed between 1976 and 1984 fall under an old law entitled the Unit Ownership—Condominium Acts of 1976.

Types of Communities

Common interest communities are legally defined as one of three types: a condominium, cooperative, or planned community. A *condominium* is a community where the units are owned separately and the common areas are owned by all of the unit owners together as tenants in common. In a *cooperative,* all the real property is owned by an association (even the units). The unit owners are members of the association and have the right to exclusive possession of a particular unit. A *planned community* is a catchall category, including any type of common interest community that is not a condominium or cooperative. Typically, PUDs, where the unit owners own their lots and an association owns the common areas, would be a planned community. (Note that if the common areas were owned by the unit owners as tenants in common, this PUD would be a condominium, not a planned community.)

Leasing

Common interest units may be leased under certain conditions specified in the bylaws. When a unit is leased, written notice must be given to a tenant informing him or her that the unit is in a common interest community. An explanation of the rights, privileges, and obligations of the tenant is most important.

Management Services

Those who offer or provide association management services to condominium or other common interest communities are required to obtain a *Certificate of Registration* from the Department of Consumer Protection. Certificates of Registration expire annually on January 31. Also, anyone who has access to association funds must furnish a *fidelity bond* sufficient to cover the maximum association funds in the manager's custody; in no case may the bond be for less than three months' assessments plus reserve funds. A separate bond is required for each association. All contracts to provide association management services must meet certain minimum standards, and specific practices are prohibited.

Condominium developers are required to register as community association managers if they receive compensation for any management function performed in developing communities. The law applies to developers of developments greater than four units, and where the developer controls more than two-thirds, but fewer than all, the votes within an association. If the law applies, in addition to registering, a developer also has to be bonded for the maximum amount of funds under the association's control.

Lien for Assessments

The association has a statutory lien on a unit for any unpaid common charges, assessments, and fines. This lien is known as a *super lien* because it takes priority over many other liens or encumbrances that may attach to the real estate, including mortgages recorded after the date of delinquency of the unpaid charges. The association is not required to record a separate notice of lien because recording of the declaration creating the community constitutes record notice and perfection of the lien. The lien may be foreclosed on in the same manner as a mortgage foreclosure.

Creation—Declaration

Common interest ownership communities are created by recording a *declaration* in the land records of the town(s) where the common interest ownership property is located. In general, the declaration must contain the following information:

- The name of the common interest community and the community association
- A statement that the common interest community is a condominium, cooperative, or planned community
- The name of every town in which any part of the common interest community is located
- A legally sufficient description of the real property included in the community
- A statement of the maximum number of units that the owner/developer reserves the right to create
- For a condominium or planned community, a description of the boundaries of each unit, including an identifying number
- The interests allocated to each unit

- A description of any limited common element
- A description of any development rights
- Any restrictions on use, occupancy, and alienation of the units
- The recording date for any easements and/or appurtenances

In addition to these general requirements, the declaration has other requirements for a developer to reserve future development rights and for cooperatives. At the time the declaration is recorded, the owner/developer must also record a set of floor plans, a land survey, and a copy of the association's bylaws.

Initial Sale—Public Offering Statement

An owner/developer of a common interest ownership property must provide all initial purchasers with a *public offering statement*. The public offering statement provides purchasers with full disclosures regarding the common interest community. This statement must be provided to all prospective purchasers not later than the date of the contract of sale. The requirements for the public offering statement are very detailed and designed to protect the purchasing public. A purchaser, before conveyance, *may cancel a contract* of sale within *15 days* after both executing it and receiving the public offering statement.

Exception: Common interest communities that contain no more than 12 units (and that may not be further developed) do not need to provide a public offering statement or resale documents as discussed below.

Resale of Units

After the initial sale by the developer, sellers of a common interest ownership unit must give potential buyers a package of resale disclosure documents. These documents consist of a copy of (1) the declaration that created the community; (2) the current association bylaws, rules, and regulations; and (3) a resale certificate prepared by the association. The *resale certificate* must provide the following information:

- The effect of the sale on any right of first refusal
- The amount of the monthly common expense assessment and any unpaid common expense or special assessment currently due from the owner
- Any other fees payable by the owner
- Any capital expenditures in excess of $1,000 approved by the executive board for the current and next succeeding fiscal year
- The amount of any reserves for capital expenditures
- The current operating budget of the association
- Any unsatisfied judgments against the association and any pending suits in which the association is a defendant
- The insurance coverage provided for the benefit of unit owners
- Any restrictions in the declaration affecting the amount that may be received by a unit owner on the sale, condemnation, casualty loss to the unit or the common interest community, or termination of the common interest community

- In a cooperative, an accountant's statement, if any was prepared, as to the deductibility for federal income tax purposes by the unit owner of real property taxes and interest paid by the association
- If the association is unincorporated, the name of the statutory agent for service of process filed with the Connecticut Secretary of State
- A statement of any pending sale or encumbrances of common elements
- A statement disclosing the effect on the unit to be conveyed of any restrictions on the owner's right to use or occupy the unit or to lease the unit to another person
- A statement disclosing the number of units whose owners are at least 60 days' delinquent in paying their common charges on the date of the statement
- A statement disclosing the number of foreclosure actions brought by the association during the past 12 months and the number of actions pending on a specified date within 60 days of the date of the statement
- Any established maintenance standards adopted by the association

Right to cancel.   Resale documents must be furnished to a buyer or his or her attorney before the closing or transfer of possession. Before conveyance, *buyers have a right to cancel a purchase contract until five business days after the resale documents have been delivered* to the buyer or buyer's attorney (or seven days after they are sent by registered or certified mail).

Obtaining resale documents.   When a unit owner (seller) requests a resale certificate from the association in hard copy or electronic writing, the association must provide it within ten business days of the request. The maximum fee the association can charge for preparation of the resale certificate and accompanying documents is $125 plus either five cents for each copied page of document or ten dollars for an electronic document.

Sellers of common interest community units can obtain resale documents by contacting the association. The association must file the name of the contact person, whether it is a property manager or an association officer, with the town clerk in the town where the community is located. In January of each year, the association must file the contact person name again; any change to the contact person data must be filed within 30 days.

Condominium Conversion

The Common Interest Ownership Act prohibits municipalities from banning the conversion of buildings to condominiums and other types of common interest housing.

The Common Interest Ownership Act also protects the tenants living in units undergoing conversion and requires that owners and/or developers give tenants at least 180 days' notice of the conversion, a public offering statement, and a conversion notice. The conversion notice must include information on the rights of tenants during this transition period. Certain tenants may qualify for relocation assistance, based on their age and gross adjusted income of the tenants. During the transition period of the conversion, tenants' rents may not be increased for any reason.

Time Shares

A separate law, known as the Time Share Act, regulates the sale of time-share interests in Connecticut. Any time-share being offered or sold in Connecticut must be registered with the Connecticut Department of Consumer Protection (with certain exemptions). Additionally, developers of time-shares located in Connecticut must record a time-share plan in the municipal land records where the property is located. Time-share developers must provide time-share purchasers with a time-share disclosure statement. Purchasers then have five days to cancel a contract after the signing of the contract and receiving the disclosure statement. A time-share resale broker must hold an appropriate state real estate license.

■ WEB LINKS

Connecticut General Statutes, Title 34 (Partnerships):
www.cga.ct.gov/2009/pub/Title34.htm
Connecticut General Statutes, Title 33 (Corporations):
www.cga.ct.gov/2009/pub/Title33.htm
Connecticut General Statutes, Title 47, Chapter 828 (Common Interest
Ownership Act): *www.cga.ct.gov/2009/pub/Chap828.htm*
Connecticut General Statutes, Chapter 400b (Community Association
Managers): *www.cga.ct.gov/2009/pub/Chap400b.htm*
Connecticut Department of Consumer Protection, Application for Registration
as Community Association Manager:
www.ct.gov/dcp/cwp/view.asp?a=16228q=446730

CHAPTER 4 QUIZ

1. Which form of ownership is *NOT* recognized under Connecticut law?
   a. Tenancy in common
   b. Joint tenancy with survivorship rights
   c. Condominium
   d. Tenancy by the entirety

2. The maximum fee that can be charged for the condominium resale documents is
   a. $75.
   b. $125.
   c. $180.
   d. $225.

3. To obtain resale documents to give to a buyer, a seller should contact the condominium association contact person whose name is on file with the
   a. Connecticut Real Estate Commission.
   b. Connecticut Secretary of State.
   c. Community Managers Association.
   d. town clerk's office in the town where the association is located.

4. Connecticut law will allow the partition of concurrent ownership in real estate
   a. when it is voluntary.
   b. when it is involuntary.
   c. voluntarily and involuntarily.
   d. only on the death of a tenant in common.

5. Alex and Adam own property as tenants in common. Alex requests a court to partition the property, but the court finds that it is physically impossible to do so. Therefore, the court may
   a. refuse the request to partition.
   b. require the sale of the property and a distribution of the proceeds of sale.
   c. instruct Alex to purchase Adam's interest at market value.
   d. escheat the property to the state until a satisfactory settlement can be made between Adam and Alex.

6. A husband and wife who own their home as joint tenants obtain a divorce. At that time, the joint tenancy
   a. extinguishes and becomes a tenancy in common.
   b. continues until one of them dies.
   c. extinguishes and becomes a tenancy at sufferance.
   d. reverts to common interest ownership

7. What types of properties are governed by the Common Interest Ownership Act?
   a. Condominiums
   b. Condominiums and cooperatives
   c. Planned unit developments (PUDs)
   d. Condominiums, cooperatives, and planned communities

8. A condominium is created by filing in the land records a
   a. public offering statement.
   b. unit deed.
   c. declaration.
   d. resale certificate.

9. On the initial sale of a cooperative unit, the developer must give the purchaser a
   a. resale certificate.
   b. proprietary lease.
   c. public offering statement.
   d. conversion notice.

10. Bob has just entered into a contract to buy a condominium unit from Cal (who originally bought the unit from the developer and has lived there for the past ten years). Cal has delivered the resale documents to Bob. Bob has a right to cancel the contract within
    a. 5 business days of receipt of resale documents.
    b. 15 business days of receipt of resale documents.
    c. 5 days from the date Bob executed the contract.
    d. no time period because Bob does not have the right to cancel a signed contract in this situation.

CHAPTER 5

Legal Descriptions

■ OVERVIEW

Real estate can be identified by either a formal legal description or an informal street reference. Connecticut law requires that a legal description be used to identify real estate in conveyance documents, such as in a deed. However, the law does not require that real estate be identified with a legal description in a contract, such as a listing agreement or purchase contract, but can be identified by reference to street address.

For legal descriptions of property, Connecticut predominantly follows the metes-and-bounds method. The government survey system is not used in Connecticut. When a parcel of land is a lot within an approved subdivision or has been subdivided out of a larger tract, the legal description will often identify and refer to the original subdivision map.

Although a metes-and-bounds description is legally preferred in Connecticut, other less exact descriptions are generally considered a valid description for purposes of describing real estate in a listing agreement and purchase contract. Therefore, most real estate contracts do not contain a full legal description but informally refer to the real estate using a street location.

■ METES-AND-BOUNDS DESCRIPTION

A typical full legal description accurately describes of the boundaries of the real estate. An example is given in following paragraphs. Monuments are used to establish boundaries. Commonly, these monuments are iron pins, concrete posts, or bronze discs set in rock or other permanent structures. (Note that it is unlawful to disturb boundary markers set by a surveyor.) Benchmarks are types of monuments that are the basis not only for horizontal measurements but also for elevation.

■ **FOR EXAMPLE** A certain piece or parcel of land with the buildings and improvements thereon situated on the southerly side of Woodmont Drive in the Town of East Hartford, County of Hartford and State of Connecticut, known and designated as Lot No. 57 on a map entitled "Section A Subdivision Plan 'Eastonbury Estates' Town of East Hartford, Conn. Owner—Arbeiter Liedertafel, Inc., Subdivider—Harry James and Edwin Hoberman, 303 Burnside Ave., E. Hartford, Conn. Everett O. Gardner and Assoc., 576 Old Post Road, Tolland, Connecticut, Professional Engineers Land Surveyors. Scale 1" = 40". Date 1/20/76" which map is on file in the Town Clerk's Office in said Town of East Hartford.

Said premises are more particularly bounded and described as follows:

Northerly: by Woodmont Drive a distance of One Hundred Seventy-Eight and Thirty-Nine One-Hundredths (178.39) feet;

Easterly: by land now or formerly of Hand J. Builders and Developers, Inc., being Lot No. 56 on a map for "Section B Subdivision Plan Eastonbury Estates" a distance of Two Hundred Twenty-Seven and Fifty-Eight One-Hundredths (227.58) feet;

Southerly: by land now or formerly of Anna S. Holm and Ellis O. Sahlberg situated in the Town of Glastonbury as shown on said map One Hundred Eighty-Five (185) feet; and

Westerly: by Lot No. 58 as shown on said map a distance of Two Hundred Fifty-One and Sixty One-Hundredths (251.60) feet.

Said premises are also known as 61 Woodmont Drive in said Town of East Hartford.

In some instances, the distances between monuments or benchmarks may not be mentioned in the description unless it becomes absolutely necessary to establish the boundaries. Thus, a description may indicate the boundaries as public roads and thoroughfares or even lands "now or formerly of" rather than using precise distances and courses. The following example of a legal description is acceptable in most instances even though it makes no specific reference to every linear dimension of the parcel.

■ **FOR EXAMPLE** All that certain piece or parcel of land with the buildings and all other improvements thereon and the appurtenances thereto, located and situated in the Town of South Windsor, County of Hartford and State of Connecticut, containing approximately One Hundred (100) acres, and being more particularly bounded and described as follows, to wit:

Easterly: by Sullivan Avenue and Pierce Road, so-called;

Southerly: by land now or formerly of Harold J. A. Collins, Stanley H. Lorenson, Asher A. Collins, and Strong Road, in part by each;

Westerly: by West Road, so-called; and

Northerly: by land now or formerly of Herbert Tomlinson, et ux., and land now or formerly of Annette Frink partly by each.

Said premises are the same as were conveyed by Ella A. West, to the grantor herein by Warranty Deed dated August 8, 1958, and recorded in Volume 66 at Page 330 of the South Windsor Land Records.

■ LAND SURVEYORS

The Connecticut Department of Consumer Protection sets forth standards for the accuracy, content, and certification of land surveys and maps. A person that measures and maps property boundary lines must be licensed as a land surveyor. (CGS Chapter 391)

■ GOVERNMENT SURVEY SYSTEM

The Public Land Survey system is a way of describing land in the United States by rectangular surveys dividing land into six-mile-square townships (and further subdivided into smaller sections). The public land survey system is not used in Connecticut; however, the Connecticut legislature has created a coordinated system for the purpose of defining geographic locations of points. Referring to the system of plane coordinates established pursuant to the system is considered a sufficient legal description describing a land boundary corner. (CGS Section 13a-255)

■ LOST BOUNDARY

In the event of a lost or uncertain boundary, Connecticut law provides for the establishment or re-establishment of the boundary on the complaint of one of the adjoining landowners to the Superior Court. The court will appoint a committee of not more than three persons to investigate the situation and erect and establish the lost or uncertain boundary. The committee may engage a surveyor to assist and will record a certified copy of the findings to establish the boundary between the adjoining landowners. Unless it can be proven that the committee made an error of law in reaching its conclusion, the findings of the committee are held to be conclusive. (CGS Section 47-34)

■ COMMON INTEREST OWNERSHIP

The conveyance of any legal interest in a condominium unit is treated in a manner similar to any other real estate conveyance. The essential difference lies in the description of the unit's undivided interest in the common areas and facilities. The Connecticut Common Interest Ownership Act (see Chapter 4) dictates that a legally sufficient description of a common interest ownership unit must contain: (1) the name of the common interest community, (2) the recording data for the original declaration, (3) the town in which the common interest community is located, and (4) the identifying number of the unit. An example of a legal description of a condominium unit is described below.

■ **FOR EXAMPLE**   Unit No. 62 of South Mountain Townhouses, Bristol, Connecticut, together with an interest in the common areas and facilities, appurtenant said unit and common areas and facilities being more specifically designated and described in the Declaration of Condominium establishing the plan for Unit Ownership under the "Unit Ownership Act" of the State of Connecticut made by the Grantors entitled "South Mountain Townhouses Declaration of Condominium" dated May 31, 1973, and recorded in Volume 614 at Pages 310 through 340 inclusive of the Land Records of said City of Bristol, the floor plans of which are set forth on drawings entitled "South Mountain Townhouses, Bristol, Connecticut, David Butts Associates, architect, 1019 Farmington Avenue, Bristol, Conn."

Said premises are conveyed together with and subject to all of the covenants, restrictions, reservations, limitations, conditions, uses, agreements, easements, appurtenances, and other provisions set forth in the aforesaid Declaration of Condominium.

Said premises are further subject to any and all provisions of any ordinance, municipal regulation, or public or private laws; and to easements as of record appears.

■ WEB LINK

Standards for Surveys and Maps in Connecticut (Connecticut Association of Land Surveyors):   *www.ctsurveyor.com/connecti.htm*

CHAPTER 5 QUIZ

1. The principal method of delineating property boundaries or legal descriptions in Connecticut is known as the
   a. colonial block grant system.
   b. system of principal meridians and baselines.
   c. system of metes and bounds.
   d. rectangular survey system.

2. An iron pin, used as a point on a property boundary, would be the same thing as a
   a. monument.
   b. meridian.
   c. base point.
   d. plat.

3. When an adjoining property owner files suit to establish or reestablish a lost boundary, a committee to carry out the task is usually appointed by the
   a. Real Estate Commission.
   b. Superior Court.
   c. Court of Appeals.
   d. Town Clerk for the town in which the property is located.

4. The findings of a committee appointed to establish a lost boundary are considered conclusive unless it can be proven that the
   a. adjoining landowners are related.
   b. committee made an error of law.
   c. committee did not employ a surveyor.
   d. boundary was between three or more properties.

5. A legally sufficient description of a condominium unit must contain all of the following EXCEPT the
   a. name of the condominium unit.
   b. identifying unit number.
   c. boundaries of the common interest community property.
   d. recording data for the original declaration.

6. Ken has agreed to buy Mary's house, and they draw up their own purchase contract. The contract describes the property as "90 Fairweather Lawn, Bridgeport." Based on the property description, is this contract binding?
   a. No, Connecticut requires a metes-and-bounds description.
   b. No, at the minimum, a reference to a subdivision map must be made.
   c. Yes, such a simple description may be used for purposes of a purchase and sale contract.
   d. Yes, Ken was fully aware of the boundaries of the property.

C H A P T E R

Real Estate Taxes and Other Liens

■ OVERVIEW

Real estate is taxed at the municipal level in Connecticut. The amount of tax is based on the value of the property. Unpaid municipal property taxes become a lien on the property and take precedence over all other liens. In addition to tax liens, Connecticut recognizes the other types of liens that are described in the principles texts.

■ PROPERTY TAXES

Title 12 of the Connecticut General Statutes provides local municipalities with broad powers to assess and evaluate real property and to levy local property taxes. The real property tax in Connecticut is the exclusive domain of the local municipality and is considered to be an *ad valorem* tax (based on value). The local tax rate is set by each individual town according to its estimated expenses for the forthcoming year and the property list provided by the local assessor's office. The state itself does not levy a real property tax.

Assessment

Local tax assessors are required to maintain a list of taxable properties in their municipalities, including real estate and such tangible personal property as automobiles. This list, often called the *Grand List*, also contains an estimate of the value of these properties. Properties owned by nonresidents are assessed and taxed in the same manner as those owned by residents. The state requires that the values placed on all properties reflect their *market value*.

Periodic revaluation. Few towns have either the manpower or financial resources to annually reassess each parcel of real estate in the town to establish current market values (although municipal assessors may hire a revaluation company to assess property within a town). Connecticut law requires that towns revalue properties every five years, by either physical observation or statistical analysis (there are some provisions for delays to the five-year schedule, including for a town's participation in a regional revaluation program). Revaluation based on a physical inspection is required every ten years. Additionally, towns can phase in all or part of the effects of revaluation for up to five years.

Farm, forest, and open-space lands. Specific categories of land have been established by the state of Connecticut. For tax purposes, farm, forest, and open-space lands are not assessed at market value. If the owners of such land follow the proper registration procedures, their assessments are lowered to provide considerable tax relief.

Assessment appeals. A property owner who feels that his or her property has been assessed incorrectly may appeal to the local *board of tax review* for a revaluation of the property. Such appeals must be made during the appropriate month (usually February or March) for the upcoming tax year unless, by a special act, the town provides additional time periods. Assessment appeals can be made during the intervening years between revaluations. Appeals from the municipal board of tax review are made to the Connecticut Appeals Board for Property Valuation.

Exempted Properties

The law provides for the exemption of certain kinds of property from local property taxes. Most of these exempted properties correspond to those mentioned in the principles texts. In addition, there are statutory provisions that allow for possible reduction or elimination of taxes for certain kinds of property or properties owned by certain classes of owners. The following is a representative (though not a complete) list of these "special" properties and owners:

Tax Abatement

- Structures of architectural or historical merit
- Environmentally impacted or contaminated sites—if remediated and redeveloped
- Various types of low-income and moderate-income housing
- Corporations (under specified circumstances)
- Others (by authority of the taxing body)

Tax Relief

- Persons over 65 years old
- Disabled or handicapped persons
- Veterans (usually limited to a $1,000 exemption)
- Farm, forest, and open-space lands (as discussed earlier)
- Others (by authority of the taxing body)

Calculation of Property Taxes

While the exact procedure used to calculate an individual property owner's tax bill might vary somewhat from town to town, there are some generally accepted principles. Most towns have a *tax assessor* whose duty it is to determine the market value and assessed value of properties located within the town.

A town first determines a property's *market value*, using appraisal and valuation techniques. Based on the market value, the town then calculates the property's *assessed value* by multiplying the market value by the assessment ratio. Connecticut law requires an *assessment ratio* of 70 percent for all towns. Therefore, a property's assessed value is 70 percent of its market value. To determine annual taxes, the assessed value is multiplied by the town tax rate (mills) and divided by 1,000.

The town property tax rate is expressed in *mills* and is equivalent to dollars of tax per thousand dollars of assessed value (a mill is technically a tenth of a penny, which is then one thousandth of a dollar). It is calculated on the basis of the revenues required by the municipality and the total list of taxable property. Each town sets its own mill rate. Some municipalities also have different mill rates for different districts within that town.

To illustrate the calculation of property tax:

■ **FOR EXAMPLE**

Property: single-family home and lot

Appraised market value: $500,000

Assessment ratio: 70 percent

Assessed value: $500,000 × 0.70 = $350,000

Tax rate: 20 mills (or $20 per $1,000 of assessed value)

Compute: $350,000 × (20 mills/$1,000)

Indicated property tax: $7,000

Special Taxes or Assessments

Every parcel of real estate in a Connecticut town does not necessarily carry an equal tax burden. Frequently, a special service—a fire district or a sewer facility—that benefits only properties within a given area will require that a special tax or assessment be levied on the properties in that area. Special taxes or assessments may be separately levied on these benefiting properties only. Owners of properties within these special service areas, then, must pay not only the standard property tax rate but also an additional rate for the special facility.

Timing of Property Tax Payments

The tax year in Connecticut is generally the same as the state's fiscal year and runs from July 1 to June 30. In the majority of Connecticut towns, real property taxes are payable for the current tax year on July 1 and January 1 (six-month taxes on

each date). Typically, there is a 30-day grace period after these dates before any penalties (interest) begin to accrue. In several towns, however, payments are made quarterly. In any real estate sales transaction, one should be particularly careful to determine the timing and manner of local tax payments well ahead of any closing to avoid unanticipated problems with pro rata adjustments. (Calculations of prorations are discussed in Chapter 16 of this text.)

Assessment dates.   Property on the Grand List for the next tax year must be assessed by October 1 of the preceding year. Thus, taxes payable on July 1, 2011, and January 1, 2012, are determined from assessments computed by the town assessor prior to October 1, 2010.

Tax bills issued.   Although the exact timing may vary somewhat from town to town, tax bills are issued at least 30 days prior to the date on which the first installment is due and payable (and often earlier).

Property Tax Liens

In the event that real property taxes or assessments are not paid in accordance with the legally prescribed schedule, such taxes become a lien on the property until they are paid or the property is sold at public auction to satisfy the delinquent sums owed. From a strictly legal standpoint, the taxes are actually a lien on the property from the date of assessment (generally October 1), but this lien is never enforced by law unless the taxpayer violates the prescribed payment schedule. As stated previously, municipal tax liens take precedence over all other liens. The possible exception would be a federal tax lien recorded against the property that became attached to the property and was completed prior to the municipal lien.

The statutes generally hold tax liens to a 15-year maximum, although this period may be extended by court order. To be valid, tax liens must be recorded by the agency levying the tax within two years from the due date of the taxes in question.

A municipality may, through superior court action, foreclose a tax lien, take possession of the delinquent taxpayer's property, and order it sold at a tax or sheriff's sale. However, the taxpayer has a period of six months from the date of the sale to exercise his or her *right of redemption* as described in the principles texts. (The redemption period may be as short as 60 days if the property was abandoned or meets other conditions established by local ordinance.) If the sale produces a sum in excess of that needed to satisfy the lien and any other costs of the sale, the excess will be turned over to the taxpayer.

■ CAPITAL GAINS TAX

The full amount of capital gains is taxed as income by the state of Connecticut. The tax is calculated in the same manner as that of the federal government. Hence a separate state tax is imposed. The law also requires that a husband and wife who file a single return jointly for IRS tax purposes file a single return jointly for the tax imposed under Connecticut General Statutes.

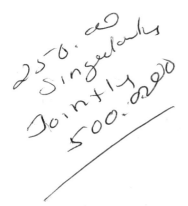

The state capital gains tax applies to both residents and nonresidents on gain realized from the sale or exchange of real estates located in Connecticut. If a nonresident is a party in a partnership that sells or exchanges realty in Connecticut and realizes a gain, that individual shall be taxed for each gain in the same manner as occurs with the federal tax. Similar taxes are also levied for individuals as shareholders in S corporations or beneficiaries of trusts or estates that sell or exchange real estate located in Connecticut.

■ CONVEYANCE TAX

Connecticut levies two types of taxes on the seller at the time of transfer of title: a state conveyance tax and a municipal conveyance, both based on a percentage of the selling price. These are paid at the time of closing (transfer of title). A more detailed explanation of these taxes is presented in Chapter 8.

■ OTHER LIENS AND TRANSFER TAXES

Mechanics', judgment, and other liens generally operate as described in the principles texts. Additionally, in Connecticut, a broker who has performed services relating to real estate has the right to place a lien on the real estate to secure payment of compensation. (See Chapter 1 for a discussion of the broker's lien.)

The usual test applied to establish the *priority* of liens other than tax or municipal liens is the *date of recording.* However, with respect to mechanics' liens, the primary test for priority lies with the establishment of the date on which the mechanic in question delivered materials or commenced work. To be valid, a mechanic's lien must be recorded within 90 days from the time the mechanic's work ceases and will extinguish in one year from that date unless action to foreclose is begun. (CGS Sections 49-33–49-38)

In Connecticut, mechanics' liens can attach to leasehold interests as well as the underlying interest of leased property, if certain conditions are met. Additionally, a property owner who has a lien placed on his property can seek a court order substituting a bond for the lien.

Connecticut also allows for a purchaser's lien to secure a purchaser's deposit paid in connection with a purchase and sale contract. The actual contract can be recorded as evidence of the lien, or a notice of contract can be recorded. In order to be valid, the recorded document must be signed by the owner of the property. This lien takes priority over any liens or encumbrances placed on the property after its recording. It can be foreclosed in the same way a mortgage lien is foreclosed.

■ WEB LINKS

Connecticut General Statutes, Title 12 (Taxation):
  www.cga.ct.gov/2009/pub/Title12.htm
Connecticut Department of Revenue Services (state income tax
  information): *www.ct.gov/drs*
Connecticut town mill rates: *www.ct.gov/opm/site/default.asp*

CHAPTER 6 QUIZ

1. In Connecticut the real property tax is essentially a(n)
   a. ad hoc tax.
   b. ad valorem tax.
   c. state tax.
   d. title lien.

2. With respect to real property taxation, Connecticut statutes require that assessments reflect
   a. reproduction value.
   b. insurable value.
   c. intrinsic value.
   d. market value.

3. The Connecticut statutes require a complete physical revaluation of real estate in any given town once every
   a. five years.
   b. year.
   c. four years.
   d. time the Grand List increases by 10 percent.

4. Certain types of land are eligible for tax relief through special assessment allowances under the general statutes. Which does not fall into this category?
   a. Farm land
   b. Open-space land
   c. Forest land
   d. Wetlands

5. The basic unit of real property tax rate in Connecticut is called a(n)
   a. quota.
   b. mill.
   c. percentum.
   d. assessment ratio.

6. Bill has just bought a home in Glastonbury for $150,000. The town has calculated its market value at $100,000. Glastonbury's mill rate this year is 20 mills. Bill has asked you to compute his yearly property taxes. You tell him
   a. you need to know the assessment ratio in Glastonbury before you can do so.
   b. $1,400.
   c. $2,000.
   d. $2,100.

7. From a strictly legal standpoint, real property taxes become a lien on the property as of the
   a. due date.
   b. 30th day from the due date.
   c. date of assessment.
   d. date a foreclosure suit is filed and recorded.

8. Jen contracted with ABC Construction Company to put a new deck on her house. They began work on May 1 and finished on June 1, but Jen never paid them. On July 1, Jen sold her house to Tom, who received a mortgage loan from Country Bank and a mortgage loan from City Bank. City Bank recorded its mortgage on July 1. Country Bank recorded its mortgage on July 2. ABC Construction Company records a mechanic's lien on July 3. What is the priority of the liens?
   a. ABC Construction, City Bank, Country Bank
   b. City Bank, Country Bank, ABC Construction
   c. ABC Construction, then City Bank and Country Bank equal
   d. City Bank and Country Bank equal, then ABC Construction

9. The conveyance tax levied by the state on the seller of the property is based on the
   a. selling price.
   b. earnest money.
   c. amount of the mortgage.
   d. time of the purchase.

10. The town of Goshen has recently revalued a piece of property at a market value of $200,000. Goshen's mill rate is 25 mills. How much property tax will be owed on the property this year?

   a. $5,000
   b. $500
   c. $3,500
   d. $350

CHAPTER 7

Real Estate

■ OVERVIEW

Purchase and sale contracts are legally enforceable agreements whereby the seller has agreed to sell real estate and the buyer has agreed to buy the real estate, upon the terms and conditions listed in the contract. A purchase and sale contract does not transfer title (a document called a deed transfers title); it is the contractual agreement to transfer title in the future.

Connecticut requires that all contracts affecting title to real estate must be in writing to be enforceable and that all contracts for over $500 must be in writing (Statute of Frauds).

Connecticut also requires that sellers provide prospective purchasers with a property condition report in all residential real estate transactions (with few exceptions).

Electronic contracts (including e-mails and faxes) must meet federal and state guidelines for electronic documents and signatures. See Appendix E for a discussion of the requirements.

■ BROKER'S AUTHORITY TO PREPARE DOCUMENTS

Connecticut laws are somewhat vague regarding the extent to which a broker is authorized to prepare documents and contracts associated with the sale of real property. The law, however, clearly *prohibits brokers and salespersons from engaging in activities that require a license to practice law*. This would seem to restrict the broker's authority to prepare contracts, such as sales or listing contracts. The use of standardized contract forms drawn up and approved by attorneys and Boards of REALTORS® is so widespread among real estate brokers that there are few instances that would require a broker to prepare his or her own documents. The law would not, however, keep a broker from preparing sales or listing contracts, subject to approval of legal counsel, if desired.

It is customary practice, then, for brokers to *use preapproved forms* for almost all their day-to-day operations. Frequently, local real estate boards or broker offices retain attorneys to draw up an appropriate array of standard contracts for affiliated brokers and salespersons to use. In the event that a broker is faced with an unusual situation for which no standard form is appropriate, it would be wisest to consult legal counsel rather than struggle with the preparation of an appropriate and acceptable contract document.

Brokers and salespersons should *not modify* a preapproved form without consulting with an attorney. Even a slight modification could have an unforeseen legal effect.

■ STANDARD CONTRACTUAL REQUIREMENTS

Written Contracts

Like other contracts, real estate contracts must contain the basic legal elements to be valid and enforceable. These include legally competent parties, offer and acceptance (mutual agreement), valid consideration, and legality of object. In Connecticut, it is presumed that the mutual agreement of the parties to a contract is not marred by mistakes, misrepresentation, fraud, duress, or undue influence.

Real estate purchase and sale contracts require three additional elements: (1) *be in writing*, (2) *identify the property*, and (3) *be signed* by all the parties to the contract. In Connecticut, the writing element is associated with Connecticut *Statute of Frauds* that requires that all contracts involving consideration in excess of $500 be in writing to be legally enforceable.

Connecticut real estate regulations also require that all *listing and buyer brokerage agreements be in writing*. Because these contracts represent a broker's contract of employment, it would be important to a broker to have the contract in writing. Verbal contracts are not enforceable by law, so brokers are urged to avoid them.

Capacity of Parties

In Connecticut, the attainment of the age of majority (currently 18) gives a person the capacity to enter into legally enforceable contracts. While minors may enter into contracts prior to attaining majority (the law sets no absolute minimum), other parties to the contract should understand that minors generally are permitted to void their contracts at their own discretion. Because of this, it is important to ascertain the capacity of an individual to sign a legally enforceable contract,

particularly with reference to his or her age. Also, any person signing a contract on behalf of a corporation must have the corporation's authority to act.

Offer and Acceptance

The Connecticut laws requiring written contracts for real estate transactions make it easier to determine whether an offer and acceptance have occurred. When the seller signs the buyer's offer, that constitutes the seller's acceptance, and the signed written document is a sales contract, if all the contractual elements are present.

■ REAL ESTATE CONTRACTS

Listing and Buyer Brokerage Contracts

Listing agreements and buyer brokerage agreements are primarily contracts of employment, with the client employing the broker. Because these agreements do not have direct application to the actual conveyance of title to real estate, they are not usually considered to fall within the jurisdiction of the Statute of Frauds. The Connecticut real estate regulations do require, however, that to be enforceable, agency agreements must be in writing and contain a minimum of information. As discussed in Chapter 2, these contracts must contain the following *additional provisions* besides those found in an ordinary contract:

■ Terms and conditions essential to the purchase or sale
■ Compensation to be paid
■ Expiration date of the contract
■ A statement of the broker's adherence to the General Statutes pertaining to Fair Housing (See Chapter 2 for a complete inventory of listing requirements.)

While other items might be added to the contract at the specific request of either party, as long as the minimal elements are present, the contract will be enforceable. See the sample Connecticut listing and buyer brokerage agreements provided in Chapter 2.

Listing contracts are *bilateral contracts* in which a client promises to pay a commission or other compensation to a broker and the broker promises to attempt to procure a ready, willing, and able buyer (with the exception of an open listing contract, which is a unilateral contract). Similarly, buyer agency agreements are bilateral contracts.

Purchase and Sale Agreements

Note that the agreement between a buyer and seller of real estate is referred to in many different ways. It is called a *purchase and sale agreement or contract*, a *purchase agreement or contract*, a *sales agreement or contract*. Regardless of what it is called, it is the instrument that establishes the *rights and obligations of the buyer and seller of real estate*.

A standard Purchase and Sale Agreement form currently in use in Connecticut (Figure 7.1), Combined Contingency Addendum to Purchase and Sale contract (Figure 7.2), Hubbard Clause contract addendum (Figure 7.3), and a Binder of Sale (contract) (Figure 7.4) appear later in this chapter, along with a Residential Property Condition Disclosure Report (Figure 7.5).

One of the broker's primary responsibilities is to negotiate a valid sales contract between the buyer and the seller. Once signed, a purchase and sale agreement is *legally binding* on both the buyer and the seller. It is, therefore, quite important that brokers be fully aware of the legal implications of all of the provisions of such agreements. It is common practice in Connecticut for brokers and salespersons to use forms that have been prepared by an attorney on behalf of the Connecticut Association of REALTORS®, Inc., local real estate boards, or broker offices.

The sales agreement is considered to be a *bilateral contract* in Connecticut because it involves a promise for a promise. The buyer promises to pay an amount of money for the seller's property as of a certain date, and the seller promises to convey his or her property to the buyer in exchange for the stipulated amount.

Contingency provisions. The purchase and sale contract may contain contingency provisions that would allow the buyer to be excused from the contract. These might include a *mortgage contingency* and *building inspection contingency*. Note that home inspectors are required to be licensed in Connecticut; brokers and salespersons who are not licensed in home inspection should be careful not to offer building inspection opinions that could be interpreted as fact.

Personal property and items of real estate. In general, the law presumes that if the sales contract is silent on the point, any items of real estate attached to the property being sold will be conveyed with the property, and any items of personal property will be removed before the buyers take possession. If the sale is to include any items of personal property (such as drapes, lawn furnishings or equipment, aboveground pools, movable appliances, and so on), that personal property must be specifically identified in the sales contract. No separate bill of sale is drawn up for the personal property, and the sales agreement for the real property doubles as a bill of sale for the personal property. The opposite is true for items attached to the real estate, such as built-in appliances, in-ground pools, sconces, and chandeliers. Any such attached items that will not be conveyed must be so specified in the sales contract.

Deposit money—escrow accounts. Generally, the real estate sales contract provides that the broker will hold the deposit money deposited by the buyer. In such cases, Connecticut laws expressly forbid a commingling of personal funds with those held as deposits on listed properties. A salesperson must immediately assign or pay over directly to his or her broker all funds received from a real estate transaction. Brokers must maintain a *separate escrow or trust account* for the deposit of all monies received on behalf of their clients. These deposits must be made *within three banking days* from the date of obtaining all signatures from all parties to the transaction.

Interest earned on real estate broker accounts is paid to the Connecticut Housing Finance Authority to benefit a program for first-time homebuyers. A buyer and seller may decide, however, to allow the buyer's deposit to bear interest for the buyer or seller. In such case a separate account is maintained in the name of the parties involved. See Chapter 10 for more details on escrow accounts for real estate deposits.

Because the sales contract will generally identify the amount of money deposited with the broker or escrow agent, a receipt is not always required, though one may be drawn up on the buyer's request. Unless the deposit is made in cash, a canceled check will always serve as a receipt. Connecticut law provides for a procedure allowing brokers to hand over a deposit to a court when there is a dispute regarding the sale.

Destruction of the premises.   In Connecticut, if the sales contract is silent on this point, it is presumed that the seller will carry the risk of loss and maintain fire insurance coverage until the date of closing. Most contracts do provide that the seller will bear the risk of loss if the premises are destroyed before the closing.

Defaults.   If either the buyer or the seller breaches a real estate sales contract, the contract is said to be in default. The remedies for default in Connecticut are essentially the same as those mentioned in the principles texts. However, the nature of the default relates directly to a broker's right to collect compensation. The real estate broker's right to compensation is discussed in Chapter 1.

Leases

Connecticut law requires that leases for a term of more than one year be in writing. To be valid, written lease contracts must describe the property leased, identify the parties, state the amount of rental and manner of payment, indicate dates, describe any other desirable terms and conditions, and contain the signatures of the parties to the contract. Leases are discussed in Chapter 12.

A broker who is entitled to a future commission for a commercial lease transaction can protect his or her right to receive that commission in the event the landlord sells the property by recording a Notice of Commission Rights in the municipal land records in the municipality where the leased property is located. A sample notice is provided in Chapter 1.

Escrow Agreements

Connecticut allows the conveyance of real estate interests by way of the escrow procedure. The laws pertaining to such transactions are generally the same as those described in the basic principles text.

■ RESIDENTIAL PROPERTY CONDITION DISCLOSURE

Sellers are required to provide prospective purchasers with a property condition report in all residential real estate transactions (with few exceptions). The law applies to both for-sale-by-owner (FSBO) and real estate agent–assisted transactions.

Covered Property

The property disclosure requirement applies to the following property:

- Residential real estate containing one to four dwelling units (including condominiums and cooperatives)
- Transfers by sale, exchange, or lease with an option to buy

Exclusions

Exclusions to the property disclosure requirement include transfers

- from co-owner to co-owner;
- for no consideration to spouse, mother, father, brother, sister, child, grandparent, or grandchild;
- pursuant to a court order;
- of newly constructed residential real property that carries an implied warranty pursuant to CGS Chapter 827;
- made by executors, administrators, trustees, or conservators;
- by the federal government or federal quasi-governmental entity;
- by deed in lieu of foreclosure;
- by the state of Connecticut or any political subdivision; and
- by strict foreclosure, foreclosure by sale, or deed in lieu of foreclosure.

Timing

Residential property condition disclosure reports have the following timing requirements:

- Disclosure reports must be delivered by the seller to a prospective purchaser at any time prior to the purchaser's signing a written offer to purchase, a binder, a contract, an option, or lease containing a purchase option.
- A photocopy, facsimile transmission, or duplicate original of the report signed by the purchaser must be attached to any written offers, binders, contracts, options, or leases containing a purchase option.
- A photocopy, facsimile transmission, or duplicate original of the report, containing both the seller's and purchaser's signatures, must be attached to any purchase agreement.

Role of Seller

The responsibility for completing the form lies with the seller of the property. The disclosures are only required to be based on the seller's actual knowledge of the condition of the prop[...]

required to respond yes, [...]

tions, the seller must ex[...]

report as required, the se[...]

held liable for failure to [...]

Role of Real Esta[...]

Agents should advis[...] accurately. This law[...] material facts about[...]

Role of Buyer

Seller's disclosur[...] is urged to carefully inspec[...] inspected by an expert.

Obtaining Forms

The required property disclosure report form has been developed by the Department of Consumer Protection. The form is shown in Figure 7.5. Copies of the form can be obtained at the Department Web site.

Connecticut Real Estate Practice & Law Twelf[...]

88

FIGURE 7.1
Purchase and Sale Agreement

(T[...]

This is a legally[...]
attorney befo[...]
and Buyer[...]

1.

■ DISCLOSURE OF OFF-SITE CONDITIONS

A residential seller and the seller's agent have satisfied their duty to disclose off-site waste conditions if, before entering into the contract, the seller gives the buyer written notice of the availability of lists of hazardous waste facilities and properties on which hunting and shooting take place. A sample notice is provided in Chapter 17; the Purchase and Sale Contract provided in this chapter also contains this notice provision.

■ WEB LINKS

Connecticut Department of Consumer Protection: *www.ct.gov/dcp*

Chapter 392 of Connecticut General Statutes, Real Estate Brokers and Salespersons: *www.cga.ct.gov/2009/pub/Chap392.htm*

Connecticut Residential Property Disclosure Form: *www.ct.gov/dcp/lib/dcp/pdf/realestate_licensing_forms/disclose.pdf*

Information for Buyers (Connecticut Association of REALTORS®, Inc.): *www.ctrealtor.com/mt_consumers/buyerInfo.shtml*

Information for Sellers (Connecticut Association of REALTORS®, Inc.): *www.ctrealtor.com/mt_consumers/sellerInfo.shtml*

Purchase and Sale Agreement

(This form is not intended for use with commercial property or new construction)

binding contract. If there are any legal questions about any part of this transaction, consult with an
e signing this Agreement or request an attorney-approval contingency. **This is an "As Is" agreement,**
should make as thorough an investigation of the Property as Buyer deems necessary.

Parties.

Buyer(s):_____
    Name(s)

    _____
    Address   Phone

Seller(s):_____
    Name(s)

    _____
    Address   Phone

2.   Property. Buyer agrees to purchase from Seller and Seller agrees to sell to Buyer certain real property
known as:_____, Connecticut
("Property") along with the following personal property_____
_____.

3.   Purchase Price. The Purchase Price for the Property is $_____.

    $_____   Initial Deposit receipt of which is hereby acknowledged.
    $_____   Additional Deposit to be paid on or before _____.
    $_____   Balance of Purchase Price to be paid at closing.

4.   Mortgage Contingency. Buyer will make diligent, good faith efforts to obtain a written commitment for a
mortgage loan ("Mortgage") from a bank or other institutional lender on or before _____
("Mortgage Contingency Date"). Buyer will provide Seller and Broker, no later than the Mortgage Contingency
Date, with a copy of any written commitment for a Mortgage obtained by Buyer. Buyer will pay all application fees,
points (not to exceed _____), and other charges in accordance with the policies established by the applicable lender.

The Mortgage must be on the following terms:

    (a) Loan Amount $_____ (b) Maximum initial interest rate _____ % per annum.
    (c) Minimum term _____ years.

Types of mortgage: (CHECK THE FOLLOWING AS APPLICABLE)
☐ Conventional Fixed Rate   ☐ CHFA   ☐ FHA   ☐ Other (Describe)
☐ Conventional Variable Rate   ☐ VA   ☐ Seller (Attach Seller Financing Addendum)

If Buyer cannot obtain a written commitment for the Mortgage (free of any conditions that are unacceptable to
Buyer), Buyer may terminate this Agreement by providing Seller and Broker, not later than the Mortgage
Contingency Date, with written notice of Buyer's inability to obtain such commitment. If Buyer does not elect to so
terminate, then this Agreement will remain in full force and effect, unless Seller, within seven (7) days from the
Mortgage Contingency Date, gives written notice to Buyer and Broker that Seller has elected to terminate this
Agreement as a result of Buyer's inability to obtain such commitment. If either party so terminates this Agreement,
then all deposits will be returned to Buyer, and the obligations of the parties under this Agreement shall end. If
Buyer applies for a different type of mortgage other than Conventional, Buyer shall provide Seller with prompt,
written notice of such application. Seller shall have three (3) business days after receiving such written notice within
which to elect to terminate this Agreement as a result of Buyer's application for a different type of mortgage than
that checked above.

_____   _____
Buyer's Initials   Seller's Initials
©2005-2010 Connecticut Association of Realtors®, Inc.
Revised September 30, 2008; Revised July 15, 2010

Page 1 of 6

F I G U R E 7.1 (continued)

Purchase and Sale Agreement

5.   Combined Contingency Addendum. ☐ If checked, the Combined Contingency Addendum attached is made a part of this Agreement.

6.   Deposits. The deposits specified in Paragraph 3 shall be made at the stated times. All deposits shall be made by check payable to the Listing Broker as escrow agent. Prior to the Closing of Title, the Listing Broker may pay the deposit funds to the Seller's attorney who shall hold them as escrow agent pending the Closing of Title. In the event any deposit funds payable pursuant to this Agreement are not so paid by Buyer, Seller may give written notice of such failure to Buyer(s) at the address specified in Paragraph 1 by certified mail, and if such notice is given and a period of five (5) days thereafter elapses without Buyer having corrected such failure, Seller may (1) declare Buyer to be in default, and (2) terminate this Agreement and the Seller shall be relieved of all obligations hereunder. In the event that this Agreement is terminated, Seller and Buyer agree to provide such permissions for release of the escrow monies as escrow agent may reasonably require. In the event of a dispute concerning the return of deposits held in escrow which results in court action, both the prevailing party and the escrow agent shall be entitled to reasonable attorney's fees from the losing party. In the event that the escrow agent commences a court action to determine the rights of the parties to deposits held in escrow, the escrow agent shall be entitled to attorney's fees, marshal's fees and docket fees to be paid out of the escrowed deposits. The parties agree that escrow agent will not be liable for the release of escrow monies in accordance with this Agreement or for errors of judgment in the release of escrowed deposits unless such errors are the result of gross or intentional misconduct.

7.   Property to be Maintained; Property Condition Disclosure. Except as may be set forth elsewhere in this Agreement, Property is being sold "as is". Seller agrees to maintain Property with all buildings, landscaping and other improvements thereon, all appurtenances thereto, and any personal property included in the sale in the same condition, reasonable wear and tear excepted, as they were on the date of this Agreement. Buyer shall have the right to make a final inspection of the Property during a 48-hour period prior to closing. In the event Seller has failed to provide Buyer with a copy of the Uniform Property Condition Disclosure Report required by Public Act 95-311 and is not exempt from the Act, Seller shall credit Buyer with the sum of $300.00 at closing as required by law.

Buyer is notified that the Department of Environmental Protection is required pursuant to Section 22a-134f of the Connecticut General Statutes to furnish lists of hazardous waste facilities located within the town to the Town Clerk's office. Buyer should refer to these lists and the Department of Environmental Protection for information on environmental questions concerning the Property and the lands surrounding the Property.

Buyer is notified that a list of local properties upon which hunting or shooting sports regularly take place may be available at the Town Clerk's office.

Buyer is notified that information concerning environmental matters on the Property and surrounding properties is available from the federal Environmental Protection Agency, the National Response Center, the Department of Defense and third-party providers.

8.   Insurance/Risk of Loss. The risk of loss or damage to Property by fire or other casualty until the delivery of the deed is assumed by the Seller. Seller shall keep the Property insured, at Seller's expense, against loss by fire and other casualties, with Extended Coverage provisions, in an amount equal to at least 80% of the market value of any improvements on the Property or in the alternative, replacement cost coverage until the delivery of the deed. In case of any loss, the Seller shall pay over or assign to the Buyer upon payment of the balance of the Purchase Price all sums recovered on account of said insurance, or the Buyer may, at Buyer's option, terminate this Agreement and the deposits shall be refunded to the Buyer, unless the Seller shall have restored the Property substantially to its former condition. This paragraph shall also apply to the items listed as fixtures in Paragraph 9 and the personal property set forth in Paragraph 2.

9.   Fixtures. Included in this sale as part of the Property are the buildings, structures and improvements now thereon, and the fixtures belonging to the Seller and used in connection therewith, including, if any, all blinds, window shades, screens, doors, door and window hardware, wood and gas stoves, storm windows, landscaping, awnings, shutters, electrical and lighting fixtures, door mirrors, pumps, mailboxes, plumbing fixtures, cabinetry, door and cabinet hardware, pool houses and other outbuildings, mantles, flagpoles, alarm system and codes, swimming pool and swimming pool pumps and equipment (if any), garbage disposal, automatic garage openers, central air conditioning equipment, and built-in dishwashers (Cross out and initial any items in this paragraph present on the Property but not included in the sale).

FIGURE 7.1 (continued)

Purchase and Sale Agreement

10.   Title, Affidavits and Releases. (A) Seller covenants and warrants that Seller is the fee title owner of the Property and has the authority and capacity to enter into this Agreement and consummate the transaction contemplated herein. The Property is to be conveyed by a good and sufficient Warranty Deed of the Seller (unless Seller is an executor, conservator, or administrator, in which case Buyer will receive a Fiduciary's Deed), conveying a good, insurable, and marketable title to the Property, free from all encumbrances, except as may be acceptable to Buyer and Buyer's Lender, if any, and except zoning and other municipal regulations, the Inland-Wetlands law and any state of facts that an accurate survey of the Property may reveal. Buyer shall at Buyer's own expense conduct a title examination of the Property within thirty (30) days of the date of acceptance of this Agreement. Buyer shall notify Seller of any defects in title that render title to the Property unmarketable, as defined by the Standards of Title of the Connecticut Bar Association, disclosed by such examination. If Seller is unable to remove such title defects within thirty (30) days of notification or the Closing of Title, whichever date is later, Buyer shall have the option to: (a) accept such title as Seller is able to convey without abatement or reduction of the Purchase Price, provided however, Seller shall pay any additional premium or post whatever bond and execute such affidavits and indemnity agreements as may be required by Buyer's title insurer to write title insurance over the defect or (b) cancel this Agreement and receive a return of all deposits, and, in addition, Seller shall pay to Buyer any expenses actually incurred by Buyer for attorney fees, nonrefundable fees of lending institutions, survey costs and inspection fees. Seller shall pay any nonrefundable fee actually incurred by Buyer to extend, refresh or renew any mortgage commitment granted Buyer by Buyer's lender pursuant to the provisions of Paragraph 4 that expires while the Seller is attempting to remove such title defect.

(B) Seller agrees to furnish such affidavits concerning title, encroachments, mechanic's liens and other items and in such form as Buyer's title insurance company may require in order to obtain owner's title insurance coverage on the Property or to waive exceptions to the title policy that are objectionable to Buyer's lender.

11.   Closing and Delivery of Possession. The closing will take place on _____ or at such other date as mutually agreed by the parties. The closing will be held at the offices of Seller's attorney unless Buyer has obtained a mortgage loan, in which event the closing will be held at the office of Buyer's lender's attorney. Upon the Closing of Title, Seller shall deliver exclusive occupancy to the Property, if the Property is a single-family residence, along with the keys, alarm codes and garage door transmitters, to the Buyer in a "broom clean" condition. "Broom clean" shall mean that the Property shall be empty of all personal property, except as may be included in the sale, free of all trash, garbage, junk, building materials, litter, cans of paint or stain, broken or discarded items, and vacuumed or swept. If the Property is a multi-family dwelling, Buyer shall take the Property subject to the rights of tenants to occupy the Property unless otherwise noted in this Agreement.

12.   Adjustments. The following are to be apportioned as of 11:59 p.m. of the day before closing:

(a)   Taxes, special tax districts, municipal water taxes and sewer taxes using the uniform fiscal year method;

(b)   Fuel oil (using the stated capacity of the storage tank);

(c)   Rents as and when collected;

(d)   Rental securities plus interest due thereon as provided by law; and

(e)   Utilities (for those utilities for which a separate meter reading and final billing cannot be obtained at closing based on the usage for the previous billing period).

If the closing shall occur before a new tax rate is fixed, the apportionment of taxes shall be upon the basis of the old tax rate for the preceding period applied to the latest assessed valuation.

Special assessment liens shall be ☐ paid by the Seller ☐ assumed by the Buyer. Pending special assessment liens or special assessments that are pending but have not yet been fixed as to an amount shall be assumed by the Buyer, provided however, that if the improvement has been substantially completed as of the date of this Agreement, the Seller shall credit the Buyer at closing with an amount equal to the latest estimate by the public body charged with levying the special assessment for the improvement.

Any errors or omissions in computing apportionments at closing shall be corrected. This provision shall survive the closing.

F I G U R E   7.1 (continued)

Purchase and Sale Agreement

13.   Seller's Representations. The Seller represents, to the best of the Seller's knowledge, information and belief without due inquiry, that, at the time of Closing of Title: (a) Seller has good, marketable title to all personal property and fixtures included in the sale and there is no leased or rented personal property or fixtures located on the Property, except as may be noted below; (b) Seller is in material compliance with all State and municipal zoning, environmental and health regulations affecting the Property and has no notice of any investigations, deficiencies, cease and desist orders, inspections or violations, actual or threatened, involving the Property, except as may be noted below; (c) Any buildings located on the Property are entirely within the boundary lines of the Property; (d) The subsurface sewage disposal and/or private water supply system, if any, and all utilities servicing the Property are located entirely within the boundary lines of the Property; (e) There is no violation of any restriction, covenant, agreement or condition affecting the Property; and (f) During the period of Seller's ownership, the Property has not been used for any commercial, industrial or other non-residential purpose and there has been no discharge, spillage, uncontrolled loss, seepage or filtration of oil, petroleum, or chemical liquids or other hazardous waste onto or emanating from the Property.

14. Multi-family Property Provisions (not applicable unless Property is a multi-family). The Seller represents that: (1) no tenant is currently in default of any material obligation under any lease or if no lease, that all tenants are current with their rental obligations; (2) that Seller has not collected rental in advance from any tenant (except for such advance rental securities as are permitted by statute) and (3) that Seller has not been notified of any claim by a tenant against Seller.

Seller agrees to provide Buyer with a statement within ten (10) days of the Date of Acceptance, certified true and correct by Seller, setting forth the amount of rent payable by each tenant, whether such rent is payable monthly or otherwise, the amount of advanced rental security Seller currently holds for each tenant and the date on which the advanced rental security was paid to the Seller. Seller agrees not to collect rent in advance for periods of time after the Date of Closing, without the Buyer's express, written permission.

15. Common Interest Ownership Property (not applicable for other types of property)

(a)   Buyer understands that the property is a unit in a condominium or planned unit development and that the property will be conveyed subject to all of the terms, conditions, covenants, restrictions, agreements, obligations, assessments and lien rights as set forth in the declaration applicable to the property, the by-laws and the rules and regulations including any exhibits attached, as they may be amended or supplemented, including, but not limited to, the obligations to make payment of common charges included therein, and all facts shown on the survey and floor plans filed with the declaration.

(b)   Seller agrees to comply with those requirements of the declaration or by-laws that create a right of first refusal, if any, in connection with the property. If any such right of first refusal is exercised, any sums paid hereunder shall be immediately returned to Buyer and both parties shall be relieved of any further liability hereunder.

(c)   Buyer will examine the Resale Certificate, if the unit owner's association is required by law to furnish a Resale Certificate, and if this Agreement is not voided within the rescission period permitted by statute, Buyer agrees that Buyer is then relying on the representations and disclosures appearing in the Resale Certificate if different or inconsistent with other representations or understandings given or inferred by Seller or real estate brokers.

(d)   Seller agrees that at the time of closing all installments of common expense assessments or other association assessments then due and payable will be paid. In consideration of the purchase price, Seller shall pay in full at the Closing of Title all special assessments whether or not such special assessment is payable in installments.

16. Lead-Based Paint. If the Property is "target housing" under federal law (meaning, with some exceptions, housing built before 1978), Seller must permit Buyer a 10-day period (unless the parties mutually agree in writing to a different time period) to conduct a risk assessment or inspection of the Property for the presence of lead-based paint and lead-based paint hazards before Buyer is obligated under this Agreement. Buyer may waive this right of inspection in writing.

EQUAL HOUSING OPPORTUNITY   REALTOR®

F I G U R E 7.1 (continued)

Purchase and Sale Agreement

This Agreement is made subject to an inspection or risk assessment of the Property for the presence of lead-based paint or lead-based paint hazards at the Buyer's expense. This contingency shall be deemed waived unless Buyer provides the Seller or the Seller's attorney with written notice of the presence of defective lead-based paint or lead-based paint hazards along with a copy of the inspection and/or risk assessment within _____ days (insert the number of days mutually agreed upon. If left blank, the number shall be "ten") of the date of acceptance of this Agreement. If such notice is given and Seller and Buyer cannot reach a mutually satisfactory agreement within fourteen (14) days of said notice regarding the defective lead-based paint or lead-based paint hazards, either party shall have the option of terminating this Agreement, and this Agreement shall be null and void. The Buyer may waive this contingency at any time without cause.

17. Default/Liquidated Damages. If Buyer defaults under this Agreement and Seller is not in default, all initial and additional deposit funds provided in Paragraph 3 shall be paid over to and retained by Seller, less commissions due, if any, as liquidated damages, and both parties shall be relieved of further liability under this Agreement. If Seller defaults under this Agreement and Buyer is not in default, Buyer shall be entitled to any and all remedies provided by law including, without limitation, specific performance and recovery of amounts spent for mortgage application, appraisal, title search, and tests or inspections.

18. Assignment and Survivorship. This Agreement may be assigned by either party without written consent of the other, and shall be binding upon the heirs, executors, administrators, successors and assigns of the parties hereto. No assignment shall act as an extension or modification of any provision of this Agreement, and shall not serve as a release of the assigning party's obligations under this Agreement. However, if this Agreement contains a provision for Seller financing, it may not be assigned without the express written consent of the Seller.

19. Use of Electronic Record. The parties agree that they may use an electronic record, including fax or e-mail, to make and keep this Agreement. Either party has the right to withdraw consent to have a record of this Agreement provided or made available to them in electronic form, but that does not permit that party to withdraw consent to the Agreement itself once it has been signed. A party's agreement to use an electronic record applies only to this particular real estate transaction and not to all real estate transactions.

For access to and retention of faxed records, there are no special hardware or software requirements beyond access to a fax machine or fax modem and accompanying software connected to a personal or laptop computer. For access to and retention of e-mail records, you will need a personal or laptop computer, Internet account and e-mail software.

Seller electronic addresses: ☐ Fax number is: _____
                               ☐ E-mail address is: _____
Buyer electronic addresses: ☐ Fax machine. Fax number is: _____
                               ☐ E-mail. E-mail address is: _____

Each party will promptly inform the other of any change in e-mail address or fax number in writing.

18.   **Brokers Recognized.** The parties recognize _____
as the Listing Broker and _____ as the Selling Broker in this transaction.

19.   **Additional Provisions.** _____

_____

_____

_____

_____

_____.

F I G U R E 7.1 (continued)

Purchase and Sale Agreement

20.   Modifications. Acceptance. Date of Acceptance. We, the parties hereto, each declare that this instrument contains the entire agreement between us, subject to no understandings, conditions, or representations other than those expressly stated herein. This Agreement may not be changed, modified or amended in whole or in part except in writing, signed by all parties. The "Date of Acceptance of this Agreement" shall be the latest date noted below on which a party accepts the Agreement.

WITNESS the signatures of the parties below on the date(s) set forth beside their respective names.

Acceptance by Seller: **Acceptance by Buyer:**

_____   _____   _____   _____
Seller   Date   Buyer   Date

_____   _____   _____   _____
Seller   Date   Buyer   Date

_____   _____
Buyer's Initials   Seller's Initials
©2005-2010 Connecticut Association of Realtors®, Inc.
Revised September 30, 2008; Revised July 15, 2010

FIGURE 7.2

Combined Contract Contingency Addendum to Purchase and Sale Agreement

Combined Contingency Addendum to Purchase and Sale Agreement

The following provisions and contingencies are hereby made a part of the Purchase and Sale Agreement referred to hereunder (Purchaser and Seller are construed to be singular or plural as appropriate):

Purchaser: _____

Seller: _____

Property Address: _____

This Agreement is made subject to:
[to include a provision, both Seller and Purchaser should initial in the space marked "Included"]

(1)   Attorney Approval
        Approval by Purchaser's and Seller's attorney within _____ days of the Date of Acceptance of the Agreement. The parties agree that such approval shall be deemed to have been given and this contingency is satisfied or waived unless a statement withholding approval is made in writing within the period set forth above.

        Included _____   Not included _____

(2)   Home Inspection
        A building inspection by a licensed home inspector reporting the dwelling to be structurally sound and its mechanical systems (including, but not limited to, plumbing, heating, central air conditioning, built-in swimming pools, and electrical) to be functioning properly. Individual repairs or replacements that cost less than $100.00 shall not be considered structural or mechanical defects unless the aggregate of such individual repairs or replacements exceeds $500.00. Failure of any component to comply with the building or health code in effect on the date of this Purchase and Sale Agreement shall not be considered a structural or mechanical defect if the component complied with the building code at the time of its installation and is, in the opinion of the health authority or municipal building inspector having jurisdiction over the Property, grandfathered under the building or health code in effect on the date of this Purchase and Sale Agreement. This contingency shall be deemed satisfied unless Purchaser gives written notice of any structural and/or mechanical defects and a copy of the inspector's report to the Seller on or before _____ days from the Date of Acceptance of the Agreement. If such notice is given and Seller and Purchaser cannot reach a mutually satisfactory agreement within fourteen (14) days of said notice regarding said defects, either party shall have the option of terminating this Agreement, upon written notice of termination and this Agreement shall become null and void. Any redecorating is considered to be normal maintenance, and therefore, the responsibility of Purchaser and exempt from this provision.

        Included _____   Not included _____   Inspection paid by: Seller ☐ Buyer ☐

(3)   Pest Inspection
        A report by a licensed pest control operator that all buildings on the property are free from infestation or damage by termites or any other wood-boring or wood-destroying insects. This contingency shall be deemed satisfied unless Purchaser gives written notice of infestation or damage and a copy of the pest control operator's report to Seller within ___ days from the Date of Acceptance of the Agreement. If Seller and Purchaser cannot reach a mutually satisfactory agreement for the necessary extermination and/or repairs, within ten (10) days of said notice, either party has the option to terminate this Agreement upon written notice of termination and this Agreement shall become null and void.

        Included _____   Not included _____   Inspection paid by: Seller ☐ Buyer ☐

(4)   Radon Concentration Test
        A radon concentration test of the air and well water (if the source of domestic water for the property is by a private water well) indicating that, in the case of the air, the screening measurement is equal to or less than 4.0 pCi/l, and in the case of the well water, the average of at least two measurements is equal or less than 5,000 pCi/l. Seller shall grant Purchaser's testing company reasonable access to the property to perform the tests and agree to comply with all conditions necessary to obtain an accurate reading. This contingency shall be deemed satisfied unless Purchaser gives written notice of a measurement in excess of 4.0 pCi/l for the air or that the average of at least two measurements of radon in the well water exceeds 5,000 pCi/l and a copy of the test report to Seller within _____ from the Date of Acceptance of the Agreement. If Seller and Purchaser cannot reach a

REALTOR®

F I G U R E 7.2 (continued)

Combined Contract Contingency Addendum to Purchase and Sale Agreement

mutually satisfactory agreement for the measure necessary to reduce the concentration of radon gas to 4.0 pCi/l or below in the case of the air and 5,000 pCi/l in the case of well water, within ten (10) days of said notice, either party has the option to terminate this Agreement upon written notice of termination and this Agreement shall become null and void. If measures are undertaken to reduce the concentration of radon gas in either the air or the well water, the reduction in concentration level shall be confirmed prior to closing by a radon measurement conducted in the same manner as the Buyer's measurements but to be paid for by Seller.

Included _____ Not included _____ Initial Inspection paid by: Seller ☐ Buyer ☐

(5) Water Potability/Mineral and Chemical Analysis
A report of testing performed by a laboratory authorized to perform such test in the State of Connecticut demonstrating that the water supplied by the private water supply system meets Connecticut Department of Public Health Services guidelines, if any, for each of the following items: coliform bacteria, nitrate, nitrite, sodium, chloride, iron, manganese, sulfate, pH, hardness, turbidity and apparent color. In addition, if testing for herbicide or pesticide residues or volatile organic chemicals is required by the health district or municipal health department having jurisdiction over the private water supply system, the water supplied by the private water supply system shall also meet Connecticut Department of Public Health guidelines for those herbicide or pesticide residues or volatile organic chemicals for which testing is performed. Where no guideline or standard exists for private water supply systems for the item tested, the action level required by the Connecticut Department of Public Health for public water supply systems shall be used as the guideline or standard. This contingency shall be deemed satisfied unless Purchaser gives written notice of test results not in conformance with the standards set forth in this paragraph and a copy of the test report to Seller within _____ days from the Date of Acceptance of the Agreement. If Seller and Purchaser cannot reach a mutually satisfactory agreement for the measures necessary to treat the water so the water meets the Connecticut Department of Public Health guidelines, within ten (10) days of said notice, either party has the option of terminating this Agreement upon written notice of termination and this Agreement shall become null and void. If measures are undertaken to treat the water, the effectiveness of treatment shall be confirmed prior to closing by a water test to be paid for by Seller.

Included _____ Not included _____ Analysis paid by: Seller ☐ Buyer ☐

(6) Private Well Water System Inspection
An inspection of the well water system, including all components and/or a yield test, to be performed by a competent well inspector showing that the private well water system serving the property is satisfactory (based on recommendations published by the State of Connecticut or municipality in which the property is located). This contingency shall be deemed satisfied unless Purchaser gives written notice that the private well water system is unsatisfactory and a copy of the inspector's report to Seller on or before____days from the Date of Acceptance of this Agreement. If such notice is given and Seller and Purchaser cannot reach a mutually satisfactory agreement concerning any repairs of and/or defects of such well system, within ten (10) days of said notice, either party shall have the option of terminating this Agreement and this Agreement shall become null and void.

Included _____ Not included _____ Inspection paid by: Seller ☐ Buyer ☐

(7) Septic Inspection
A report by a licensed septic installer, professional sanitary or civil engineer, registered sanitarian or a sanitarian certified by the Connecticut Department of Public Health to perform inspections, or an inspector accredited by the National Association of Waste Transporters (NAWT), National Small Flows Clearinghouse, National Sanitation Foundation (NSF) or any State of Connecticut sponsored inspection certification program using the Connecticut Recommended Existing Septic System Inspection Report. The subsurface sewage disposal system shall be pumped at Seller's expense unless the system has been pumped within 6 months of the date of the inspection. Purchaser may withdraw from the Agreement by providing written notice along with a copy of the report to Seller within _____ days from the Date of Acceptance of the Agreement if the report notes any of the following conditions: (a) system operating at capacity under current usage levels; (b) need for component replacement due to structural damage; (c) further investigation of leaching system with machine digging is recommended; (d) evidence of prior high liquid levels in system components; or (e) sewage overflow observed, repair required under permit of local health department. If the report notes any of the following conditions: (a) plumbing leaks or wastewater routing problems in home; or (b) soil testing recommended to determine expansion/repair area, Seller may agree in writing to rectify leaks and routing problems and perform soil testing at Seller's expense, to be completed by the date of Closing, in which event the Agreement will remain in full force and effect.

F I G U R E 7.2 (continued)

Combined Contract Contingency Addendum to Purchase and Sale Agreement

Note: Purchaser acknowledges that: (a) there are many different types of septic system designs and construction; (b) Purchaser's experience with the septic system will depend on many factors (including intensity of use, materials disposed of in the system, family size) and may differ greatly from the previous user's experience; and (c) the Connecticut Department of Public Health, local Health District or Town Sanitarian may be able to provide an evaluation of the operation and design of the septic system serving the property and furnish further information regarding the construction, use, and maintenance of septic systems.

Included _____ Not included _____   Inspection paid by: Seller ☐ Buyer ☐

(8)   Septic System Cost Estimate
Purchaser to obtain a price estimate not to exceed $_____ on or before _____, 20____ for the installation of a system suitable for Purchaser's intended use (including the number of bedrooms) of the property. If the price estimate exceeds the price noted above and Purchaser notifies Seller thereof on or before the above date, Purchaser shall have the option of terminating the Agreement and all sums paid as deposit shall be promptly returned to Purchaser and this Agreement shall become null and void.

Included _____ Not included _____

(9)   Home Owners Insurance
Purchaser(s) to obtain a binder for property/casualty insurance from an insurer licensed to do business in the State of Connecticut on such terms and conditions as may be acceptable to the Purchaser and the Purchaser's lender _____ days from the Date of Acceptance of the Agreement. If Purchaser cannot obtain such binder on or before the above date, Purchaser shall have the option of terminating the Agreement and all sums paid as a deposit shall be promptly returned to Purchaser and this Agreement shall become null and void.

Included _____ Not included _____

(10)   General Provisions
When written notice is required by this Addendum, such notice may be made by one of the following methods: (1) first-class mail, postage prepaid to the address set forth in the Agreement next to the recipient's name or to the recipient's attorney at the attorney's office address; (2) facsimile transmission to the recipient, the recipient's real estate agent or the recipient's attorney; or (3) hand delivered to the recipient or the recipient's attorney.

Seller shall grant reasonable access to the property to Purchaser and Purchaser's inspectors and laboratories for the purpose of conducting the inspections and tests required by this Addendum.

The term "days" as used throughout this Addendum shall mean "calendar days."

In the event that the Agreement is null and void for reasons as set forth in this Addendum, all monies paid as deposit(s) will be promptly returned to Purchaser. Seller and Purchaser agree to provide such permissions for release of escrow monies as escrow agent may reasonably require. The parties agree that escrow agent will not be liable for the release of escrow monies in accordance with this Agreement or for errors of judgment in the release of escrowed deposits unless such errors are the result of gross or intentional misconduct.

_____   _____
Purchaser   Date

_____   _____
Purchaser   Date

_____   _____
Seller   Date

_____   _____
Seller   Date

FIGURE 7.3

Hubbard Clause Contract Addendum

Addendum For Sale of Buyer's Real Estate

This Addendum is intended to amend a certain Purchase Agreement or Contract dated _____ (the "Agreement") concerning real property located at _____ _____ between the undersigned parties.

The parties each acknowledge that the Buyer owns real estate located at _____ _____(the "Buyer's Property") which must be sold in order for the Buyer to meet its obligations under the Agreement. If the Buyer fails to notify the Seller in writing on or before _____ that the Buyer has received a purchase agreement for the Buyer's real estate, which purchase agreement is either without contingencies expressed in the purchase agreement or contract or has all the contingencies waived or fulfilled, either party shall have the option of terminating this Agreement upon written notice of termination, and this Agreement shall become null and void. All monies paid as deposit(s) will be promptly returned to Purchaser. Seller and Purchaser agree to provide such permissions for release of escrow monies as escrow agent may reasonably require. The parties agree that escrow agent will not be liable for the release of escrow monies in accordance with this Agreement or for errors of judgment in the release of escrowed deposits unless such errors are the result of gross or intentional misconduct.

It is also further agreed and understood that the Seller may continue to market Seller's Property by any means, with the following conditions:

1. Seller shall cease marketing Seller's Property upon Seller's receipt of written notification by the Buyer that the Buyer is prepared to close in accordance with the terms of the Agreement.

2. Seller shall provide Buyer with written notice if Seller accepts any bona fide offer for the purchase of the Premises. Such written notice shall be signed by the Seller and contain a copy of the bona fide offer Seller intends to accept. Buyer shall then have until 6:00 pm on the third business day, time being of the essence, after the Buyer's receipt of Seller's notice in which to agree to close in accordance with the terms of the Agreement without any contingency for the sale of Buyer's real estate. If the Buyer does not notify the Seller in writing of the Buyer's agreement to close in accordance with the terms of the Agreement without any contingency for the sale of Buyer's real estate by 6:00 pm on the third business day after the Buyer's receipt of Seller's notice, time being of the essence, then any deposit monies paid by the Buyer shall be returned to the Buyer and this Agreement shall be of no further force and effect. An offer which contains a contingency for the sale of the offeror's real estate shall not be considered a "bona fide offer" for purposes of this paragraph.

3. In the event Buyer agrees to close as set forth in 2 above, Buyer may not assign the purchase agreement without Seller's express, written consent notwithstanding any other provision to the contrary in the Purchase Agreement.

4. When written notice is required by this Addendum, such notice may be made by one of the following methods: (1) first-class mail, postage prepaid to the address set forth in the Purchase Agreement or to the recipient's attorney at the attorney's office address; (2) facsimile or e-mail transmission to the recipient, the recipient's real estate agent or the recipient's attorney; or (3) hand delivered to the recipient or the recipient's attorney.

_____   _____
Buyer   Date   Seller   Date

_____   _____
Buyer   Date   Seller   Date

©2001-2007 Connecticut Association of Realtors®, Inc.
Revised July 15, 2002; October 8, 2004; April 12, 2007; October 4, 2010

F I G U R E 7.3 (continued)

Hubbard Clause Contract Addendum

Waiver of Contingency For Sale of Buyer's Real Estate

Property:_____

Seller(s):_____

Buyer(s):_____

Purchase Agreement or Contract Date:_____

The Buyers in the above-referenced Purchase Agreement or contract hereby waive their rights under a certain Addendum for Sale of Buyer's Real Estate dated _____ _____which Addendum amends the Purchase Agreement or contract referenced above.

Buyer acknowledges that by waiving this contingency, and deposit Buyer has paid will be at risk of forfeiture to the Seller in the event that Buyer cannot close because Buyer's Property has not sold.

In all other respects the Purchase Agreement or contract referenced above remains in full force and effect.

Seller _____   Buyer _____

Seller _____   Buyer _____

Date _____   Date _____

R
REALTOR®

FIGURE 7.4

Binder (Offer to Purchase)

The Greater Bridgeport Board of REALTORS®, Inc.
OFFER TO PURCHASE

EQUAL HOUSING
OPPORTUNITY

RECEIVED OF _____

Address _____

the sum of $ _____ as a deposit for the Purchase of the Property known as

at the Full Purchase Price of _____ Dollars.

This offer is given contingent upon the Purchaser's ability to obtain a _____ Mortgage
in the amount of _____ Dollars,
for a term of _____ years at the Prevailing Interest Rate by _____ (date).

THIS IS NOT A CONTRACT OF SALE, a Formal Contract shall be prepared by Seller's Attorney and shall be executed by Purchaser and the **Balance of Deposit $** _____ shall be paid on or before _____ to the Seller's Attorney and/or the Listing Agency, pursuant to Connecticut General Statutes 8-265F, to be held in trust until closing of title.

The Seller does not know and represents that he/she has no reason to believe that ureaformaldehyde foam insulation has ever been installed on the premises of the Listed Property, and if it has that it **is** _____ **(is not** _____ **)** still present.

The **Sale to be consummated** on or before _____

INSPECTIONS

If checked, this Offer to Purchase is subject to the following inspections and/or tests to be paid by the Purchaser:

    ❑ Wood Destroying Insects   ❑ Physical/Structural   ❑ Well   ❑ Septic   ❑ Radon
    ❑ Lead Substances/Paint   ❑ UFFI   ❑ Asbestos
    ❑ Other _____
    a) Inspection to be completed on or before _____ 19 _____ .
    b) Notification of results to be within _____ business days after inspection date.

Included in the sale are the following: _____

Other terms: _____

Purchaser acknowledges that Seller **has** _____ **(has not** _____ **)** furnished Purchaser with the Uniform Property Condition Disclosure Form required by Connecticut Public Act 95-311 prior to Purchaser's execution of this Agreement. If such Disclosure has been furnished, a copy is attached hereto. If such Disclosure has not been furnished, Seller shall give and Purchaser shall receive a credit of $300 against the purchase price at closing.

LEAD-BASED PAINT AND LEAD-BASED PAINT HAZARDS
[Required if Subject Real Property Consists of or Contains a Residential Unit Built Before 1978]

Lead Warning Statement

Every purchaser of any interest in residential real property on which a residential dwelling was built prior to 1978 is notified that such property may present exposure to lead from lead-based paint that may place young children at risk of developing lead poisoning. Lead poisoning in young children may produce permanent neurological damage, including learning disabilities, reduced intelligence quotient, behavioral problems, and impaired memory. Lead poisoning also poses a particular risk to pregnant women. The Seller of any interest in residential real property is required to provide the buyer with any information on lead-based paint hazards from risk assessments or inspection in the Seller's possession and notify the Buyer of any known lead-based paint hazards. A risk assessment or inspection for possible lead-based paint hazards is recommended prior to purchase.

    ❑ A completed *Disclosure of Information on Lead-Based Paint and Lead-Based Paint Hazards* is attached.
    ❑ This Offer to Purchase is contingent upon a risk assessment or inspection of the property for the presence of
        lead-based paint and/or lead- based paint hazards at the PURCHASER'S expense until 9 p.m. on:
        ❑ the <u>tenth</u> calendar-day after signing of the Offer to Purchase by all parties; -OR-
        ❑ the _____ calendar-day after signing of the Offer to Purchase by all parties; -OR-
        ❑ _____ (mutually agreed upon date).

(Intact lead-based paint that is in good condition is not necessarily a hazard. See EPA pamphlet *Protect Your Family From Lead in Your Home* for more information). This contingency will terminate at the above predetermined deadline unless the PURCHASER (or agent) delivers to the SELLER (or SELLER'S agent) a written contract addendum listing the specific existing deficiencies and corrections needed, together with a copy of the inspection and/or risk assessment report. The SELLER may, at the SELLER'S option, within _____ days after delivery of the addendum, elect in writing whether to correct the condition(s) prior to settlement. If the SELLER will correct the condition(s), the SELLER shall furnish the PURCHASER with certification from a risk assessor or inspector demonstrating that the condition has been remedied before the date of the settlement. If the SELLER does not elect to make the repairs, or if the SELLER makes a counter-offer, the PURCHASER shall have _____ days to respond to the counter-offer or remove this contingency and take the property in an "as is" condition or this Offer to Purchase shall become void. The PURCHASER may remove this contingency at any time without cause.

SELLING AGENT   ACCEPTED BY PURCHASER(S)

Signed _____ Date _____   Signed _____ Date _____

Name _____   Name _____

Firm _____   Signed _____ Date _____

Address _____   Name _____

City/Town _____ State _____ Zip _____   Telephone _____

Telephone _____

ACCEPTANCE BY SELLER(S) - The foregoing terms and conditions are agreed to and accepted by Seller(s).

LISTING AGENT   SELLER(S)

Signed _____ Date _____   Signed _____ Date _____

Name _____   Name _____

Firm _____   Signed _____ Date _____

Address _____   Name _____

City/Town _____ State _____ Zip _____   Address _____

Telephone _____   City/Town _____ State ____ Zip ____ Telephone _____

© 1996 GBBR, Inc. (Form 3.2)

FIGURE 7.5

Residential Property Condition Disclosure Report

Note: The Connecticut Real Estate Commission is in the process of updating this report, per Public Act 09-60 to include (1) municipal contact information if the property is located in a historic district or is a historic property and (2) a statement listing all leased appliances and other leased items.

RE DISC Rev. 6/02

STATE OF CONNECTICUT
DEPARTMENT OF CONSUMER PROTECTION
165 Capitol Avenue ✦ Hartford, CT 06106

RESIDENTIAL PROPERTY CONDITION DISCLOSURE REPORT

Seller's Name:		
Property Street Address:		
Property City:	State:	Zip Code:

The Uniform Property Condition Disclosure Act <u>Connecticut General Statutes Section 20-327b</u> requires the seller of residential property to provide this disclosure to the prospective purchaser prior to the prospective purchaser's execution of any binder, contract to purchase, option or lease containing a purchase option. These provisions apply to the transfer of residential real property of four dwelling units or less made with or without the assistance of a licensed broker or salesperson. The seller will be required to credit the purchaser with the sum of $300.00 at closing if the seller fails to furnish this report as required by this act.

Please note that Connecticut law requires the owner of any dwelling in which children under the age of 6 reside to abate or manage materials containing toxic levels of lead

Pursuant to the Uniform Property Condition Disclosure Act, the seller is obligated to disclose here any knowledge of any problem regarding the following:

YES	NO	UNKN	I. GENERAL INFORMATION

1. How long have you occupied the property? _____ Age of structure _____

☐ ☐ ☐   2. Does anybody other than yourself have any right to use any part of your property or does anybody else claim to own any part of your property? If yes, explain
_____

☐ ☐ ☐   3. Is the property in a flood plain area or an area containing wetlands?
_____

☐ ☐ ☐   4. Do you have any reason to believe that the municipality may impose any assessment for purposes such as sewer installation, sewer improvements, water main installation, water main improvements, sidewalks or other improvements?
_____

☐ ☐ ☐   5. Is the property located in an historic village or special tax district?
Explain _____

F I G U R E 7.5 (continued)

Residential Property Condition Disclosure Report

YES	NO	UNKN		II. SYSTEM/UTILITIES	

☐ ☐ ☐   6. HEATING SYSTEM problems? Explain_____
          a. Heating System and Fuel Type_____
          b. Is there an underground fuel tank? If yes, location and age_____
          _____

☐ ☐ ☐   7. HOT WATER HEATER problems? Explain
          Type of hot water heater_____ Age _____

☐ ☐ ☐   8. PLUMBING SYSTEM problems? Explain_____
          _____

☐ ☐ ☐   9. SEWAGE SYSTEM problems? Explain_____
          a. Type of sewage disposal system
             (central sewer, septic, cesspool, etc.)_____
          b. If private: (a) Name of service company_____
                         (b) Date last pumped _____ Frequency _____
          c. If public:
             (1) Is there a separate charge made for sewer use? yes___ no ____
             (2) If separate charge, is it a flat amount or metered? _____
             (3) If flat amount, please state amount and payment dates
             _____
             (4) Are there any unpaid sewer charges, and if so state
                 the amount _____

☐ ☐ ☐   10. AIR CONDITIONING problems? Explain_____
          Air Conditioning type: Central _____Window _____ Other_____

☐ ☐ ☐   11. ELECTRICAL SYSTEM problems? Explain_____

☐ ☐ ☐   12. DRINKING WATER problems? Quality or Quantity? Explain_____
          _____

          If public drinking water:
          a. Is there a separate charge made for water use? Yes_____ No_____
          b. If separate charge, is it a flat amount or metered?_____
          c. If flat amount, please state amount and payment dates

          d. Are there any unpaid water charges, and if so state the amount _____

☐ ☐ ☐   13. ELECTRONIC SECURITY SYSTEM problems? Explain_____

☐ ☐ ☐   14. CARBON MONOXIDE OR SMOKE DETECTOR problems? Explain_____

☐ ☐ ☐   15. FIRE SPRINKLER SYSTEM problems? Explain_____

FIGURE 7.5 (continued)

Residential Property Condition Disclosure Report

YES	NO	UNKN		III. BUILDING/STRUCTURE/IMPROVEMENTS

☐ ☐ ☐ 16. FOUNDATION/SLAB problems/settling? Explain_____

☐ ☐ ☐ 17. BASEMENT Water/Seepage/Dampness? Explain amount, frequency and location.
_____

☐ ☐ ☐ 18. SUMP PUMP problems? If yes, explain_____

☐ ☐ ☐ 19. ROOF leaks, problems? Explain _____
Roof type _____ Age _____

☐ ☐ ☐ 20. INTERIOR WALLS/CEILING problems? Explain_____

☐ ☐ ☐ 21. EXTERIOR SIDING problems? Explain_____

☐ ☐ ☐ 22. FLOOR problems? Explain_____

☐ ☐ ☐ 23. CHIMNEY/FIREPLACE/WOOD OR COAL STOVE problems? Explain:_____
_____

☐ ☐ ☐ 24. Any knowledge of FIRE/SMOKE damage? Explain_____

☐ ☐ ☐ 25. PATIO/DECK problems? _____
If made of wood, is wood treated or untreated?_____

☐ ☐ ☐ 26. DRIVEWAY problems? Explain_____

☐ ☐ ☐ 27. TERMITE/INSECT/RODENT/PEST INFESTATION problems? Explain_____
_____

☐ ☐ ☐ 28. IS HOUSE INSULATED? Type _____ Location _____

☐ ☐ ☐ 29. ROT AND WATER DAMAGE problems? Explain_____

☐ ☐ ☐ 30. WATER DRAINAGE problems? Explain_____

☐ ☐ ☐ 31. Are ASBESTOS CONTAINING INSULATION OR BUILDING MATERIALS present?____
If yes, location_____

☐ ☐ ☐ 32. Is LEAD PAINT present? If yes, location_____

☐ ☐ ☐ 33. Is LEAD PLUMBING present? If yes, location_____

☐ ☐ ☐ 34. Has test for RADON been done? If yes, attach copy.
State whether a radon control system is in place_____

F I G U R E 7.5 (continued)

Residential Property Condition Disclosure Report

The Seller should use this area to further explain any item above. Attach additional pages if necessary and indicate here _____ the number of additional pages attached.

I. Seller's Certification

To the extent of the Seller(s) knowledge as a property owner, the Seller acknowledges that the information contained above is true and accurate for those areas of the property listed. In the event a real estate broker or salesperson is utilized, the Seller authorizes the broker or salesperson to provide the above information to prospective buyers, selling agents or buyer's agents.

DATE _____ SELLER _____ SELLER _____

(Signature)   (Type or Print)

DATE _____ SELLER _____ SELLER _____

(Signature)   (Type or Print)

II. Responsibilities of Real Estate Brokers

This report in no way relieves a real estate broker of his or her obligation under the provisions of Section 20-328-5a of the Regulations of Connecticut State Agencies to disclose any material facts. Failure to do so could result in punitive action taken against the broker, such as fines, suspension or revocation of license.

III. Statements Not to Constitute a Warranty

Any representations made by the seller on this report shall not constitute a warranty to the buyer.

IV. Nature of Disclosure Report

This residential disclosure report is not a substitute for inspections, tests, and other methods of determining the physical condition of the property.

V. Information on the Residence of Convicted Felons

Information concerning the residence address of a person convicted of a crime may be available from law enforcement agencies or the department of public safety.

VI. Buyer's Certification

The buyer is urged to carefully inspect the property and, if desired, to have the property inspected by an expert. The buyer understands that there are areas of the property for which the seller has no knowledge and this disclosure statement does not encompass those areas.   The buyer also acknowledges that the buyer has read and received a signed copy of this statement from the seller or seller's agent.

DATE _____ BUYER _____ BUYER _____

(Signature)   (Type or Print)

DATE _____ BUYER _____ BUYER _____

(Signature)   (Type or Print)

Questions or Comments? Consumer Problems?
Contact the Department of Consumer Protection at (860) 713-6150 or occprotrades@po.state.ct.us

CHAPTER 7 QUIZ

1. The Connecticut Statute of Frauds requires that all contracts for more than _____ must be in writing to be enforceable.
   a. $500
   b. $1,000
   c. $5,000
   d. $2,000

2. A real estate broker who redrafts a provision in a purchase and sales contract on behalf of his client has most likely
   a. met his fiduciary duties to the client.
   b. met his employment duties under a real estate listing agreement.
   c. engaged in the practice of law, which is legal with a broker's license.
   d. engaged in the practice of law without a license, which is illegal (unless the broker is also an attorney).

3. In Connecticut, an individual may enter into legally enforceable contracts when he or she reaches the age of
   a. 16.
   b. 18.
   c. 19.
   d. 21.

4. Listing and buyer brokerage contracts are considered to be
   a. bilateral contracts.
   b. implied contracts.
   c. parol contracts.
   d. unilateral contracts.

5. A purchase and sale contract signed by both the seller and buyer
   a. is legally binding on the parties.
   b. is of no effect until endorsed by on attorney.
   c. transfers the real estate identified in the contract.
   d. must also be signed by the real estate broker involved in the transaction.

6. A seller is required to give a buyer a Property Condition Disclosure Report in all of the following transactions EXCEPT
   a. when the seller is not assisted by a licensed real estate agent.
   b. if the seller has not resided on the property in the last year.
   c. when the transaction is the sale of commercial property.
   d. if the buyer has lived on the property as a tenant.

7. Property Condition Disclosure Reports must be delivered to the buyer
   a. prior to the buyer's making a written offer.
   b. at the time the buyer makes a written offer.
   c. prior to the buyer's signing a purchase and sale contract.
   d. at the time of the home inspection.

8. A seller has no knowledge of any plumbing system problems on the property being sold. In actuality, however, the pipes are seriously corroded and will need to be replaced soon. In the Property Condition Disclosure Report, when responding to whether the seller has any knowledge of plumbing system problems, the seller should respond
   a. yes.
   b. no.
   c. unknown.
   d. by saying that the seller is not required to respond to this question.

9. All funds received by a broker on behalf of his or her client must be deposited in an escrow or trust account within three
   a. days of receiving the deposit.
   b. days of obtaining all signatures.
   c. banking days of receiving all signatures.
   d. working days of receiving all signatures.

10. A lease must be in writing if it is for a period in excess of
    a. 60 days.
    b. 90 days.
    c. six months.
    d. one year.

Transfer of Title

■ OVERVIEW

Title to real estate can be transferred in Connecticut in the following ways: voluntarily (by deed), involuntarily (by operation of law), and at the time of death (by will or intestate distribution). Wording and forms of deeds are set forth in Connecticut General Statutes at Chapter 821a, but other deed forms can also be used.

Connecticut charges a two-part conveyance tax when real estate is transferred. Details of the conveyance tax can be found at Chapter 223 of the Connecticut General Statutes.

■ DEEDS OF CONVEYANCE

In Connecticut the primary function of a deed is to convey or pass title (ownership) to land. Connecticut requires that certain elements be in a deed. (CGS Section 47-5) A deed transferring an interest in real estate must be

- in writing;
- signed by the grantor (if the grantor is a legal entity, it must be signed by a authorized person);
- acknowledged by the grantor to be his or her free act and deed; and
- signed by two witnesses.

Courts are generally liberal in their interpretation of these deed requirements. Therefore, if a deed does not have these exact statutory requirements, a court may still rule that a conveyance has still taken place.

While any legal form of deed may be used, the Connecticut statutes set forth *statutory forms* for deeds that may be used. (CGS Chapter 223) The deed must state the parties' full *legal names*. If the grantor has changed his or her name since acquiring the property to be conveyed, both names should be included.

A deed signed by the grantor and delivered to the grantee conveys title to the property (assuming the grantor had the title to convey). Deeds are recorded in the land records to give third parties notice of the transfer of title. If a deed is executed by power of attorney, the power of attorney must be recorded with the deed unless it was previously on record and reference to it is made in the deed.

Types of Deeds

The two most common forms of deeds of conveyance are the *warranty and quitclaim*. While both deeds convey title, a warranty deed contains warranty covenants while a quitclaim deed does not. The *warranty covenants* are guarantees made from the grantor (seller) to the grantee (buyer) that

- the grantor owns the property in fee simple;
- there are no encumbrances to the ownership of the property, except those that have been disclosed;
- the grantor has the legal authority to sell the property to the grantee; and
- the grantor will defend the title against claims by third persons.

These guarantees do not clear up a title defect, but they do give the grantee the right to sue the grantor for any defect that was not disclosed.

A variety of other deed types are also used in Connecticut. Because Connecticut is a modified title-theory state with regard to mortgage financing, a *mortgage deed* is used to convey an interest in property used as collateral for a loan. If the mortgage is later foreclosed, a certificate of foreclosure is executed by court order, which serves to convey full possession to the mortgage holders, who may then subsequently convey title by warranty deed if they choose.

Administrator and executor deeds are used to convey property of a person who has died, as part of a probate procedure. Conservator deeds are used to convey property of an incapable person, also as part of a probate procedure. *Tax collector deeds* are given to the purchaser of property at a tax or sheriff's sale.

■ REAL ESTATE CONVEYANCE TAXES

Connecticut imposes a *two-part tax* on the sale or transfer of an interest in real property; the two-part tax is payable at the time and place of recording the instrument of conveyance. One part is for the benefit of the municipality. The *municipal conveyance tax* rate is *0.11 percent* of the total selling price of the property. The second part of the tax is for the benefit of the state and is required to be forwarded to the State Commission of Revenue Services by the town clerk collecting the tax. The *state conveyance tax* rate is *0.5 percent* of the first $800,000 of the selling price. The amount over $800,000 is taxed at the rate of 1 percent. (The state conveyance tax rate for all nonresidential property sales is a straight 1 percent of the total selling price.)

Note: The municipal conveyance tax rate has been "temporarily" increased to 0.25 percent from March 15, 2003, multiple times to June 30, 2011. On July 1, 2011, the municipal conveyance tax rate is scheduled to revert back to 0.11 percent. There is a possibility that the Connecticut legislature will extend the temporary increase or to even make it permanent, but as of the writing of the text, it has not.

In addition to the above state conveyance taxes, 18 "targeted investment communities" had the option of imposing an added 0.25 percent to the municipal conveyance tax, which increased the total municipal conveyance tax in those communities to 0.36 percent *(0.50 percent until July 1, 2011)*. The municipalities that have the option of adding to the conveyance tax are Bloomfield, Bridgeport, Bristol, East Hartford, Groton, Hamden, Hartford, Meriden, Middletown, New Britain, New Haven, New London, Norwalk, Norwich, Southington, Stamford, Waterbury, and Windham. All of these municipalities have taken advantage of this option and have increased their municipal conveyance tax by 0.25 percent; Stamford has increased its rates by 0.10 percent.

Unless otherwise stated, for purposes of all examples and questions in this book, the 0.11 percent municipal tax rate is used. Adjustments would have to be made in real life accordingly if the town or time frame required one of the different rates.

The following are examples showing the calculation of the real estate conveyance tax. Additional examples can be found in Appendix D.

■ **FOR EXAMPLE** A residential property sells for $210,000. The conveyance tax is calculated as follows:

Municipal Conveyance Tax	=	Selling Price × 0.0011
	=	$210,000 × 0.0011
	=	$231

State Conveyance Tax	=	(Selling Price up to $800,000 × 0.005) + (Selling Price over $800,000 × 0.01)
	=	($210,000 × 0.005) + N/A
	=	$1,050

■ **FOR EXAMPLE** A residential property sells for $950,000. The conveyance tax is calculated as follows:

Municipal Conveyance Tax	=	Selling Price × 0.0011
	=	$950,000 × 0.0011
	=	$1,045

State Conveyance Tax = (Selling Price up to $800,000 × 0.005) + (Selling Price over $800,000 × 0.01)

= ($800,000 × 0.005) + ($150,000 × 0.01)

= $4,000 + $1,500

= $5,500

■ **FOR EXAMPLE** A commercial property sells for $375,000. The conveyance tax is calculated as follows:

Municipal Conveyance Tax = Selling Price × 0.0011

= $375,000 × 0.0011

= $412.50

State Conveyance Tax = Selling Price × 0.01

= $375,000 × 0.01

= $3,750

Taxes must be paid to the town clerk prior to recording, and the fact that they have been paid is noted by the town clerk on the deed.

Various categories of conveyances are *exempted* from the municipal portion of the conveyance tax. These include the following: mortgage deeds; transfers to government agencies and divisions; gifts; dedications; condemnations; tax deeds; mortgage releases; partitions; mergers and deeds between a parent company and its subsidiaries involving no consideration other than cancellation of stock and land transfers of $2,000 or less; and transfers that make only a change of identity or a change in the form of ownership or organization rather than a change in beneficial ownership. Also exempt are employer and relocation company resales of residential property acquired through relocation plans, if the resale occurs within six months of the employee conveyance. Additionally exempt are deeds in lieu of foreclosure for a primary residence and any transfer of a primary residence where the purchase price is less than the mortgage and property taxes due on sale.

Calculation of Purchase Price Based on Conveyance Tax

Connecticut does not require that a deed state the actual consideration paid for property. Many times an agent may need this information to conduct a market study or better advise a buyer or seller. Because the amount of town conveyance tax paid is always stamped on a recorded deed, the purchase price can be calculated. This is done by dividing the town conveyance tax paid by the conveyance tax rate in effect at the time of conveyance *Note that the rate is currently 0.11 percent, but it may be different in the past and future. For the period March 15, 2003, to June 30, 2011, it is 0.25 percent.*

■ **FOR EXAMPLE** A recently recorded deed does not state the actual purchase price, but the conveyance tax stamp indicates that $165 was paid for town conveyance tax. By dividing $165 by the current town conveyance tax rate of 0.11 percent (165 ÷ 0.0011), you can calculate that the purchase price was $150,000.

Conveyance of Farm, Forest, and Open-Space Lands

As indicated in Chapter 6, various types of real estate may be classified as farm, forest, or open-space land and are assessed and taxed at a lower rate than other properties.

The reason for this special classification and the resultant tax advantage is the state's desire to preserve such land and encourage agricultural and recreational land usage throughout the state. In recent years farm, forest, and open-space land has been difficult to preserve because of the burdens of high property taxes.

A special conveyance tax has also been instituted by the state for land under this classification. If the property is sold before ten years after the date the classification was obtained, a *penalty conveyance tax* must be paid in addition to the standard conveyance tax. The amount of the additional conveyance tax is based on a sliding scale of 0 percent to 10 percent of the total sales price. If the owner conveys within the first year of such classification, the penalty is 10 percent of the sales price. If he or she conveys within the second year, the penalty is 9 percent, and so on until, after the tenth year, no penalty taxes will be levied against the conveyance. The reason for this special conveyance tax is to discourage large landowners from applying for such classification merely to avoid paying higher taxes.

ADVERSE POSSESSION

Connecticut recognizes adverse possession as a way to obtain title to real estate. The adverse possessor must claim the right to possess the property, possess the property without the owner's consent, and possess the property openly, continuously, exclusively, and uninterrupted for *15 years*. (CGS Section 52-575)

To acquire title by adverse possession, a *quiet title* action must be brought in civil court. The burden of proof rests with the person claiming right to the title, and the decision as to whether all the requirements for the acquisition of title by adverse possession have been met will be made by the court *according to the facts* presented. Courts adhere strictly to the statutory requirements necessary to acquire by adverse possession. The adverse possessor's factual proof must be clear and positive. (CGS Section 52-575)

A property owner can *stop* adverse possession by serving a notice on the adverse possessor and recording it in the land records. The property owner must also go on the property and assert his or her possessory interest and then bring a court action within one year of serving the notice.

Certain property cannot be obtained through adverse possession, including land owned by investor-owned water companies, land belonging to a nonprofit land conservation or preservation corporation, and certain railroad and canal land.

■ TRANSFER OF A DECEASED PERSON'S PROPERTY

If a *sole owner* of real estate dies, the owner's real estate transfers according to the owner's will, or if no will, then according to state law. When a *joint tenant co-owner* of real estate dies, the property automatically transfers to the other joint tenant(s). If a *tenancy in common co-owner* of real estate dies, the property transfers according to the owner's will, or if no will, then according to state law.

Wills

In Connecticut, a will may be prepared by anyone of sound mind who is at least 18 years of age. The document must be in writing and be signed by at least two witnesses in the presence of the person making the will (the testator). The beneficiaries of a will may not sign as witnesses unless they are also heirs of the testator. A beneficiary who is not an heir runs the risk of being excluded from his or her devise if he or she signs as a witness.

On the death of the testator, the executor of the estate must submit the will to the probate court within 30 days. Once received by the court, notice of the hearing must be given to all interested parties. This is usually done by placing an announcement in the newspaper. Wills may be contested in court if they are felt to be illegal in their manner and order of distribution or statutory construction. Thus, if an heir, beneficiary, or other interested party feels that the will unfairly denies an inheritance or was prepared illegally, he or she has the right to contest the will in court.

Title to real estate passes to those persons listed in the will as of the date of the testator's death and is never really held by the executor or administrator of the estate. If a person to receive real estate according to a will has died himself or herself, then the real estate would pass to that person's heirs or assigns.

Intestate Distribution

If the owner of real estate dies without a will, then the real estate is transferred according to Connecticut *intestate distribution* laws. If the owner of real estate who died is survived by a spouse, issue (children and their direct descendants), or other blood relatives, his or her interests pass to these individuals according to the *order of descent* outlined in Figure 8.1. Note that the survivorship rights of a spouse in the property of his or her spouse, as discussed in Chapter 4, take priority over this distribution. (CGS Sections 45a-43 –45a-452)

The distribution of such an estate may be determined in three distinct ways: (1) by a fiduciary (often an attorney); (2) by a committee of three disinterested parties appointed by the probate court; or (3) by mutual agreement of all the parties interested in the estate. When an estate is distributed by mutual agreement, all the interested parties who are legally capable execute and file with the court a mutual distribution agreement. However, a regular probate decree ordering the distribution of an intestate estate stands above all others. Thus, the court may

F I G U R E   8.1

Intestate Distribution

Survivors	Distribution
Spouse and children* of both decedent and spouse	Spouse takes first $100,000 plus half of the remainder. Children take the other half.
Decedent's spouse and children,* one or more of whom is not the child of the spouse	Spouse takes half. All the children* share the other half equally.
Spouse and parent or parents (no children†)	Spouse takes the first $100,000 + three-fourths of the remainder. Parents take the other fourth.
Spouse only (no children†, no parents)	Spouse takes all.
Children* only (no spouse)	All goes to children.*
Parents (no spouse, no children†)	All goes to the parents.
Brothers* and sisters* (no spouse, no parents, no children†)	All goes to the brothers and sisters.
Next of kin (no spouse, no children†, no parents, no brothers† or sisters†)	All goes to next of kin.

If there is no next of kin, but there is a stepchild,* he or she will be the next in line to take. If there is no kin and no stepchild, all goes to the state of Connecticut.

*   If this person (persons) has (have) died before the decedent, his or her descendants may take instead.
†   or descendants.

override distributions occurring under any of the three traditional methods if it feels the situation calls for such action.

The Connecticut General Statutes also provide for the manner of distribution of an estate under a variety of unusual circumstances. If the owner of real estate was murdered, the person guilty of the murder cannot inherit the owner's property. Also, in the event that no legal heirs or assigns can be identified within 20 years of the owner's death, the owner's real estate would be transferred to the state by *escheat*. The statutes also pursue the inheritance problems related to absentee heirs, heirs from foreign countries, and a variety of other situations. In the event that a difficult inheritance problem is encountered, the wisest advice is to seek legal counsel specializing in inheritance cases.

■ WEB LINKS

Connecticut General Statutes Chapter 821a (forms of deeds):
www.cga.ct.gov/2009/pub/chap821a.htm

Connecticut General Statutes Chapter 223 (conveyance tax):
www.cga.ct.gov/2009/pub/chap223.htm

Connecticut Law about Adverse Possession (Judicial Law Library):
www.jud.state.ct.us/LawLib/Law/possession.htm

Guidelines for Administration of Decedent's Estate (Connecticut Probate Courts
Web site):   www.jud.ct.gov/probate/GuideDecEstate.pdf

CHAPTER 8 QUIZ

1. To be valid, a deed must contain all below *EXCEPT*
   a. the signature of the grantor.
   b. the signature of the grantee.
   c. the signature of witnesses.
   d. an acknowledgment.

2. How many witnesses must sign a deed?
   a. One
   b. Two
   c. Three
   d. Four

3. A warranty deed differs from a quitclaim deed in that it
   a. is valid.
   b. conveys fee simple title.
   c. cures any title defects.
   d. contains guarantees made by the grantor to the grantee.

4. A seller sold residential property to a buyer for $450,000. The total municipal and state conveyance tax on the transaction was
   a. $7,245.
   b. $4,995.
   c. $2,745.
   d. $495.

5. A recently recorded deed states that the purchase price was "$10 and other good and valuable consideration." The conveyance tax stamp indicates that $192.50 was paid for town conveyance tax. What was the property sold for?
   a. $175,000
   b. $192,500
   c. $21,175
   d. $10

6. The state of Connecticut wishes to widen a highway; it has exercised its right of eminent domain and taken a portion of Alice Field's property through condemnation proceedings. The conveyance tax on Field's conveyance to the state of Connecticut would be
   a. one-half the usual.
   b. zero.
   c. the same as usual but picked up by the state.
   d. $250, regardless of the consideration amount.

7. Since acquiring a piece of property, a woman has legally changed her name. To convey that property by valid deed, the woman should use the
   a. name as it appears in the deed.
   b. present legal name.
   c. name on the deed and the present legal name.
   d. name she wishes to use.

8. A farmer obtained a forest land classification on the farm's rear 100-acre parcel on January 1, 2001, and thus reduced the tax assessment substantially. On June 30, 2007, the farmer sold the property to a residential land developer for $2,250,000. In addition to the standard municipal and state conveyance tax, the farmer paid a "penalty" tax of
   a. $225,000.
   b. $90,000.
   c. $112,500.
   d. $135,000.

9. The prescriptive period in the state of Connecticut to acquire title to real property through adverse possession is
   a. 7 years.
   b. 10 years.
   c. 15 years.
   d. 20 years.

10. How old must a citizen of Connecticut be before he or she may prepare a legally binding will?
    a. 15 (as long as real property is not involved)
    b. 18
    c. 21
    d. Any age (as long as the will is legally witnessed and recorded)

11. In terms of a married couple, if the man were to die without a will, his entire estate would be taken by his wife if the
    a. man had no previous spouses.
    b. man had no surviving children, grandchildren, or parents.
    c. man's estate was valued at less than $100,000.
    d. man's estate was created after he married his current wife.

12. Unclaimed estates escheat to the state after a period of
    a. 5 years.
    b. 10 years.
    c. 15 years.
    d. 20 years.

9

Title Records

■ OVERVIEW

Town Clerk

Documents related to ownership and other interests in real estate are required to be recorded in the *municipal land records* in the town where the property is located. Each of the 169 towns in Connecticut maintains extensive public records of real estate and other documents, including deeds, mortgages, leases, and liens. The *town or city clerk* is responsible for receiving documents for recording and for the maintenance of these records.

The town clerk makes copies of documents submitted for recording (originals of documents are sent back to the property owner), and the town clerk assigns each document a land record volume and page number. The documents are indexed according to grantor (seller) and grantee (buyer). Copies of the documents and the indexes are *available for the public* to physically view in the land records, in paper and in some cases electronic version. Some municipalities are also now beginning to put digital copies of land record documents and indexes online.

■ THE NECESSITY TO RECORD

Constructive Notice

In Connecticut, title to real estate passes on delivery and acceptance of a deed, not recording. Documents affecting the title to real estate are recorded to give other persons *constructive notice* of the status of title. Further, the date of recording of documents affects the *priority* that the law will give to the documents; priority basically has to do with which interests in the real estate are legally recognized first.

Establishes priority of liens

The law will generally not void a transfer of an interest in real estate simply because a deed was not recorded, although the interest conveyed in that deed may lose priority over other transactions. Also note that the act of recording a deed or document does not automatically make the transfer valid, if there were reasons that it was not valid.

The Connecticut policy requiring that realty conveyances be recorded is summed up well in the following quote from the 1840 Connecticut Supreme Court case of *North v. Belden:*

> *. . . It has even been the policy of our law, that title to real estate should appear upon record, that it might be easily and accurately traced. This policy has added greatly to the security of our land titles, and has prevented much litigation, which would otherwise have arisen. And our courts have even considered it their duty to give as much construction to our statutes as will continue this salutary protection. It is true, there has been some diversity of opinion as to the precise extent of this doctrine; and cases will sometimes arise where there may be a doubt as to its application. One principle seems to be definitely settled, that the real nature of the transaction, so far as it can be disclosed, must appear upon the record, with reasonable certainty; and if the deed does not actually give notice of any condition or other circumstance, which might be important, it should at least point out a track, which the enquirer might pursue to obtain it.*

Reasonable Time

Connecticut law requires that deeds conveying title must be recorded in the municipal land records within a reasonable time from delivery of the deed to the buyer or other grantee. No specific minimum or maximum "reasonable time" has been set.

Recording Fees

Connecticut municipalities charge a recording fee of $53 for the first page of a document (scheduled to revert to $43 on July 1, 2011) and $5 for each additional page, plus a supplementary $3 per document (this supplementary fee is used for the preservation of historic documents). Thus, for example, the total recording fee for a four-page document would be $71 ($53 for the first page, $15 for three additional pages, and $3 for the document).

Volume and Page References

Copies of recorded documents are available for viewing in the Land Records. Each document recorded is assigned a unique volume (or book) and page reference, so that the documents can later be found. These references are basically assigned in chronological order based on the time of recording.

Grantor/Grantee Indexes

The land records are indexed under the names of the *grantors* (sellers or those conveying an interest in real estate) and *grantees* (buyers or those receiving an interest in real estate). Because the basic land records for any town are simply a chronological compilation of all types of documents received for recording, the grantor/grantee index makes it easier to trace a specific parcel's chain of title to pinpoint the volume and page number of a given transaction.

Day Book

There is sometimes a few days' time lapse between the recording of a document and the town clerk's indexing it in the grantor/grantee lists. Such documents are catalogued in a day book. When searching for information on a real estate transaction, the day book should always be referred to, along with the grantor/grantee lists.

Change of Name or Status

If an individual or legal business entity owner of real estate undergoes a change of name or status—for example, a marriage or business merger—such change must be filed and recorded with the town clerk of the town where the real estate is located within 60 days from the date of such change. A legal entity, such as a corporation, may also be required to file the name change with the Connecticut Secretary of State.

■ EVIDENCE OF TITLE

In Connecticut, the status of the title or ownership interest in a piece of real estate is determined by conducting a *title search*, which basically consists of examining all relevant land records related to the property. A purchaser typically assumes this responsibility. These searches are usually carried out by attorneys, and their cost is borne by the individual commissioning the search. However, there is no law requiring that the purchaser actually conduct a title search; it is merely in his or her best interest to have one done to determine the status of the interest in real estate and whether the seller has the right to sell that real estate. If the purchaser finances the property, many lenders do require evidence of title through title insurance.

Title Searching

Searching a title is a complicated procedure that involves not only knowing what public records to look at but also the legal implication of the documents found. A full title search should be performed only by someone experienced and qualified to do so.

In general, title searching involves looking up the records of transactions in the grantor/grantee indexes and referring to copies of actual documents in the volumes. To *begin* a title search, you would look up the name of the *current owner* of the property (this can be obtained from the street cards in the tax assessor's office if it is not known) *under the grantee index* for the time of conveyance. The seller to the current owner would be referred to as the grantor. You would then find the seller's immediate predecessor in title by looking up the seller's name in the grantee index. This process of *searching back in time* would be continued until the original owner of the property was found. Then a *forward search* is made through the grantor indexes for each owner of the property for the time he or she held the property to find any mortgages, liens, and recorded interests of others. The last step would be to check the day book for any documents affecting the title to the property that are not yet indexed in the grantor/grantee indexes.

Title Search Preparation

Typically, the results of a title search are presented as either: a brief summary of the status of the title (certificate of title), a detailed accounting of the status of the title (abstract of title), or an insurance policy insuring the status of the title (title insurance).

If the purchaser is paying cash or the seller is providing any needed financing by taking back a purchase-money mortgage, the purchaser's attorney, at the purchaser's request, will conduct the title search. If the purchaser obtains a mortgage from a financial institution as a portion of his or her financing package, Connecticut statutes require that a title search (or at least a certificate of title) be prepared. The bank's closing attorney customarily conducts this search. Note that the bank's closing attorney and the purchaser's attorney may be the same person. In the first instance, where the purchaser is paying cash, the search would be conducted exclusively on behalf of the purchaser. In the second case, where the purchaser has a mortgage from a bank, the search would benefit both the purchaser and the bank.

Regardless of whether a certificate of title or complete abstract is prepared, such searches are *not absolute guarantees* of clear title. The complexity of real estate conveyances often leaves room for error in the most diligent title searches.

Certificate of Title

An attorney's certificate of title is a summary of the status of the title found while conducting a title search. The certificate of title generally includes a brief opinion about the marketability of the title and lists any encumbrances that the examining counsel has identified—utility easements, sewer liens, and so on. While not as detailed as an abstract, certificates of title are used as evidence of title in many real estate conveyances. A copy of a typical certificate of title is set out in Figure 9.1.

FIGURE 9.1

Certificate of Title

TITLE RECORD

CERTIFICATE OF TITLE
Storrs, Connecticut
October 11, 2010

To: Mansfield Federal Savings and Loan Association
33 Storrs Road
Storrs, CT 06268

THIS IS TO CERTIFY that I have examined the title to the premises situated on the southerly side of Merrow Road in Mansfield, Connecticut, and being known as Lot No. 19 in the "GLENWOOD ACRES" Subdivision, and being more particularly described in a certain Mortgage Deed from Samuel L. and Patricia D. Jones to the Mansfield Federal Savings and Loan Association, Storrs, CT, dated October 9, 1990, and recorded in Volume 120, Page 89 of the Mansfield Land Records, and I am of the opinion that said mortgagors have a good and sufficient title thereto of record, free and clear of all recorded and property indexed encumbrances, except:

1. Any and all provisions of any ordinance, municipal regulations, and public and private law.
2. Taxes to become due the Town of Mansfield on the List of October 1, 2006.
3. A possible pole line easement in favor of the Connecticut Light and Power Company more fully appearing of record.
4. A mortgage in the original principal amount of $182,000 from Samuel L. and Patricia D. Jones to the Mansfield Federal Savings and Loan Association, Storrs, CT, dated October 9, 1990, and recorded on October 11, 1190, in Volume 120, Page 89 of the Mansfield Land Records.
5. Any statement of facts that an accurate survey may disclose.

Clarence Darrow

Attorney-at-Law

Abstract of Title   *More detailed*

A title abstract is similar to a certificate of title but is more detailed. A title abstract includes a history of the transfers of the real estate, as well as a listing of all potential encumbrances and claims that could be made against the title by other people. The listing of all previous transactions and owners for a piece of real estate is referred to as a *chain of title*.

All the previous transaction + chain of title

Title Insurance

Title insurance is a type of insurance policy that protects a real estate buyer against defects in the title that were not found during a title search. If a defect was found during a title search, the title insurance policy would not correct it (the policy would disclose the defect). While mortgage lenders require that a buyer purchase mortgagee title insurance policy to protect the mortgage lender, a buyer can also purchase owners title insurance to protect him or her.

Torrens System

With a Torrens land registration system, the government keeps a master record of land ownership and encumbrances. Connecticut does not recognize or employ the Torrens system or any other system of land title registration.

■ MARKETABLE RECORD TITLE ACT

A marketable record title is one that is *unbroken for a period of 40 years*. This does not mean that an owner must possess the property for 40 years before he or she has marketable record title. Instead it means that the *chain of title can be traced back* at least 40 years without encountering a "break," such as, for example, some unverified conveyance, encumbrance, or other interest. Establishing a marketable record title voids any claims recorded prior to that time. (*Example:* A mortgage with a 50-year term is recorded 41 years ago. A deed conveying the property free of the mortgage is recorded 40 years ago. Under the Marketable Record Title Act, the mortgage would be extinguished.) Certain interests are exempted from the act's operation (i.e., government entities, certain easements). (CGS Sections 47-33b–47-33l)

Marketable record title is the best and most desirable form of title. Notice of claim to an interest in land must be recorded within the 40-year period to remain effective against the property. If an individual has held a parcel of land for 40 years, during which time no transactions involving the parcel have taken place and no claims of interest have been filed and recorded against it, the owner's period of possession is enough to establish marketable record title in most cases. An attorney's title search generally indicates the degree to which a title is considered marketable or the limitations to its marketability if it is not completely free of encumbrances.

Native American Land Claims

Many recognized and unrecognized Indian tribes throughout the state have made legal claims to old tribal lands. Many of these lands were conveyed by the Native Americans or governing bodies back in the 1700s and 1800s and have for many years been owned by private individuals. Obviously, the Native Americans' claims to lands have prompted questions as to why the Marketable Record Title Act or adverse possession would not defeat the Native Americans' claims. Basically, this is because Native American title is a matter of federal law and cannot be extinguished without federal consent (even by a conveyance by the Native Americans). State statutes dealing with the marketable title, adverse possession, or the like cannot be enforced against the federal law mandates.

■ WEB LINKS

Connecticut municipality Web sites:　*www.ct.gov/ctportal/cwp/view*
　　.asp?a=843&q=257266
Vision Appraisal (brief ownership history for properties in many towns, as
　　compiled by municipal tax assessor's office):　*www.visionappraisal.com*
Research Guide to Connecticut Land Records (Connecticut State
　　Library):　*www.cslib.org/landrec.htm*

CHAPTER 9 QUIZ

1. Max has recorded his deed to 180 Shore Drive in the land records. The primary purpose of this recording is to
   a. enforce the transfer.
   b. give others constructive notice of the transfer.
   c. give others actual notice of the transfer.
   d. give notice to the town clerk of the transfer.

2. A buyer enters into a purchase and sale contract to buy a house on October 15. The closing occurs on November 15, at which time the seller delivers the deed. The deed is recorded on November 17. The buyer moves into the property on November 18. In Connecticut, title would have passed from the seller to the buyer on
   a. October 15.
   b. November 15.
   c. November 17.
   d. November 18.

3. What types of documents are required to be recorded in the land records?
   a. Only deeds
   b. Only deeds and mortgages
   c. All documents affecting the title to real estate
   d. All legal documents

4. Deeds must be recorded in the land records within _____ of the date of conveyance.
   a. a reasonable time
   b. one business day
   c. three business days
   d. one month

5. The local official who maintains the municipal land records in Connecticut is the
   a. first selectman.
   b. assessor.
   c. tax collector.
   d. town clerk.

6. A certificate of title is a
   a. brief opinion about the marketability of the title.
   b. guarantee of clear title.
   c. guarantee of marketable title.
   d. summary of the chain of title.

7. To establish a "marketable record title," an unbroken chain of title must be established for a period of at least
   a. 15 years.
   b. 20 years.
   c. 40 years.
   d. 60 years.

8. Title insurance insures that the title is free of
   a. any title defects.
   b. any title defects recorded in the past 40 years.
   c. all title defects that were not discovered during a title search.
   d. encumbrances that would make the property unmarketable.

9. Any change of name or status of an individual or corporate owner of real estate must be recorded with the town clerk in the town where the real estate is located within
   a. 30 days.
   b. 60 days.
   c. 90 days.
   d. 180 days.

10. Connecticut land records are indexed through
    a. a Torrens system.
    b. lot, block, map numbers.
    c. the location of the property.
    d. grantor/grantee indexes.

10
CHAPTER

Real Estate License Law

■ OVERVIEW

A person or entity engaging in the real estate business in Connecticut must have a Connecticut *real estate license*. There are two categories of license: broker and salesperson (both are referred to as *licensee*). A salesperson must be affiliated with and can only work on behalf of a broker.

Connecticut licensing law is enforced by the Connecticut Real Estate Commission (the Commission), which is part of the Department of Consumer Protection. Specific state statutes governing the licensing and conduct of real estate licensees can be found at Title 20, Chapter 392 of the Connecticut General Statutes. The Commission has the authority to and has enacted regulations implementing the statutes.

■ CONNECTICUT REAL ESTATE COMMISSION

CGS SECTIONS 20-311a–20-311f, 20-314, 20-314a, 20-326

The Connecticut Real Estate Commission administers the Connecticut licensing laws. Its primary duties are to issue licenses; arbitrate disputes between brokers and salespersons; investigate and prosecute complaints against licensees; and formulate and enforce rules and regulations regarding licensing and conduct of licensees. The Commission is part of the Connecticut Department of Consumer Protection. It must keep records of all its activities and submit an annual report to the governor.

Structure

The Commission is made up of

- eight members—five in real estate business (three licensed brokers and two licensed salespersons at the time of appointment) and three members of the public;
- at least one member from each congressional district; and
- not more than a bare majority from the same political party.

Members of the Commission

- must be electors in the state;
- are appointed by the governor;
- take an oath to perform faithfully the prescribed duties; and
- may be removed from office for cause by the governor after being given an opportunity to be heard.

The Commission members select a chairperson. The chairperson of the Commission must be bonded in accordance with the requirements of the State Insurance Purchasing Board.

- When voting on issues, a majority of the members constitutes a quorum.
- Seats vacated through resignation, death, or removal are filled by appointees of the governor.
- Commission members are not paid for their services but are reimbursed for necessary expenses incurred in the performance of their duties.

Fees

The Commission collects licensing fees as outlined in Figure 10.1. All fees collected are deposited with the state treasurer and become part of the general fund (except the portion of license fees payable to the University of Connecticut in conjunction with the operation of the Center for Real Estate and Urban Economic Studies).

Approval of Courses and Schools

The Commission evaluates and approves courses and schools that fulfill the prelicensing educational requirement and continuing education requirements discussed later in this chapter. Courses that have not been approved by the Commission do not count towards licensing or license renewal.

■ ACTIVITIES REQUIRING A LICENSE

CGS SECTIONS 20-311, 20-312, 20-325, 20-329

Any *person who engages in the real estate business* must have a real estate license. A person engaging in the real estate business without a license can be fined and/or imprisoned. Also, an unlicensed person cannot use the state courts to attempt to collect any commission or compensation owed.

There are two categories of licensure: broker and salesperson. A *broker* is a person who performs real estate activities for a real estate consumer. A *salesperson* works on behalf of a broker, either as an employee or independent contractor. A salesperson cannot perform real estate activities on his or her own but must be affiliated with and supervised by a broker.

Definitions

It is important to be familiar with the terms defined below.

Person—A *person* includes individuals, partnerships, associations, limited liability companies, or corporations.

Engaging in the real estate business—This includes any person *acting for another and for a fee*, commission, or other valuable consideration, who performs or offers or attempts to perform brokerage activities (listed under the definition of a broker).

Real estate broker—This is any person or entity who, for another and for a fee, performs, offers to perform, or attempts to perform any of the following activities pertaining to real estate:

- Lists real estate for sale
- Sells real estate
- Exchanges real estate
- Buys real estate
- Rents or collects rent for the use of real estate
- Resells a mobile home

Real estate salesperson—This is any person *employed* by a real estate broker or *affiliated* with a real estate broker as an independent contractor who performs or offers or attempts to perform any of the activities listed above on behalf of a real estate broker.

Exemption from Licensure

The following persons are exempted from the licensing requirement:

- Clerical or custodial employees of a real estate broker
- Real estate owners and landlords who are not primarily in the real estate business
- Employees of real estate owners or landlords who are employed as on-site residential superintendents or custodians when any real estate activities are conducted in the regular course of their business (The Commission has interpreted this law as requiring all of the following conditions for the exception to apply: the individual must (1) be a regular employee, (2) be employed as a superintendent or custodian, (3) work on a residential site where he or she engages in licensed activities, and (4) reside at the location where he or she works and engages in those licensed activities.)
- Attorneys at law when serving as legal counsel to their clients
- Receivers, trustees in bankruptcy, administrators, executors, or other fiduciaries, while acting as such

- Persons selling real estate under court order
- Trustees acting under a trust agreement, deed of trust, or will and their regular salaried employees
- Witnesses in court attesting to the value of real estate, who are exempt from brokerage license but must be licensed as appraisers
- Government employees acting within the scope of their regular employment responsibilities
- Any employee of any nonprofit housing corporation that manages a housing project assisted in whole or in part by the federal government pursuant to Section 8 of the United States Housing Act of 1937, as amended, while performing such duties

Personal assistants. Brokers and salespersons are allowed to use unlicensed assistants to assist them in their business. However, unlicensed assistants are not allowed to engage in real estate activities that require a license. For a list of activities that can be performed by an unlicensed assistant, see Chapter 1.

LICENSING PROCEDURE

CGS SECTIONS 20-312–20-319a

A summary of licensing requirements and fees can be found in Figure 10.1.

Application

A license candidate must submit an application to the Department of Consumer Protection along with a nonrefundable application fee ($120 for brokers, $80 for salespersons as of 2010). Each application fee entitles the applicant to take the licensing exam four times within a one-year period.

If the application is approved, the Department of Consumer Protection will notify the testing vendor of applicant's eligibility to sit for the licensing examination. The testing vendor will then notify the applicant that he or she has been approved and can register for the examination.

Any individual who willfully misrepresents any facts required to be disclosed on the application or in any other document to be filed with the Commission in connection with the application for a license may be fined up to $500, imprisoned up to six months, or both.

Education

Applicants for a real estate license must take an approved *60-hour course* in real estate principles and practices. In addition, applicants for a broker's license must also take a 30-hour course in real estate appraisal and a 30-hour course in an elective real estate topic.

Experience

To qualify for a real estate broker's license, applicants must have been actively engaged for at least *two years* as a Connecticut licensed salesperson under the supervision of a Connecticut licensed broker. There is no experience required for obtaining a salesperson's license.

Examination

Applicants for either a broker's or salesperson's license must pass a *written examination* before a license can be issued. The licensing examination is administered by a state selected *private testing vendor*. The actual vendor can change over time due to state contract and bidding procedures. The current testing vendor is *PSI*. A *candidate handbook* that outlines exam content, fees, procedures, and test site locations can be found at the testing vendor's Web site.

FIGURE 10.1

Connecticut Real Estate Brokers and Salespersons Requirements Summary

Note these requirements and fees may change; current information can be found at the Department of Consumer Protection Web site.

	Broker	Salesperson
Education	60 hours—Real Estate Principles and Practices 30 hours—Real Estate Appraisal 30 hours—Other Real Estate Course	60 hours—Real Estate Principles and Practices
Experience	2 years' experience as a Real Estate Salesperson	None
Testing	Broker's Licensing Exam (score of 75% or better)	Salesperson's Licensing Exam (score of 70% or better)
Sponsor	No	Yes (by a broker)
Minimum Age	18	18
Renewal	March 31, annually	May 31, annually
Continuing Education	12 hours every two years	12 hours every two years

FEES		Broker	Salesperson
	Application	$120	$80
	Testing – Initial	$52	$52
	Testing – Retake	$52	$52
	License - Initial Year	$565	$285
	License - Renewal	$375	$285
	Continuing Education Processing (Biennial)	$8	$8
	Guaranty Fund (One time)	$20	$20
	Change of Broker Affiliation	n/a	$25

The exam is divided into two sections: general content and state-specific content. The *general content* section consists of *80 questions* (plus *5 pretest questions*) on general real estate principles and practices such as ownership, contracts, valuation, agency relationships, brokerage operations, fair housing, financing, and leasing. The *state content* section of the exam consists of *30 questions* for salespersons and *40 questions* for brokers (plus *5 pretest questions* for both) on state-specific real estate principles and practices and licensing law. The state content outline is set forth in Figure 10.2.

The testing vendor charges a fee for taking the licensing examination as well as a fee for retaking the exam.

After an applicant completes the examination, the testing vendor will issue a score report that states whether the applicant passed or failed. The testing vendor sends the results of passing applicants to the Department of Consumer Protection. Applicants who fail the examination will receive statistical information about their performance and can schedule to retake it.

License Issued

Once an applicant meets all the Commission's requirements and passes the license examination, the Department of Consumer Protection will issue a Certificate of Licensure. This is when an applicant is actually considered licensed. Although a licensee may be asked to produce the Certificate, the law does not require that it be publicly displayed. Once licensed, the applicant is entitled to perform all the acts of a real estate broker or salesperson as described earlier in this chapter.

Grounds for Refusal of a License

Even though an applicant meets the licensing requirements and passes the license examination, there are still circumstances under which an application could be refused or a license withheld. The Commission will generally refuse to issue a license to any applicant who

- has been refused a real estate broker's or salesperson's license in any state within the year preceding the current application;
- has had a real estate broker's or salesperson's license revoked in any state within the year preceding the current application; or
- is not yet 18 years old.

Any applicant who is refused a license will be notified and given an opportunity for a hearing according to regulations established by the Commissioner of the Department of Consumer Protection.

Convicted felons.   A convicted felon is allowed to apply for and obtain a real estate license. The Commission can, however, determine that a felony conviction makes an applicant not suitable for a license. In making such a determination, the Commission will consider

- the nature of the crime and its relationship to the job for which the person applied;

FIGURE 10.2

Connecticut Real Estate Exam—State Content Outline

I. Connecticut Real Estate Commission and Licensing Requirements
   a. Real Estate Commission Powers and Duties
   b. Activities Requiring a License
   c. Exemptions from Licensure
   d. License Types and Qualifications
   e. License Renewal, Continuing Education, and Transfer
   f. Real Estate Guaranty Fund
   g. License Suspension and Revocation

II. Connecticut Laws Governing the Activities of Licensees
   a. Broker/Salesperson Relationship
   b. Duties to Parties
   c. Handling of Deposits and Other Monies
   d. Misrepresentation
   e. Disclosure of Nonmaterial Facts
   f. Advertising
   g. Commissions and Compensation
   h. Unlicensed Personal Assistants

III. Connecticut Real Estate Agency
   a. Agency: Representing a Client vs. Working with a Customer
   b. Agency Agreements
   c. Agency Disclosure
   d. Subagency Limitations
   e. Dual Agency
   f. Designated Agency
   g. Confidential Information
   h. Interference with Agency Relationship

IV. Connecticut-Specific Real Estate Principles and Practices
   a. Connecticut-Specific Property Ownership and Transfer Issues
      i. Co-ownership Forms and Shares
      ii. Adverse Possession/Prescriptive Easement Time
      iii. Land Records and Recording
      iv. Real Property Taxes and Assessments
      v. Conveyance Tax
      vi. Residential Property Condition Disclosure
   b. Connecticut Landlord-Tenant Act
   c. Connecticut Common Interest Ownership Act
   d. Connecticut Fair Housing Law
   e. Connecticut Lead Paint Laws
   f. Connecticut Disclosure of Off-site Conditions Law
   g. Connecticut Uniform Electronic Transactions Act

V. For Broker's Exam Only
   a. Record Keeping
   b. Escrow Accounts
   c. Brokers Lien
   d. Notice of Commission Rights in Commercial Transactions
   e. Cooperation with Out-of-State Brokers
   f. Interstate Land Sales
   g. Mortgage Brokerage Fees Charged by Brokers
   h. Real Properties Securities/Syndication

- information pertaining to the degree of rehabilitation of the convicted person; and
- the amount of time that has elapsed since the applicant's conviction or release.

Licensing Corporations and Other Entities

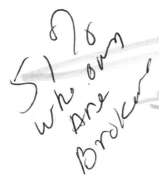

Any business entity—corporation, limited liability company, partnership, or association—that engages in the real estate brokerage business *must obtain a real estate broker license* in the name of the legal entity. To be eligible for a broker's license, all active owners, members, partners, and officers in the business entity must be licensed as a salesperson or a broker, and 51 percent or more of those individuals who own or control the entity must be licensed brokers. When a business entity applies for a broker's license, the entity must designate one individual to serve as the firm's broker under the license. Unlicensed business entities engaging in the real estate brokerage business are subject to fines and may be precluded from bringing any action to recover fees and commissions owed.

Licensing Nonresidents

A person who is not a resident of the state of Connecticut may obtain a Connecticut real estate broker's or salesperson's license by meeting all the state licensing education, experience, and examination requirements.

A person who holds a real estate broker's or salesperson's license issued by a state that has a *reciprocal agreement* with Connecticut does not need to meet the state licensing requirements to obtain a license. The Commission has entered into reciprocal agreements with states that have licensing requirements that are substantially similar to or higher than the requirements in Connecticut.

A list of reciprocal states can be found at the Department of Consumer Protection Web site. As of the writing of this edition, those states were Alabama, Colorado, Florida, Georgia, Illinois, Indiana, Massachusetts, Mississippi, Nebraska, New York, North Carolina, Ohio, Oklahoma, Rhode Island, and Tennessee. Connecticut also recognizes a reciprocal agreement with Illinois, Indiana, and Ohio, but persons applying for a Connecticut license from those states are required to still take the state content section of the Connecticut licensing examination.

Nonresident holders of license-by-reciprocity who become Connecticut residents have a valid Connecticut license and are not required to qualify with course, experience, and examination requirements in order to maintain the validity of their license.

All nonresident applicants must file an *irrevocable consent to suit* with the Commission. This consent enables lawsuits and legal actions to be brought against the nonresident licensee in Connecticut.

■ MAINTAINING A REAL ESTATE LICENSE

CGS SECTIONS 20-314, 20-319, 20-319a, 20-322, and 20-328-10a

Connecticut law does *not* require that a real estate licensee maintain a definite place of business or display either a license or a sign indicating that the licensee is a real estate broker or salesperson.

License Renewal

All real estate licenses expire annually and are renewable on payment of the appropriate fee. Brokers' licenses expire on *March 31*; salespersons' licenses expire on *May 31*. The Commission has the authority to change the expiration date.

If, for any reason, the license is not renewed on request, the fee is returned. All renewal refusals by the Commission are written and may be challenged on the licensee's written request for a hearing or appeal according to the regulations established by the Commissioner of the Department of Consumer Protection.

As long as a licensee has all the qualifications specified by the law and has complied with all the regulations of Chapter 392, his or her license must be renewed.

Continuing Education

Licensees must take 12 hours of continuing real estate education every two years. This continuing education must be complete in even-numbered years, by March 31 for brokers and May 31 for salespersons.

Continuing education courses must be approved by the Real Estate Commission. The Commission may require specific mandatory courses during a continuing education cycle. The Commission posts the mandatory course requirement for a continuing education cycle at the Department of Consumer Protection Web site. Continuing education courses can be offered and taken in an online format.

In lieu of taking continuing education courses during the two periods, a licensee has the option of either (1) taking and passing a continuing education exam administered by the state testing vendor, or (2) proving to the Commission that he or she has experience or education that amounts to the equivalent of continuing education.

Change of Broker Affiliation

A licensed real estate salesperson must be supervised by a designated broker. A salesperson can change his or her affiliation from one designated broker to another. To change affiliation, a salesperson must register the change with the Real Estate Commission and pay a $25 transfer fee.

Furthermore, upon change of broker affiliation, a licensee is required to return all records and information collected during his or her affiliation with the original designated broker to that broker. Within 10 days of the return of such information (or within 45 days of the termination of the relationship), the original designated broker is required to give the licensee a written account of all active listing agreements, agency agreements, transactions, and commissions and compensation involving that licensee. The accounting must include a statement of the commission or compensation that the broker intends to pay the licensee.

DCP Notification Registry

The Connecticut Department of Consumer Protection (DCP) maintains an e-mail registry. All licensees can register their e-mail address on the registry to receive important updates regarding real estate licensing laws, policies, and procedures. Registration is electronic, on the DCP Web site.

▉ CONDUCT OF LICENSEES

Connecticut Regulations

Connecticut license law regulates the manner in which licensees conduct themselves in the real estate brokerage business. A licensee owes certain duties to parties above and beyond the fiduciary duties owed to clients under agency law.

Interest in property. If a licensee has a present or contemplated interest in real estate, the licensee must disclose the interest to all parties concerned. A licensee must also disclose to the buyer or seller any relationship that exists to the seller or buyer, such as immediate family member or member of the same real estate firm. A sample disclosure form is found in Figure 10.3.

Material facts. A licensee has a duty to *disclose material facts* about a property or transaction and cannot misrepresent or conceal a material fact. This duty applies even when the licensee does not represent a party; for example if a licensee represented a seller in the sale of real estate, the licensee has a duty to disclose material facts about the property to potential buyers.

A *material fact* is generally characterized as an important fact about real estate or the transaction involving the real estate which, if known, may persuade a buyer or seller of the real estate to make a different decision as to whether to purchase or sell the real estate and at what price. In other words, a material fact is a fact that might change a reasonable person's mind about buying the property or the price offered.

Nonmaterial facts. By law, a fact related to whether a property occupant has or had a *disease* listed by the Public Health Commissioner, or the fact that there was a *death or felony* on the property, is *not considered material*. Therefore, sellers, landlords, and licensees are not liable for failure to disclose these issues. However, if a purchaser or tenant advises the owner or licensee in writing that this information is important to their decision, then the owner or licensee does have a duty to disclose in writing any knowledge about whether a suicide, murder, or other felony

Disclosure of Interest in Property

Disclosure of REALTOR® Interest in Property
or in Purchaser or Tenant

Property Address: _____

_____

The undersigned Realtor® discloses the following interest in the Property: (check appropriate box)

☐ The Realtor® has or will present an offer for the Realtor® , a member of the Realtor® 's immediate family, the Realtor® 's firm or a member of the Realtor® 's firm, or an entity in which the Realtor® , the Realtor® 's immediate family or the Realtor® 's firm has an ownership interest.

☐ The Realtor® owns or has an interest in the Property.

_____   _____

Realtor®   Date

I received a copy of this Statement on _____, 20____.

_____

occurred on the property (but not the disease status of persons who lived on the property). (CGS Sections 20-329cc–20-329gg)

Sales price.   Licensees are required to accurately represent the sales price of a property. In other words, in any documentation required to be submitted to a lender, government office, or other person or entity, the licensee must state the actual selling price of the property and not a lower or higher number.

Property condition disclosure.   Sellers are required to provide prospective buyers with a *property condition report* in all residential real estate transactions (with few exceptions). Real estate licensees should advise a seller-client of the seller's responsibility. The state form and more information about this disclosure is presented in Chapter 7. (CGS Section 20-327b)

Off-site conditions.   Sellers and agents are potentially liable to a buyer for failure to disclose off-site hazardous waste conditions. Connecticut law excuses both the seller and the seller's agent of any such liability if the seller provides a written notice to potential purchasers of the availability of Connecticut Department of Environmental Protection lists. The notice needs to be given either before or at the time the purchase contract is signed; in practice, notice is often contained as a provision in the purchase contract. More detail about this and other environmental disclosures is provided in Chapter 17. (CGS Section 20-327f)

Hunting or shooting properties.   Owners of property where hunting or shooting regularly takes place can enter the property information on a list kept by the town clerk in the town where the property is located (owners have no liability for not entering property on the list). A seller and a licensee representing the seller have met any duty of disclosure of such information to potential buyers, if the seller provides a written notice about the town clerk's list of hunting and shooting properties prior to, or upon, entering into a purchase and sale contract (however, the law does not require such a duty of disclosure). (CGS Section 20-327g)

Agency disclosure.   A licensee representing a seller, buyer, landlord, or lessee is required to make a written disclosure of whom he or she represents in the transaction to any *unrepresented party* in the transaction. The state mandates the form to be used; see Figure 1.3 and refer to Chapter 1 for a complete discussion of this agency disclosure requirement. (CGS Section 20-325d)

Advertising

Real estate *advertising* is broadly defined to include all forms of identification, representation, promotion, and solicitation disseminated in any manner and by any means of communication to the public for any purpose related to licensed real estate activity.

A licensee is required to diligently obtain and present accurate information in advertisements and other representations to the public. No blind ads are allowed. Full disclosure of the broker's name is required.

To advertise *property listed with another broker,* the licensee must get permission of the other broker. That listing information can't be changed in any way without the permission of the other broker, and must be updated at least every 72 hours.

Internet advertising must include, on every page of the site,

- the licensee's name and office address,
- the name of the real estate broker the licensee is affiliated with,
- all states where the licensee is licensed, and
- the last date when the site property information has been updated.

Electronic communication, including e-mail and bulletin-board postings, must contain on the first or last page of the communication

- the licensee's name and office address,
- the name of the real estate broker the licensee is affiliated with, and
- all states where the licensee is licensed.

Agency Agreements

A written contract between a broker and client is required before any attempt can be made by the broker or broker's salespersons to negotiate a sale, exchange, purchase, or lease. This written agreement must

- identify the property correctly, and
- contain all terms and conditions, including
  — compensation to be paid,
  — beginning and expiration dates,
  — type of agency agreement, and
  — signatures and addresses of all parties concerned.

Refer to Chapter 2 for further information on agency representation agreements.

Diligent effort.   If a broker enters into an *exclusive agency* listing agreement with a seller or landlord client, the broker and salespersons working for the broker are required to *make a diligent effort* to sell or lease the property. Likewise, if a broker enters into an exclusive buyer or tenant agency agreement, the broker and salespersons working for the broker are required to make a diligent offer to find a property within the prospective buyer's or tenant's specifications. Diligent effort includes keeping a client apprised of what is happening with the process on a regular basis.

Signs.   A licensee must obtain the written consent of an owner of property to put a sign on the owner's property. Also, note that even if an owner consents, some towns have restrictions on the placing and dimensions of signs.

Offers.   When a licensee writes up an offer, the offer must include essential terms and conditions, including the manner in which the purchase is to be financed. When a licensee receives an offer on behalf of a client, the licensee must submit the offer to the client as quickly as possible.

Unless agreed otherwise, a listing broker is not obligated to market property and a buyer broker is not obligated to search for property, once the broker's client has an accepted offer or counteroffer.

Commissions and Compensation

A licensee cannot share compensation (either in the form of a commission or other type of fee) with unlicensed persons engaging in the real estate business for another person. Also, a licensee cannot demand compensation unless the licensee has reasonable cause for payment.

Agency agreements that set compensation must contain the following statement in not less than ten-point boldface type (or in some manner that stands out significantly from the text preceding it):

> **NOTICE: THE AMOUNT OR RATE OF REAL ESTATE BROKER COMPENSATION IS NOT FIXED BY LAW. IT IS SET BY EACH BROKER INDIVIDUALLY AND MAY BE NEGOTIABLE BETWEEN YOU AND THE BROKER.**

Additionally, the regulations specify the following about compensation:

- A licensee shall receive compensation only when reasonable cause for such exists.
- When a party fails to proceed with a transaction, the real estate broker has no right to any funds deposited with the broker, even though compensation may have been earned.
- A licensee shall receive no compensation for expenditures made for his or her client without the knowledge and consent of the client.
- Compensation from more than one party to a transaction cannot be accepted without all parties to the transaction agreeing to it prior to the closing.
- No part of any real estate compensation can be given to a person who was nonlicensed at the time services were rendered.
- A licensee must assign or pay over directly to his or her real estate broker all funds received from a transaction.
- Real estate brokers cannot compensate another broker's salespersons directly. All compensations are paid to the real estate broker of the cooperating agency.

Agreements with out-of-state brokers. In general, an unlicensed person cannot engage in the real estate business in Connecticut, and a Connecticut licensee cannot share compensation with an unlicensed person engaging in the real estate business on behalf of another person. This means that a Connecticut licensee cannot share compensation with an out-of-state broker or salesperson who is licensed in another state but not in Connecticut. However, an exception exists for certain commercial transactions. Compensation can be shared with persons who are licensed in another state but not in Connecticut in a commercial real estate transaction if various conditions are met, including that the out-of-state licensee affiliate with a Connecticut licensed broker.

Referral fees. Connecticut prohibits a broker from paying a referral fee to an unlicensed person engaging in the real estate business. To meet this license requirement, the person receiving the fee can be licensed in either Connecticut or another state.

A licensee cannot demand a referral fee, unless a reasonable cause for payment exists. Through policy guidance, the Commission has stated that a reasonable cause for payment (which would allow a licensee to demand a referral fee) means that

- an actual introduction of business has been made;
- a subagency relationship exists;
- a contractual referral fee relationship exists; or
- a contractual cooperative brokerage relationship exists.

Cooperation

Connecticut law also regulates the manner in which licensees cooperate in the real estate business.

With other licensees. Licensees are required to cooperate with other licensees when it is in the best interest of the client. A licensee cannot, however, negotiate directly with another licensee's client, unless the other licensee consents or a diligent effort is made to contact the other licensee without success.

With the state. A licensee is required to cooperate truthfully with the Department of Consumer Protection, Real Estate Commission, and staff personnel investigating possible law violations.

Interfering with agency relationships. Connecticut prohibits a licensee from interfering with the agency relationship of another licensee. Further, a licensee is prohibited from advising a client of another licensee to break his or her agency contract with the other licensee. When interpreting these mandates, the Commission has stated that an agency relationship is not established until a written agency agreement (either a listing or buyer agency agreement) is entered into.

The Commission has defined interference with the agency relationship of another licensee to include

- demanding a referral fee from another licensee without reasonable cause;
- threatening to take harmful actions against the client of another licensee because of the agency relationship; or
- counseling a client of another licensee on how to terminate or amend an existing agency contract.

While relocation companies have to follow these rules also, the communication of corporate relocation policies or benefits to a transferring employee is not considered interference, provided that the communication does not involve advice or encouragement on how to terminate or amend an existing agency contract.

Fair Housing

A licensee cannot discriminate against any person on the basis of race, color, creed, sex, age, physical, mental or learning disability, ethnic or national origin, marital status, sexual orientation, lawful source of income, or familial status. All agency agreements must include the statement:

> "This agreement is subject to the Connecticut General Statutes prohibiting discrimination in commercial and residential real estate transactions." (CGS Title 46a, Chapter 814c)

Fair housing law is discussed in greater detail in Chapter 15.

Handling Monies

All monies accepted or held by a licensed broker on behalf of a client must be placed in a trust or an escrow account. The account must be distinct and separate from the broker's personal account and maintained in a bank doing business in Connecticut. When a salesperson receives deposits or other monies as part of a transaction, the salesperson must promptly give it to the salesperson's designated broker. Brokerage firms often have policies allowing salespeople to make deposits but not withdraw funds.

Any monies accepted by a broker from a client or other person to which the broker is not personally or legally entitled (including such items as down payment, earnest money, deposit, rental money, and rental security deposit), must be deposited within three banking days from the date the agreement evidencing such transaction is signed by all necessary parties. Any broker who violates this section of the licensing law can be fined up to $2,000 or imprisoned up to six months or both. The Commission has the right to inspect broker accounts at any time.

Connecticut law provides for a procedure allowing a broker to hand over a deposit to a court when there is a dispute regarding a transaction or the deposit. If a broker does this, then the broker is no longer liable for the legal distribution of the money. (CGS Section 20-324k)

Interest earned on real estate deposits. There is a program for the use of interest earned on real estate broker escrow or trust accounts. All brokers are required to participate in the program by depositing down payment money in interest-bearing accounts specifically established for use in this program. The interest earned from these amounts is paid to the Connecticut Housing Finance Authority. This interest is used for mortgage assistance for first-time homebuyers and low-income and moderate-income families. A client may request that his or her deposit not be part of this program (regardless of amount of deposit or duration), in which case the deposit is to be put in a separate interest-bearing account. (CGS Sections 8-265f–8-265h)

■ SUSPENSION OR REVOCATION OF A LICENSE

CGS SECTIONS 20-320–20-323

The Commission has the power to suspend temporarily or revoke permanently the license of any broker or salesperson and/or impose a fine of up to $2,000, if it finds that the licensee (or person fraudulently obtaining a license) is guilty of any of the following activities:

■ Making any material misrepresentation (i.e., failing to disclose or misrepresenting a material fact)

■ Making any false promise of a character likely to influence, persuade, or induce

■ Acting for more than one party in a transaction without the knowledge of all parties for whom the licensee acts

■ Representing or attempting to represent a real estate broker other than the licensee's employer or the broker with whom the licensee is affiliated, without the express knowledge and consent of the licensee's employer or affiliated broker

■ Failing to account for or remit within a reasonable time any monies coming into the licensee's possession that belong to others

■ Entering into an exclusive listing contract or buyer agency contract that provides for an automatic extension of the contract beyond the stated termination date

■ Failing to deliver immediately a copy of any instrument to any party executing it, when the licensee has prepared or supervised the preparation of the instrument and the instrument relates to the licensee's employment or to any real estate transaction with which the licensee is involved

■ Being convicted in a court of competent jurisdiction in any state of forgery, embezzlement, obtaining money under false pretenses, larceny, extortion, conspiracy to defraud, or other like offense (in such cases the Commission must consider the circumstances discussed earlier in this chapter under "Convicted felons")

■ Collecting compensation in advance of services to be performed and failing, on the demand of the person paying the compensation or the commission, to account for this money

■ Commingling funds of others with the licensee's own, or failing to keep these funds in an escrow or a trust account

■ Performing any act or conduct that constitutes dishonest, fraudulent, or improper dealings

■ Failing to provide agency disclosures as required by Section 20-325c

■ Violating any provision of the license law or any of the Commission's regulations

The Commission may suspend or revoke a license on its own initiative or in response to a verified written complaint that supplies evidence and documentation to warrant the Commission's action.

Prior notice and hearing.   Before refusing, suspending, or revoking a license or imposing any fine, the Commission must notify the licensee of the charges. The licensee is then given the opportunity of a hearing in front of the Commission.

Appeal of Commission ruling.   Any person who feels that the Commission's decisions, orders, or regulations are unfair or unjust may appeal to the Superior Court for the New Britain judicial district or the judicial district in which he or she resides. Any corporation aggrieved by such decisions, orders, or regulations must appeal to the Superior Court for the New Britain judicial district or the judicial district in which it maintains its principal place of business. For additional information see CGS Section 4-183.

License revocation on conviction of crime.   Any licensee who is convicted of any of the offenses listed above (forgery, embezzlement, obtaining money under false pretenses, larceny, extortion, conspiracy to defraud, or other like offense) forfeits his or her license and all fees paid. The clerk of the court in which the conviction takes place forwards a certified copy of the conviction to the Commission. Within ten days after receiving this notice, the Commission will notify the licensee in writing that his or her license has been revoked. Any application for reinstatement must conform to the requirements discussed earlier in this chapter under "Convicted felons."

■ REAL ESTATE GUARANTY FUND

CGS SECTIONS 20-324a–20-324f

The license law directs and authorizes the Commission to maintain a Real Estate Guaranty Fund from which persons may recover compensation if they are aggrieved by the following actions of a licensed real estate broker, salesperson, or unlicensed employee of a broker:

- The embezzlement of money or property
- Obtaining money or property from persons by false pretenses, trickery, or forgery
- Fraud, misrepresentation, or deceit by or on the part of the licensed broker, salesperson, or unlicensed employee of the broker

The maximum compensation paid in connection with any single claim or transaction is $25,000, regardless of the number of persons aggrieved or parcels of real estate involved.

Any person who obtains a real estate broker's or salesperson's license for the first time must pay a one-time fee to the Real Estate Guaranty Fund in the amount of $20. By state law, this fee as well as $3 of each annual license renewal fee and all fines imposed against licensees for certain unethical or illegal acts must be credited to the fund. The level of this fund cannot exceed $500,000.

Procedures.   Any actions that might involve subsequent recovery from the Guaranty Fund must be initiated no later than *two years* from the date of the final judgment or on expiration of time for an appeal.

To collect from the fund, an aggrieved person must sue the licensee or unlicensed employee and obtain a court judgment against him or her. Any person commencing legal action that might involve a subsequent recovery from the Guaranty Fund

must notify the Commission, in writing, at the time
notified, the Commission has the right to enter an app
defend an action.

Once the aggrieved person obtains a final judgment in court,
period expires, the aggrieved person applies to the Real Estate Com
order directing payment from the Guaranty Fund. The Commission
a hearing where the aggrieved person will be required to show certain
particularly that he or she has unsuccessfully tried to collect the judgment.
aggrieved person makes a showing that is satisfactory to the Commission, th
Commission will approve payment from the fund.

Once it has made any payment from the fund, the Commission has the right to
seek repayment from the licensee. Any monies, including interest, subsequently
recovered by the Commission must be redeposited in the fund.

Revocation of license. When the Commission makes a payment from the
fund to satisfy a judgment claim, the license of the broker or salesperson whose
actions were the cause of claim will automatically be revoked. The license will
not be reissued until the person has repaid the entire sum, plus interest at a rate
determined by the Commission. Bankruptcy does not extinguish this penalty.

■ OTHER LICENSING LAWS

There are other Connecticut licensing laws related to real estate. A real estate
broker or salesperson's license does not authorize licensees to perform activities
that require another license.

Only *attorneys* who are admitted to the Connecticut bar are authorized to give
legal advice or counsel in the state. Real estate brokers and salespersons are not
authorized to act as attorneys and cannot provide legal advice or counsel. Real
estate licensees are allowed to complete forms prepared by an attorney but cannot
write legal agreements and cannot attempt to provide legal advice. If a client has
a legal question, licensees should suggest that the client speak with an attorney.

Connecticut requires certification of real estate *appraisers*. Real estate brokers and
salespersons cannot perform appraisals unless they are also a certified appraiser.
Brokers and salespersons, however, are allowed to estimate the value of real estate
as part of a market analysis for a brokerage client, as long as the value estimate is
not referred to as an appraisal. Also, any fee paid in valuing a one- to four-family
residence must be credited against future compensation owed the licensee. The
law governing certification and conduct of appraisers, as well as this exemption for
real estate brokers and salespersons, is discussed in Chapter 13.

Mortgage lenders, brokers, and originators must hold an appropriate license from
the Connecticut Department of Banking. Real estate licensees cannot act as a
mortgage broker or lender without also obtaining the appropriate mortgage
license. Moreover, in the case of one- to four-family residential property, a real
estate licensee cannot receive a fee for mortgage brokerage services in addition

...te brokerage services, unless specific disclosure is made to the buyer.
...licensees are excluded from the definition of mortgage originator (and
...om originator licensing requirements) unless the real estate licensee is
...ed by a mortgage lender or broker. Details of the laws in this area can
... Chapter 11.

...ty securities dealers must hold a real estate broker's license in Connecti-
...ate license law contains specific provisions covering their operations
...ng. Details of the law in this area can be found in Appendix A.

Connecticut General Statutes, Chapter 392 (Real Estate Brokers and
 Salespersons):   *www.cga.ct.gov/2009/pub/Chap392.htm*

Connecticut Department of Consumer Protection Web site (includes real estate
 licensing requirements, information, and forms):
 www.ct.gov/dcp (select Real Estate)

Connecticut Licensing Info Center: *www.ct-clic.com* (select Trade/
 Occupational Licenses)

Connecticut Department of Consumer Protection License Look-up (search
 status of licensees, verify status complaint and discipline history of licensees,
 download rosters of licensees):   *www.elicense.ct.gov*

Connecticut Real Estate Commission (lists Commission members, links to
 monthly meeting minutes):
 www.ct.gov/dcp/cwp/view.asp?a=1624&Q=276076&PM=1

PSI Web site (licensing and continuing education testing vendor; includes a
 license applicant candidate handbook):   *www.psiexams.com*

CHAPTER 10 QUIZ

1. The real estate license law is administered by
   the
   a. Department of Banking.
   b. Real Estate Commission.
   c. Connecticut Association of REALTORS®.
   d. Department of Housing.

2. A person must be licensed as a real estate broker
   or salesperson if that person is
   a. selling his or her house.
   b. buying a house for his or her personal use.
   c. engaging in the real estate business.
   d. constructing houses.

3. "Engaging in the real estate business" consists
   of acting for another and for a fee in all of the
   following activities EXCEPT
   a. investing in real estate.
   b. reselling a mobile home.
   c. selling real estate.
   d. collecting rent for the use of real estate.

4. Who below is exempt from the real estate
   licensing requirement?
   a. Attorney-at-law when serving as legal
      counsel to a client
   b. Appraiser when also valuing a client's
      property
   c. Associations, partnerships, corporations
   d. Real property securities dealers

5. The primary responsibilities of an office manager for a local real estate firm include coordinating the flow of paperwork through the
   office, preparing forms and advertising copy,
   and hiring and supervising clerical personnel.
   The office manager
   a. is violating the license law.
   b. is required to have a broker's license.
   c. is required to have a salesperson's license.
   d. does not need a real estate license for this
      job.

6. Applications for any real estate license in Connecticut must
   a. be completed before taking the written
      exam.
   b. contain a picture of the applicant.
   c. be made before May 31 of each year.
   d. be accompanied by a sworn statement
      attesting to the applicant's character.

7. You are employed by an apartment complex as
   a residential on-site property custodian. Part of
   your duties involves negotiating leases for the
   apartments. In this position you
   a. must have a salesperson's license.
   b. must have a broker's license.
   c. are exempt from the licensing requirements
      if you reside at the apartment complex.
   d. are violating the license law.

8. In addition to a course in real estate principles
   and practices, a broker applicant must also take
   a course in
   a. real estate law.
   b. the law of contracts.
   c. real estate finance.
   d. real estate appraisal.

9. Applicants who fail a license examination
   a. are notified of the results at the examina-
      tion site.
   b. must wait 180 days before a retake.
   c. are scheduled for a review session with the
      Commission.
   d. must score 80 percent on a subsequent
      retake to pass.

10. The initial salesperson's license fee is presently
    _____, and annual renewals are _____.
    a. $285/$285
    b. $565/$285
    c. $285/$75
    d. $565/$375

11. After moving to Connecticut, Alan applies for a real estate salesperson's license. The Commission discovers from his application that he was refused a license in his former state because he was not yet 18 years old. Alan is now 18 and possesses all the other qualifications. How long from the date of the earlier refusal must Alan wait to be issued a Connecticut license?

    a. He must wait one year.
    b. He must wait five years.
    c. He can be issued a license immediately.
    d. He is ineligible until he has been a resident of Connecticut for one year.

12. A nonresident license applicant must file with the Commission a(n)

    a. certificate of specific performance.
    b. irrevocable consent to suit.
    c. copy of his or her birth certificate.
    d. corpus delicti.

13. All real estate salespersons' licenses

    a. are granted in perpetuity.
    b. do not need to be renewed unless previously revoked.
    c. expire annually on March 31.
    d. expire annually on May 31.

14. To maintain their licenses, real estate licensees are required to take _____ of continuing education every _____.

    a. 6 hours, one year
    b. 12 hours, one year
    c. 12 hours, two years
    d. 60 hours, two years

15. All listings in Connecticut must include all of the following EXCEPT

    a. written confirmation.
    b. date of expiration.
    c. signatures of owners and brokers.
    d. certificate of title insurance.

16. To change broker affiliation, a salesperson must

    a. register the change with the Commission.
    b. register the change with his or her new broker.
    c. apply for a new license.
    d. apply for a broker's license.

17. Kathleen accompanies a young couple during an open house on a property listed with her agency. The couple is so impressed with the house and Kathleen's response to their questions that they decide to make an offer. Before the offer is presented to the principal, they ask Kathleen's personal opinion as to whether they should require that the seller give them a warranty deed or a quitclaim deed at the closing. Kathleen should

    a. make a decision and support it with facts.
    b. refer the couple to an attorney for legal advice.
    c. assure the couple that either is acceptable.
    d. admit she does not know.

18. If a broker tells a lender that the sales price on a property is something above its actual sales price, the

    a. broker has done nothing wrong as long as the appraisal substantiates this price.
    b. buyer is likely to receive an interest rate break.
    c. broker can lose his or her license and be fined and imprisoned.
    d. buyer can receive a higher mortgage amount.

19. The Commission has the power to revoke a salesperson's license, if the salesperson

    a. attempts to represent a real estate broker other than his or her employer, after obtaining the employer's consent.
    b. attempts to represent a buyer.
    c. enters into an exclusive listing contract.
    d. deposits a buyer's down payment in his or her own bank account.

20. A licensee represents a seller in the sale of the seller's house. The licensee is aware that the seller's basement periodically floods, but the seller has instructed the licensee not to disclose this fact to potential purchasers. In this case, the licensee

    a. must disclose the flooding because it is a material fact.

    b. is not required to disclose the flooding because it is not a material fact.

    c. must disclose the flooding because the licensee owes fiduciary duties to the potential buyers.

    d. cannot disclose the flooding because the licensee owes fiduciary duties to the seller.

21. A licensee represents a seller in the sale of the seller's house. The licensee is aware that the seller's husband had been murdered in the house, but the seller has instructed the licensee not to disclose this fact because she is fearful that people may not want to buy a house where someone recently was killed. In this case, the licensee

    a. must disclose the murder because it is a material fact.

    b. is not required to disclose the murder because it is not a material fact.

    c. must disclose the murder because the licensee owes fiduciary duties to the potential buyers.

    d. cannot disclose the murder because the licensee owes fiduciary duties to the seller.

22. A saleswoman regularly communicates with all of her clients and potential clients via e-mail. The licensing law requires that her e-mail contain all of the following EXCEPT

    a. her name and office address.

    b. the name of the broker she is affiliated with.

    c. her license certificate number.

    d. all the states where she is licensed.

23. Ben Broker maintains a Web site that highlights all of the property listings that he has. Ben knows that the licensing law requires that he include certain information on this Web site, including the

    a. address of all properties listed.

    b. seller's contact information for all of the properties listed.

    c. last date when Ben showed any of the properties listed.

    d. last date when the Web site property information was updated.

24. Ben Broker wishes to include information about other property listed with another broker on his Web site. To do so, Ben must

    a. get the permission of the other broker.

    b. get the permission of the Commission.

    c. include a disclosure on his Web site that he may not have the rights to all properties advertised.

    d. forget the idea because he cannot advertise property listed with another broker.

25. Ben Broker has entered into an agency agreement with Sallie Seller. Such an agency agreement imposes a duty on Ben to

    a. make a diligent effort to sell the property.

    b. accept all offers on Sallie's behalf.

    c. update the property information on his Web site every 72 hours.

    d. buy the property if it does not sell quickly.

26. Ben Broker has entered into an agency agreement with Sallie Seller and has been marketing her property. Several potential buyers are interested in the property, and he has appointments to show the property throughout the next week. The first buyer he shows the property to makes an immediate offer. Ben does not tell Sallie about the offer right away, thinking that additional offers may come in over the next few days, and he will present them all to her at the end of the week. Ben has

 a. violated the licensing law because he planned to continue to show the property after an offer was submitted to him.
 b. violated the licensing law because he did not submit the offer received to Sallie as quickly as possible.
 c. taken Sallie's best interests into account and is in compliance with the licensing law.
 d. made a diligent effort to sell the property and has therefore not violated the licensing law.

27. Ben Broker has entered into an agency agreement to sell Sallie Seller's property. A salesperson affiliated with another broker introduces a buyer to the property, and that buyer actually purchases it. Ben would like to share some of his commission earned from Sallie with the salesperson. Can he do so?

 a. Yes, he can do so as long as the salesperson is licensed.
 b. Yes, he may do so as long as Sallie agrees.
 c. No, the compensation from Sallie cannot be paid to more than one party in a transaction.
 d. No, a real estate broker cannot compensation another broker's salesperson directly.

28. Ben Broker has entered into an agency agreement to sell Sallie Seller's property. Sallie meets Betty, another broker, at a church event. Betty tells Sallie that she could do a much better job advertising Sallie's property and suggests that Sallie terminate her agreement with Ben and enter in a listing agreement with her. Betty's action amounts to

 a. interfering with an agency relationship, which violates the licensing law.
 b. protecting the fiduciary duties of her potential client, which is in keeping with the licensing laws.
 c. counseling a potential client, which is in keeping with the licensing laws.
 d. fair dealing because Ben has not actually sold the property.

29. Who may receive compensation from the Real Estate Guaranty Fund?

 a. A broker who does not receive an earned commission
 b. A seller who pays a commission to a broker under false pretenses
 c. A buyer who pays a fee to a broker under a buyer agency agreement
 d. A cooperating broker who does not receive a commission split

30. The maximum compensation that will be paid from the Real Estate Guaranty Fund for any single transaction is

 a. $5,000.
 b. $10,000.
 c. $25,000.
 d. $50,000.

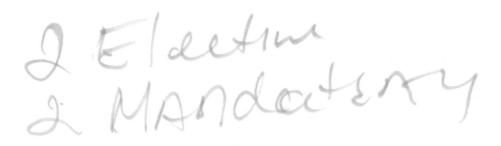

11

CHAPTER

Real Estate Financing: Principles/Practice

CT title theory State

■ OVERVIEW

A lender who lends money to a borrower requires that the borrower pay the money back with interest. The borrower promises to do so in a document called a *note*. When the money is lent to purchase real estate, often the lender will require that the real estate be pledged as collateral for repayment of the note. The borrower transfers a collateral interest in the real estate to the lender by giving the lender a *mortgage*.

Legally, Connecticut is a title theory state, so that technically a mortgage conveys title to the real estate from the borrower to the lender; therefore, the actual mortgage document is referred to as a *mortgage deed*. However, in practice, Connecticut holds a *modified* position with respect to mortgages. Although the lender receives a mortgage deed, the borrower is permitted to continue in possession of the property and to retain title as long as the terms of the mortgage are complied with (e.g., payment of principal, interest, taxes, and insurance). Basically, the lender's right to exercise ownership through possession is restricted as long as the monthly payments are made on time and all the conditions of the mortgage are met.

Connecticut statutes relating to mortgage financing can be found at Title 49 of the Connecticut General Statutes (Mortgages and Liens).

■ MORTGAGE DEED AND NOTE

The standard clauses included in mortgage deeds and notes used in Connecticut relate primarily to the rights and obligations of both the mortgagee/lender and mortgagor/borrower (such as prepayment privileges, assignments, and defaults). There may be subtle variations in these clauses from institution to institution.

Usury

Mortgage loans for more than $5,000 are automatically *exempted* from usury regulations. Thus, there is no ceiling on the interest rates that may be charged on these real estate loans in Connecticut.

Recording

Mortgages in Connecticut are recorded for at least two reasons. First, the application of *title theory* gives rise to mortgage deeds, and all deeds must be recorded under state law. Second, in the event of a default on the part of the mortgagor, the date of recording generally establishes the order of *priority* for the satisfaction of claims. This second point is particularly significant for lenders who rewrite or refinance existing first mortgages without paying off an existing second mortgage (or equivalent junior financing). If the lender who rewrites the existing first mortgage is unaware of the secondary financing or fails to obtain a subordination agreement from the second mortgagee, its mortgage will stand second in line to be satisfied in the event of a default and/or subsequent foreclosure action because the newly refinanced mortgage was recorded after the existing secondary financing. Thus, it is important for lenders to be aware of the necessity to record mortgages and deeds and to conduct proper title searches to ascertain the existence of prior liens (particularly those still outstanding).

1st Recorded State Law
2nd priority of liens

Releases

Once the mortgage loan has been fully paid, the lender is required by law to execute and deliver a *release of the mortgage*. Releases are recorded and indexed by the town clerk under the names of the mortgagor/borrower and mortgagee/lender. In addition, a marginal entry is made on the record of the original mortgage referring to the release. This release basically clears the title, so that the land records reflect that the property is no longer collateral for a loan.

Releases drawn up in the following form are considered sufficient:

■ FOR EXAMPLE

Know all persons by these presents, that _____ of _____ in the county of _____ and state of _____ do hereby release and discharge a certain (mortgage, mechanic's lien, or power of attorney for the conveyance of land) from _____ to _____ dated _____ and recorded in the records of the town of _____ in the county of _____ and state of Connecticut, in book _____ at page _____. In witness whereof _____ have hereunto set _____ hand and seal, this _____ day of _____ , AD. Signed, sealed, and delivered in the presence of _____.
    (Seal)
    (Acknowledgment)

This is a general release form and can be used in a number of circumstances.

In the case of partial releases from a construction loan, the instrument must clearly identify the extent (dollar amount) to which the mortgage is released and the portion of the property being released from the mortgage.

Assignments

A lender may assign (transfer its right in) its interests in a mortgage to another party by completing an instrument of assignment, such as the following:

■ **FOR EXAMPLE**

Know all persons by these presents, that _____ of _____ in the county of _____ and state of _____ does hereby grant, bargain, sell, assign, transfer and set over a certain (mortgage, assignment of rents and leases, or assignment of interest in a lease) from _____ to _____ dated _____ and recorded in the records of the town of _____ county of _____ and state of Connecticut, in book _____ at page _____ in witness whereof _____ have hereunto set _____ hand and seal, this _____ day of _____, AD. Signed, sealed, and delivered in the presence of _____.
　　　　(Seal)
　　　　(Acknowledgment)

This is a general form that may be used to assign a number of different interests in real estate. Instruments of assignment are recorded in the same manner as mortgages and releases.

■ MORTGAGE BROKERAGE

Connecticut has numerous mortgage-related licensing requirements. Any person or entity who for a fee either (1) takes a residential mortgage loan application or (2) offers or negotiates terms of a residential mortgage loan must have a license. At the company level, a *mortgage broker license* is required. At the individual level, a *mortgage originator license* is required. Officers, partners, and members of a mortgage loan lender entity must be licensed as mortgage loan originators if they fit the definition above.

Mortgage brokers and originators are licensed by the Connecticut Department of Banking. There are prelicensing education, examination, and continuing education requirements for mortgage loan originators. A surety bond is required of mortgage brokers.

Additionally, any person or entity who for a fee takes a residential mortgage loan application or offers or negotiates terms of a residential mortgage loan must have a *mortgage broker license*.

Real Estate Broker Assisting in Mortgage Transaction

A real estate broker or salesperson cannot be compensated by a mortgage lender or broker for negotiating or arranging a mortgage loan for a real estate client unless the real estate licensee *also* holds a mortgage loan originator license. However, a real estate licensee can be compensated by a client for assisting with securing a mortgage loan for the client (this does not fall under the definition of mortgage loan originator). If a real estate licensee receives a fee or commission for the sale of one- to four-family residential real estate, the licensee can only receive a fee or commission for assisting the buyer in the sale in obtaining a mortgage loan *if* there is a written agreement between the broker or salesperson and buyer, and certain *disclosures* are made. The disclosure must be in writing (in at least ten-point bold-face capital letters) and given to the buyer before the buyer signs the contract for mortgage brokerage services. (CGS Section 20-325c)

The disclosure must be as follows:

> I UNDERSTAND THAT THE REAL ESTATE BROKER OR SALES-PERSON IN THIS TRANSACTION HAS OFFERED TO ASSIST ME IN FINDING A MORTGAGE LOAN. ADDITIONALLY, I UNDER-STAND THAT THIS REAL ESTATE BROKER OR SALESPERSON DOES NOT REPRESENT ANY PARTICULAR MORTGAGE LENDER AND WILL ATTEMPT TO OBTAIN THE BEST TERMS AVAILABLE WITHIN THE MORTGAGE LOAN MARKET FOR MY SPECIFIC HOME FINANCING NEEDS. IF THE REAL ESTATE BROKER OR SALESPERSON DOES NOT FULFILL HIS FIDUCIARY OBLIGA-TION I MAY FILE A COMPLAINT WITH THE DEPARTMENT OF BANKING. I ALSO UNDERSTAND THAT I MAY ATTEMPT TO FIND A MORTGAGE LOAN TO FINANCE THE PURCHASE OF MY HOME WITHOUT THE ASSISTANCE OF THE REAL ESTATE BROKER OR SALESPERSON IN WHICH CASE I WILL NOT BE OBLIGATED TO PAY A FEE TO THE REAL ESTATE BROKER OR SALESPERSON.

Any fee or commission received by a broker or salesperson for assisting a buyer with a mortgage loan *must be related to the services actually performed based* on reasonable hourly rates. The compensation *cannot* be imposed for the *mere referral* of the buyer to a mortgage lender and must be paid directly to the broker or salesperson by the buyer rather than from the mortgage loan proceeds at the time of closing.

Consumer Credit Licenses

A person who negotiates short sales or foreclosure rescue services must obtain a debt negotiation license from the Department of Banking. There are no exceptions for real estate licensees.

Residential Mortgage Fraud

In Connecticut, it is a felony for a mortgage professional to make or use any material misstatements, misrepresentations, or omissions during the mortgage lending process.

PREDATORY LENDING

Predatory lending is a general term used to describe illegal, unfair, and/or abusive lending practices whereby lenders induce borrowers to take out loans that they cannot afford. Connecticut has laws prohibiting unscrupulous lending practices. In addition, there are limits placed on "high cost loans," including mandatory disclosures and prohibited practices and provisions. Also, limitations on prepaid finance charges apply even if a loan is not high cost. The Connecticut Office of Legislative Research Web site provides a summary of state antipredatory lending laws.

MORTGAGE FORECLOSURE

When a mortgage falls into default due to the borrower's failure to make required payments or other violations of the terms of the mortgage contract, foreclosure is the usual result. If a lender agrees, a borrower may avoid a foreclosure action by granting the lender a *deed in lieu of foreclosure* (a voluntary deed). This presumes, however, that the mortgagee is agreeable to this alternative. In this case, the defaulting borrower would convey the title to the property to the lender outright rather than face the prospects of a strict foreclosure and its attendant costs. These costs would range from the incidental expenses associated with court and legal fees to the long-term penalty of the poor credit rating almost certain to accompany a foreclosure action. In general, however, strict foreclosures and foreclosures by sale represent the most common methods by which real property interests are foreclosed on in Connecticut.

Strict Foreclosure

Under a strict foreclosure, the lender/mortgagee first files a suit to foreclose. As part of the suit, the lender is required to submit a current real estate appraisal on the property to be foreclosed, prepared by a Connecticut licensed or certified appraiser. Notice, in the form of a summons, of the impending foreclosure is delivered to all parties having a recorded interest in the property. Such notice directs them to appear in court on a specified date set by the court. A notice of the foreclosure action, *lis pendens* (litigation pending), is also recorded in the land records of the town in which the property is located. On the court date, any arguments for and against the foreclosure action will be heard, and the appraisal will be entered into the proceedings to establish the value estimate of the court-appointed appraisers.

If the parties to the foreclosure suit take no action to extend the date on which a foreclosure judgment will be effective, the court will enter a judgment of foreclosure, set a law day on which the property will pass to the foreclosing creditor if no one redeems the property, and establish a day in court on which each of the intervening creditors will have the opportunity to redeem the mortgage and take over the property. If neither the defaulted mortgagor nor any of the other creditors has the capacity or desire to redeem the property, it goes to the foreclosing mortgagee and the slate is wiped clean; that is, all other claims are extinguished except delinquent taxes, valid mechanics' liens, and liens that were recorded before the mortgage.

Thus, if First National Bank, the first mortgagee, forecloses on property on which Home Finance holds a second mortgage, Home Finance may redeem the bank's mortgage and take title by paying off the first mortgage and whatever other costs might have resulted from the foreclosure action. If there are any intervening creditors (debts that are recorded and stand ahead of the redeeming creditor), the redeeming creditor must also pay them before acquiring title.

Certificate of satisfaction.   Once either the defendant (defaulted borrower/mortgagor) or another creditor redeems the property from foreclosure, the plaintiff (mortgagee initiating the suit) must execute and deliver to the defendant a certificate of satisfaction. This certificate is signed by the plaintiff and evidences the fact that the debt and costs of foreclosure have been satisfied. It must be filed by the defendant with the court in which the original foreclosure judgment was entered and recorded in the records of the town in which the property is located, as discussed earlier in this chapter.

Modifying judgments of foreclosure.   As discussed above, if no one redeems the property within the time period established by the court, title will rest in the foreclosing creditor. After a judgment of foreclosure has been rendered by the court, the judgment may be reopened at the court's discretion at any time before the title to the property passes to the foreclosing creditor. The court may reopen the judgment to make any modifications it feels are equitable on the written motion of any person having a legitimate interest in the foreclosure action. Once title has passed, the judgment cannot be reopened. Note, however, that judgments are not reopened at the whim and fancy of the party who makes such a request before the court. Because it is at the court's discretion to reopen judgment, the reasons for doing so must be substantial, such as fraud, misrepresentation, or an error of the court. The court will not reopen judgment merely to give the defendant another shot at redeeming the property.

Foreclosure certificates.   Once title to a foreclosed property rests in the person or persons who initiated the suit, that person or persons must record a foreclosure certificate in the land records of the town in which the property is located. The certificate must contain at least the following information:

- A description of the property foreclosed
- The mortgage deed on which the foreclosure took place
- The volume and page number where the above deed was recorded
- The time at which the title became absolute in the foreclosing party
- The signature of the person taking title (or his or her agent)

Ejectment and possession.   Under any foreclosure judgment, the foreclosing party may issue a complaint to the court demanding possession of the property he or she is foreclosing. If the court upholds the plaintiff's request, the defendant may be ejected from the property. Note that tenants of the property who are not involved in the foreclosure suit generally are protected from ejectment.

Foreclosure by Sale

A foreclosure by sale typically is requested by a creditor whose claim is subordinate to that of the foreclosing lender/mortgagee. Under a strict foreclosure, this lender would be compelled to redeem the foreclosing mortgage and debts to all other intervening creditors to take the property. Under a foreclosure by sale, he or she need only be the highest bidder. Thus, the sale offers a junior lienholder the opportunity to acquire the property at a lesser cost than under strict foreclosure. Any deficiencies would be the problem of the original debtor—not the purchaser at the sale.

A foreclosure by sale would begin in essentially the same manner as a strict foreclosure and would follow all the steps identified above up to the point of notifying the parties to the foreclosure suit. Under Connecticut mortgage law, any party to the foreclosure suit may request that the court order a foreclosure by sale instead of a strict foreclosure. If the court so orders, it will appoint a committee to conduct the sale and require that notice of the sale be advertised (in accordance with specific notice requirements). The date of the sale is decided on by the court on the advisement of the parties to the suit and their respective counsel.

The sale is conducted by the court-appointed committee and is similar to an auction. *Anyone* may bid on the property, including the party being foreclosed and the junior lienholders. The purchasing bidder on the property is required to post a deposit on the property and is given a period of time to procure the additional funds to complete the sale. Both the amount of the deposit and the time allowed are determined by the court or its appointed committee. The proceeds of a foreclosure by sale would be used to satisfy the claims against the property in order of court-established priority (date of recording), with any excess returned to the mortgagor. If the sale fails to yield sufficient funds to satisfy the mortgage or lien foreclosed on, the court may order a *deficiency judgment* against the party liable for this mortgage or lien. The other creditors would be squeezed out and would receive nothing. At the sale the purchaser would receive a sheriff's deed and would acquire the same title that would have passed to the foreclosing creditor under a strict foreclosure.

Foreclosure Mediation

A Foreclosure Mediation Program is available in Connecticut to assist any borrower/mortgagor whose primary residence (one- to four-family) is the subject of a mortgage foreclosure action. To initiate the mediation, a borrower must file foreclosure mediation forms with the court after the lender/mortgagee files a suit to foreclose. The borrower then meets with a mediator and the lender to try to restructure the mortgage debt and avoid foreclosure. The program is run through the Connecticut Judicial Department and is mandatory in all foreclosure actions through June 30, 2012.

Deed in Lieu of Foreclosure

As discussed earlier in this chapter, there are some instances in which a borrower/mortgagor may wish to simply deed the property over to the potentially foreclosing mortgagee rather than face the costs and trial of a foreclosure suit. The lender/mortgagee, however, should exercise caution in agreeing to such a deed in lieu of foreclosure, particularly if there are other delinquent loans on the property. Other creditors, clamoring that the conveyance was effected to squeeze them out, could make life very difficult for the mortgagee accepting the deed. Typically, a lender would agree to such an arrangement only if it were the sole (or at least principal) creditor. The presumed advantages of this method or alternative to foreclosure are found in the time and expense saved by both parties.

Redemption

The defaulted borrower/mortgagor has only two opportunities to redeem the property. Under strict foreclosure he or she may redeem the property on the *law day* provided by the court. Under a foreclosure by sale, he or she may redeem by *bidding successfully* on the property. In most foreclosure cases there is no other redemption period. The only exception is in the case of property foreclosed for delinquent taxes; in such cases the property owner has six months to redeem the property (unless the property was abandoned, in which case the redemption period is reduced to 60 days).

Deficiency Judgments

Should a *foreclosure by sale* not produce enough funds from a sale to satisfy the foreclosing creditor, the court may order a deficiency judgment against the debtor liable for the debt or lien. This becomes a general lien.

If, however, a foreclosure by sale produces a sales price below the value established by the court-ordered appraisal, the court requires that the debt(s) outstanding as of the date of sale be reduced (credited) by one-half the difference between the appraisal value and the sales price before it will grant a deficiency judgment. Thus, if a property foreclosed by sale yields a $400,000 sales price and has a court appraisal indicating a value of $420,000, the foreclosing creditor must credit $10,000 to the money owed before obtaining a deficiency judgment.

Under a *strict foreclosure*, the plaintiff (foreclosing mortgagee) may be awarded a deficiency judgment based on the difference between the amount of its claim and the court appraisal. The idea behind allowing deficiency judgments is to prevent waste on the part of the defaulted borrower by making him or her liable for the difference between the appraisal and the claim of the mortgagee. It serves to prevent these borrowers from walking away from their investments when they experience problems. In the case of a strict foreclosure, the plaintiff must make an application for a deficiency judgment within 90 days of the end of the time period allowed for redemption.

Deficiency judgments must be recorded within four months from the time they are awarded to become valid liens on the property of the debtor. When and if the lien is satisfied, a discharge of lien must be prepared and recorded in the appropriate town land records (generally in the town in which the property is located).

■ SOURCES OF MORTGAGE FUNDS

The funds available for financing the purchase of or investment in real estate flow from a variety of sources in the mortgage market. The principal sources of mortgage financing are financial institutions. Individuals and other private sources make up the remainder of the mortgage market. Different financial institutions came into being over the years to meet different credit or savings needs. This helps to explain the great diversity that exists in the mortgage market. Because of these differences, some lending institutions are better equipped than others to make certain types of real estate loans. Depending on the regulatory limitations placed on them and their methods of operation, investment policies, and organizational structures, the different types of institutions provide mortgage funds to different categories of borrowers or market segments.

It is important that real estate brokers and salespersons have a thorough knowledge of the mortgage market to effectively counsel their clients and customers. The following discussion provides a brief analysis of some of the different types of loan programs in Connecticut.

Connecticut Housing Programs

The Connecticut Department of Economic and Community Development offers many different programs to provide loans and grants for the development and purchase of low-income housing.

The *Home Investment Partnerships Program* provides grants to localities to build, buy, and/or rehabilitate affordable housing for rent or home ownership. It also provides direct rental assistance to low-income people.

The *Federal Section 8 Housing Payment Assistance Program* and the *State Rental Assistance Program* each provide rent subsidies to low-income and moderate-income persons. They provide an opportunity to afford quality housing. There are prescribed income levels and property rental levels applicable to this program.

Financial services are available to business firms and homeowners. Tax credit vouchers are available to business firms that make contributions to nonprofit organizations to develop, sponsor, and manage housing programs for low-income and moderate-income families.

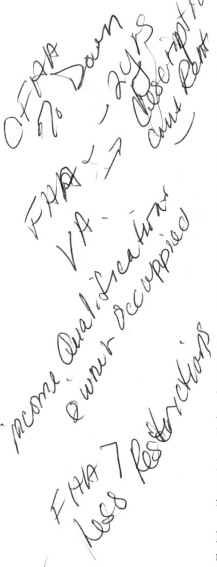

Connecticut Housing Finance Authority

Connecticut provides an additional source of mortgage financing for low-income and moderate-income families through the Connecticut Housing Finance Authority (CHFA). The CHFA offers a below-market interest rate (BMIR) program through approved lenders to qualified applicants. To become an approved lender, an institution is required to submit an application to the CHFA detailing its ability to handle the program and service any loans it makes under the program. In general, the approved lender must also be willing to write FHA and VA loans. The CHFA provides specific amounts of funds to its approved lenders to originate mortgages. When the lender's allocated funds are depleted, the lender may apply for an additional allocation.

Qualification for the program is based on a sliding income scale related to family size that stipulates a maximum sales price for properties that can be financed through the program. Both incomes and sales prices are modified by geographic areas within the state to reflect differences in the cost of living.

Applicants register their loan applications with an approved CHFA lender. Once the loan is approved by both the lender and CHFA and the papers are signed, the loan is assigned to the CHFA (the lender retains the service fee). The funds for the program are provided through bond issues of the CHFA. A CHFA program also exists to finance development projects of housing for low-income and moderate-income families.

It is important that brokers and salespersons be aware of programs like the CHFA (and the FHA and VA as well) to assist their clients in obtaining mortgage loan financing.

Following is a sampling of the CHFA programs. Borrower income limits apply to most programs.

Homebuyer mortgage program. Below-market-interest-rate 30-year mortgage loans (as much as 1 percent below comparable rates) for first-time homebuyers (persons who have not owned their own residence within the last three years).

Homeownership program. Below-market interest rates on 30-year mortgage loans for police and public school teachers who are first-time homebuyers. Local police must buy in the community they serve. State police must buy in one of Connecticut's 20 most populous cities. Teachers have some location restrictions and must be teaching in certain priority school districts.

Rehabilitation mortgage loan. Below-market-interest-rate loans to finance the purchase and rehabilitation (or refinance) of homes in need of repair. Available to first-time homebuyers and any homebuyer in certain targeted areas.

Alternative Mortgage Loans

State-chartered financial institutions are allowed to offer alternative mortgage loans. The law states that financial institutions must disclose alternative mortgage information to loan applicants at the same time that information on all types of mortgage loans is disclosed. Mortgage loan applicants have the choice of applying for conventional mortgage loans or alternative mortgage loans offered by the institutions. (CGS Section 36a-265)

Before a state-chartered financial institution makes an alternative mortgage loan available, the Connecticut Banking Department must approve a prototype plan. Many alternative mortgage instruments are offered in Connecticut, such as graduated payment mortgage (GPM), reverse annuity mortgage (RAM), growing equity mortgage (GEM), and variable-rate mortgage (VRM).

■ HOME MORTGAGE DISCLOSURE ACT

Redlining = process of denying loans in specific areas

The Home Mortgage Disclosure Act (HMDA) of 1975 requires that all depository institutions with assets in excess of $10 million and with one or more offices in a Standard Metropolitan Statistical Area (SMSA) disclose where they made their mortgage loans. The purpose of HMDA is to aid in the identification of *redlining* practices, which accelerate the decline of our inner cities and other neighborhoods. *Redlining* is defined as *the process of denying loans in specific geographic locations*. This practice is usually, if not always, associated with the decline in property values and the deterioration of housing in certain areas of a city.

Title III of HMDA requires that lenders covered by this act disclose where residential loans were made during the year by census tract number. The act pertains to all types of residential loans—conventional, FHA, FNMA, DVA, multifamily, and home improvement loans. Disclosures are made on an annual basis. Connecticut General Statutes Section 36-466 also requires that lenders disclose the reason for denial of each mortgage loan application on the HMDA forms.

As reported, information will be broken down into major categories: loans made by the lender and loans purchased by the lender (including participations). Each of these categories will be further broken down into loans within the relevant SMSA and those outside. The relevant SMSA is defined as an SMSA within which the lender maintains the home or a branch office. Loans made outside the relevant SMSA need only be disclosed by number and amount, rather than by census tract number.

■ WEB LINKS

Connecticut General Statues Title 49 (Mortgages and Liens):
www.cga.ct.gov/2009/pub/Title49.htm

Connecticut Law about Foreclosure (Connecticut Judicial Branch Law
Libraries): *www.jud.state.ct.us/LawLib/Law/foreclosure.htm.*

Verify a mortgage brokers license (Connecticut Department of Banking):
www.ct.gov/dob

Connecticut Department of Community and Economic Development programs
(choose Community/Housing Development): *www.ct.gov/ecd*

Connecticut Housing Finance Authority: *www.chfa.org*

Home Mortgage Disclosure Act data: *www.ffiec.gov/hmda*

Summary of Connecticut predatory lending laws:
www.hud.gov/local/ct/homeownership/predatorylending.cfm

Connecticut Foreclosure Mediation Program: *www.jud.ct.gov/foreclosure/*

CHAPTER 11 QUIZ

1. Generally, what establishes the priority of claims if the mortgagor defaults and a foreclosure suit is initiated?
   a. The date of recording
   b. The dollar amount
   c. The party initiating the action
   d. The order of redemption

2. A property has a recorded first mortgage. The property owners now wish to take out a home equity loan and will give that lender a mortgage interest in the property. Once the home equity lender records the home equity mortgage, the priority of the home equity lender
   a. will be nonexistent.
   b. will be paramount.
   c. will be first.
   d. will be behind the first mortgage lender.

3. At a minimum, a person receiving compensation from a mortgage lender for negotiating a mortgage loan must have
   a. a mortgage broker license.
   b. a mortgage loan originator license.
   c. a real estate salesperson license.
   d. a real estate broker license.

4. Which document must be recorded?
   a. A mortgage release
   b. A mortgage commitment
   c. A listing contract
   d. A sales contract

5. A man owes $200,000 mortgage on a house worth $150,000, so he hands the keys to the bank and walks away. After the foreclosure sale fails to cover the outstanding loan owed, the lender can
   a. collect only the proceeds from the sale.
   b. have the man arrested.
   c. do nothing to the man.
   d. collect a deficiency judgment against the man.

6. Before title passes under a strict foreclosure of a first mortgage, other creditors have an opportunity to
   a. redeem the foreclosing mortgage interest.
   b. refinance the foreclosing mortgage interest.
   c. rewrite the foreclosing mortgage interest.
   d. do nothing in regard to the foreclosing mortgage interest.

7. A foreclosure by sale is conducted by
   a. the court.
   b. a court appointed committee.
   c. the foreclosing lender or creditor.
   d. the borrower who has failed to pay his or her mortgage.

8. Once a judgment has been rendered by the court in a strict foreclosure action, the court may reopen the judgment
   a. at any time.
   b. at any time prior to the passing of title.
   c. within 60 days from the passing of title.
   d. at no time because the court cannot reopen judgments under strict foreclosure.

9. A bank has acquired title to a defaulted mortgagor's property through a strict foreclosure action. What must the bank now record?
   a. A mortgage deed
   b. A dissolution certificate
   c. An irrevocable consent of subrogation
   d. A foreclosure certificate

10. A homeowner's property is being foreclosed through a strict foreclosure process. The homeowner has the right to redeem the property by
    a. redeeming the property before title passes to the foreclosing creditor.
    b. being the successful bidder at the foreclosure sale.
    c. redeeming the property within one year of title's passing to the foreclosing creditor.
    d. matching the successful bidder's bid within one year of the foreclosure sale.

12 CHAPTER

Leases

■ OVERVIEW

Connecticut has comprehensive statutory laws regarding residential landlord-tenant matters governing rights and responsibilities, habitability, rental payments, security deposits, and remedies. Tenants who intentionally damage leased property may be prosecuted criminally. The statutory law can be found under Title 47a of the Connecticut General Statutes, entitled Landlord and Tenant.

■ LEASE

In Connecticut, the statute of frauds requires that *leases for a term of more than one year must be in writing* to be enforceable. However, inasmuch as Connecticut law requires that all contracts for greater than $500 be in writing and it considers leases as contracts, all leases regardless of term should be in writing (although this is not a legal requirement and does not affect the validity of the lease). This includes leases that are month-to-month, week-to-week, and less than one year.

Connecticut law also requires that leases for more than one year be *recorded* in the local land records to give constructive notice to a third party (future purchaser of the property, future recourse to a landlord's action, etc.) in a manner similar to recording deeds. Alternatively, a *notice of lease* may be recorded in lieu of the lease itself, provided that the notice of lease discloses at least the following pertinent information:

- The names and addresses of the parties to the lease
- The lease term with beginning and termination dates

■ A description of the property
■ Reference to the lease, including its date of execution
■ Notice of any right of extension or renewal
■ Date by which an option to purchase (if any) must be exercised
■ Reference to the place where the lease is kept on file

Leases and leasehold estates are considered to be personal property under Connecticut statutes, even though the operation of long-term leases, such as a 99-year lease, gives rise to possession that is tantamount to ownership.

It is advisable to remember that a lease is a tool to create a harmonious relationship between landlord and tenant. The completeness and full understanding of its clauses by both landlord and tenant can accomplish this. Without this clear understanding and cooperation, problems are inevitable. A lease form in plain language is shown in Figure 12.1.

■ LEASEHOLD ESTATES

Connecticut recognizes a term lease (for a specific period of time) and a periodic lease (from period to period, such as month-to-month). If a tenant holds over after the expiration of his or her lease, the law construes the tenancy as a month-to-month occupancy and not an agreement for a further lease. In all cases where a tenancy is not subject to an agreed-on term or expiration date, it is construed as a month-to-month tenancy. Unless the rental agreement fixes a definite term, the tenancy is month-to-month, except in the case of a tenant who pays weekly rent; then the tenancy is week-to-week.

■ LANDLORD AND TENANT ACT

Connecticut has a comprehensive statute relating to the rights and responsibilities of landlords and tenants, rental payments, security deposits, and summary process (evictions). The legislation relates primarily to residential dwelling units. The current law is found under Title 47a—Landlord and Tenant—of the Connecticut General Statutes and includes several important provisions.

Lease Provisions

Leases and other rental agreements may contain any terms and conditions agreeable to both parties that are not in violation of state laws. These terms and conditions may include the rent payable, the length of the term of the agreement, and any other provisions that would act to govern the rights and obligations of each party.

Prohibited clauses.   The lease agreement may not contain clauses by which the tenant (lessee)

■ agrees to waive his or her legal rights under the Connecticut General Statutes;

- allows the landlord to automatically obtain a judgment in court against the tenant without the tenant's knowledge (see discussion of judgment clauses in the text);
- agrees to excuse the landlord from any damages that the tenant suffers that would normally be the legal responsibilities of the landlord;
- agrees to waive his or her right to interest on the security deposit;
- agrees to allow the landlord to evict or dispossess him or her without court order;
- consents to the seizure of property as security for rent; or
- agrees to pay the landlord's attorney's fee in excess of 15 percent of any judgment against the tenant in the event the landlord must take the tenant to court.

Nonallowable clauses in a lease are unenforceable.

Security Deposits

Legislation regulating security deposits is found in Sections 47a-21 through 47a-22a (Advanced Rental Payments, Security Deposits) of the Connecticut General Statutes. A landlord is not required to charge a security deposit. The maximum security deposit a landlord can demand is *two months' rent*. In the case of tenants 62 years old or older, however, landlords can require only one month's rent.

Security deposits must be kept in an *escrow account* and separate from the other funds of the landlord. The escrow account must be maintained in a financial institution. The Banking Commission has enforcement powers over this portion of the Landlord and Tenant Act. The landlord must pay the tenant the earned interest on the deposit at the anniversary of the lease. The penalty for not doing so is a fine of $100. A landlord who knowingly and willfully neglects to return the security deposit to the tenant on termination of the lease will be fined $250, unless there is evidence that the landlord was entitled to the funds for damages created by the tenant. A fine of up to $500 and/or 30 days of imprisonment can be levied on a landlord who does not hold the security deposit in escrow.

Interest on Security Deposits

The current law stipulates that landlords must pay tenants interest on their security deposits only in residential units. The rate of interest payable is a *floating rate* tied to the average savings deposit rate as published in the Federal Reserve Bulletin. The rate is set annually on the first of the year and published by the Commissioner of Banking. It can never go lower than 1.5 percent. Exemptions to this regulation are for residential units owned or controlled by an educational institution for housing its students and their families, for mobile homes, or for space, lots, or parks for mobile homes.

The interest must be *paid on every anniversary* of the lease (typically each year). It may be paid directly to the tenant or subtracted from the next monthly rent payment at the option of the lessor. If any rental payment is received later than ten days after the scheduled due date, the tenant forfeits the interest for the month he or she is late in paying the rent. If the lease (rental agreement) is terminated prior to an anniversary, the lessor is required to pay interest up to a date within 30 days of actual termination.

Returning the security deposit.   Within *30 days* of the date the tenancy ends, the landlord must return the deposit (and applicable accrued interest) to the tenant, unless there have been damages to the property by the tenant. The landlord can deduct from the security deposit any amount of damages caused by the tenant through violation of the rental agreement if the landlord provides the tenant with a written notification of the nature of the damages within 30 days of the date the tenancy ends. In the case of such notification, the balance of any security deposit and interest due and an itemized statement of damages must be delivered to the tenant at his or her forwarding address within 30 days after termination of the tenancy. Should the landlord fail to observe any of these requirements and provisions, the tenant may recover up to twice the security deposit due the tenant (except if the landlord fails to deliver only the interest, in which case the tenant can recover up to twice the interest due). In addition, there is a $250 penalty for each failure of the landlord to return a security deposit plus interest due.

Security deposits can be held by the landlord for rent owed. Any person may bring an action for repossession of confiscated property or for money damages in any court of competent jurisdiction to reclaim any part of the security deposit. This does not preclude the landlord or tenant from recovering other damages.

Landlord's Rules

The landlord may adopt and enforce rules and regulations regarding a tenant's use and occupancy of the property only if such rules or regulations

- promote the convenience, safety, or welfare of the tenants; equitably distribute services to all the tenants; or protect the property from abusive use;
- are related reasonably to the purpose for which they were adopted;
- apply to all tenants equally and fairly;
- are clear enough to be understood by the tenants; and
- are made known to the tenant when he or she enters into the rental agreement or at the time a new rule or regulation is adopted.

Any new rule or regulation that substantially modifies a current tenant's agreement is invalid unless the tenant consents to it in writing.

If the rental unit is in a condominium, the condominium association has the right to change rules at any time and to bind the owner (landlord) to such new rules and fine the owner for any violations committed by the tenant. Therefore, the language of the lease should state that the "tenant shall abide by all the rules, including any that may be hereafter adopted by the condominium association."

Landlord's Right to Enter

The landlord has the right to enter the dwelling unit of a lessee to make inspections, repairs, alterations, and so on when entry is made at *reasonable times*. The landlord's entry must be made after giving the tenant *reasonable notice* and in a manner that does not constitute harassment of the tenant (such as repeated entries). Entry in the case of emergency may be made by the landlord without the tenant's consent. The landlord may also enter the unit if the tenant has surrendered or abandoned it. Either party may seek a judgment or injunctive relief if the tenant refuses to allow entry or if the landlord makes repeated, supposedly legal, entries that have the effect of harassment.

Landlord's Obligations

Landlords must provide tenants with a written notice indicating the name and address of the manager of the property and the name of the person on whom any legal process may be served. In lieu of such a notice, the person who, under the landlord's authorization, entered into the lease agreement with the tenant will be considered the manager and person on whom legal process may be served.

It is also the duty of the landlord to comply with all applicable laws and ordinances in his or her operation of the property. These duties extend but are not necessarily limited to the following:

- Adhering to applicable building and housing codes
- Keeping the property in *fit and habitable* condition (unless the property is intentionally made unfit for occupancy by the tenant, his or her family, or others on the property without the landlord's consent—in which case the repair becomes the tenant's responsibility) (Property containing defective lead-based paint is considered uninhabitable.)
- Keeping all common areas in clean and safe condition
- Maintaining in good and safe working condition all equipment supplied by the landlord, used by the tenant, and necessary to permit occupancy, including appliances, heating and ventilating equipment, sanitary facilities, and so on
- Providing and maintaining trash receptacles as needed
- Supplying heat, running water, and reasonable amounts of hot water at all times (unless the law does not require it or the unit occupied is constructed so that the tenant has a direct public utility connection and controls these amenities)

The landlord and tenant may make a good-faith written agreement that provides that the tenant perform specified maintenance or repairs, as long as the agreement does not cover or diminish the obligations of the landlord under the six items listed above.

If a landlord sells the property to another person, he or she is relieved of liabilities under the rental agreements concerning the property as soon as written notice of the new owner is sent to the tenant.

Managers of rental properties represent the landlord and are not personally liable for violations of rental agreements.

Unlawful occupancy. A certificate of occupancy is issued by the local building inspector and certifies that a structure is habitable for the purpose intended. If a landlord allows or permits a tenant to occupy a building that has not received a certificate of occupancy (where required), he or she is prohibited from recovering rent during the period of this unlawful occupancy. If the tenant voluntarily pays rent during this period, the landlord is obligated to put it in an escrow account and not withdraw it until a certificate of occupancy has been issued.

Receipt of payment of rent.   A landlord must provide a tenant with a *receipt for a cash payment*, even if no receipt is requested.

Tenant's Obligations

In using property, tenants are generally obligated to conduct themselves and to use the property in accordance with both state and local laws and ordinances and without infringing on the rights of others, particularly those occupying other portions of the same property. State law further provides that a tenant

- comply with all building, housing, or fire codes materially affecting health and safety;
- keep his or her unit as clean and safe as the general condition of the premises permits;
- remove all trash and rubbish to places and/or receptacles provided by the landlord;
- keep all plumbing fixtures and appliances as clean as the condition of such fixtures and appliances permits;
- use all equipment and appliances in a reasonable manner;
- not willfully destroy, damage, impair, or remove any part of the property or permit another person to do so;
- not disturb his or her neighbors' peaceful enjoyment of the property;
- occupy a dwelling unit only as a dwelling unit; and
- notify the landlord of anticipated extended absences from the premises.

Criminal damage.   A tenant who intentionally damages leased property (including damage due to reckless action) is considered to have committed a crime and can be criminally prosecuted. If damage to the property exceeds $1,500, the crime is criminal damage to the landlord's property in the first degree, which is a *class D felony*. If the damage exceeds $250 but is less than $1,500, the crime is criminal damage of a landlord's property in the second degree, a *misdemeanor*.

Landlord's Recourse (Remedies)

If a tenant fails to pay rent within *nine days* of the due date, the landlord may terminate the lease and evict the tenant under the procedures described later in this chapter.

With respect to breaches of the lease by the tenant that do not involve nonpayment of rent, the landlord may deliver a written notice to the tenant citing the breaches and notifying the tenant that unless these breaches are remedied, the lease will terminate in 15 days. The tenant has 15 days from the date of the notice to cure the breaches by repair or payment to the landlord. At the end of this 15-day period, if the tenant takes no action to correct the breach, the lease is effectively terminated.

Actions by the landlord.   The landlord may initiate or maintain legal actions against the tenant in a variety of different circumstances. The landlord may maintain an action to recover possession of a dwelling unit under the eviction procedure (summary process) discussed later in this chapter if the

- tenant is using the unit in an illegal manner, or in a way that is prohibited by the lease agreement;
- tenant has not paid the rent;
- landlord is making a good-faith attempt to recover possession to use the unit as his or her own home;
- tenant's guests or family, with his or her consent, have willfully damaged the property or otherwise violated his or her legal obligations; or
- landlord is seeking to recover possession after giving proper notice to terminate the tenant's periodic tenancy, especially when this notice was given to the tenant prior to any complaints made by the tenant.

Tenant's protection against retaliatory action.   Rent is determined by the rental agreement. With a month-to-month tenancy, however, a landlord can raise rent after giving the tenant one month's notice. Landlords cannot raise rent as retaliatory action, within six months after

- the tenant made a good-faith attempt to legally remedy the landlord's violations of his or her legal obligations or of any other state or local laws and ordinances;
- any municipal agency or official has filed a notice, order, or complaint regarding any violations by the landlord;
- the tenant has made a request in good faith that the landlord make needed repairs; or
- the tenant has organized or become a member of a tenants' association or union.

Raising rents would not be deemed retaliatory and will be allowed when costs due to the tenant's lack of care of the property or property taxes or other operating expenses have increased substantially at least four months before the landlord's request for the additional rent. Any increase cannot exceed each unit's pro rata share of the higher tax or cost.

Abandonment of property (and landlord's duty to mitigate damages).   In the event that a tenant abandons the property, the landlord is required to make a *reasonable effort to rent* the property to minimize the tenant's liabilities. The landlord must begin efforts as soon as he or she receives notice of the abandonment and must seek to obtain a fair market rent for it. Thus, if a tenant on a 12-month lease abandons the property after three months, the landlord cannot merely sit back and allow the overdue rent to pile up under the assumption that he or she can eventually sue the abandoning tenant for the full amount. The landlord must make a reasonable effort to rent the abandoned unit to keep the loss, the amount for which he or she could sue the previous tenant, to a minimum.

Tenant's Recourse (Remedies)

If the landlord breaches the rental agreement or fails to fulfill any of his or her legal obligations, the tenant may terminate the agreement. To terminate the lease agreement, the tenant must give the landlord 15 days from the receipt of written notice of the acts and/or omissions that provoked the breach. If the landlord has not taken any action at the end of the 15-day period, the lease is effectively terminated.

In the event that the same problem giving rise to a current breach has occurred within the previous six months (for example, a leaking ceiling) the tenant can terminate the agreement on 14 days' written notice, as long as the notice specifies the date on which the breach (the leak in this case) occurred and the date on which the tenant intends to vacate. This must still be within 30 days of the breach. Note, however, that if the breach is the result of the tenant's (or member of the tenant's family, or another person on the leased property with the tenant's consent) *willful or negligent act or omission*, he or she may not terminate the agreement by the means indicated above.

Supplying essential services.   If a landlord fails, for reasons *not* beyond his or her control, to supply such essential services as heat, water, or electricity, the tenant(s) may give notice to him or her by identifying the breach and may subsequently elect to provide for the services in the following manner:

- The tenant may provide the service at his or her own expense and then *deduct* this amount from the scheduled rental payment.
- If the lack of any services makes the occupancy of the premises impossible, the tenant may *procure substitute housing* until the services are restored. Note that the landlord must be given two days to remedy the breach before this alternative may be used. If the same breach has occurred within the previous six months, the two-day period is eliminated and substitute housing may be procured immediately. Under this alternative, the tenant is not liable for rent and may recover any costs exceeding the regular rent, if the substitute housing is more expensive.
- If the failure was willful, the tenant can *terminate* the rental agreement as described above and recover an amount equal to the greater of two months' rent or twice actual damages.

In all the cases above, the tenant may recover reasonable attorney's fees if incurred in defense of an action relating to the landlord's failure to provide essential services. Prepaid rent, security deposits, and interest are recoverable under any of the above actions, in addition to other damages.

Damage or destruction of property.   If property is damaged or destroyed so that the tenant can no longer occupy or enjoy occupancy of the unit, and the damage is the result of the landlord's willful act or negligence, the tenant is *not liable to pay rent*. At the option of the tenant, he or she may vacate the premises and notify the landlord of intention to terminate the lease agreement within 15 days. In this case, the landlord must return all prepaid rent and security deposits to the tenant. The tenant's other alternative is to adjust his or her rental payment to reflect the reduction in fair market rental value caused by damage to the premises.

Action to enforce landlord's responsibilities.   If a landlord has failed to perform any of his or her legal duties, a tenant may institute an action in superior court to enforce those responsibilities. The court may grant the following types of relief:

- Order the landlord to comply with his duties
- Appoint a receiver to collect rent and correct defective conditions
- Stop other proceedings concerning the property
- Award the tenant money damages, which may include a retroactive abatement of rent
- Other appropriate relief

After a tenant has filed such an action, he or she pays the court all rent when due.

SUMMARY PROCESS (ACTUAL EVICTION)

Suits to recover possession of property that is illegally occupied by a tenant due to termination of a lease, violation of its terms, nonpayment of rent, and so on, generally fall under the provisions of *summary process*. Summary process is usually equated with actual eviction proceedings. This section will provide you with a discussion of the basic elements of Connecticut's laws regarding summary process. Because the legal nature of summary process is so complex and could change over time, you are advised to consult the statutes and competent legal advice whenever you have a question about it.

Notice to Quit Possession

The first step in a residential eviction is the service of a Notice to Quit. This is a *written notice* given by the landlord to the tenant calling for the tenant to quit possession. The landlord must have a valid reason to ask the tenant to quit possession, such as nonpayment of rent or violation of the rental agreement. Service of this Notice to Quit has the effect of terminating the tenant's right to occupy the property.

If a tenant or a person occupying property uses the property illegally (for example, as a betting parlor or in violation of vice laws), this automatically serves to void any lease that might be in effect and precludes the necessity for the landlord to provide a notice to quit possession.

Court Action

If the tenant does not leave after the time to quit possession has passed, the landlord can *file a complaint* in Superior Court for immediate possession. If the tenant fails to appear in court, the court will file a judgment and award the landlord possession and his or her court costs. If the tenant appears in court, a hearing is conducted, and the court will order the tenant to deposit with the court an amount equal to the fair market rental value of the property for the court proceeding period. The court will then make a determination as to possession of the property.

Appeals

The court requires that tenants making appeals in an eviction action *post a bond for all rents* accrued and those that will become due during the appeal. If there is no lease in effect that identifies the rental amount, the bond will be based on fair market rental value.

Appeals must be made within five business days after court judgment is rendered. As long as the court does not feel that the appeal is being made solely to delay execution, it will accept the application for appeal, and the execution of the judgment (eviction) will be *stayed*, or put off.

Stay of Execution

Unless the landlord is evicting the tenant for nonpayment of rent, nuisance, the use of the property for immoral or illegal purposes, or no initial right to occupy the property, there will be a five-day stay of execution. In addition to this stay of execution, a tenant may, upon application to court, be granted additional time to vacate the premises if the court finds the reasons valid and acceptable and his or her application for this additional time is made before the expiration of the basic five-day period.

Ejection and the Removal and Sale of Personal Effects

On the expiration of any stay(s) of execution or the date on which a judgment is permitted to be executed, the tenant/occupant/defendant must remove himself or herself and all belongings from the property. If the tenant does not do this, the landlord may request an execution of the summary process judgment and have the tenant's goods and belongings removed by a state marshal and placed on the adjacent sidewalk, street, or highway.

The state marshal must make a reasonable effort to locate the tenant and inform him or her of the action to be taken and of the possibility of a sale of the belongings if they are not claimed within 10 days.

If the tenant does not claim the goods removed from the property immediately, they will be removed and stored for a period of 15 days. The storage expense will be borne by the tenant. Assuming no claim is made, the property will be sold at public auction. Once the sale has occurred, the tenant may claim the proceeds (less expenses) within 30 days. After 30 days, all the proceeds are turned over to the town treasury.

Actions of Summary Process by Other Parties

Landlords are not the only parties who may bring actions of summary process to recover possession. Assignees, mortgagees, and reversioners/remaindermen are also permitted by the statutes to bring such actions. The selectmen of a town owning property may also initiate and maintain actions against tenants occupying the town's property in the same manner as illustrated for landlords.

Eviction of Elderly, Blind, or Disabled

Landlords are *prohibited* from evicting these protected classes from five-or-more-unit dwellings *except* for nonpayment of rent, refusal to pay a fair and equitable rent increase, noncompliance with adopted rules and regulations, voiding of the rental agreement, permanent removal from the dwelling, or landlord's bona fide intention to use that unit as his or her own principal residence. This law also covers those tenants who have as permanent residents in their household a spouse, sibling, parent, or grandparent over 62 years of age, as well as a member of the family who is blind or physically disabled.

■ FAIR RENT COMMISSION

Municipalities where renter-occupied dwellings exceed 5,000 units are required to have a fair rent commission unless a municipality voted against it. Two or more towns not subject to this requirement can form a joint fair rent commission.

The fair rent commission regulates and eliminates excessive charges for residential rental property. Other housing problems are also considered by the commission. It is a forum for both tenants and landlords.

The commission cannot accept complaints from any tenant who owes back rent or who currently is being evicted by a landlord. The tenant is required to pay the "last agreed-on rent" on time each and every month pending the results of the hearing. As a result of a formal hearing, the commission's decision may require that the tenant pay any rent increase retroactive to its effective date.

■ NONRESIDENT LANDLORD REGISTRATION

Connecticut municipalities are allowed to pass laws requiring *absentee landlords* to register their residential addresses with the city or town that houses their rental property. An *absentee landlord* is a landlord who does not reside on the property. The registration is intended to provide a current physical address in the event the landlord must be contacted. If an owner landlord does not register his or her address if required, then the address the municipal property tax bill is sent to will be considered the landlord's address, or if the landlord is a legal entity, then the address of the agent in charge of the building will be considered the landlord's address.

■ WEB LINKS

Connecticut General Statutes Chapter 830 (Rights and Responsibilities of
   Landlords and Tenants):   *www.cga.ct.gov/2009/pub/Chap830.htm*

Connecticut Department of Banking (choose Landlord/Tenant for regulatory
   information on security deposits and current-year security deposit interest
   rates):   *www.ct.gov/dob*

Connecticut Law about Landlord/Tenant Law (Connecticut Law Library,
   includes landlord's and tenant's guide to summary process eviction):
   www.jud.state.ct.us/LawLib/Law/landlord.htm

Apartment Owners Association of Connecticut (information for landlords):
   http://aoact.wordpress.com/

Fair Rent Commission Information (including list of Connecticut towns
   that have a fair rent commission; Legal Assistance Resource Center of
   Connecticut):   *www.larcc.org/pamphlets/housing/tr_fair_rent.htm*

FIGURE 12.1

Residential Lease

Residential Lease

1. Date of Lease; Parties

This Lease is made on _____ , 20__ , between _____ ,
Landlord, and _____ and _____ , Tenant(s).
The parties shall be referred to as "Landlord" and "Tenant" in the remaining provisions of this Lease.

2. House or Apartment Leased

Landlord hereby leases to Tenant the apartment or house and grounds located at _____
_____ , Connecticut 06____ referred to in this Lease as "the Premises."

3. Term of Lease

The term of this Lease is one year. It begins on _____ , 20__ and ends on __
_____ , 20__ at 11:59 p.m.

4. Rent; Time and Manner of Payment of Rent

The total rent for the term of this Lease is $_____.   The rent must be paid in equal
monthly installments of $_____ the first day of each month of the term of the Lease. Tenant
has paid the sum of $_____ , receipt of which is acknowledged, as a deposit in order to hold the
house open for rental. Tenant shall pay the additional sum of $_____ as an
additional deposit upon the execution of this Lease. The deposit sums shall be non-refundable except that
the deposit shall be applied to the first monthly installment of rent.

5. Use of Premises

The Premises must be used and occupied only and solely as a private dwelling for Tenant and Tenant's
immediate family, to live in. It may not be used for any other purpose. Any full-time occupancy by any other
party is prohibited unless Landlord consents in writing, which consent shall not be unreasonably withheld.

Tenant will not store any unregistered automobiles, motorized contrivances, building materials, hazardous
materials, or other personal property on or upon the outside grounds of the Premises.

Tenant may keep _____ as pet(s) on the Premises and outside grounds.
Tenant shall keep the pets healthy and well groomed. Tenant shall also keep the Premises and outside
grounds free from animal waste, litter and other noxious or unhealthy animal byproducts.

6. Condition of Premises

It is understood that Tenant will take possession of the Premises in its present condition.

Any appliances located in the Premises on the date of this Lease are furnished solely for the convenience of
Tenant and are not a part of this Lease. Tenant shall perform, at Tenant's sole expense, any maintenance
required on the appliances.

☐ *(Applicable if checked)* Tenant shall keep the outside driveways and walkways free from snow and
ice and accumulations of litter and debris and shall mow the lawn when necessary to maintain a neat
appearance to the outside grounds.

©2002-2010 Connecticut Association of Realtors® Inc.
Revised October 4, 2010

Page 1 of 4

FIGURE 12.1 (continued)

Residential Lease

Tenant acknowledges that there are smoke detectors present at the Premises. Tenant will not do any act which serves to disable or damage the smoke detectors. In the event that a smoke detector malfunctions, Tenant will promptly notify Landlord of the malfunction.

7. Requirements of Law

Tenant is to comply with all the sanitary laws, ordinances and rules, and all orders of the local department of health or health district or other authorities, including zoning authorities, affecting the cleanliness, occupancy, use and preservation of the Premises and the sidewalks to the Premises during the term of the Lease.

8. Access to Premises

Tenant agrees that Landlord, Landlord's agents, servants and contractors shall have the right to enter into and upon the Premises, or any part thereof, at all reasonable hours for the purpose of examining same, or making emergency repairs or alterations as may be necessary for the safety and preservation thereof.

9. Fuel, Heat, Gas, Electricity, Telephone and other Utilities

Tenant shall pay all charges for the following:

☐ fuel (including fireplace wood, propane, oil, and gas) needed to heat the Premises

☐ hot water ☐ electricity

☐ cable television ☐ municipal water

☐ telephone ☐ other (specify) _____

☐ snow removal ☐ lawn care including mowing

☐ *(Applicable if checked)* Tenant shall light and maintain the furnace which heats the Premises including cleaning

10. Damage by Fire or Other Casualty

If the Premises, or any part thereof, shall be slightly damaged by fire or other casualty during said term, the Premises shall be promptly repaired by Landlord and an abatement will be made for the rent corresponding with the time during which and the extent to which said Premises may have been untenantable, but if the building should be so damaged that Landlord shall decide to rebuild, the term of this Lease shall cease and the rent be paid up to the time of the fire or other casualty.

11. Alterations by Tenant

Tenant shall not make any alterations, additions, or improvements to the Premises without the written consent of Landlord. The kinds of alterations, additions or improvements referred to are those which are of a more or less permanent nature, such as new floors, partitions, wallpaper and paneling. If consent of Landlord is given, then any or all such alterations, additions or improvements, may, if Landlord wishes, become the property of Landlord at the end of the term of the Lease. However, if Landlord wishes, Landlord may require Tenant to remove any or all of such alterations, additions or improvements at the end of the term of the Lease and restore the Premises to the condition it was in when the term of this Lease began.

12. Liability of Landlord; Reimbursement by Tenant; Insurance

If Landlord must pay any damages for a claim arising from the fault of Tenant, then Tenant must reimburse Landlord for any such sums paid. In addition, Tenant must reimburse Landlord for any expense Landlord

FIGURE 12.1 (continued)

Residential Lease

incurred in defending against such claim, whether or not Landlord has to pay any damages.

During the term of this Lease, Tenant, at its expense, shall carry public liability insurance not less than the following limits: Bodily injury - $_____,000; property damage - $_____,000. Tenant agrees to furnish Landlord, prior to occupancy, with a certificate of insurance evidencing that Tenant has secured the insurance required by this paragraph and that Landlord is named as an additional insured or loss payee of such insurance. Tenant also agrees to insure his/her own personal property located in the Premises.

13. Assignment and Sublease

This Lease may not be assigned, nor may the Premises be sublet, without the advance written consent of Landlord. Such consent shall not be unreasonably withheld. Any such assignment or sublease does not relieve Tenant of any of Tenant's obligations or liability under this Lease. The subtenant shall be bound by and subject to all the terms of this Lease.

14. Quiet Enjoyment by Tenant

As long as Tenant pays the rent and is not in default on any of the conditions of this Lease, Tenant shall peaceably and quietly have, hold and enjoy the Premises during the term of the Lease.

15. Warranty of Habitability

Landlord represents and states that the Premises and all areas used in connection with it are fit for human life and for the use reasonably intended by the parties and there are no conditions dangerous, hazardous or detrimental to life, health and safety.

16. Security

In addition to the sums set forth above, Tenant, prior to occupancy, shall deposit with Landlord the sum of _____ Dollars as security for the performance of Tenant's obligations under the Lease. Landlord shall hold such sum or deposit the same in a bank as may be required by law. Under the law, Tenant may be entitled to interest on such security deposit. If such is the case, interest will be paid to Tenant minus the sum Landlord is permitted to keep under the law.

If Tenant fails to make any payments of rent or defaults under any other obligations of this Lease, Landlord may use the security in payment of such rent or in payment of any sums Landlord may be forced to spend because of Tenant's default. If Landlord does so use the security, then he shall notify Tenant in writing of the amount so used, and Tenant shall immediately forward a like amount to Landlord. There shall always be deposited with Landlord a sum not less than the amount originally deposited as security.

If at the end of the term of the Lease Tenant has made all payments of rent required and fully complied with all the other obligations under the Lease, then Landlord shall return the security to him together with any interest that may be required by law.

17. Waiver by Landlord or Tenant Limited

If either Landlord or Tenant waives or fails to enforce any of their rights under the Lease, this does not mean that any other rights under the Lease are waived. Further, if Landlord or Tenant waives or fails to enforce any of their rights under a specific paragraph of the Lease, such waiver or failure to enforce such rights is

Residential Lease

limited to the specific instance in question and is not a waiver of any later breaches of such paragraph.

18. Invalidity or Illegality of Part of Lease

If any part of this Lease is invalid or illegal, then only that part shall be void and have no effect. All other parts of the Lease shall remain in full force and effect.

19. Modification or Change of Lease

The only way in which any of the provisions of this Lease can be changed or modified is by a written agreement signed by both parties.

20. Persons Bound by Lease

It is the intent of the parties that this Lease shall be binding upon Landlord and Tenant and upon any parties who may in the future succeed to their interests.

21. Surrender of Premises

At the expiration of the term of this Lease, Tenant will surrender the Premises in as good a state and condition as they were in when the term began, reasonable use and wear thereof accepted.

22. Captions for Paragraphs of Lease; Use of Form

The captions of the various paragraphs of this Lease are for convenience and reference purposes only. They are of no other effect. The parties acknowledge, agree and understand that this form has been furnished by the Connecticut Association of REALTORS®, Inc. for the sole use of its members and assumes no responsibility for its use or content and is not a party to this Lease.

23. Purchase by Tenant; Listing Agreement Amendment

☐ *(Applicable if checked)* The parties recognize as the listing real estate broker and as the cooperating real estate broker _____. Landlord agrees that the listing agreement dated for the rental of the Premises is hereby amended to provide that in the event this Tenant purchases the Premises during the term of this Lease or within days after the termination of this Lease, the Landlord will pay compensation to the listing real estate broker calculated as follows _____and the term of the listing shall be extended to days after the term of this Lease.

_____   _____
Landlord   Landlord

_____   _____
Tenant   Tenant

CHAPTER 12 QUIZ

1. With respect to leases for terms in excess of one year, the landlord may record, instead of the actual lease, a
   a. lis pendens.
   b. rent supplement notice.
   c. notice of constructive occupancy.
   d. notice of lease.

2. In Connecticut when there is no agreement on the part of the landlord and tenant as to the term or expiration date of the tenancy, the tenancy is construed to be
   a. ad limbonium.
   b. month-to-month.
   c. constructive occupancy.
   d. illegal.

3. Two roommates have an agreement to lease a unit in an apartment complex. There is a provision in the lease to waive their rights to the interest earned from the security deposit. This provision is
   a. unenforceable, thus making the lease invalid.
   b. unenforceable, but the lease is still valid.
   c. enforceable because all parties agreed to it.
   d. enforceable only for the term of the lease.

4. Rules and regulations for tenants of leased property must be presented initially to the tenants by the landlord at the time
   a. the tenant first violates them.
   b. the tenant requests such.
   c. during the rental agreement.
   d. the tenant enters into the rental agreement or at the time the rules or regulations are adopted.

5. Through the landlord's negligence and inaction, the heat in an apartment complex is shut off, and a tenant moves into a furnished apartment until repairs are completed. The most the tenant can recover for the cost of this substitute housing is
   a. its actual cost plus regular rent.
   b. the excess of its cost over regular rent.
   c. nothing.
   d. an amount up to, but not over, the regular rent.

6. The landlord may terminate the rental agreement if a tenant fails to pay rent within how many days of the scheduled due date?
   a. 7 days
   b. 9 days
   c. 10 days
   d. 30 days

7. A landlord cannot retaliate against a month-to-month tenant requesting needed repairs by raising rent within _____ of the request?
   a. One month
   b. Four months
   c. Six months
   d. Zero time

8. A woman leased a condominium and put down a two-month security deposit. What percentage of interest does her security deposit earn as long as she does not pay her rent late?
   a. 2%
   b. 4%
   c. 5¼%
   d. Percent that is tied to the average savings deposit rate

9. If a monthly rental payment is made more than ten days after the due date, how much must the tenant forfeit on his or her security deposit?
   a. One month's interest
   b. The whole year's interest
   c. No interest
   d. One-half the interest

10. A tenant skips out on his last scheduled monthly payment on a one-year lease. The landlord may
    a. keep the tenant's belongings.
    b. sue the tenant for the back rent.
    c. do nothing because the lease is terminated.
    d. extend the lease automatically because the tenant gave no notice.

11. If an evicted tenant does not move his or her belongings, under summary process the belongings of the evicted tenant may be
    a. used by the landlord.
    b. sold by the landlord.
    c. placed on the street by the marshal.
    d. brought to the town dump.

12. If no one claims the proceeds of sale resulting from the sale at public auction of the belongings of an evicted tenant within 30 days from such sale, these proceeds are turned over to the
    a. landlord in order to offset the judgment.
    b. sheriff who executed the eviction.
    c. town treasury.
    d. state's general fund.

13. Which statement below about security deposits is *FALSE*?
    a. Security deposits are required for residential units.
    b. Landlords must pay tenants interest on their security deposits.
    c. At the end of the lease, the landlord can apply the security deposit to rent owed by the tenant.
    d. Unless there have been damages, the landlord must return the security deposit to the tenant within 30 days of the end of the lease.

14. In a fit of rage, a tenant intentionally punches a wall, causing approximately $500 in damage to the leased property. The tenant may
    a. be arrested because the tenant committed a crime.
    b. lose his or her entire security deposit of $1,000.
    c. be subject to a rent increase to cover the damage.
    d. abandon the property because it is no longer fit for living.

Real Estate Appraisal

■ OVERVIEW

3 types in Ct

Connecticut requires that real estate appraisers be licensed. There are three categories of licensure: certified general appraiser (all property types), certified residential appraiser (residential property), and provisional appraiser (in training).

The Connecticut law governing the licensing and conduct of real estate appraisers can be found at Title 20, Chapter 400g of the Connecticut General Statutes and its associated regulations.

■ CONNECTICUT REAL ESTATE APPRAISAL COMMISSION

The Connecticut Real Estate Appraisal Commission administers the Connecticut appraisal licensing laws and oversees the approval of state appraisal education schools and courses. The Appraisal Commission is a part of the state Department of Consumer Protection.

8 member Governor

The Commission consists of *eight members* appointed by the Governor. Five of these members must be either certified general appraisers or certified residential appraisers, and three are public members. No more than a bare majority can be members of the same political party, and there must be at least one member from each congressional district. A majority of its members constitutes a quorum.

State E-mail Notification Registry

The Connecticut Department of Consumer Protection maintains an e-mail list. Licensed appraisers can register their e-mail address on this list to receive important notifications of state appraisal licensing related issues.

■ WHO MUST BE LICENSED

[handwritten: Real Estate Appraiser / Provisional]

Any person who acts as a real estate appraiser or provisional appraiser or who engages in the real estate appraisal business must have the appropriate license. *Engaging in the real estate appraisal business* is defined as *the act or process of estimating the value of real estate for a fee or other valuable consideration.*

Any person who engages in the real estate appraisal business (or holds himself or herself out as an appraiser) without a license can be fined up to $1,000 and/or be imprisoned up to six months.

Exemption

[handwritten: Mandatory Appraisal State 1-4 unit]

The following persons are exempted from the licensing requirements:

- Any person under contract with the municipality to perform a revaluation of real estate for tax assessment purposes.
- Any licensed real estate broker or real estate salesperson estimating the value of real estate as part of a market analysis; this value estimate must
  — be for the purpose of a prospective listing or sale of the real estate, providing information to the owner under a listing agreement, or providing information to a prospective buyer or tenant under a buyer or tenant agency agreement; and
  — not be referred to or construed to be an appraisal.
  — For 1–4-unit residences, if the owner enters into a listing with the broker or salesperson, any fee paid for the value estimate must be credited against compensation owed under the listing.

Connecticut is a mandatory appraisal state. This means that exemptions to licensing requirements pursuant to FDIC regulations are not recognized in Connecticut. (CGS Section 20-526)

■ LICENSE CATEGORIES

The appraisal law establishes the categories of appraisal license listed below. No appraiser is permitted to perform appraisal work that is beyond the scope of practice for his or her license category.

Certified General Appraiser

A certified general appraiser is allowed to appraise *all types* of real estate.

Certified Residential Appraiser

A certified residential appraiser is allowed to appraise *residential* real estate.

Residential real estate is defined as property improved with 1–4-unit residential structures and vacant or unimproved land where the highest and best use analysis is for 1–4-unit residential purposes. This does not include land where a development analysis/appraisal, such as a subdivision development analysis or condominium development analysis, is necessary or utilized.

Provisional Licensed Appraiser

[handwritten: Entry Level 4 yrs]

The purpose of this category is to provide an *entry level* that will allow appraisers to develop the appraisal experience needed to qualify for a category of certified or licensed appraiser. A person can be a provisional licensed appraiser for only four years. *[handwritten: Less Expensive]*

A provisional licensed appraiser is allowed to appraise real estate while under the direct supervision of a certified appraiser or licensed appraiser, for the types of property and in the types of transactions the *supervising appraiser* is permitted to appraise. A supervising appraiser can only sponsor up to three provisional appraisers, unless the supervising appraiser obtains a waiver of this limit by the Real Estate Appraisal Commission. *[handwritten: Supervisor 3 only]*

■ OBTAINING A LICENSE

[handwritten: 75 Percent 24 month]

To obtain a real estate license, there are *education*, *experience*, and *examination* requirements. These license requirements are summarized in Figure 13.1.

All applications for licenses must be in writing on forms prescribed by the Department of Consumer Protection. A written examination is required to obtain a certified license; to pass the exam an applicant must obtain a score of at least 75 percent. A passed exam is good toward the licensing requirement for 24 months.

Education

Note that the education requirements for all categories of appraisal licensing have recently changed, with requirements for certified general and certified residential appraisers changing significantly. Reported in this text are the requirements that are effective January 1, 2008.

Provisional appraiser. To qualify as a provisional appraiser, a person must have 75 hours of approved appraisal coursework, including 30 classroom hours of basic appraisal principles, 30 hours of basic appraisal procedures, and 15 hours of *Uniform Standards of Professional Appraisal Practice (USPAP)*, discussed below in Appraisal Standards. The *USPAP* course is only good for six years prior to the date of the application.

Certified general appraiser.   To qualify as a certified general appraiser, a person must meet requirements *1 and 2* below.

1. *300 classroom hours* of study in the following *required core curriculum* areas as follows:

    (A)   Basic Appraisal Principles (30 hours)
    (B)   Basic Appraisal Procedures (30 hours)
    (C)   The 15-hour National USPAP Course or its equivalent (15 hours)
    (D)   General Appraisal Market Analysis and Highest and Best Use (30 hours)
    (E)   Statistics, Modeling, and Finance (15 hours)
    (F)   General Appraiser Sales Comparison Approach (30 hours)
    (G)   General Appraiser Site Valuation and Cost Approach (30 hours)
    (H)   General Appraiser Income Approach (60 hours)
    (I)   General Appraiser Report Writing and Case Studies (30 hours)
    (J)   Appraisal Subject Matter Electives (30 hours)

2. A *bachelor's degree* from an accredited college
    or
    30 semester hours of in the following college-level courses (3 hours each):

    ■ English composition
    ■ Macroeconomics
    ■ Microeconomics
    ■ Finance
    ■ Algebra, geometry, or higher level mathematics
    ■ Statistics
    ■ Computers (introductory level course), including word processing and spreadsheets
    ■ Business law or real estate law
    ■ Two (2) elective courses in any of the following subject matters: accounting, geography, ag-economics, business management, or real estate

Certified residential appraiser.   To qualify as a certified residential appraiser, a person must meet requirements *1 and 2* in the following.

1. *200 classroom hours* of study in the following *required core curriculum* areas as follows:

    (A)   Basic Appraisal Principles (30 hours)
    (B)   Basic Appraisal Procedures (30 hours)
    (C)   The 15-hour National USPAP Course or its equivalent (15 hours)
    (D)   Residential Market Analysis and Highest and Best Use (15 hours)
    (E)   Residential Appraiser Site Valuation and Cost Approach (15 hours)
    (F)   Residential Sales Comparison and Income Approaches (30 hours)
    (G)   Residential Report Writing and Case Studies (15 hours)
    (H)   Statistics, Modeling, and Finance (15 hours)
    (I)   Advanced Residential Applications and Case Studies (15 hours)
    (J)   Appraisal Subject Matter Electives (20 hours)

2.   A minimum of an *associate's degree* from an accredited college
or
21 semester hours of in the following college-level courses (3 hours each):

- English composition
- Principles of economics, either macroeconomics or microeconomics
- Finance
- Algebra, geometry, or higher level mathematics
- Statistics
- Computers (introductory level course), including word processing and spreadsheets
- Business law or real estate law

Qualifying Experience

A provisional appraiser does not require any previous experience to qualify for a license. A state-certified general or residential appraiser requires numerous hours of real estate appraisal experience. Appraisal experience includes performing fee and staff appraisals, ad valorem tax appraisals, mass appraisals, review appraisals, appraisal analyses, and feasibility analyses or studies, and teaching appraisal.

To obtain this experience, an appraiser must work under the supervision of a licensed appraiser as a *provisional licensed appraiser*. Experience is documented in the form of an *appraisal log*. In addition, reports and file memorandum need to be available to support the experience claimed.

The *supervising appraiser* must be responsible for the direct supervision of a provisional licensed appraiser. This means that the supervising appraiser must

- accept responsibility for the appraisal work performed (and indicate so in any written appraisal report by signing and certifying the report is in compliance with USPAP);
- review the provisional licensed appraiser's reports; and
- personally inspect each appraised property with the provisional licensed appraiser until a reasonable appraiser would judge the provisional licensed appraiser to be competent in accordance with the competency provision of USPAP.

See Figure 13.1 for a brief summary of Connecticut appraisal certification and licensing requirements.

■ FEDERAL REGISTRY

The Appraisal Subcommittee of the Federal Financial Institutions Examination Council requires that each state submit a roster of licensed appraisers to it along with an annual registry fee of $25 from each appraiser.

LICENSE RENEWAL

Appraisal licenses expire on April 30 of each year. Appraisers must apply each year for renewal of their certifications or licenses. Renewal fees for each category are listed in Figure 13.1.

Continuing Education

In every even-numbered year, appraisers must submit proof of compliance with continuing education requirements with their renewal applications (28 hours, including specific topics). Only continuing education courses approved by the Appraisal Commission qualify. See Figure 13.1 for a list of requirements.

[handwritten margin note: 28 hours Every other yr]

APPRAISAL STANDARDS

An appraiser is required to follow the *Uniform Standards of Professional Appraisal Practice (USPAP)* adopted by the Appraisal Standards Review Board of the Appraisal Foundation that are in effect at the time the services are performed. Copies of *USPAP* are available upon request from the Appraisal Commission.

An appraiser who wishes to enter in or on any real estate not the subject of appraisal to conduct a market comparison must obtain permission from the owner or occupier of the real estate and must identify himself or herself as an appraiser.

Every appraisal, review appraisal, or consulting report must contain the following (for each appraiser signing the report):

- The appraiser's name, either printed or typed
- The category of license held and license number
- The state of issuance
- The expiration date of the license

APPRAISERS LICENSED IN ANOTHER STATE

A person licensed as an appraiser in another state may become an appraiser in Connecticut by meeting all the requirements for a category of license as described above. The Connecticut Appraisal Commission has developed some *reciprocity agreements* with other states so that an appraiser from another state who holds a valid certification or license from that other state can obtain the same level of licensure in Connecticut without going through the full qualifying process. This arrangement also allows an appraiser from Connecticut to more easily obtain an out-of-state appraisal license from a reciprocal state. Information about specific state reciprocity can be obtained through the Appraisal Commission.

[handwritten margin note: CT 6 months]

Connecticut has a *temporary* license that allows nonresident appraisers to conduct appraisal work on a temporary basis within the state. The nonresident appraiser must hold a valid certification or license from another state and submit an application to the Commission with a fee. Temporary licensure is effective for six months

FIGURE 13.1

Connecticut Real Estate Appraisal Certification/Licensing Requirements Summary— New Fees Effective October 1, 2009

Category	Qualified for Appraisal Of	Minimum Requirements		
		Education	Experience	Testing
Certified General Appraiser	All property types for all types of transactions (1)	300 hours of Required Core Curriculum including 15 hours *USPAP* Bachelor's degree or 30 semester hours of specific college course work (2) (3)	3,000 hours over at least 30 months with 50% minimum spent on appraising income properties	General Appraiser Examination (7)
Certified Residential Appraiser	All 1–4-family properties for all types of transactions (1)	200 hours of Required Core Curriculum including 15 hours *USPAP* Associate's degree or 21 semester hours of specific college course work (2) (3)	2,500 hours over at least 2 years	Residential Appraiser Examination (7)
Provisional Appraiser	Must be under supervision of licensed appraiser Practice limited to the types of properties and transactions for which supervising appraiser is qualified (4)	75 hours including 30 hours of basic appraisal principles 30 hours of basic appraisal procedures 15 hours of *USPAP* in past six years (2) (3)	None, but time spent as a provisional licensed appraiser is limited to 4 years	None

(1) Shall not sponsor more than three provisional appraisers unless by waiver of the Connecticut Real Estate Appraisal Commission.

(2) Courses must be a minimum of 15 hours including an examination. No time limit on education, except *USPAP: Principles and Practices of Real Estate* taken after 9/1/00 does not qualify for prelicensing or license upgrade.

(3) The 15-hour *USPAP* course with exam must have been successfully completed within the six-year period preceding the date of application.

(4) May have more than one sponsor.

(5) Continuing education offerings must be at least two hours in length.

(6) Submission for continuing education credit is in even-numbered years.

from issuance and applies to one appraisal assignment, which must be specified in the application. If the appraiser is unable to complete the assignment in six months, the appraiser may request an extension.

Nonresident appraisal *reviewers* who are performing an appraisal review on Connecticut real estate do not need to be licensed in Connecticut (permanent or temporary) as long as the reviewer is not conducting any fieldwork in Connecticut. *Appraisal review* is defined as "the act or process of developing and communicating an opinion about the quality of another appraiser's work."

FIGURE 13.1 (continued)

Connecticut Real Estate Appraisal Certification/Licensing Requirements Summary—New Fees Effective October 1, 2009

Continuing Education	Fees				
	Application	Testing	Initial Year	Renewal	Continuing Education
28 hours every 2 years, including 3 hours on appraisal legislation, *USPAP*, and 7 hours national *USPAP* (5) (6) (10)	$45 *90*	$65 (7)	$375 plus $25 annual registry fee (9)	$285 plus $25 annual registry fee	$16
28 hours every 2 years, including 3 hours on appraisal legislation, *USPAP* (8) and equal opportunity laws, and 7 hours national *USPAP* (5) (6) (10)	$45 *90*	$65 (7)	$375 plus $25 annual registry fee (9)	$285 plus $25 annual registry fee	$16
28 hours every 2 years, including 3 hours on appraisal legislation, *USPAP* and equal opportunity laws, and 7 hours national *USPAP* (5) (6) (8) (10)	$40 *80*	N/A	$100	$100	$16

(7) The applicant may take exam up to four times in a one-year period.
(8) No continuing education requirement for first renewal of provisional license.
(9) Initial (first license only) license fee is prorated on a quarterly basis.
(10) Effective January 1, 2003, the 7-hour national *USPAP* course must be taken every two years and taught by an Appraisal Qualifications Board (AQB) Certified Instructor.
NOTE: This figure is a summary intended to give an overview. For specific questions consult statutes and regulations.

◼ APPRAISAL MANAGEMENT COMPANIES

Appraisal management companies must register with the Connecticut Department of Consumer Protection before doing business in Connecticut. Appraisal management companies are required to annually certify that they maintain detailed records of each appraisal request or order they receive and of the appraiser who performs each appraisal. Companies are required to pay appraisers within 60 days of completing an appraisal report and are prohibited from attempting to influence an appraiser to misstate or misrepresent a property's value.

■ WEB LINKS

Connecticut General Statues Chapter 400g (Real Estate Appraisers): *www.cga.ct.gov/2009/pub/Chap400g.htm*

Connecticut Department of Consumer Protection (Regulations, License Information, and Applications): *www.ct.gov/dcp*

Connecticut Department of Consumer Protection E-mail Notification Registry (to receive notification of licensing issues): *www.das.state.ct.us/dcp/list/*

State Licensing Database (searchable database of state licensed appraisers): *www.ct-clic.com*

Appraisal Foundation and USPAP Standards (click USPAP): *www.appraisalfoundation.org*

National Appraisal Registry (searchable database of licensed appraisers in all states): *www.asc.gov.*

CHAPTER 13 QUIZ

1. A real estate appraisal license is required to _____ real estate for a _____.
   a. broker/commission
   b. value/fee
   c. sell/determined price
   d. assist in buying/value

2. All certified residential appraisers can appraise
   a. any property in Connecticut.
   b. a three-family house in Connecticut.
   c. a strip shopping center in Connecticut.
   d. a six-unit apartment complex in Connecticut.

3. A licensed real estate salesperson is exempt from the appraisal licensing requirements when the salesperson
   a. has taken an appraisal course.
   b. does not charge a fee.
   c. performs what are referred to as *appraisal services* for real estate clients only.
   d. estimates the value of real estate as part of a market analysis conducted for a prospective seller.

4. A provisional license
   a. lasts for only four years.
   b. is renewable in four years.
   c. automatically renews for four years.
   d. can be reinstated every four years.

5. A supervising appraiser can sponsor _____ provisional appraiser(s).
   a. one
   b. three
   c. ten
   d. an unlimited number of

6. An appraiser is required to follow *USPAP,* the
   a. *United States Principles of Appraisal Practice.*
   b. *United States Appraisal Principles and Practices.*
   c. *Uniform Standards of Professional Appraisal Practice.*
   d. *Uniform Standards of Practical Appraisal Principals.*

7. To qualify as a certified general appraiser, a person must meet how many hours of experience?
   a. 3,000
   b. 2,500
   c. 2,000
   d. 0

8. What are the requirements to qualify as a provisional licensed appraiser?
   a. 75 hours of education, four years of experience, and an exam
   b. 75 hours of education, no experience, and an exam
   c. 75 hours of education, no experience, and no exam
   d. 30 hours of education, no experience, and no exam

9. A certified or licensed general or residential appraiser must take how many hours of continuing education every two years?
   a. 12
   b. 15
   c. 20
   d. 28

10. A person may obtain a temporary license to conduct real estate appraisals in Connecticut if
    a. the property to be valued is less than $100,000.
    b. the person holds a valid Connecticut real estate broker or salesperson's license.
    c. the person holds a valid appraisal license in another state.
    d. the person applies for one.

14 CHAPTER

Land-Use Controls and Property Development

■ OVERVIEW

Land use and development are regulated by both the state and municipality. The numerous state laws include environmental regulations, affordable housing initiatives, building accessibility and safety standards, and interstate land sales registration. All cities and towns have enacted zoning regulations, which dictate the use that can be made of land within its borders. Zoning regulations vary significantly between municipalities and also have a significant impact on what property owners can and cannot do with their property. Municipalities also have subdivision and inland wetland regulations.

In terms of residential *construction*, new home contractors and home improvement contractors are required to be registered with the state. There is both a New Home Construction Guaranty Fund and a Home Improvement Guaranty Fund from which a consumer can seek reimbursement for uncollectible damages. In terms of commercial construction, private contracts for building, renovating, or rehabilitating commercial or industrial buildings must contain payment schedule provisions.

■ PLANNING AND ZONING

Connecticut state law authorizes municipalities to enact planning and zoning regulations. *Planning* has to do with determining a plan of development for the town. *Zoning* divides the town into various zones and dictates the type of land use that can occur in each zone. To accomplish these activities, towns are authorized to form and operate local planning and zoning commissions (which can operate as two separate commissions or a combined commission).

Zoning

A local zoning commission is a legislative body, separate from and not controlled by the town government. (In towns of under 5,000 population and some of the larger cities, however, the town council members can act as the zoning commission.) Depending on local ordinance, the members of the zoning commission may be elected or appointed, but in all cases they must be *electors* (resident voters) of the town. A zoning commission must have between five and nine members, can have up to three alternate members, and designates one member to be the chairperson.

Zoning commissions are authorized to *control land use* by enacting and enforcing zoning regulations that are necessary to safeguard the health and general welfare of the public and to oversee the prudent and productive development of the town's land resources. Zoning regulations have two important components: a *zoning map,* which divides the town into different zoning districts, and the actual *zoning regulations*, which dictate what type of land use can occur in each district.

Chapter 124 of the Connecticut General Statutes outlines the more specific aspects of land use and property development that can be regulated by a local zoning commission. They include the following:

- Height, size, and number of stories of various buildings and structures
- Percentage of a lot that a structure may cover
- Density of population
- Permitted uses within designated areas
- Height, size, and location of advertising signs
- Location of specific areas for trade, industry, and residences

When any use or condition is found that violates zoning regulations, the *local zoning officer* (typically an employee of the town that assists the zoning commission) or other designated authority has the power to order the violation corrected and to impose fines until the situation is remedied.

If the zoning commission seeks to establish new regulations, designate new zones, or change the permitted uses in any area of an existing zone within 500 feet of a town boundary, it must hold a public hearing before formally adopting any of these changes or new regulations. All such proposals must be referred to the local planning commission and regional planning agency before the required public hearing.

Variances and special permits.   Two types of exceptions to the zoning regulations may be obtained by a property owner: the variance and the special permit.

A *variance* is a permit to employ a particular use in an area that is not zoned for that use, and it runs with the land. A person seeking a variance must apply to the *zoning board of appeals,* a five-member to eight-member board that may be elected or appointed. The zoning board of appeals must hold a public hearing and act on

requests for variances within 65 days after proper applications have been submitted. The board will grant a variance if it determines that the characteristics of the site, unlike other similar sites, would cause the owner exceptional difficulty and *unusual hardship* in employing a permitted use. Economic hardship alone is not considered sufficient reason to grant a variance.

In contrast to the variance, there are certain uses that are permitted by the zoning regulations only if specific standards are met. An owner may obtain a *special permit* or *special exception* for such uses by applying to the zoning commission, the planning commission, or the zoning board of appeals. Before granting a special permit, the agency involved must first hold a hearing to determine if the required standards are fulfilled. Note that while all three agencies are empowered to grant special exceptions, only the zoning board of appeals may grant a variance.

Planned unit developments. Municipalities can adopt the state's uniform regulations governing planned unit developments, commonly referred to as *PUDs*. The regulations, if adopted as a part of the local zoning regulations, outline the standards, conditions, and application procedures for evaluating and approving PUDs. However, because of the flexibility given to local planning and zoning commissions in designing controlled projects, Connecticut municipalities are not required to adopt these regulations.

Town planning and zoning regulations may allow *cluster developments*, which are building patterns concentrating units on a parcel with at least one-third of the parcel left as open space for recreational, conservation, or agricultural purposes.

Village districts. Local zoning commissions are authorized to establish village districts as part of a municipality's zoning regulations. These districts can have their own land-use regulations protecting the district's historic, natural, and/or community character.

Planning

Chapter 126 of the Connecticut General Statutes authorizes a town to form a *planning commission* for the purpose of preparing, adopting, and amending a *plan of development* for the town. This plan is essentially a statement of goals, policies, and standards relating to the town's physical and economic development. Any proposed zoning regulations or boundaries or any changes to existing zoning regulations or boundaries must be reviewed to determine whether such proposals are consistent with the plan of development.

The planning commission also has the authority to adopt *subdivision regulations* and to evaluate and approve new subdivision proposals submitted to it. It is important to recognize the amount of *interaction* between the state and local laws (such as inland wetlands legislation, discussed later in this chapter) in the overall process of subdividing and land development. Thus, a subdivider/developer must take all of these regulations into consideration before he or she makes a move on any particular project.

Although it is common to see combined planning and zoning commissions in Connecticut, state law allows a municipality to maintain separate commissions. Planning commissions are composed of no fewer than five electors and three alternates.

Subdivisions. Connecticut requires that the subdivision of a parcel of land into *three or more parts* must be approved by the local planning commission. Approval requires that the developer of the parcel submit subdivision plans to the planning commission. Any plans submitted must conform to the subdivision regulations and other applicable development laws of the municipality in which the proposed subdivision will be located.

Although the specific requirements for subdivisions vary from locality to locality, virtually all planning commissions require the submission of an accurate development plan indicating the physical layout of the lots to be created, the roads to be constructed, the manner in which utilities will be provided to each of the proposed lots, and any other pertinent engineering or development data. The subdivision plans must be drawn up by a licensed surveyor and must meet the requirements of both local ordinances and state laws. Planning commissions are required to consider information on passive solar energy techniques (site techniques maximizing solar heat gain) when deciding a subdivision application. Once approved by the commission, all subdivision plans and maps must be filed in the town clerk's office within 90 days from the expiration of the appeal period (or in the case of an appeal, within 90 days of the resolution of that appeal).

The legal descriptions of each lot generally make specific reference to the original subdivision map and identify the lot in question by the number appearing on the original document. A typical plot map for a subdivision (Figure 14.1) appears along with a plot plan, which focuses on one property (Figure 14.2). The plan is one that a lender would typically require to make sure that the property is not in violation of any zoning, subdivision, or building line restrictions.

Open space. Towns may require a dedication of open space land as part of a subdivision. In lieu of a land dedication, towns may allow applicants for subdivision approval to pay a fee (or combination fee and land). The fee is limited to 10 percent of the fair market value of the land to be subdivided prior to approval of the subdivision. The town must deposit such funds into a special account for open-space, recreational, or agricultural purposes. Exemption to this provision is granted for subdivisions of less than five parcels transferred for no consideration to certain members of a family or for subdivisions providing 20 percent of their development for "affordable" housing purposes.

Inland Wetlands

Chapter 440 of the Connecticut General Statutes requires all municipalities to have an *inland wetlands commission*. The purpose of the inland wetland commission is to establish the boundaries of inland wetlands and watercourses within the municipality and regulate the types of activities that can be conducted in these areas. No regulated activity can be conducted in an inland wetlands without a permit from the inland wetlands commission. The commission must consider a

FIGURE 14.1

Subdivision Plan

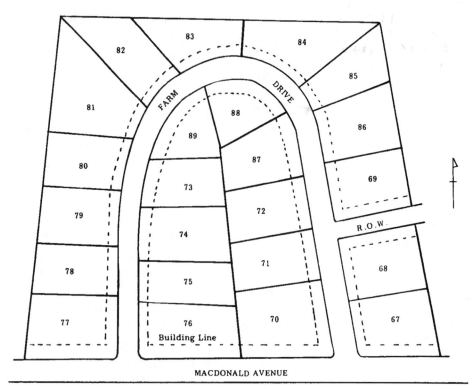

MACDONALD AVENUE

SCALE 1" = 100'

SUBDIVISION PLAN
OF
"COUNTRY FARM ESTATES"

John L. Sullivan Const. Co.
Willimantic, Conn.

Prepared by:

George Washington
Licensed Surveyor and
Professional Engineer

Accepted:

Tom K. Smith
Tom K. Smith, Chairman
Zoning Commission
7-4-76

number of factors when deciding on an application, the most important of which is the environmental impact of the regulated activity. State statute requires that a permit shall not be issued by the commission unless it finds that a feasible and prudent alternative to the regulated activity does not exist. *Feasible* means "able to be constructed or implemented consistent with sound engineering principles"; *prudent* means "economically and otherwise reasonable in light of the social benefits to be derived from the proposed regulated activity, provided cost may be considered in deciding what is prudent and further provided a mere showing of expense will not necessarily mean an alternative is imprudent."

Connecticut also has a Tidal Wetlands Program that is run at the state level by the Department of Environmental Protection.

FIGURE 14.2

Plot/Plan Mortgage Survey

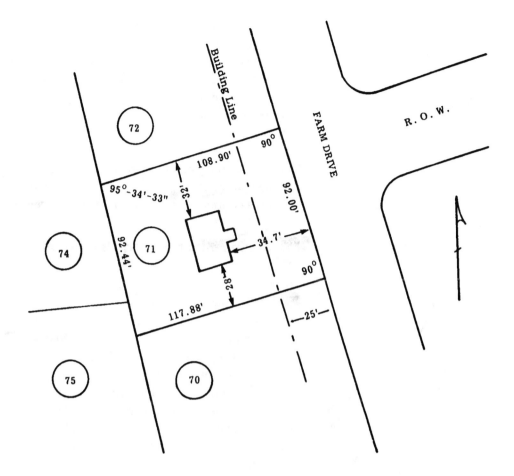

I HEREBY CERTIFY THAT THIS MAP IS SUBSTANTIALLY CORRECT. NO ZONING, SUBDIVISION, OR BUILDING LINE VIOLATIONS.

George Washington
Surveyor

PLOT PLAN/MORTGAGE SURVEY
JOHN L. SULLIVAN CONST. CO.
WILLIMANTIC, CONN.

SCALE 1" - 40'   DEC. 20, 1976

Regional Planning Agencies

Connecticut allows for regional planning agencies in any of the planning areas defined by the Connecticut Office of Policy and Management (OPM). The OPM is responsible for guiding and coordinating the direction of land use in the state through its liaison work with the regional agencies and its own research efforts. The areas it defines as planning regions correspond roughly to the county jurisdictions that existed prior to the demise of county government in Connecticut. However, it is up to the director of the OPM to actually determine the area.

Regional planning agencies prepare comprehensive plans of development that encompass all the towns located within their jurisdictions. With these plans of development, planners make general recommendations for land use as well as recommendations concerning principal highways and freeways, airports, parks, playgrounds, recreational areas, schools, public facilities, and so on. After this comprehensive plan has been presented at a public hearing, it must be approved by a majority of the local representatives to the agency if it is to be adopted. Local representatives may be elected or appointed by the legislative authorities of the town they represent. Once adopted, the plan becomes a model to advise those implementing the planning process at the local level and, thus, may have some impact on any locally proposed land use that conflicts with its recommendations. But, more important, the regional plan is used in reviewing certain government grants to municipalities for land development, and it may have substantial impact in those cases.

Regional planning agencies are also authorized to assist local planning agencies in implementing the regional development plan and may provide technical assistance on a contract or voluntary basis to member municipalities.

Affordable Housing Land-Use Appeals

Chapter 126a of the Connecticut General Statutes provides an *affordable housing appeals procedure* when a municipality denies an affordable housing development application. Its purpose is to encourage the development of affordable housing in the state. The act defines *affordable housing* as either "assisted housing" (through which one receives financial assistance under any government program for the construction or rehabilitation of low- and moderate-income housing and housing occupied by persons receiving rental assistance) or housing where not less than 30 percent of the units will be conveyed by deeds containing covenants and restrictions that require that such units be sold or rented at or below prices that will preserve the units as affordable (as defined in the law according to area median income) for at least 40 years.

The act shifts the burden of proof in an appeal of a development application denial from the developer to the municipality. The municipality must prove that denial of an affordable housing development (1) is supported by sufficient evidence in the record; (2) is necessary to protect substantial public interests in health, safety, or other matters that it may legally consider; (3) is necessary because such public interests clearly outweigh the need for affordable housing; and (4) is necessary because such interests cannot be protected by reasonable changes to the proposed affordable housing development.

Municipalities are exempt from the act if at least 10 percent of the municipal housing is deemed affordable by the Commissioner of Economic and Community Development. Towns are also allowed a moratorium from appeals of certain types of projects for four years after completion of other certain types of affordable housing projects in the town.

City and Town Development

The comprehensive City and Town Development Act (CTDA) aids municipalities in their attempts to reverse their deteriorating employment, housing, and land resource conditions. The act deals with *development properties,* which are defined as any real or personal properties, including land, buildings, and other structures, acquired or to be acquired by the municipality and dedicated to the purposes of the CTDA. The CTDA empowers municipalities to do any of the following with respect to these development properties: (1) buy, (2) sell, (3) lease, (4) construct, (5) reconstruct, (6) rehabilitate, (7) improve, (8) finance, and (9) foreclose.

The CTDA, then, would allow a municipality to purchase structures in a deteriorated neighborhood, demolish them, erect new construction (for example, a new civic center) on the vacant parcels, sell the improved parcel, and finance the entire deal for the investors purchasing the property. CTDA allows Connecticut's municipalities to initiate programs on their own.

NEW HOME CONSTRUCTION

Implied Warranties

In addition to any express warranties that a new home builder gives to a purchaser, Connecticut law imposes an *implied warranty* that the home is

- free from faulty materials;
- constructed according to sound engineering standards;
- constructed in a workmanlike manner; and
- fit for habitation at the time of delivery of a deed (or completion of improvement if not complete when deed is delivered).

The implied warranty does not apply to a defect that could have been reasonably discovered by an inspection before the contract to purchase is signed by the purchaser. This warranty lasts for one year after transfer (or if an improvement was not complete until after transfer, then one year after the completion of the improvement).

Additionally, when a certificate of occupancy is issued for a new home from the town, the new home builder guarantees to the buyer that the home is in compliance with the *building code*. This implied warranty lasts for three years. (CGS Chapter 827)

Contractor Registration

New home contractors must register with the Department of Consumer Protection. A new home contractor is defined as someone who *contracts with a consumer to build a new home* or a portion of one before it is occupied. Additionally, new home contractors must include their registration number in all advertisements and must provide certain disclosures to consumers before entering into a contract. (CGS Chapter 399a)

Building officials must check registration certificates before issuing a contractor a building or construction permit. If requested by a consumer, a contractor must return a deposit if 30 days have passed since work was to have begun and no substantial portion of the work has been completed.

Real estate licensees are specifically exempted from the new home construction registration requirements as long as the licensee is working within the scope of his or her license.

Guaranty Fund

A consumer may seek *reimbursement* from the Department of Consumer Protection New Home Guaranty Fund for damages caused by a new home contractor that the consumer is unable to collect. The reimbursement for a single claim is capped at $30,000.

■ HOME IMPROVEMENT CONTRACTORS

Home improvement contractors and salespeople must *register* with the Department of Consumer Protection. Home improvements are defined as repairs, replacement, remodeling, alteration, modernizing, and rehabilitation of any private or public dwelling in which the total cash price for all work agreed on between contractor and owner exceeds $200. It does *not* include (1) construction of new homes, (2) sale of goods by a seller who neither directly nor indirectly performs any labor in connection with installation or application of goods or materials, (3) sale of goods or services furnished for commercial or business use or resale, (4) sale of appliances, or (5) any work provided by an owner. (CGS Chapter 400)

Municipalities are prohibited from issuing a building permit to a contractor who is not registered.

Home Improvement Contract

Eight items are required in a home improvement contract. To be valid and enforceable, a home improvement contract must

1. be in writing,
2. be signed by both owner and contractor,
3. contain the entire agreement,
4. contain the date of the transaction,
5. contain the name and address of the contractor,
6. contain a notice of the owner's cancellation rights,
7. contain a starting date and completion date, and
8. be entered into by a registered contractor.

A contractor who has complied with 1, 2, 6, 7, and 8 but not 3, 4, and 5 is not precluded from recovering payment for work based on the reasonable services requested by the owner if the court determines that it would be inequitable to deny such a recovery.

Exemptions

Certain professionals and tradespeople are exempt from registering as home improvement contractors while working in their own profession or trade, for example, (1) government agencies and departments, (2) those who are involved with construction of a new home, (3) sellers of goods who neither arrange to perform nor perform any work in connection with an installation, (4) sellers of goods for commercial or business use, (5) sellers of appliances designed for easy installation, or (6) owners performing work on their own premises.

Home Improvement Guaranty Fund

A fund administered by the Commissioner of Consumer Protection has been established to reimburse homeowners who have suffered loss or damage by reason of the performance or nonperformance of registered home improvement contractors. A $10,000 bond is required of each contractor for the use of the state or any person aggrieved by the contractor's action. The maximum that may be paid out of the Home Improvement Guaranty Fund on a single claim is $15,000. This fund also permits a homeowner to be reimbursed from the fund for attorney's fees.

■ COMMERCIAL/INDUSTRIAL CONSTRUCTION

Private contracts for building, renovating, or rehabilitating commercial or industrial buildings must contain a payment schedule. Unless agreed otherwise, owners must pay general contractors within 15 days after receiving a payment request, and general contractors must pay subcontractors within an additional 15 days. Also, *retainage*, defined as the amounts withheld from progress payments to a general contractor or subcontractor, under a construction contract is limited to 7.5 percent of the amount owed.

■ PRIVATE LAND-USE CONTROL

Private regulations affecting subdivision, land development, and land consist almost exclusively of deed restrictions and covenants. These are, essentially, voluntary restrictions that may or may not stand up under close scrutiny in a court of law.

■ BUILDING ACCESSIBILITY

All units in R-2 buildings (multifamily dwellings) with elevators and ground floor units constructed or substantially renovated after July 1, 1991, as well as R-2 buildings without elevators, must be adaptable for use by people with disabilities. In dormitories and boarding houses, 1 in 25 beds must be accessible to the disabled. The requirement for one-family and two-family attached dwellings constructed after July 1, 1991, is that 1 in 10 units be accessible to people with disabilities.

■ CONNECTICUT INTERSTATE LAND SALES

Protect from Swamp land

Occasions arise when real estate located in states other than Connecticut is advertised for sale and sold in Connecticut. Such activity can take place only under the provisions of *either* the Federal Interstate Land Sales Full Disclosure Act or the Connecticut Real Estate Licensing Laws Concerning the Advertising, Sale, Exchange or Other Disposition of Certain Real Estate Located in Another State (CGS Sections 20-329a–20-329m). The general purpose of the Connecticut law is to cover those instances that fall outside the jurisdiction of the federal laws. Appropriate filings with the Federal Office of Interstate Land Sales will generally exempt parties or individuals from the registration and compliance requirements of the Connecticut laws.

Whether the offering in Connecticut involves the sale of condominiums in Florida or raw land in Alaska, it must be registered with the Real Estate Commission and the Connecticut Secretary of State's office. The offer must comply with the law, unless specifically exempted from the disclosure requirement by virtue of prior compliance with the federal law(s).

Under the Connecticut law, registration and compliance involve the following five general steps, although not necessarily in this order:

1. The offeror must submit documents, promotional plans, and advertising materials to the Real Estate Commission.
2. The offeror must appoint the Connecticut Secretary of State as the agent through whom actions and proceedings against the offeror may be served. Such appointment must be in writing.
3. The offeror must post a bond, as deemed appropriate by the Real Estate Commission, in favor of the state. The bond must be made with a surety company authorized to do business in Connecticut.
4. The applicant/offeror must apply for and receive a license from the Real Estate Commission that authorizes the offering and disposition in Connecticut of the property that is the object of the application and registration. Fees for such licenses are based on a sliding scale.
5. The offeror must appoint a resident Connecticut broker, who is responsible for compliance, as his or her representative in the state.

Once approved by the Real Estate Commission, the sale of properties outside Connecticut may proceed legally in accordance with the prescribed plan.

72 hrs

Only licensed real estate brokers in Connecticut are authorized to *dispose* of interstate land in state. *Dispose* is defined as sell, exchange, lease, and award. Under no circumstances can brokers or parties to the disposition in any way advertise that the property in question has been inspected and/or approved by the Real Estate Commission or any other official, department, or employee of the state of Connecticut.

When an individual purchases property covered under Connecticut's Interstate Land Sales Act, he or she must be presented with a clearly identified copy of the prospectus, property report, or offering statement within 72 hours before signing a sales contract. The broker will retain a signed receipt.

Subdivisions of less than five parcels or lots; shares in real estate investment trusts; cemetery lots; and leases pertaining to apartments, stores, or offices generally are exempted from Connecticut interstate land sales regulations.

■ EMINENT DOMAIN

Connecticut *limits* the use of eminent domain by state municipalities. Of particular importance, a municipality cannot use eminent domain solely for the purpose of increasing local property taxes. A taking of property for redevelopment purposes requires a public hearing and certain other procedural safeguards. If a municipality does not make use of a property acquired by eminent domain and seeks to sell the property, it must first offer the property to the former owner (or the former owner's heirs) at a price that does not exceed the amount the municipality paid for the property.

■ WEB LINKS

Connecticut General Statutes Chapter 124 (Zoning):
  www.cga.ct.gov/2009/pub/Chap124.htm
Connecticut General Statutes Chapter 126 (Planning):
  www.cgact.gov/2009/pub/Chap126.htm
Connecticut General Statutes Chapter 440 (Inland Wetlands):
  www.cga.ct.gov/2009/pub/Chap440htm
Online examples of zoning map and regulations, subdivision regulations, and
  inland wetlands regulations:
  www.cityofstamford.org/content/34/1219/default.aspx
Municipal Web sites (Many town sites contain detailed information on local
  land use regulations.): *www.munic.state.ct.us/townlist.htm*
Connecticut Regional Planning Organizations:
  www.ct.gov/opm/cwp/view.asp?a=2986&q=383046
Connecticut General Statutes Chapter 126a (Affordable Housing Land Use
  Appeals): *www.cga.ct.gov/2009/pub/Chap126a.htm*
Connecticut General Statutes Chapter 827 (New Home Implied
  Warranty): *www.cga.ct.gov/2009/pub/Chap827.htm*
Connecticut General Statutes Chapter 399a (New Home Contractor
  Registration): *www.cga.ct.gov/2009/pub/Chap399a.htm*
Connecticut General Statutes Chapter 400 (Home Improvement Contractor
  Registration): www.cga.ct.gov/2009/pub/Chap400.htm
Connecticut Building Code: *www.ct.gov/dps/cwp/view.asp?a=2148&Q=305412*
Connecticut Fire Safety Code:
  www.ct.gov/dps/cwp/view.asp?a=2148&Q=308964&dpsNav=|.

CHAPTER 14 QUIZ

1. Local planning and zoning commissions
   a. are always separate entities.
   b. may be a combined commission.
   c. must be separate entities.
   d. must be a combined commission.

2. A local law that restricts a property to only residential use would be an example of
   a. subdivision law.
   b. inland wetland law.
   c. housing land use law.
   d. zoning law.

3. Which local authority has jurisdiction over subdivision regulation?
   a. Planning commission
   b. Board of tax review
   c. Town clerk
   d. Assessor's office

4. The state law governing planned unit developments (PUDs) is incorporated into which ordinances if adopted by a municipality?
   a. Subdivision regulations
   b. Zoning regulations
   c. Plan of development
   d. Building code

5. A homeowner is interested in building a deck off the back of his or her new house, but such a structure would not be in keeping with the zoning regulations. The most likely procedure would be for the homeowner to apply for a
   a. special permit.
   b. zone change.
   c. hardship exemption.
   d. variance.

6. Subdivision plans in Connecticut must be drawn up by a
   a. local planning commission.
   b. building architect.
   c. licensed mechanical engineer.
   d. licensed surveyor.

7. Once approved by the planning commission, subdivision plans must be filed at the town clerk's office
   a. within 15 working days.
   b. within 90 days from the expiration of the appeal period.
   c. by the chairperson of the commission.
   d. by the tax assessor.

8. A new home comes with an implied warranty from the builder that it is constructed in a workmanlike manner that lasts how long?
   a. Zero months
   b. Three months
   c. One year
   d. Three years

9. A homeowner plans on hiring a contractor to build an addition. All statements below are true about the home improvement business in Connecticut EXCEPT
   a. home improvement contractors must be registered with the state.
   b. home improvement contracts must be in writing to be enforceable.
   c. a homeowner is prohibited from hiring a contractor that is not registered with the state.
   d. a homeowner may be able to collect losses caused by a registered home improvement contractor from a state fund.

10. Which is excluded from Connecticut's law governing interstate land sales?
    a. Subdivisions under 50 lots
    b. Improved land up to 25 lots
    c. Condominiums
    d. Real estate investment trusts

11. How long before the signing of a sales contract for recreational lots outside Connecticut must the seller present a purchaser with a prospectus?
    a. 24 hours
    b. Within 72 hours
    c. Five business days
    d. One week

12. The Affordable Housing Land Use Appeals Act gives a developer the right to
    a. sue a town that denies a land use application.
    b. build affordable housing in certain towns.
    c. build affordable housing in all towns.
    d. appeal the denial of an affordable housing development application.

15

Fair Housing

■ OVERVIEW

Connecticut's fair housing law can be found at Chapter 814c of the Connecticut General Statutes.

Connecticut fair housing law is substantially equivalent to Title VIII of the Federal Civil Rights Act. Although there is similar coverage in many areas of both state and federal laws, there still remains a certain amount of overlap and "underlap." In some instances, federal law provides greater coverage than state law, and in other instances state law provides greater coverage than federal law.

In Connecticut, it is illegal for a real estate licensee in the conduct of his or her business to discriminate against any person on the basis of a *protected class*. Real estate licensees who violate these laws, whether by accident or design, risk serious civil and criminal penalties, including substantial fines and possible revocation of their real estate licenses. Although there are exceptions for some property owners, there are *no exceptions* for real estate licensees. The safest way to avoid problems and ensure compliance with the law is simply not to discriminate or to participate in the discriminatory practices of others.

The combined state and federal protected classifications are: race, religion, color, national origin, ancestry, sex, marital status, age, lawful source of income, familial status, physical disability, mental disability, learning disability, or sexual orientation.

■ UNDERSTANDING FAIR HOUSING LAWS

There is no single, all-inclusive, all-controlling fair housing law. Instead, there are *various laws* and regulations enacted or adopted by *federal, state, and local governments*. Each of these laws can apply to different protected classes (e.g., race, national origin, families with minor children), different kinds of real estate transactions (e.g., residential properties versus commercial properties), and different kinds of discriminatory practices (e.g., residential racial steering, discriminatory advertising, or blockbusting). Each level of government also has its own practices and procedures for enforcing its fair housing laws. To complicate things further, these laws can overlap. A given act of discrimination (e.g., denial of an apartment because of race) can violate a number of different laws and may be enforceable in federal court and in a state or local administrative agency, all at the same time.

The first step to understanding fair housing law is to know the *classes of persons it protects,* the acts of discrimination it prohibits, and how it is enforced. Because more than one law may apply to the same act of discrimination, it is important to be familiar with the provisions of every law that may apply to any given set of facts or real estate transactions.

Fair housing laws are intended to eliminate the effects of *unintentional as well as intentional* discrimination. The focus of fair housing laws is on the effect of a given act or omission, not on the state of mind of the principal. Therefore, practices and procedures that are perfectly innocent and benign in motive may violate the law if the effect is to discriminate because of membership in one of the classes protected by the law. To ensure compliance with fair housing laws, the professional conduct of real estate brokers and salespersons must be firmly based on their clients' legal and legitimate business needs as well as their own.

A popular misconception regarding fair housing laws is that they are designed to protect only minorities. While it is true that such laws arose out of discrimination against racial and ethnic minorities, the protection of the law is available to all. Anyone may file a fair housing complaint if they have been discriminated against because of their race, sex, religion, or other protected class status.

■ PROTECTED CLASSES IN CONNECTICUT

A *protected class* is a group of persons protected by statute from unlawful discrimination. Discrimination *on the basis* of any of the protected classes listed in Figure 15.1 is illegal.

FIGURE 15.1

Protected Classes in Connecticut

Race	Categories of race can include American Indian or Alaskan Native, Asian, Black or African American, Hispanic, Native Hawaiian or other Pacific islander, and White.
Religion/Creed	Religious observances, practices and beliefs.
Color	Skin color.
National Origin	A person, or their ancestor's, country or place of origin.
Ancestry	A person's family lineage and/or heritage.
Sex	Male versus female; includes discrimination related to pregnancy, child-bearing capacity, sterilization, fertility, or related medical conditions. Also includes sexual harassment, such as sexually offensive comments and requests for sexual favors.
Marital Status	Single, married, widowed, or divorced. Note that Connecticut recognizes same sex marriages.
Age	How old.
Lawful Source of Income	Income derived from a legal source, including income derived from Social Security, housing assistance, child support, alimony, or welfare.
Familial Status	Whether a person has or does not have children under the age of 18 living with them (or is pregnant).
Physical Disability	Chronic physical handicap, infirmity, or impairment (that either a person was born with or resulted from an injury or illness); includes epilepsy, hearing impairment, or reliance on a wheelchair or other remedial device.*
Mental Disability	A mental disorder (as defined by the American Psychiatric Association) that includes mental illness and mental retardation.*
Learning Disability	Refers to a person who is of at least average intelligence but has a diminished ability to listen, speak, read, write, spell, or do mathematical calculations. *(This is a protected class only under the Connecticut fair housing law, currently not under the federal law.)*
Sexual Orientation	A preference for heterosexuality, homosexuality, or bisexuality (or having a history of such preference or being identified with such preference); excludes any behavior that constitutes an illegal sex offense. *(This is a protected class only under the Connecticut fair housing law, currently not under the federal law.)*

* The federal Fair Housing Act does not use the word disability, but it rather prohibits discrimination on the basis of a person's handicap. The federal definition of handicap includes any physical or mental impairment that substantially limits one or more major life functions.

■ DISCRIMINATORY HOUSING PRACTICES

Connecticut's fair housing laws apply to residential transactions when a *dwelling* is involved. A dwelling is real estate used or intended to be used as a single-family house or *multifamily* housing. The exact statutory definition of *dwelling* is:

> *Any building, structure, manufactured mobile home park, or portion thereof that is occupied as, or designed or intended for occupancy as, a residence by one or more families, and any vacant land that is offered for sale or lease for the construction or location thereon of any such building, structure, manufactured mobile home park, or portion thereof.*

In Connecticut, the following 11 *discriminatory practices* are prohibited:

1. To refuse to *sell or rent* a dwelling on the basis of a protected classification.

2. To discriminate against any person on the basis of a protected classification in the terms, conditions, privileges, or *provision of services* or facilities in connection with the sale or rental of a dwelling.

3. For purposes of items 1 and 2, discrimination against a person because of the physical, mental, or learning disability of any other person *associated* with such persons or any other person residing or intending to reside in the dwelling is also prohibited.

4. For purposes of items 1, 2, and 3, discrimination against a person with a physical, mental, or learning disability includes (a) refusing to permit the person to make *reasonable modifications* at the person's own expense to afford such person full enjoyment of the premises (permission may be conditioned upon a renter's agreeing to restore the interior of the premises to its original condition); (b) refusing to make *reasonable accommodations* in rules, policies, practices, or services if necessary to afford such person equal opportunity to use and enjoy a dwelling or premises; and (c) failure to design and construct certain multifamily dwellings that will be initially occupied after March 13, 1991, in accordance with the federal Fair Housing Act or after July 1, 1991, under state building codes (this includes buildings with four or more units and one or more elevators and ground-floor units in other four-plus unit buildings).

5. To *advertise* with respect to the sale or rental of a dwelling in a way that indicates any preference, limitation, or discrimination based on a protected classification.

6. To represent to any person because of a protected classification that any dwelling is *not available* for inspection, sale, or rental when such dwelling is so available.

7. To restrict or attempt to *restrict the choices* of any buyer or renter to purchase or rent a dwelling to an area that is substantially populated by persons of the same protected class as the buyer or renter (this is often termed *steering*).

8. To induce or *attempt to induce* any person to sell or rent any dwelling by representations regarding the entry or prospective entry into the neighborhood of a person or persons of a particular protected class (this is often termed *blockbusting*).

9. For any person engaging in *residential real estate–related transactions*, to discriminate against any person in making available such a transaction or in the terms or conditions of such a transaction because of a protected classification. (Note that a "*residential real estate–related transaction* is defined as either (a) the making or purchase of loans or providing other financial assistance for purchasing, constructing, improving, repairing, or maintaining a dwelling, or secured by residential real estate or (b) the selling, brokering, or appraising of residential real estate.")

10. To *deny any person access* to or membership or participation in any *multiple listing service*, real estate brokers' organization, or facility relating to the business of selling or renting dwellings or to discriminate against him or her in the terms or conditions of such access, membership, or participation on account of a protected classification.

11. To *coerce, intimidate, threaten, or interfere* with any person in the exercise or enjoyment of, or on account of his or her having aided or encouraged any other person in the exercise or enjoyment of, any of the above-granted rights.

Exceptions for Property Owners

Considerable caution must be exercised when relying on the exceptions contained in the state fair housing law. Many of the federal laws discussed in the main principles texts apply to situations that come within one of the exceptions to the state law. None of the exceptions in Title VIII, for example, applies to single-family housing sales or rentals involving the services or facilities of a real estate broker, agent, or salesperson. Two other federal fair housing statutes (i.e., Sections 1981 and 1982 of the Civil Rights Act of 1866) contain *no exceptions whatever*. Because the Connecticut Commission on Human Rights and Opportunities has authority to prosecute violations of these federal laws, the Commission can still receive and act on complaints that fall outside the coverage of the state law. In questionable situations it is far easier and safer not to discriminate than to rely on statutory exceptions, which reliance may lead to loss of a license or substantial financial penalties.

Because of the broad way in which the state fair housing law is written, its protections extend to persons who are injured, financially or otherwise, because of discrimination directed at someone else. For example, a white tenant who is evicted from an apartment because he or she has black friends can file a race complaint with the Commission, even though the discrimination is not because of the tenant's own race but the race of his or her friends. Similarly, a real estate agent who loses compensation because a client refuses to sell to a family with children may file a familial status discrimination complaint based on the familial status of the home seeker.

The following are exceptions under Connecticut fair housing law:

- *In general.* Does not apply to the rental of a unit in a dwelling containing living quarters occupied or intended to be occupied by no more than two families if the owner actually lives in one of the two units (four units for sexual orientation category); does not apply to the rental of a room or rooms in a single-family dwelling unit if the owner actually maintains and occupies part of such living quarters as his or her residence
- *Marital status.* Does not prohibit the denial of a dwelling to a man and a woman who are both unrelated by blood and not married to each other
- *Age.* Does not apply to minors or to "housing for older persons"
- *Familial status.* Does not apply to "housing for older persons" or to a unit in a dwelling containing units for no more than four families living independently of each other, if the owner of such dwelling resides in one of the units
- *Lawful source of income.* Does not prohibit the denial of full and equal accommodations solely on the basis of insufficient income
- *Sex.* Does not apply to the rental of sleeping accommodations provided by associations and organizations that rent all such sleeping accommodations on a temporary or permanent basis for the exclusive use of persons of the same sex to the extent that occupants utilize shared bathroom facilities (based on considerations of privacy and modesty)
- *Sexual orientation.* Does not apply to an owner-occupied dwelling of single-family to four-family units, without the services of an agent and where no advertising has occurred

Housing for older persons is specifically defined in the law as housing that is

■ provided under any state or federal program that the Secretary of the U.S. Department of Housing and Urban Development determines is specifically designed and operated to assist elderly persons;

■ intended for, and solely occupied by, persons 62 years of age or older; or

■ intended and operated for occupancy by at least one person 55 years of age or older per unit in accordance with the standards set forth in the federal Fair Housing Act and regulations.

No Exceptions for Licensees

While there are certain exemptions for others, discrimination based on a protected classification is illegal for Connecticut real estate licensees. Licensees are *not exempt* from housing discrimination. In addition, racial discrimination has no exceptions under the Civil Rights Act of 1866.

■ ADMINISTRATIVE ENFORCEMENT

The primary federal fair housing law, Title VIII of the federal Civil Rights Act of 1968, may be enforced by filing a *private lawsuit* in federal court or by *filing an administrative complaint* with the federal Department of Housing and Urban Development (HUD). Where a state or local government has enacted fair housing laws that are *substantially equivalent* to Title VIII, HUD is required to defer all fair housing complaints it receives from within that jurisdiction to the state or local fair housing enforcement agency created by that state or locality. A state or local fair housing law is considered to be substantially equivalent to Title VIII if its prohibitions and remedies are comparable to those of that federal law.

In Connecticut only the city of New Haven and the state, itself, have enacted laws substantially equivalent to Title VIII. Connecticut's fair housing laws are enforced by the *Connecticut Commission on Human Rights and Opportunities*. The New Haven Commission on Equal Opportunities is the enforcement agency for the city of New Haven.

Connecticut Commission on Human Rights and Opportunities

The Connecticut Commission on Human Rights and Opportunities (CHRO) is the state administrative agency that has the authority to receive, initiate, and investigate complaints that are alleged to be violations of the fair housing statutes. It has offices throughout the state and employs its own legal counsel, staff, and investigators. It has the power to adopt, publish, amend, and rescind regulations consistent with and to effectuate the carrying out of its duties under the state law.

Complaint procedures.   Any person claiming to be discriminated against may file a complaint with CHRO within *180 days* of the act of discrimination. The *complaint* must be in writing *under oath* and include the name and address of the person alleged to have committed the discriminatory practice and the details of the discrimination.

CHRO then serves the complaint on the person alleged to have committed the discriminatory practice, and the person has the opportunity to file a written response to the charges. CHRO investigates the complaint to determine if there is reasonable cause to believe a discriminatory practice has been committed as alleged. CHRO may conduct conferences during the investigatory practice for the purpose of finding facts and promoting a voluntary resolution.

Findings and damages. If CHRO determines that a discriminatory act did take place, there will be an attempt to determine the damages suffered by the person discriminated against as a result of this discriminatory act. *Damages* can include expenses incurred for obtaining alternate housing, storage of goods, moving costs, other costs actually incurred as a result of such discriminatory practice, and reasonable attorney's fees.

If the alleged discriminator does not agree to settle at this stage, a *public hearing* is scheduled. Such hearing is held before an impartial attorney, known as a *hearing officer*, appointed for that purpose. After a full public hearing, the hearing officer renders a decision and orders the relief appropriate to his or her determination. CHRO hearing decisions may be appealed in state court. CHRO may also seek the assistance of the state courts in enforcing any decision issued by a hearing officer. Such decisions may include an order requiring the sale or rental of the property at issue in the case, substantial money damages, and other forms of affirmative relief.

In addition, up to $50,000 of *punitive damages* can be awarded to the person discriminated against. CHRO can also impose a *state penalty* against a discriminator payable to the state to vindicate the public interest in an amount (1) up to $10,000, if the discriminator has not been adjudged to have committed any prior housing discriminatory practice; (2) up to $25,000, if the discriminator has been adjudged to have committed one other discriminatory housing practice in the past five years; and (3) up to $50,000, if the discriminator has been adjudged to have committed two or more discriminatory housing practices during the previous seven years.

Civil action. Any person who has filed a timely complaint with CHRO and received a release from CHRO can also file a *civil suit* against the alleged discriminator in Connecticut superior court. Such a civil action must be bought within *two years* of filing the complaint with CHRO.

Connecticut Real Estate Commission Regulations

The Connecticut Real Estate Commission has direct authority over the licensing and regulation of the real estate licensees in Connecticut. Administrative regulations adopted by the Commission require real estate salespersons and brokers to comply with fair housing laws.

The Commission requires that all real estate *listing agreements* contain words to the effect that "This agreement is subject to the Connecticut General Statutes prohibiting discrimination in commercial and residential real estate transactions (CGS Title 46a, Chapter 814c)." This regulation ensures that all parties to a real estate listing agreement have clear notice that such agreements must comply with the requirements of the fair housing law.

Enforcement procedures.   The Connecticut Real Estate Commission has the authority to accept complaints alleging violations of its regulations. If, after investigation, the Commission finds merit to a complaint, it will endeavor to eliminate the violation voluntarily. If those efforts fail, a formal public hearing will be held by the Commission. The Commission has the authority to *suspend or revoke* a license and/or *fine* a licensee for failure comply with fair housing laws. Decisions of the Commission can be appealed to a state court.

NONMATERIAL FACT

Brokers, salespeople, and owners are not liable to buyers or tenants for failure to disclose that (1) a property occupant has or had a disease listed by the Connecticut Public Health Commissioner (such as the fact that an occupant is HIV-positive) or (2) a suicide, murder, or other felony occurred on the property. By law these circumstances are deemed nonmaterial. (CGS Sections 20-329cc–20-329ff)

Disclosure of knowledge about suicide, murder, or other felony is deemed material, however, if the purchaser/tenant advises the owner or licensee in writing that such information is important for his or her decision. (Note, however, that information about disease status still need not be disclosed.)

ACCESSIBILITY REQUIREMENTS

New multifamily buildings containing *four or more units* must be constructed according to certain *accessibility* standards. Common areas must be accessible to persons with physical disabilities, and doors and hallways must be wide enough for wheelchairs. All units must have: (1) an accessible route into and through the unit; (2) kitchens and bathrooms that can be used by people in wheelchairs; (3) accessible light switches, electrical outlets, thermostats, and other environmental controls; and (4) reinforced bathroom walls to allow for later installation of grab bars.

PUBLIC ACCOMMODATIONS LAW

Connecticut law prohibits discrimination in any place of public accommodation. A place of public accommodation is defined as any establishment that caters or offers its services, facilities, or goods to the general public, such as a real estate brokerage office. The Connecticut law specifically states that this prohibition does not require that persons modify their property in any way. The federal Americans with Disabilities Act (ADA), however, does provide that structural changes to public accommodations must be made when they are "readily achievable." (CGS Section 46a-64)

■ IMPLICATIONS FOR CONNECTICUT REAL ESTATE BROKERS AND SALESPEOPLE

Because of their critical function in the housing market, real estate salespersons and brokers have a key role to play in the enforcement of fair housing laws. If real estate salespersons and brokers make an effort to comply with the letter and spirit of fair housing laws and cooperate with state and local fair housing enforcement agencies, they can make a substantial contribution to eliminating discrimination in Connecticut. They can also serve as an important source of information and education for the general public. If, on the other hand, real estate licensees look for loopholes in the law and cooperate with persons who wish to discriminate, they risk serious legal consequences and perform a disservice to themselves, their profession, and their community.

Licensed brokers and salespeople are legally bound and ethically obligated to know and obey state and federal fair housing laws. Failure to do so will result in substantial financial penalties and possible license suspension or revocation. Equal housing opportunity is a legitimate and necessary component of everyone's civil rights. It is the duty and responsibility of the licensed broker or salesperson to ensure that this right is available to everyone.

■ WEB LINKS

Connecticut General Statutes Chapter 814c (Human Rights and Opportunities): *www.cga.ct.gov/2009/pub/Chap814c.htm*

Connecticut Commission on Human Rights and Opportunities: *www.ct.gov/chro*

Connecticut Fair Housing Center: *www.ctfairhousing.org*

CHAPTER 15 QUIZ

Are the examples below acts of housing discrimination under either the state or federal fair housing laws? Answer *yes* or *no* and explain.

1. In your capacity as a real estate agent, you receive a call from a landlord who owns a two-family house. Although the landlord does not live in the house, the landlord's mother lives on the first floor. The landlord wants you to rent out the second floor but says he does not want you to rent it out to any family with small kids. Is this discrimination? If so, what law or laws are being violated?

2. You are a real estate agent and you have a client with two small children who is interested in buying a condominium with two bedrooms. You find one for sale through the MLS but have learned that the condominium has a bylaw prohibiting minor children from living there. Could they refuse to sell to your client because she has small children if she is otherwise qualified to buy? What additional information may you need to know?

3. You have a client in a wheelchair who is looking for an apartment to rent. You find him a first-floor apartment in a three-family house where the owner lives on the second floor. Your client says the apartment is fine, but he would like to install grab bars in the bathroom at his expense. The owner says he will rent your client the apartment but refuses to allow him to install grab bars regardless of who pays. Is your client being discriminated against? If so, what law or laws are being violated?

4. You own a single-family house and are renting out three rooms in the house to different tenants. You live in the house, and you have decided you want to rent out the rooms only to women. A man applies for one of the rooms that you have advertised for rent in the newspaper. Is it discrimination if you refuse to rent to him because he is male? If so, what law or laws are being violated?

5. You are renting out a guest room in a house you own and live in. You do not advertise or use an agent but are renting it strictly by word of mouth. Is it discrimination if you refuse to rent to a black person because you would feel uncomfortable having that person live there?

6. You have just finished remodeling your three-family house on the east side of Bridgeport. You live on the first floor, and you decide you want to rent only to tenants who are gainfully employed. Is it discrimination if you refuse to rent to someone who is on welfare because they are on welfare? Is it discrimination if you refuse to rent to someone on Section 8 because they are on Section 8? If so, what law or laws are being violated?

7. You are a real estate agent and have a married couple in their mid-20s as clients who are interested in buying a co-op unit advertised in the MLS. They have no children, but they are refused by the board of directors of the co-op because they are only selling to people 35 and over. This has always been the policy of the co-op since it was first built. Is this discrimination? If so, what law or laws are being violated?

8. You are a real estate agent and have a married couple in their late 20s with two minor children as your clients. They want to buy a two-bedroom co-op unit that has been advertised in the MLS. They are refused for the same reason as the couple in item 7. The co-op is selling only to people 35 and over, which has always been its policy. Is this discrimination? If so, what law or laws are being violated?

9. You have a friend who is a single man in his late 40s who is confined to a wheelchair. He wants to buy a co-op unit that is being sold strictly by word of mouth without advertising and without the use of an agent. He has requested that he be allowed to build a ramp at his own expense. The board of directors of the co-op have decided they will sell him the unit but refuse to allow him to construct a ramp. Is this discrimination? If so, what law or laws are being violated?

10. You own a rooming house and live in a first-floor unit. There are seven rooms in all, which you rent out. You have decided you do not want to rent to any members of the Jehovah's Witnesses religion. You don't advertise or use an agent but rent out the rooms strictly by word of mouth. If you refuse to rent to someone because he or she is a member of this religion, would that be discrimination? If so, what law or laws are being violated?

11. You are an agent and receive a call from the owner of a single-family home who recently purchased a second home and wants you to rent out his first home. Although the home has three bedrooms, he does not want you to rent it to any family that has small children because he would eventually like to have his own daughter move into the house after she gets married and wants to make sure it remains in good shape. Can you legally take this listing and abide by the owner's wishes not to rent to any family with small children? Explain why it is or is not discrimination. If it is, what law or laws are being violated?

12. You own a seven-unit rooming house and someone who is handicapped and uses a wheelchair wants to rent one of the units. You live in the house and are willing to let him rent one of the rooms, but you have refused him permission to build a ramp at his expense. Are you guilty of discrimination? If so, what law or laws are being violated?

13. In the sale of a house you represent the seller, who has AIDS. You do not mention this fact to the buyer, and after the closing the buyer learns about it from a neighbor. The buyer threatens to sue you and the owner for not disclosing a material fact. Are either of you potentially liable?

16

Closing the Real Estate Transaction

■ OVERVIEW

The *closing* is the final procedure in a real estate transaction, where the *deed is delivered* from the seller to the buyer (and then recorded in the land records) and the seller receives the purchase money. Upon delivery of the deed, *title passes* from the seller to the buyer. Other documents are also signed at closing, and adjustments are made for expenses associated with the transfer.

Most closings are conducted *face-to-face* in Connecticut, although it is not uncommon to have an *escrow* closing in commercial and some residential transactions. The title procedures (with the exception that the buyer is typically responsible for title work) and closing statements are handled basically as described in the principles texts.

■ CLOSING PROCESS

Although closings customarily are executed under the direction of legal counsel, a knowledgeable broker or salesperson can be invaluable to the buyer and/or seller.

Between the signing of the contract and the final settlement, both the buyer and the seller need direction, support, and encouragement. They must comply with time requirements to fulfill their obligations set forth in the contract. They must work diligently toward the final consummation of the contract completion. The buyer promises to obtain sufficient financing; the seller promises to obtain a clear, unencumbered title. Each promises to exchange one for the other at a designated date and hour at a specific location according to the contract. It is frequently the broker or salesperson who is instrumental in keeping the action flowing systematically toward settlement.

Financing

A buyer's broker or salesperson may assist the buyer in securing a mortgage loan. Recall from Chapter 11, however, that a licensee cannot act as a mortgage broker, unless licensed as a mortgage broker, and cannot accept a referral fee from a lender for merely referring a buyer to a lender. A licensee assisting a client must always act in the client's best interest not in the licensee's best interest. If an agent is asked to recommend a mortgage broker, the agent should always recommend at least two or three mortgage brokers that the agent knows are qualified.

The mortgage process is typically explained to the borrower by the lender. It may be helpful, however, for the buyer's broker or salesperson to suggest questions the borrower may wish to ask to help him or her understand the mortgage obligations and alternatives more easily. Such questions might be: What points may I pay rather than having them taken from the loan? What is the capped rate for the life of the mortgage? What happens when I pay more principal than is required in the monthly payment? What are the alternatives to this particular mortgage? How often will the rate change? What is the rate based on?

Inspections

Inspections usually are needed before the closing can be planned. These will vary from building inspections to termite inspections to inspections by appraisers, surveyors, and systems operations experts (i.e., heating/cooling, electrical). A broker or salesperson representing the buyer may coordinate these various inspections and frequently accompanies the inspectors in order to open the building and assist in whatever way possible. If an agent is asked to recommend an inspector, the agent should always recommend at least two or three inspectors that the agent knows are qualified.

A walk-through inspection is a good practice that most agents require of both the buyer and the seller. This occurs immediately prior to the closing itself. Through this inspection, the buyer and the seller can be assured that all systems function properly and can be aware of the final condition of the property. Any adjustments necessary are resolved at the closing.

Appraisals

Lenders require that an appraisal be rendered by a qualified appraiser approved by the lending institution. A real estate licensee should cooperate with the appraiser's request for data. This not only creates professional teamwork but also develops the attitude of trust and confidence that better serves the client and customer and protects the public. Gathering data is only part of the appraiser's work. Those data must then be analyzed and substantiated to document the estimated value of the property. A buyer is entitled to a copy of the appraisal.

Confidential Information

The broker and salesperson are not permitted to reveal details of the transaction to those who are not parties to the transaction. The purchase price and terms of a sale are considered private information—not to be shared with anyone—until recorded for public record. Further, licensees must keep a client's private personal information confidential (such as financial data, reasons for buying or selling, etc.) even after the client's agency agreement has expired and the client's transaction has concluded.

■ AT THE CLOSING

Because of the complexity of real estate ownership rights and the various forms used in the conveyance process, there is almost always at least one attorney involved in a conveyance, and in most cases two. The seller's attorney is responsible for preparing any documents necessary to convey title to the buyer, and the buyer's attorney conducts any title searches that might be required. Additionally, both attorneys offer legal counsel to their respective clients. The actual closing meeting takes place at either attorney's office.

When a real estate closing involves a mortgage loan, another attorney is needed to conduct the closing for the lender. Thus, the legal representation for most closing situations can generally be divided into three areas: the seller's counsel, the buyer's counsel, and the lender's settlement (or closing) agent. Many banks allow the buyer to choose the attorney who will do the closing work for the bank, and, as a result, it is common for the buyer's and bank's attorneys to be the same person. However, some banks still require that their own attorney do their closing work and will not allow the buyer's attorney to fill the dual capacity. In either event, it is the responsibility of the closing attorney to calculate the prorations between buyer and seller, search the title, and prepare the mortgage note and deed. Real estate closings generally are held at the office of the closing attorney. There may be some instances, however, when a lender requires that the closing take place at the institution's offices.

Under no circumstances should a broker or salesperson advise a buyer against the use of legal counsel or attempt to offer legal advice. Both these actions are in violation of the license law and could cost brokers and salespeople their licenses. Although the real estate agent typically attends the closing to collect the commission, he or she does not actually participate in it.

Face-to-Face versus Escrow Closing

Most residential real estate closing are held *face-to-face*, meaning all of the parties involved in the transaction actually meet together to sign documents and exchange funds. However, closings *in escrow* are allowed, where the buyer and seller sign documents ahead of time and instruct their attorneys to exchange documents and funds without the buyer and seller being physically present.

Prorations or Adjustments

In Connecticut, it is customary for the seller to pay the property expenses for the day of closing. Therefore, the seller's obligation for any accrued expenses ends on the day of closing, and the buyer reimburses the seller for any prepaid expenses beginning with the day after the closing.

When an item covering a period of time is prorated, or adjusted, between the buyer and the seller, it is the usual practice in Connecticut to use a 12-month (30 days each) or 360-day year to calculate the prorations (although actual days in the month are used for commercial real estate prorations). Of course, the buyer and seller may agree to waive or adjust the payment in accordance with their own agreement. An adjustment example would be the elimination of a property tax proration as an inducement to get the buyer to close earlier.

In Connecticut real property taxes are usually paid twice a year, on July 1 and January 1, for a tax year running from July to June. However, in several municipalities taxes are paid quarterly. The broker must understand the local tax payment schedule to provide accurate information to his or her clients regarding the tax proration.

Net data sheets may be used to the advantage of both the buyer and the seller. This information will give an estimate of what expenses to expect and what benefits can be anticipated. This information will include the following:

- The contract sales price
- Earnest deposit money
- The real property tax
- Insurance
- Prorated rents
- Security deposits
- The private mortgage insurance premium
- The assessments/special tax
- The loan origination fee
- Points
- Fees for appraisals, credit checks, recordings, inspections, surveys, etc.
- The broker's commission
- The mortgage amounts (first, second, assumable, etc.)
- Liens
- Title insurance
- Attorney fees
- The conveyance tax
- The transfer tax
- Warranties
- Utilities (prorations)

Refer to Appendix D for math problems, including prorations.

CHAPTER 16 QUIZ

1. In Connecticut who is responsible prior to closing for calculating the prorations between the buyer and seller, searching the title, and preparing the mortgage note and deed?
   a. Closing attorney
   b. Salesperson
   c. Broker
   d. Lender

2. In Connecticut, most residential closings are typically held
   a. in limbo.
   b. in escrow.
   c. at noon.
   d. face-to-face.

3. Where do closings usually take place?
   a. Broker's office
   b. Lender's office
   c. Attorney's office
   d. Town clerk's office

4. A seller has paid the monthly condominium common charges of $180 for the month of June. If the closing occurs on June 20, what type of adjustment would usually be made?
   a. $120 in favor of the seller
   b. $120 in favor of the buyer
   c. $60 in favor of the seller
   d. $60 in favor of the buyer

5. The broker or salesperson may perform all of the following in preparation for the closing EXCEPT
   a. maintaining a time schedule and providing net data.
   b. explaining closing procedures to both buyer and seller.
   c. coordinating inspections and delivering documents and escrow monies to the appropriate attorney.
   d. preparing the deed.

6. A salesperson represents Buyer One in the purchase of First Avenue. The salesperson also represents Buyer Two, who is interested in making an offer on a property on Second Avenue. To make an informed offer, Buyer Two asks the salesperson what was the price Buyer One contracted to purchase First Avenue. The salesperson can disclose this information to Buyer Two only after Buyer One's
   a. offer is accepted.
   b. mortgage commitment has been signed.
   c. closing has occurred.
   d. deed has been recorded in the land records.

7. A salesperson represents both Buyer One and Buyer Two. To make an informed offer, Buyer Two asks the salesperson how Buyer One was able to afford the property that Buyer One bought. When can the salesperson disclose this information?
   a. Only after Buyer One's closing has occurred
   b. Only after Buyer One's deed has been recorded in the land records
   c. Only after Buyer One's buyer agency agreement has expired
   d. Never

CHAPTER

17

Environmental Issues and the Real Estate Transaction

■ OVERVIEW

Environmental issues and laws can have a significant impact on many real estate transactions. There is extensive federal legislation dealing with environmental problems. Connecticut has also promulgated extensive environmental legislation that in some cases mirrors and in other cases adds to the federal law. The Connecticut Department of Environmental Protection is the primary state agency that has jurisdiction over the permitting and regulating of environmental activities, although many other state agencies also have their environmental niche.

The following discussion provides a brief summary of Connecticut legislation on some of the more common environmental hazards that real estate brokers and agents should be aware of. This is by no means an exhaustive summary and does not preclude or supersede any federal law in the area.

■ ASBESTOS

Asbestos is primarily regulated at the federal level. The Connecticut Department of Health Services has regulations requiring the abatement of asbestos in schools and has regulations outlining abatement procedures that mirror the federal law. The disposal of asbestos is regulated by the Connecticut Department of Environmental Protection, Bureau of Waste Management. Asbestos contractors must be licensed. (CGS Chapters 368l and 400a)

■ LEAD-BASED PAINT

The presence of lead in paint has been identified by health professionals as a health concern. Connecticut has enacted comprehensive legislation regulating lead-based paint in *residential* properties. The law regulates when inspections and abatement are required, what type of inspections and abatement methods are allowed and how they are to be conducted, precautions to be taken when renovating or remodeling, training and certification of inspection and abatement professionals. (CGS Sections 19a-111a–19a-111f)

Under Connecticut law, *inspections* are not required on the sale or lease of property. Inspections are only required in the following circumstances: (1) when a child (defined as a person under the age of six) has been diagnosed with an elevated blood lead level, that child's dwelling must be inspected; (2) if the child with an elevated blood lead level lives in a multifamily building, the other dwelling units in the building must be inspected; and (3) all day-care centers must be inspected prior to licensure and relicensure. While Connecticut law does not require inspections on transfer, many potential buyers and tenants may negotiate for an inspection as part of the transfer. (Note that federal law provides that all potential buyers be allowed a ten-day period after signing a purchase contract to conduct an inspection.) If a lead-paint inspection reveals that there is lead paint present in a dwelling where a child resides, the lead inspector is legally required to report his or her finding to the local director of health and the state Department of Public Health (which then has the authority to order that abatement work be done).

Abatement is required in Connecticut if a child lives in the dwelling and there is defective lead-based paint. Additionally, if a child residing in the dwelling has an elevated blood lead level, certain intact surfaces must be abated (surfaces up to five feet from the floor that have a half-inch protrusion that children can chew, movable parts of windows, and surfaces rubbing against movable parts of windows). Many municipalities have also passed ordinances regulating the presence of lead paint in housing.

Lead-paint inspection and abatement contractors that contract to do work must be *licensed*. Workers who work for inspection and abatement contractors (the persons actually carrying out the work) need to be *certified*. Both licensing and certification require training courses and an application with the Department of Public Health.

There is a wave of recent litigation involving lead paint. Tenants are suing landlords for lead paint poisoning, and buyers are suing sellers and agents for nondisclosure of the presence of lead-based paint.

■ RADON

Radon is a colorless, odorless gas that is the product of uranium decay. It is commonly found in houses and other buildings in Connecticut, entering through cracks and other openings in foundations. Long-term exposure to radon has been linked to higher levels of lung cancer. The Connecticut Department of Health recommends that all homes be tested for radon gas and be mitigated when airborne radon is equal to or greater than 4 pCi/L. Contractors performing radon mitigation work must be registered with the Connecticut Commissioner of Consumer Protection under the home improvement contractor registration requirements. A radon mitigation contractor will not receive a certificate of registration unless he or she attended a radon mitigation program approved by the U.S. Environmental Protection Agency and received a passing score on the national Radon Contractor Proficiency examination. The Department of Public Health and Addiction Services publishes a list of companies that perform radon mitigation and diagnoses. (CGS Section 19a-14b)

The Department of Public Health regulations also establish safe levels of radon in potable water.

■ MOLD

Mold is a recent environmental concern. Some people are susceptible to mold toxins while others are not. The state publishes guidelines on mold remediation, which is not mandatory. Otherwise, there are no state laws dealing with mold disclosure or exposure. However, the presence of mold could potentially be considered a material property condition, and therefore any knowledge about mold should be disclosed by a property seller/landlord/agent to a potential buyer/tenant.

■ FOAM AND DRYWALL

Connecticut law has prohibited urea-formaldehyde foam insulation (UFFI) from being installed in any building or structure after June 1, 1981 (CGS Section 29-277). It has been reported that foreign-made drywall imported in 2004–2005 may be the source of noxious sulfur odors and is believed to be the source of problems with copper plumbing and electrical wiring. This foreign-made drywall is reported to be emitting higher levels of sulfur, methane, and other volatile organic compounds than is considered healthy.

■ WATER WELLS AND GROUNDWATER CONTAMINATION

The Connecticut Department of Environmental Protection (DEP) has identified and rated all of the groundwater and surface water in the state. The water quality designations of all water resources are mapped. The master map is located at the DEP; copies of the map are available from the DEP Natural Resource Center. (CGS Sections 22a-351–22a-352)

The Connecticut Commissioner of Public Health has adopted regulations regarding the testing of water quality in private residential wells. The regulations cannot require that a test be conducted as a consequence or condition of the sale of property containing a private residential well; however, water quality test results on a private residential well must be reported within 30 days of the test to the municipality's public health authority. (CGS Section 19a-37)

WATER DIVERSION

The Connecticut Water Diversion Policy Act prohibits a diversion of state waters unless a permit is obtained. This permitting process is required for use of both surface waters and ground waters. *Waters* are defined as

> *all tidal waters, harbors, estuaries, rivers, brooks, water courses, waterways, wells, springs, lakes, ponds, marshes, drainage systems and all other surface or underground streams, bodies or accumulations of water, natural or artificial, public or private, which are contained within, flow through or border upon this state.*

Application to divert waters must be made to the DEP. There are activities that are exempt from requiring a permit, such as certain wells, storm drainage systems, and roadway crossings or culverts. (CGS Sections 22a-365–22a-378)

The DEP also regulates discharges into the waters of the state. A permit must be obtained to discharge pollutants. The issuance of such a permit does not convey any property rights; therefore, discharges may still be in violation of the common law under riparian rights theories. (CGS Section 22a-427)

UNDERGROUND STORAGE TANKS

Property owners in Connecticut can be held liable for cleanup costs and damage associated with leaking underground storage tanks, and sellers who do not disclose the presence of an underground tank to buyers may have to take back the property. Many municipalities in Connecticut have enacted ordinances requiring the removal of older residential underground storage tanks. The Commissioner of Environmental Protection regulates nonresidential underground storage tanks and requires that certain underground storage tanks on residential property must be removed. (CGS Section 22a-449d)

Connecticut has established an Underground Storage Tank Petroleum Fund for expenses related to releases of petroleum from underground storage tanks and third-party damages. The party responsible for the release must still bear all costs of the release that are less than $10,000 or more than $1 million. (CGS Section 22a-449c)

HAZARDOUS WASTE AND OTHER CONTAMINATION

Property owners in Connecticut can be held liable for cleanup costs associated with hazardous waste on their property, even if they were not responsible for the spill or discharge. Connecticut does have an innocent landowner defense for those acquiring polluted property after a spill or discharge, but it only limits liability to the imposition of a lien against the property. The state's lien on a polluted parcel is limited to the appraised value as if uncontaminated plus administrative costs.

Liability for pollution cleanup costs for lenders acquiring title to property through foreclosure or a deed in lieu of foreclosure is limited to the value of the property. (CGS Section 22a-452a)

Connecticut law protects a property owner from liability to third parties for contaminated property, if the owner did not actually pollute, or was not affiliated with the polluter, and the DEP has given written approval of the owner's investigation and remedial action plan. This is a limited shield to liability, meant to encourage the acquisition and cleanup of hazardous waste properties by eliminating the risk of third party claims. (CGS Section 22a-133ee)

Property Transfer

Connecticut requires an assessment of any discharge, spillage, uncontrolled loss, seepage, or filtration of hazardous waste at an "establishment" prior to the transfer of ownership of the property. An *establishment* is defined as any (1) real estate or business operation that generated a defined amount of hazardous waste; or (2) place where hazardous waste was handled, stored, or disposed of; or (3) dry cleaning, furniture stripping, and vehicle body repair facilities. Certain forms are to be filed, an inspection must be executed, and an analysis of the findings and cleaning of land as deemed appropriate by the DEP must be performed. (CGS Section 22a-134a)

■ WASTE DISPOSAL SITES

The DEP maintains an inventory of sites in Connecticut where hazardous or toxic wastes have been disposed (these sites do not necessarily pose a threat to public health or the environment). The DEP is required to furnish the inventory list, updated quarterly, to the town clerk of each municipality, to be maintained in the land records. The list includes each site's name, the name of the town in which it is located, the type of material and disposal activity involved, the present groundwater classification of the site, and general information about the site's current status. (CGS Section 22a-8a)

The construction of hazardous waste facilities requires a Certificate of Public Safety and Necessity from the Connecticut Siting Council. (CGS Sections 22a-114–22a-133)

Disclosure of Off-site Conditions

A seller who provides written notice to a potential purchaser about the availability of the DEP inventory lists has legally met his or her duty to disclose the presence of off-site hazardous waste facilities. If such disclosure is given, the agent is also excused from liability for failure to disclose off-site hazardous waste conditions. The notice needs to be given either before or at the time of the signing of the purchase contract. The Purchase Contract in Chapter 7 contains a provision giving such notice. Figure 17.1 provides an example of this notice in combination with other notices regarding other environmental issues and about hunting properties.

■ WEB LINKS

"Environmental Hazards in the Home: A Guide for Homeowners, Homebuyers, Landlords, and Tenants" (published by the Connecticut Association of REALTORS®, Inc., and the Connecticut Department of Public Health): *www.ct.gov/dph/environmental_health/eoha/pdf/Environmental_Hazards _in_the_Home.pdf*

Connecticut Department of Environment Protection: *www.ct.gov/dep* (To find Connecticut environmental laws and regulations on this site, choose Law and Regulations.)

Connecticut Lead Poisoning Prevention and Control Program: *www.ct.gov/dph* (choose Lead)

Connecticut Radon Program: *www.ct.gov/dph* (choose Radon)

Connecticut Mold Information and Guidelines for Mold Remediation: *www.ct.gov/dph* (choose Mold)

Connecticut River Watershed Council: *www.ctriver.org*

Connecticut Underground Storage Tank Information: *www.ct.gov/dep/cwp/viewasp?A=2692&Q=322600*

Connecticut Hazardous Materials and Waste Management Information: *www.ct.gov/dep/cwp/view.asp?a=2690&q=322434&depNav_GID=1639& depNav=|*

Connecticut Contaminated Property Transfer Program: *www.ct.gov/dep/cwp/view.asp?a=2715&q=325006&depNav_GID=1626*

Connecticut Siting Council: *www.ct.gov/csc*

FIGURE 17.1

Hazardous Waste Notice

Notice of Availability of Environmental Information

Property Address: _____

Town: _____

Buyer is notified that the Connecticut Department of Environmental Protection is required pursuant to Section 22a-134f of the Connecticut General Statutes to furnish lists of hazardous waste facilities located within the town to the Town Clerk's office. Buyer should refer to these lists and the Department of Environmental Protection for information on environmental questions concerning the Property and the lands surrounding the Property.

Buyer is also notified that information concerning environmental matters on the Property and surrounding properties is available from the federal Environmental Protection Agency, the National Response Center, the Department of Defense and third-party providers.

Buyer is notified that a list of local properties upon which hunting or shooting sports regularly take place may be available at the Town Clerk's office.

_____
Firm's name

_____
Signature of Licensee

I/We acknowledge that I/We have been notified of the availability of lists of hazardous waste facilities on

_____.
Date

_____   _____
Buyer's (or Tenant's) signature   Buyer's (or Tenant's) signature

©2002-2008 Connecticut Association of REALTORS®, Inc
Revised September 30, 2008; October 4, 2010

Reprinted with permission of the Connecticut Association of REALTORS®, Inc., all rights reserved.

CHAPTER 17 QUIZ

1. The primary Connecticut state agency having jurisdiction over environmental matters is the
   a. Real Estate Commission.
   b. Department of Consumer Protection.
   c. Department of Environmental Protection.
   d. Environmental Management Commission.

2. What are the ramifications of a residential seller (who has children) allowing a potential purchaser to conduct a lead paint inspection?
   a. The seller may be ordered to abate defective lead paint.
   b. The seller will have to pay for the inspection.
   c. The potential purchaser will be prohibited from purchasing.
   d. There are no seller ramifications.

3. A couple own their own home where they live with their five-year-old son. Knowing their house contains some surfaces with lead paint, the boy was tested for elevated blood levels—the tests showed he had no lead in his system. Does Connecticut law require that the couple take any action with regard to the lead paint in their home?
   a. Yes, they must abate all lead paint.
   b. Yes, they must abate defective lead paint.
   c. No, as long as their son does not have an elevated blood lead level, they need not conduct any abatement.
   d. No, abatement of lead paint is required only in rental housing.

4. A buyer has ordered a home inspection, including testing of the well water, for the home being purchased. The results of the water quality test must be
   a. kept confidential by the firm conducting the test.
   b. reported to the buyer only.
   c. reported to the buyer and the seller of the property.
   d. reported to the municipal public health authority.

5. A purchase and sale agreement has been signed for the sale of a facility that was previously operated as a dry cleaners. Connecticut law requires
   a. an assessment of the presence of any hazardous waste prior to the transfer of ownership.
   b. a payment made to the Connecticut DEP of up to $100,000 for potential cleanup costs.
   c. that the contract be reviewed by the Environmental Protection Agency (EPA).
   d. that the seller must pay the cost to clean up any hazardous waste.

6. A woman discovers that there is an underground oil storage tank in her backyard. Which would *NOT* apply to her situation?
   a. She may be required to remove the tank.
   b. She may be held liable for cleanup costs if the tank has leaked.
   c. She should not disclose the presence of the tank to a potential purchaser.
   d. She may be able to rescind the transaction if she recently purchased the property and the seller did not disclose that the tank was there.

7. A seller provides a buyer with written notice of the availability of hazardous waste facility information but does not disclose the presence of a hazardous waste site two blocks from the seller's property. The buyer now sues the seller for nondisclosure of this material fact. Is seller potentially liable?
   a. No, providing the notice excuses the seller from failure to disclose.
   b. No, the presence of an off-site hazardous waste condition is not a material fact.
   c. Yes, providing the notice does not excuse the seller from failure to disclose knowledge of an actual site.
   d. Yes, the presence of an off-site hazardous waste condition is a material fact.

8. Asbestos contractors must be licensed in Connecticut.
   a. True
   b. False

9. Radon contractors must be registered in Connecticut.
   a. True
   b. False

10. Lead paint abatement contractors must be licensed in Connecticut.
    a. True
    b. False

APPENDIX A Real Estate Securities

■ OVERVIEW

A *real estate security* is a share of an *investment* in real estate. It is an indirect way to own real estate that is different than direct ownership. The primary reason for investing in a real estate security is to earn a financial return. An investor does not have to manage or maintain the underlying real estate asset.

Connecticut regulates the sale of real estate securities. It defines two different types of securities: *real property securities* and *real estate syndicate securities*. Each type of real estate security is regulated under a separate law. Real property securities are regulated under Connecticut General Statutes Chapter 392, which is an extension of the real estate license law. Real estate syndicate securities are regulated under Connecticut General Statutes Chapter 826, which is not part of the real estate license law. Both laws are administered by the *Connecticut Real Estate Commission*.

■ TYPES OF REAL ESTATE SECURITIES

A *real estate security* is basically a share of income-producing investment that has real estate as an underlying asset. Instead of holding title to the real estate, an investor in a real estate security holds an investment share in an entity that either owns real estate or the right to receive payments on a loan with real estate used as collateral. For example, a partnership might be formed to purchase a property. To raise sufficient funds for the purchase, the partnership might issue and sell shares to investors. In effect, the investors are financing the project, and the shares represent claims of ownership of the partnership (whose only asset is the real estate).

Packaging real estate investments for multiple or group ownership is a widely used technique to pool the financial resources of investors. Many investors have neither the financial nor managerial resources to purchase and operate large investment properties. By splitting a large real estate investment into small shares and by retaining the management responsibilities, real securities allow the investor to reap the benefits of real estate ownership without the management responsibilities. The benefits would include income, tax shelter, and capital appreciation. Specific types of securities may be structured to maximize a particular benefit, such as a tax shelter, while others may provide all three benefits.

There are many different types of real estate securities, including real estate limited partnerships, mortgage-backed securities, and real estate investment trusts. Connecticut does not regulate all types of real estate securities. Basically, Connecticut *regulates* the sale of *two types: real property securities* and *real estate syndicate securities*.

Real Property Securities

Real property securities are investments in a single *loan note or contract* secured by a parcel of real estate, where the payments on the note or contract are *guaranteed* by the person selling the security (or by that person's principal). Also included are investments in multiple loans secured by multiple parcels of real estate in the same or adjoining subdivisions.

A permit from the Real Estate Commission is required before real property securities may be sold to the *public*. The public does not include institutional investors and corporations. Also, the person who sells real property securities to the public—called a *real property securities dealer*—must be licensed as a real estate broker and have his or her license specifically endorsed by the Real Estate Commission.

Real Estate Syndicate Securities

Real estate syndicate securities are investment ownership shares in a real estate syndicate. A *real estate syndicate* is a partnership or other noncorporate entity (typically a limited partnership) set up to invest in real estate that has 18 or more investors. The person or entity that forms the partnership and sells the investment shares is referred to as the *issuer* of the real estate syndicate securities.

An *issuer of real estate syndicate securities* is not required to have a real estate license.

■ CONNECTICUT REGULATIONS ON THE SALE OF REAL ESTATE SECURITIES

The Commissioner of Consumer Protection, with the advice and assistance of the Real Estate Commission, has the authority to make and enforce whatever regulations are considered necessary to regulate the marketing and sale of both real property securities and real estate syndicate securities. In addition, the Commission may prescribe the qualifications of dealers and issuers and oversee their actions.

See Figure A.1 for an outline of the different requirements for the two types of securities.

FIGURE A.1

FIGURE A.1

Connecticut Securities Transactions

	Real Property Securities	**Real Estate Syndicate Securities**
Securities covered	Shares in loan proceeds	Shares in a syndicate—generally involve only one property
Regulated by	Real Estate License Law	Real Estate Syndicate Law
Administered by	Connecticut Real Estate Commission	Connecticut Real Estate Commission
Seller	Real property securities dealer—licensed broker + special endorsement	Issuer—no licensing required
Permit to sell	Required information submitted with application	Prospectus submitted with application
Fee	No fee	$300 to $1,500 based on total value of interests issued in Connecticut
Purchaser receives	Written statement containing required information	Prospectus containing required information
Records and reports	1. Copies of written statements to purchasers executed by purchasers retained for at least four years 2. Financial report to the Commission within 60 days from close of usual business period	Books, records, sales accounts maintained—may be subject to Commission's examination
Advertising materials must be to the Commission	Ten days before use	Three business days before use
Penalties for violation	$5,000 and/or one to five years' imprisonment	$1,000 to $10,000 and/or up to ten years' imprisonment
Civil suits must be initiated within	Three years from date of transaction	Two years from date of transaction or one year from detection of violation—whichever expires first

■ REAL PROPERTY SECURITIES

Permit to Sell

Dealers in real property securities must obtain permits from the Commission to sell any real property security in Connecticut. Applications for these permits must be in writing and accompanied by whatever information regarding the security issue and/or the applicant the Commission requests.

Fees

Although the Connecticut license law reserves the right for the Commissioner of Consumer Protection, with the advice and assistance of the Real Estate Commission, to levy a "reasonable" fee for the submission of an application or the issuance of a permit, no specific fee is prescribed at present, and the Commission does not charge any application fee.

Required Statement to Purchaser

Any dealer who sells or attempts to sell a real property security must present a written statement on the property to the purchaser. The dealer must personally sign and deliver this statement to the purchaser, who must, in turn, sign and return an executed copy to the dealer. The dealer must retain all signed statements for at least *four years*. The statement must contain the following information:

- The legal description or address of the property subject to the lien that secures the note or contract being made or sold
- The name and address of the fee owner of the property
- Available information regarding the ability of the person liable for the obligation to meet his or her contractual payments
- A description of any improvement on the property
- A description of any streets, sewers, water mains, curbs, and gutters on or adjacent to the property
- The terms and conditions of the contract or note being made or sold, including information about the principal balance owed and whether the payments are current
- A statement of the approximate balloon payment on the note or contract being made or sold, which must appear prominently in words and figures
- The terms, conditions, and balance of all prior and existing liens on the property and the status of these accounts
- The amounts and terms of tax liens and assessments
- An appraisal of the property made by either the dealer or an independent fee appraiser (the purchaser may waive this requirement by obtaining his or her own appraisal and indicating this to the dealer)
- A statement as to whether the real property securities dealer is acting as a principal or as an agent
- A statement that the transaction is in compliance with the provisions of Chapter 329 (real estate license law) that pertain to real property securities
- Any other information the Commissioner of the Department of Consumer Protection, with the advice and assistance of the Real Estate Commission, may require from time to time by regulation

Advertising

In marketing real property securities, a dealer is required to submit to the Commission for approval *at least ten days before use* any materials he or she wishes to use in advertising the securities. If the Commission disapproves of the materials because they include false or misleading statements or material omissions, it will prohibit the dealer from using them. If the Commission does not reply to the dealer within ten days after receipt of the materials, the dealer may consider them approved.

Financial Report

The Connecticut license law also requires that real property securities dealers furnish the Commission with financial data. Within 60 days from the close of the dealer's usual business period, he or she must file with the Commission a *financial report* prepared by a certified public accountant. The report must include the total number and dollar value of sales for the period (whether as principal or agent), information concerning the handling and disposition of all funds related to these sales, and any other information required by the Commissioner of the Department of Consumer Protection with the advice and assistance of the Real Estate Commission. If the dealer fails to provide an annual financial report, the Commissioner may order an audit, the cost of which will be borne by the dealer.

Exemptions

The license law requirements regarding the sale of real estate securities exempt the sale of notes or contracts under investment participation pools or to the sale of certificates based on notes or contracts used as collateral. This exemption refers primarily to sales in the secondary mortgage market through such agencies as Fannie Mae (the Federal National Mortgage Association) and Freddie Mac (the Federal Home Loan Mortgage Corporation).

Also exempted are dealers who sell other types of securities and deal with transactions involving the sale of promissory notes secured by mortgage deeds as opposed to shares of a syndication in which a trust deed is the principal asset.

Because the real property securities dealer is permitted to deal only in real estate securities, he or she is not also regulated under the laws regarding sales of other types of securities and fiduciary arrangements.

Enforcement and Penalties

Under the license law provisions relating to real property securities, any person found guilty of any of the following acts may be fined up to $5,000 by the court and/or imprisoned for one to five years:

- Knowingly making any false statement or representation, or filing or causing to be filed with the Commission any false statement or representation in a required report
- Issuing or causing to be issued any advertisement or other material concerning any real property security that contains any statement that is deliberately false or misleading
- In any respect willfully violating or failing to comply with any provision of the laws pertaining to real property securities dealers or with any order, decision, demand, requirement, or permit of the Commission
- With one or more other persons, conspiring to violate any permit or order issued by the Commission or any provision of said sections

If the Commission feels that a dealer is violating provisions of the license law as it relates to real property securities or conducting his or her business in an unsafe or fraudulent way, the Commission may follow the procedure outlined under suspension or revocation of a license. Dealers may appeal Commission decisions.

Civil actions.   Any person who sustains an injury resulting from a real property security transaction that was in violation of the license law may recover damages plus 7 percent interest through a civil action. The action must be initiated within three years from the date of the transaction.

■ REAL ESTATE SYNDICATE SECURITIES

Permit to Sell and Prospectus

Issuers wishing to sell any real estate syndicate securities in Connecticut must also apply in writing to the Real Estate Commission for a *permit*. An issuer's application must be accompanied by a copy of the *prospectus*, or a printed statement of information about the proposed issue, that will be distributed to purchasers. The Commission requires that the prospectus include the following information:

- The name, residence, and principal business address of the issuer
- The names and residences and business addresses of all officers or members of the corporation, partnership, or joint venture if the issuer is a corporation, partnership, or joint venture
- A detailed statement of the plan of syndication including, but not limited to, the form of entity and the number and aggregate amount of the real estate syndicate securities proposed to be sold
- A copy of partnership or other agreements governing the rights, duties, and liabilities of members or participants
- A legal description of the real property, including a detailed description of any existing or proposed improvements
- A true statement of the condition of the record title to the real property, including all encumbrances
- A statement disclosing any covenants, conditions, or restrictions
- The detailed terms of the property acquisition, including, but not limited to, the down payment and the amount, periodic payment, and terms of any encumbrances
- A description of the type or types of real properties intended to be acquired if the plan of syndication provides for the acquisition of unspecified property or properties
- A statement disclosing any management agreement, including the amount of any fee, compensation, or promotional interest to be received by the issuer or any other persons in connection with the formation and management of the syndicate
- The name of any escrow depository
- A statement disclosing the amount, terms, and conditions of fire, liability, and hazard insurance
- Any other information required by the Commission's regulations

Note that the information required for the prospectus is essentially equivalent to the data included in the written statement that a dealer must submit to a purchaser of a real property security. The prospectus may contain considerably more data than the minimal amount required by the Commission. However, all information that is included in the prospectus must be submitted to the Commission along with the application for a permit to sell.

Fees

Under the real estate syndicate law, an issuer must pay a fee when filing a permit application. The amount of the fee is based on a *sliding scale* from $300 to $1,500, depending on the aggregate, or maximum, value of the interests to be issued in Connecticut. For the purpose of this law, value is equivalent to the proposed sales price. A similar fee formula is used for applications involving increases and/or changes in existing security issues.

Prospectus to Purchaser

As indicated above, an issuer of syndicate securities must give a copy of the syndicate's prospectus to every purchaser of a real estate syndicate security. The prospectus essentially provides a collection of all the pertinent information about both the syndicate and the real property underlying the syndicate.

Advertising

In marketing real estate syndicate securities, an issuer must submit to the Commission for approval any advertising materials he or she wishes to use *at least three business days* before use (or whatever shorter period the Commission agrees to allow). As with real property securities, the issuer may not use any advertising materials of which the Commission disapproves. In addition, the syndication law exempts the media from any liability for advertising placed by a seller of real estate syndicate securities.

Required Records

The issuer of syndicate securities must maintain a complete set of books, records, and accounts on sales. On the Commission's request, the issuer must report to the Commission any interests sold by the syndicate (including the amount and disposition of proceeds). The Commission has the right to examine the issuer's accounts at any time and will be reimbursed by the issuer for the costs of any out-of-state travel required to make such examinations.

Exemptions

The real estate syndicate law exempts the following types of securities:

- Syndicate securities in oil, gas, or mining titles or leases
- Interests in mutual water companies
- Real estate investment trusts falling under provisions of the license law
- Syndicate securities registered under the Federal Securities Act of 1933
- Condominium interests covered under the Common Interest Ownership Act
- Syndications not construed as public offerings and involving sales or offers to fewer than 18 persons
- Any other transactions not intended by the Commission to be covered by this law

Enforcement and Penalties

The real estate syndicate law calls for punitive measures similar to those prescribed under the license law provisions regarding real property securities. The syndicate law does not, however, identify specific violations, but rather generalizes on violations and associated penalties. Any person found guilty of violating the law or any of the Commission's regulations may be fined from $1,000 to $10,000 and/or imprisoned for up to ten years.

Cease and desist orders. If the Commission feels that an issuer of syndicate securities is violating the syndicate law or conducting his or her business in an unsafe or fraudulent way, the Commission may order the issuer to desist and refrain from such conduct or to stop all security sales. The issuer may submit a written request for a hearing within ten days after receiving the order. The hearing will be held within the time limits and provisions set in the real estate license law. Decisions of the Commission can be appealed.

Civil action. As with real property securities, any person who sustains an injury as a result of a syndicate security transaction may recover damages under a civil suit. However, the law limits the conditions under which an aggrieved party may file a suit as well as the types of violations that can be considered under the real estate syndicate law. If an issuer has made false statements or if the security was unqualified for sale, the issuer may make a written *offer to repurchase* the security (plus interest and/or actual damages) from the buyer. In such cases, if the buyer either accepts the offer or fails to accept it within 30 days after it was received, he or she loses the right to sue. When the issuer does not make such an offer, the buyer may sue for the consideration originally paid for the security plus interest at the prevailing legal rate. If the original purchaser no longer owns the security, the judgment will be apportioned according to the length of time each individual owned the security.

Any actions brought under the real estate syndicate law must be initiated *within two years* of the date of the transaction or within one year from the date the violation was actually detected by the plaintiff—whichever period expires first.

■ WEB LINKS

Connecticut General Statutes Chapter 826, Sections 20-329o–20-329bb (real property securities):
www.cga.ct.gov/2009/pub/Chap392.htm#Sec20-329o.htm
Connecticut General Statutes Chapter 826 (real estate syndicates):
www.cga.ct.gov/2009/pub/Chap826.htm

APPENDIX A QUIZ

1. Under Connecticut law any person who acts as a real property securities dealer must have
   a. a real estate broker's license.
   b. his or her license endorsed by the Real Estate Commission.
   c. have both a and b.
   d. no special license.

2. Which does *NOT* have to be included in the statement that a real property securities dealer must present to a purchaser of such securities?
   a. The name of the fee owner of the property
   b. A list of improvements on the property
   c. The terms and conditions of the contract or note being sold
   d. The uses to which adjacent properties are being put

3. A real property securities dealer submits promotional material to be used in selling securities to the Commission for its approval. If the dealer does not hear anything within seven days, he or she
   a. must wait three more days before doing anything.
   b. may assume the Commission has approved the materials.
   c. must resubmit the materials.
   d. may make a written request for a hearing.

4. With a real property security, the payments to be received by the investor are
   a. never guaranteed.
   b. guaranteed by the person selling the security.
   c. tax free.
   d. automatically reinvested.

5. A civil action to recover damages from a real property security transaction must be initiated within what period?
   a. One month
   b. Six months
   c. One year
   d. Three years

6. Which is *NOT* required to sell real estate syndicate securities?
   a. A permit to sell
   b. A prospectus
   c. A real estate broker's license
   d. All of the above

7. Which investment is *NOT* regulated by the real estate syndicate law?
   a. Syndication of fewer than 18 persons
   b. Limited partnership
   c. Joint venture
   d. Syndicate in real estate titles

8. How many days prior to use must materials used in advertising a real estate syndicate security be submitted to the Commission for examination?
   a. Three business days
   b. Three calendar days
   c. One week
   d. Ten business days

9. When submitting an application for a permit to sell a real estate syndicate security, the syndicator must also include a
   a. photograph of the property.
   b. copy of the prospectus.
   c. sworn affidavit identifying the syndicator.
   d. certified partnership tax return for the most recent year.

10. Under the license law, a real property securities dealer must file with the Commission within 60 days of the close of the business period
    a. a copy of the revised statement on the offerings.
    b. a financial report showing the total number and dollar volume of sales for the period.
    c. the complete books of the firm.
    d. the names and addresses of the property owners.

State Sources of Information

State of Connecticut

State of Connecticut Web site
www.ct.gov

Real Estate License Laws/Education

Connecticut Licensing Information Center
www.ct-clic.com

Connecticut Real Estate Commission*

Connecticut Real Estate Appraisal Commission*

Department of Consumer Protection*
*165 Capitol Avenue
State Office Building
Hartford, CT 06106
860-713-6050
800-842-2649
www.ct.gov/dcp

Center for Real Estate and Urban Economic Studies
University of Connecticut
2100 Hillside Road, Unit 1041RE
Storrs, CT 06269-1041
860-486-3227
www.business.uconn.edu/realestate

PSI Real Estate Licensing Examination Services
100 West Broadway, Suite 1100
Glendale, CA 91210-1202
800-733-9267
www.psiexams.com

Test Centers:
45 S. Main Street, Ste. 209   488 Main Avenue
West Hartford, CT   Norwalk, CT

Real Estate Brokerage

Connecticut Association of Realtors®, Inc.
111 Founders Plaza, 11th Floor
East Hartford, CT 06108
860-290-6601 / 800-335-4862
www.ctrealtor.com

Connecticut CCIM Chapter
chapters.ccim.com/connecticut

Connecticut MLS Services
www.ctreal.com

Legal

General Statutes of Connecticut (updated January 2009)
www.cga.ct.gov/2009/pub/titles.htm

Connecticut State Library
www.cslib.org

Connecticut Bar Association
www.ctbar.org

Connecticut On-line Commercial Recording Database
www.sots.ct.gov

Megan's Law Sex Offender Registry
www.ct.gov/dps

Municipal Information and Records

Municipality Web sites
www.ct.gov/ctportal/cwp/view.asp?a=843&q=257266

Tax Assessors Records
www.visionappraisal.com

Property Specific Information

Comparable Sales
www.zillow.com

Maps and Satellite Images
earth.google.com

Leasing

Apartment Owners Association of Connecticut
http://aoact.wordpress.com/

Fair Housing

Commission on Human Rights and Opportunities
90 Washington Street
Hartford, CT 06106
860-566-7710
www.ct.gov/chro

Connecticut Fair Housing Center
221 Main Street, Suite 204
Hartford, CT 06106
860-247-4400
www.ctfairhousing.org

Fair Housing Association of Connecticut
45 Lyons Terrace
Bridgeport, CT 06614
203-576-8323
www.nationalfairhousing.org

Office of Protection & Advocacy for Persons with Disabilities
60B Weston Street
Hartford, CT 06120
860-297-4300
www.ct.gov/opapd

Office of Fair Housing & Equal Opportunity, HUD
www.hud.gov/local/index.cfm?state=ct

Municipal Fair Housing Offices or Commissions
Check local telephone book

Housing

Department of Economic & Community Development, Housing Department
www.ct.gov/ecd

Listing of Local Housing Authorities
www.ct.gov/ecd/cwp/view.asp?a=1098&Q=249720&ecdNav=%7C

Economic Information

Department of Economic Development
865 Brook Street
Rocky Hill, CT 06067
860-270-8000
www.ct.gov/ecd

Connecticut Center for Economic Analysis
ccea.uconn.edu

Connecticut Policy and Economic Council
www.cpec.org

Connecticut Market Data
www.ct.gov/ecd/cwp/view.asp?a=1106&q=251002

Connecticut Economic Resource Center
www.cerc.com

Mortgages

Department of Banking
44 Capitol Avenue
Hartford, CT 06106
860-240-8299
www.ct.gov/dob

Connecticut Mortgage Bankers Association
www.cmba.org

Connecticut Bankers Association
www.ctbankcom

Connecticut Housing Finance Authority
99 West Street
Rocky Hill, CT 06067-4005
860-721-9501
www.chfa.org

Environmental Issues

Department of Environmental Protection
165 Capitol Avenue, Room 117
State Office Building
Hartford, CT 06106
860-424-3000
www.ct.gov/dep

Office of Lead Paint
Department of Public Health
150 Washington Street
Hartford, CT 06106
860-509-7229
www.ct.gov/dph (choose Lead)

Underground Storage Tank Information
www.ct.gov/dep/cwp/view.asp?a=2692&q=322600

Architecture/Engineering

Architectural Licensing Board
Connecticut State Board of Landscape Architects
State Board of Examiners for Professional Engineers & Land Surveyors
www.ct.gov/dcp

Connecticut Association of Land Surveyors
www.ctsurveyor.com

Department of Transportation
www.ct.gov/dot

Connecticut Transaction Documentation

Outline of Documentation for Real Estate Licensees in Connecticut Residential Purchase and Sale Transaction	
Initially	**Written Agency Agreement** (or Consent to Subagency)
Marketing/Locating Property	**Real Estate Agency Disclosure Notice given to Unrepresented Persons** (given to unrepresented parties the agent works with) **Lead Hazard Information Pamphlet** (given to potential Purchasers if housing built before 1978)
Open House	**Post sign or display pamphlet disclosing Agent's agency relationship**
If Firm Represents Both Buyer and Seller in Transaction	**Dual Agency Consent Agreement** *- or -* **Dual Agency/Designated Agency Notice and Consent Agreement**
Prior to Offer	**Connecticut Property Condition Disclosure Form** (completed by Seller, given to Buyer, attached to offer, binder, contract) **Lead-Based Paint Disclosure Statement** (if housing built before 1978; completed by Seller, given to Buyer, attached to contract) **CIOA Public Offering Statement** (if initial sale of condo, co-op, or PUD; given to Buyer before contract signed)
At Time of Contract	**Purchase and Sale Agreement** **Hazardous Waste Notice** (can be included as part of Purchase and Sale Agreement) **Disclosure of Gun and Hunting Clubs** **Resale Certificate** (if resale of condo, co-op, or PUD; given to Buyer before conveyance)

Connecticut Specific Real Estate Math Applications

Real estate professionals must have a working knowledge of mathematics because much of real estate involves working with numbers in a variety of contexts. The principles textbooks detail the basics of real estate math; this appendix will focus only on real estate math applications where Connecticut specific law or customs dictate computations.

■ PERCENTAGES

Brokerage Commissions (Chapter 2)

A brokerage firm's compensation (under both listing agreements and buyer agency agreements) is usually set as a percentage of the sales. Further, a salesperson's share of the commission is usually set as a percentage of the broker's commission. If a co-brokerage firm is involved, the co-brokerage firm's share of the commission is usually set as a percentage of the listing broker's commission.

Remember: When converting a percentage you move the decimal point two places to the left. 50% = 0.50

■ **FOR EXAMPLE** A seller listed a home for $220,000 and agreed to pay the listing brokerage firm a commission of 6 percent of the sales price. Through the multiple listing service, the listing brokerage firm agreed to pay any brokerage firm that introduced the buyer to the property 50 percent of the commission collected. The brokerage firm that introduced the buyer to the property has agreed to pay 50 percent of its share of the commission to its salesperson working with the buyer. If the house sold for $205,000, how much commission did the salesperson receive?

Listing brokerage firm's commission = 6% of $205,000 = 0.06 × 205,000 = $12,300

Share to buyer brokerage firm = 50% of $12,300 = 0.50 × $12,300 = $6,150

Share to buyer brokerage firm's salesperson = 50% of $6,150 = 0.50 × $6,150 = $3,075

■ **FOR EXAMPLE** Seller has agreed to pay the listing broker 4.5 percent of the sales price. Listing broker will give 1.5 percent to a buyer broker who introduces a buyer to the property. If the property sells for $575,000, how much does the seller pay the listing broker? How much does the listing broker pay the buyer broker?

Listing broker's commission = 4.5% of $575,000 = 0.045 × 575,000 = $25,875

Buyer broker compensation from listing broker = 1.5% of $575,000 = 0.015 × $575,000 = $8,625

Property Taxes (Chapter 6)

Real estate is taxed at the municipal level in Connecticut. Annual property tax is calculated by dividing a property's assessed value by $1,000 and then multiplying by the town's tax rate. The assessed value of a parcel of real estate is 70 percent of its market value. Tax rates vary by municipality, but all are expressed in mills (and are equivalent to dollars of tax per thousand dollars of assessed value).

■ **FOR EXAMPLE** An office building in Wallingford has a market value of $550,000. Wallingford's mill rate is 37 mills. What should the annual property tax be?

Assessed value = 70% of $550,000 = 0.70 × $550,000 = $385,000

$$\text{Indicated annual property tax} = \frac{\$385,000}{1,000} \times 37 = \$385 \times 37 = \$14,245$$

■ **FOR EXAMPLE** A house in Madison has a market value of $910,000. Madison's mill rate is 22 mills. What should the annual property tax be?

Assessed value = 70% of $910,000 = 0.70 × 910,000 = $637,000

$$\text{Indicated annual property tax} = \frac{\$637,000}{1,000} \times 22 = \$637 \times 22 = \$14,014$$

Note that actual property taxes may vary from indicated property taxes, depending on the municipality's opinion of a property's market value.

Conveyance Taxes (Chapter 8)

Connecticut levies the following two taxes upon the conveyance of *residential* real estate:

1. A municipal conveyance tax of 0.11 percent of the sales price
2. A state conveyance tax of 0.5 percent of the first $800,000 of the sales price, and 1 percent for any amount over $800,000

For *nonresidential* property, the municipal conveyance tax rate is still 0.11 percent, but the state conveyance tax rate is a straight 1 percent.

Note: For the time period of March 15, 2003, to June 30, 2011, the municipal conveyance tax rate is 0.25 percent. After June 30, 2011, the municipal conveyance tax is scheduled to revert back to 0.11 percent (unless the legislature chooses to extend the increase).

In addition to the above state conveyance taxes, 18 "targeted investment communities" have the option of imposing an added 0.25 percent to the municipal conveyance tax, which would increase the total municipal conveyance tax in these communities to 0.36 percent (0.50 percent during the years when the base municipal conveyance tax was 0.25 percent).

Unless otherwise stated, for purposes of all questions in this book, the 0.11 percent municipal tax rate is used. Adjustments would have to be made in real life accordingly if the town/time frame required one of the different rates.

■ **FOR EXAMPLE** A house in Mansfield sells for $380,000. What is the total conveyance tax to be paid?

Municipal conveyance tax = $380,000 × 0.0011 = $418

State conveyance tax = $380,000 × 0.005 = $1,900

Total conveyance tax = $418 + $1,900 = $2,318

■ **FOR EXAMPLE** A house in Stamford sells for $1,300,000. What is the total conveyance tax to be paid?

Municipal conveyance tax = $1,300,000 × 0.0011 = $1,430

State conveyance tax = $800,000 × 0.005 = $4,000

+ ($1,300,000 – 800,000) × 0.01 = $500,000 × 0.01 = $5,000

= $4,000 + $5,000 = $9,000

Total conveyance tax = $1,430 + $9,000 = $10,430

■ **FOR EXAMPLE** Residential property sold in Meriden for $499,000. Meriden is one of the targeted investment communities that has an increased municipal conveyance tax rate, so the total municipal conveyance tax is 0.36 percent. What is the total conveyance tax to be paid?

Municipal conveyance tax = $499,000 × 0.0036 = $1,796.40

State conveyance tax =$499,000 × 0.005 = $2,495.00

Total conveyance tax = $1,796.40 + $2,495.00 = $4,291.40

■ **FOR EXAMPLE** An office building sold in West Hartford for $950,000. What is the total conveyance tax to be paid?

Municipal conveyance tax = $950,000 × 0.0011 = $1,045

State conveyance tax = $950,000 × 0.01 = $9,500

Total conveyance tax = $1,045 + $9,500 = $10,545

■ **FOR EXAMPLE** Assume in the above example that the office building sold in May 2007 for $950,000 (when the municipal conveyance tax rate was 0.25%). What is the total conveyance tax to be paid?

Municipal conveyance tax = $950,000 × 0.0025 = $2,375

State conveyance tax =$950,000 × 0.01 = $9,500

Total conveyance tax = $2,375 + $9,500 = $11,875

Calculation of Purchase Price Based on Conveyance Tax (Chapter 8)

Connecticut does not require that a deed state actual consideration paid for property, but the amount of town conveyance tax paid in relation to the sale is always stamped on a recorded deed. The sales price can be calculated by looking at the conveyance tax paid. This is done by dividing the town conveyance tax paid by the town conveyance tax rate in effect at the time of conveyance.

■ **FOR EXAMPLE** The conveyance tax stamp on a recently recorded deed states that $328.90 was paid for town conveyance tax. What was the sales price of the property?

$$\text{Sales price} = \frac{\$328.90}{0.0011} = \$299,000$$

■ **FOR EXAMPLE** The conveyance tax stamp on a deed recorded in January 2005 (when the municipal conveyance tax rate was 0.25%) states that $1,275 was paid for town conveyance tax. What was the sales price of the property?

$$\text{Sales price} = \frac{\$1,275}{0.0025} = \$510,000$$

■ PRORATIONS (CHAPTER 16)

Sometimes property-related expenses are paid or received on a monthly or yearly basis. So a seller may have to prepay a bill for services used by the buyer after the closing, or the buyer may have to pay a bill for services used by the seller before the closing. Proration is a way for the buyer to pay back the seller for bills the seller has paid in advance, or for the seller to pay the buyer for bills the buyer will pay in arrears.

Statutory Year

When an item covering a period of time is prorated, or adjusted, it is the usual practice in Connecticut to use a 12-month (30 days each) or 360-day year.

■ **FOR EXAMPLE** Seller prepays a community well water bill of $180 per year on January 1 for the year. The closing transferring the property to the buyer is scheduled for September 16. At closing, how much will buyer reimburse seller for the water bill?

Number of days bill paid for buyer = 14 (Sept) + 30 (Oct) + 30 (Nov) + 30 (Dec) = 104 days

Per day rent = $180 per year ÷ 360 days = $0.50 per day

Proration = $0.50 ÷ day × 104 days = $52

Credit to seller, debit to buyer (because bill paid in advance)

■ **FOR EXAMPLE** Seller's property is rented for $600 a month, paid on the first of the month. The closing on the property to the buyer is scheduled for April 20. At closing, how much will seller reimburse buyer for this item?

Number of days owed = 30 days – 20 days = 10 days

Per day rent = $600 per month ÷ 30 days = $20

Proration = $20 per day × 10 days = $200

Credit to buyer, debit to seller (because rent received in advance)

Through Day of Closing

In Connecticut, it is customary for the seller to pay the property expenses for the day of closing. Therefore, the seller's obligation for any accrued expenses ends on the day of closing, and the buyer reimburses the seller for any prepaid expenses beginning with the day after closing.

■ **FOR EXAMPLE** Seller paid $125 in condominium common charges for the month of July. The closing is set for July 17. At closing, how much will buyer reimburse seller for this expense?

Number of days owed = 30 days – 17 days = 13 days

Per day common charge rate = $125 per month ÷ 30 days = $4.17

Proration = $4.17 per day × 13 days = $54.21

Credit to seller, debit to buyer (because bill paid in advance)

■ **FOR EXAMPLE** Property is transferred from seller to buyer on June 14. If buyer will pay a gas bill of $400 for gas used in June, how much should seller reimburse buyer? (Note this is just an illustrative example; typically the gas company will send separate bills to both buyer and seller for only the time period each owned the property.)

Number of days owed = 14 days

Per day gas rate = $400 per month ÷ 30 days = $13.33

Proration = $13.33 per day × 14 days = $186.62

Credit to buyer, debit to seller (because bill paid in arrears)

Property Taxes

In Connecticut, real estate taxes are based on ownership of property from October 1 to September 30. That tax is then owed in two installments on the following July 1 and January 1. Given that taxes are paid in arrears, the seller will owe the buyer from the most recent payment date (July 1 or January 1) through the day of closing.

■ **FOR EXAMPLE** The annual property tax on a house is $3,600. The property is scheduled to close on March 15. What is the proration?

Number of days owed = 30 (Jan) + 30 (Feb) + 15 (Mar) = 75 days

Per day tax = $3,600 per year ÷ 360 days = $10 per day

Proration = 75 days × $10 per day = $750

Credit to buyer, debit to seller (because bill paid in arrears)

■ **FOR EXAMPLE** The annual property tax on a house is $7,120. The property is scheduled to close on April 2. What is the proration?

Number of days owed = 30 (Jan) + 30 (Feb) + 30 (Mar) + 2 (Apr) = 92 days

Per day tax = $7,120 per year ÷ 360 days = $19.78 per day

Proration = 92 days × $19.78 per day = $1,819.56

Credit to buyer, debit to seller (because bill paid in arrears)

 **APPENDIX**

Electronic Signatures and Contracts

This appendix consists of a legal alert written by Eugene Marconi, General Counsel of the Connecticut Association of REALTORS®, Inc., for the Connecticut Association of REALTORS®, Inc. It is reprinted with permission of the Connecticut Association of REALTORS®, Inc.; all rights are reserved.

ELECTRONIC SIGNATURES

Attorney Eugene A. Marconi, General Counsel

October 8, 2001

Revised July 30, 2002

Revised May 20, 2003

■ INTRODUCTION

For several years now, REALTORS® have been bombarded by pundits urging them to enter the new age of electronic communications. Web sites, e-mails, and instant messaging have become as much a part of the REALTORS®' tool kit as MLS books and the telephone were several years ago.

Many REALTORS® have adapted their practices to the electronic age by using fax machines. Most REALTORS®, however, did not realize that the law, to a large extent, had not caught up to the electronic age and was not far advanced from the days of the quill pen and ink well.

This Legal Alert will discuss Connecticut law concerning signatures and legislative attempts to bring the law (albeit kicking and screaming) into the electronic age, including the Electronic Records and Signature in Commerce Act and the Connecticut Uniform Electronic Transactions Act (CUETA).

■ CONNECTICUT LAW AND "WET" SIGNATURES

Connecticut courts have attempted to define a "signature" for many years. The last Connecticut Supreme Court case defining a signature occurred in 1975. In that case, the Court stated that "a signature is the name of a person written with his own hand to signify that the writing which precedes accords with his wishes or intentions." As you can see, the Connecticut courts traditionally favored a so-called "wet" signature, where the signer took pen in hand and signed his or her own name, or made a mark or other distinguishing writing. Using such a definition, neither a faxed signature nor an electronic signature was valid.

Connecticut courts have not been entirely oblivious to technological change, however. Connecticut had several cases in the late 19th and early 20th centuries dealing with that technological revelation, the rubber stamp. In the rubber stamp cases, the courts dealt with the question as to the validity of signing a document by means of a rubber stamp. These cases are useful for two reasons. First, this is an instance where the Connecticut courts authorized use of something other than a true "wet" signature. Second, the courts engaged in a useful discussion as to the reasons for requiring a signature. Essentially, there are two reasons for requiring a signature. The first is that a signature shows that the person intended to be bound by what is written in the document. The second reason is that the signature shows that the document is the authentic document. It is useful to keep these concepts in mind as they also carry over into the world of electronic signatures.

■ ENTER CONGRESS

Several states adopted legislation authorizing electronic signatures. This legislation varied; some were simply authorizing the electronic signature of documents and others specifying that certain technologies be used to produce an encrypted or secure signature. Congress began to get nervous over the various approaches that these states adopted. Believing that there should be one approach in use throughout the country and that this approach should not involve the adoption of any particular technology, Congress passed the Electronic Records and Signature in Commerce Act, also known as "E-sign." This Act preempts all state legislation to the contrary for contracts involving interstate commerce. Generally, real estate is so intertwined in interstate commerce that virtually all real estate transactions, especially those involving financing, are interstate commerce. Let us take a closer look at the Electronic Records and Signature in Commerce Act.

■ ELECTRONIC RECORDS AND SIGNATURE IN COMMERCE ACT

The Act applies to every sort of electronically transmitted signature. Therefore, it includes e-mails and facsimile transmissions commonly known as faxes. REALTORS®, therefore, have guidance from Congress as to how to obtain a signature on a document transmitted through a fax machine. The Act goes on to state that an electronically signed document is the equivalent of a written document with a so-called "wet" signature. This is so despite any requirement in state law that a document be in writing or be signed. As all REALTORS® will recall from their Principles and Practices course, a contract for the sale of real estate is not enforceable unless it is in writing. This is called the statute of frauds. As a result of this Act, the statute of frauds can be met electronically as well as with paper and ink. Similarly, Connecticut's statute requires that listing and buyer representation agreements be in writing and signed. The requirements for these agreements can also now be met electronically.

The Act is technology neutral. An "electronic signature" is defined very broadly. It is an "electronic sound, symbol, or process, attached to or logically associated by a person with the intent to sign the record." In other words, it does not matter whether an encrypted signature is used or whether any encryption is used. So long as the parties are agreeable to contracting electronically and can agree on what constitutes a "signature," the use of that agreed-upon signature will be adequate to properly execute the electronic document.

■ PROTECTION FOR CONSUMERS

Congress was also worried about consumers being forced to contract electronically or being put in a position where they were not able to send and receive electronic documents but were bound by the electronic documents. Therefore, Congress required that a notice be given to a consumer. A "consumer transaction" was defined as one for family or household purposes. The typical real estate transaction would, therefore, be a "consumer transaction" for purposes of the Act.

Consumers who are asked to contract electronically must be provided with a notice. As you might imagine, the notice must meet certain requirements. These are:

1. Consumers affirmatively consent to the use of electronic records.
2. Consumers receive a "clear and conspicuous" statement informing them of the right to receive records in paper or in non-electronic form, the right to withdraw consent regarding electronic transactions, and the process for requesting paper records.
3. Consumers receive a statement of the "hardware and software requirements" for access to and retention of electronic records.
4. Consumers consent electronically in a manner that "reasonably demonstrates" that they can access the information.

As can be seen from this list, the statement that "the parties agree to be bound by their faxed signatures" contained in many Board and company listing agreements, buyer representation agreements, and purchase contract forms does not meet the Act's requirements for consumer transactions. REALTORS® *should therefore not rely on these statements for the fax execution of listing agreements, buyer representation agreements, and purchase contracts in residential transactions.* A form of notice that meets the Act's requirements is attached to this Legal Alert and can be found on CAR's Fax-On-Demand service at 800-335-4862 or at *www.ctrealtor.com*. This addendum can be used in listing agreements and buyer representation agreements. It should also be noted that the CAR Purchase and Sale Agreement form incorporates the required notice and can be executed electronically.

■ ENTER THE CONNECTICUT LEGISLATURE

Congress granted permission for a state to adopt its own electronic signature legislation. Any state that adopted the Uniform Electronic Transactions Act (UETA) "substantially in its reported form" could do so without preemption by E-sign. Connecticut enacted Public Act 02-68 "An Act Concerning the Connecticut

Uniform Electronic Transactions Act" in the 2002 session. The Connecticut version of the Uniform Electronic Transactions Act is known as CUETA and took effect October 1, 2002. The Act applies to every transaction and contract except for wills and those documents that are recorded in the land records. The Act provides that an electronic record or electronic signature is attributable to a person if it was the act of the person. Whether an electronic record or electronic signature was the act of the person may be shown in any manner. In other words, evidence that a faxed signature bears a very great resemblance to the pen and ink signature of the person executing the document can be used to show that the faxed signature was the act of that person. This does not mean that the simple statement contained in board and company forms is sufficient to have a document executed by fax.

CUETA does answer certain questions that E-sign left unanswered. CUETA provides that an electronic record is "sent" when (a) it is addressed properly or otherwise directed properly to an information processing system that the recipient has designated or uses for the purpose of receiving electronic records or information of the type sent; (b) from which the recipient is able to retrieve the electronic record; (c) is in a form capable of being processed by that information processing system; and (d) enters the information processing system outside the control of the sender. In other words, a fax is "sent" when you run it through the fax machine and it enters the telephone line with the proper phone number. An e-mail is sent once the "send" button is hit and the e-mail enters the telephone line. An electronic record is "received" when it enters the information processing system of the recipient or someone the recipient has designated or uses for the purpose of receiving electronic records. So a recipient who asked that the contract be faxed to an office supply center "receives" the document when the document reaches the office supply center's fax machine. However, if the sender is aware that the electronic record was not actually sent or received, the legal effect of the sending or receipt is determined by Connecticut law governing contracts in general or by the terms of the contract itself.

In addition, CUETA states that unless otherwise expressly provided for in the electronic record or agreed upon between the sender and recipient, the electronic record is deemed to be sent from the sender's "place of business" and to be received at the recipient's "place of business." If the sender or the recipient do not have a "place of business," then the sender or recipient's residence is considered to be the "place of business." Since the parties can establish the "place of business," it is possible to use a third party, like the parties' REALTOR®, as the "place of business." However, this means that the REALTOR®'s e-mail or fax will continue to be used as the "place of business" unless the parties subsequently agree otherwise.

There are several items in CUETA that REALTORS® should note. *First, the notices required by federal law for consumer transactions apply to residential real estate transactions.* Therefore, an electronic record, which includes a fax, should not be used in the purchase and sale of a residence unless the federal law's notice requirements are met. **Please note that under both CUETA and E-sign, a simple statement in a listing, buyer representation agreement, or purchase and sale contract that the parties agree to be bound by their faxed signatures is insufficient to create a legally binding electronic signature.** Further, in order to avoid arguments over the location of the recipient's "place of business," the electronic document should indicate where the electronic record is to be faxed or e-mailed and that is the only address or telephone number that should be used. Therefore, REALTORS® electronically contracting should obtain the e-mail address or fax number where the consumer wishes to send and receive electronic documents to avoid questions over whether the consumer's residence or employer is the consumer's place of business. The CAR addendum for listings and buyer representation agreements meets the requirements of both E-sign and CUETA. The CAR form "Purchase and Sale Contract" also meets the requirements of both E-sign and CUETA.

■ ADVICE FOR REALTORS®

1. Remember that E-sign and CUETA apply to all forms of electronic contracting and electronic execution of documents including faxes, e-mails, instant messaging, and other forms of electronic communications.
2. Do not rely on statements in Board form and company form agreements stating "that the parties agree to be bound by their faxed signatures" for residential transactions. As a result of E-sign and CUETA, these statements do not meet the requirements to validate an electronic signature for a consumer transaction. Only those documents electronically executed using the proper notice mandated by E-sign and CUETA will be effective.
3. REALTORS® seeking to have documents electronically executed in foreign countries should be aware of the Acts in those countries and of the statutes in those countries concerning electronic execution of documents. They may or may not be the same as U.S. law.

■ SUMMARY

Congress and the Connecticut legislature have spoken on the electronic execution of documents and have established rules for the electronic execution of these documents. REALTORS® varying from these rules risk having consumers argue that their listing agreement, purchase and sale contract, or buyer representation agreement has not been properly executed and is therefore invalid. Since the rules are not particularly extensive or troublesome in order to execute documents electronically, REALTORS® should begin using the notice to ensure that there can be no claims that the required documents were not validly executed.

THIS LEGAL ALERT FOR REALTORS® IS INTENDED FOR GENERAL INFORMATION PURPOSES AND IS NOT INTENDED TO PROVIDE LEGAL ADVICE ON ANY SPECIFIC FACTS. IF YOU HAVE SPECIFIC QUESTIONS CONCERNING YOUR OWN SITUATION, PLEASE CONSULT YOUR ATTORNEY.

FIGURE E.1

ADDENDUM FOR USE OF ELECTRONIC SIGNATURE AND RECORD

Addendum for Use of Electronic Signature and Record

This Addendum is used with one or more of the following documents (check all that apply):

☐ Listing Agreement dated: _____

☐ Buyer Representation Agreement dated: _____

You agree that we may use an electronic record, including fax or e-mail, to make and keep this Agreement.

You need not agree to use an electronic record. By a written notice to us, you have the right to withdraw your consent to have a record of this Agreement provided or made available to you in electronic form, but that does not permit you to withdraw your consent to the Agreement itself once it has been signed. We will provide you with a paper copy of this Agreement should you request one in writing to us at the address, e-mail or fax number listed below. Your agreement to use an electronic record applies only to this particular real estate transaction and not to all real estate transactions in which you are a party.

For access to and retention of faxed records, there are no special hardware or software requirements beyond access to a fax machine or fax modem and accompanying software connected to a personal or laptop computer or a service that converts faxed documents to e-mail. For access to and retention of e-mail records, you will need a personal or laptop computer, Internet account and e-mail software or web browser.

My electronic addresses are: My fax number is:_____

My e-mail address is:_____

All electronic records will be sent to the fax number or e-mail address noted above unless you inform us of any change in your e-mail address or fax number in writing to the Brokerage Firm address, e-mail or fax number set forth.

_____	_____
Signature	Brokerage Firm
_____	_____
Print Name	Brokerage Firm address
_____	_____
Signature	Brokerage Firm e-mail
_____	_____
Print Name	Brokerage Firm fax number

©2000-2007 Connecticut Association of Realtors®, Inc.
Revised July 30, 2002; May 7, 2003; June 28, 2007; July 30, 2010

REALTOR®

ANSWER KEY

Following the answers in the Answer Key are references to pages of the text where points are discussed or explained. A brief rationale for the answer is also provided. These references are made to help you make maximum use of the tests. If you did not answer a question correctly, you may want to consider rereading the course material until you understand the correct answer.

CHAPTER 1
Real Estate Brokerage and Agency

1. **b** (2) Connecticut requires a person who engages in a real estate activity for another and for a fee to hold a Connecticut broker's license. A salesperson cannot work directly for another but, rather, can only work on behalf of a broker.

2. **a** (3) A Connecticut real estate salesperson must be affiliated with and supervised by a Connecticut real estate broker. The salesperson can be either an employee of the broker or an independent contractor. Salespersons do not enter into agency relationships with clients. Brokers *enter into* agency relationships with clients, and then salespersons work on behalf of the broker also as an agent of the broker's client.

3. **d** (3) A real estate broker's license does not allow a person to appraise real estate. A separate real estate appraisal license is required to perform appraisals.

4. **b** (3) A legal entity that engages in the real estate business in Connecticut must hold a valid broker's license. The majority of ownership in the entity must be held by Connecticut licensed brokers, and all owners must hold either a Connecticut broker's or salesperson's license.

5. **b** (5) Connecticut law allows a broker working with a buyer to be the buyer's agent. To enter into an agency relationship with the buyer, the broker would need to enter into a written buyer agency agreement. Because Connecticut limits subagency, it would not be typical that the broker working with the buyer would be the subagent of the seller.

6. **d** (6) To enter into an agency relationship with the buyer, the broker would need to enter into a written buyer agency agreement.

7. **a** (10) Agency disclosures are given to unrepresented parties. When the broker represents a seller, agency disclosure is given to the buyer, if the buyer is not represented by another broker.

8. **c** (8) Connecticut allows dual agency (representing both parties in the same transaction) if the broker obtains the informed consent of both parties. Designated agency can but does not need to be chosen with dual agency.

9. **a** (8–9) In dual agency, the broker and all the salespersons working on behalf of the broker represent both parties to the transaction. This means that they owe fiduciary duties to both parties and must keep both parties personal information confidential. Answers b, c, and d would be disclosing a client's confidential information, and such disclosure is prohibited.

10. **b** (7–8) Sal is not a dual agent because Sal no longer represents the seller. But because the seller was a former client, Sal must keep the seller's personal information that was obtained during the former agency relationship confidential. Information about the physical condition of the property is not confidential, but information about prior offers is confidential.

11. **b** (6–8) When a broker represents both the seller and buyer in a transaction (dual agency), all salespersons who are affiliated with the broker also represent both the seller and buyer (and are all dual agents). The only exception to this is when designated agency is chosen; in that case *just* the designated agents are no longer dual agents and are single agents of either the seller or buyer.

12. **c** (4) An unlicensed personal assistant cannot act as a licensee. Permitted and prohibited activities are outlined in Figure 1.1.

13. **a** (15) A real estate licensee is prohibited from receiving a referral fee for referring mortgage business to a lender.

14. **d** (14–15) A broker who has performed services relating to all types of residential and commercial property has the right to place a lien on the property to secure payment of compensation.

CHAPTER 2
Listing and Buyer Agency Agreements

1. **a** (25) All agency agreements must be in writing to be enforceable. Connecticut law allows for agency agreements with a seller (listing agreements) and buyer (buyer agency agreements).
2. **b** (31) The broker would be required to keep the agency agreement and related disclosures for seven years from the time the listing expired.
3. **d** (27) Real estate brokerage compensation is always negotiable.
4. **d** (28) Exclusive right-to-buy or right-to-sell agency agreements are allowed but must be clearly indicated as such in the agreement.
5. **c** (28) Any exclusive listing contract requires that the broker make a diligent effort to sell the property. Any exclusive buyer agency contract requires that the broker make a diligent effort to find a property for the buyer.
6. **a** (26) Without representing Betty with a written buyer agency agreement, a real estate licensee cannot ask her to disclose confidential information (qualifying for a mortgage requires discussing a buyer's finances).
7. **c** (26–27) The salesperson from Hartfield Realty is an agent of all the sellers that Hartfield has entered into listing agreements with. Therefore, the salesperson has a duty to attempt to sell those listings, including showing the listings to buyers. The salesperson and/or Hartfield do not need to also represent the buyer to show the buyer Hartfield listings; in fact the salesperson can work with the buyer as a customer. If the buyer is unrepresented by Hartfield or another broker, then the buyer must be given an agency disclosure notice.
8. **d** (28) Net listings are illegal in Connecticut.
9. **a** (31) A broker must obtain a property owner's consent before placing a sign on the property.
10. **c** (31) Salespersons can advertise, but cannot advertise listed property in their own name. All advertisements placed by a salesperson must be made in the name of the broker (or brokerage agency) under whom the salesperson is licensed.
11. **d** (31) When advertising another broker's listing, that information must be updated every 72 hours.
12. **a** (31) An e-mail related to real estate service is considered advertising. Among other requirements, Susie must include the name of the real estate broker she is affiliated with.

CHAPTER 3
Interests in Real Estate

1. **d** (53) Dower and curtesy are not recognized in Connecticut.
2. **c** (53) Under Connecticut law, the wife would be entitled to a life estate equal in value to one-third of her deceased partner's property (real and personal).
3. **d** (54) Connecticut law does not allow a homeowner to exempt any amount from a foreclosing mortgagee. A homeowner is able to exempt $75,000 from other nonvoluntary creditors.
4. **a** (55) The burden of proof in matters concerning rights-of-way and other easements lies with the user (party claiming the easement).
5. **c** (55) The time required for acquisition of prescriptive easements is 15 years.
6. **c** (55) The time required for abandonment of prescriptive easements is 15 years.
7. **b** (55) In determining whether an easement has been acquired through prescription, a court decides whether all the requirements have been met.
8. **a** (56) When the owner of a property seeks to prevent another's acquisition of a right-of-way or easement, he or she must abide by the statutory procedures. Mere signs, letters to, or verbal contact with, the persons claiming the right will not qualify as an interruption of use in most cases.
9. **c** (56) For a licensor to revoke or cancel a license under Connecticut law, there must be a valid reason; it cannot be merely at the whim of the licensor.

10. **a** (56) The most critical factor in establishing the boundary of an upland owner is the determination of whether the body of water adjoining the owner's property is navigable.

CHAPTER 4

Forms of Real Estate Ownership

1. **d** (59) Connecticut does not recognize tenancy by the entirety. Married couples wishing to hold property together with rights of survivorship would choose joint tenancy.
2. **b** (65) The maximum fee that can be charged for the preparation of common interest ownership resale documents is $125.
3. **d** (65) Sellers of common interest community units can obtain resale documents by contacting the association. The association must file the name of the contact person, whether it is a property manager or an association officer, with the town clerk in the town where the community is located.
4. **c** (60) Partition can be voluntary or involuntary.
5. **b** (60) When physical partition is not possible, a court will order the sale of the property and distribute the proceeds to the co-owners according to their ownership shares.
6. **a** (60) A divorce decree has the effect of changing a formerly married couples' co-ownership interest from joint tenancy to tenancy in common.
7. **d** (62) The Common Interest Ownership Act covers all properties where a unit owner is required to financially contribute to the maintenance of common areas. This includes three types of defined communities: condominiums, cooperatives, and planned unit developments.
8. **c** (63) All common interest ownership communities, including condominiums, are created by filing a declaration in the land records in the town where the property is located.
9. **c** (64) When a developer sells a unit in a common interest ownership community, the developer must give the initial purchaser a public offering statement.

10. **a** (65) Upon resale of a common interest ownership unit, a seller must provide the buyer with a resale certificate and other resale documents. The buyer has a right to cancel the purchase within five business days after receiving these documents.

CHAPTER 5

Legal Descriptions

1. **c** (68) Legal descriptions in Connecticut typically refer to property boundaries via the system of metes and bounds.
2. **a** (69) Monuments are used to establish boundaries; the actual monument is typically an iron pin.
3. **b** (70) To reestablish lost boundaries, application must be made to the Connecticut Superior Court. The court then appoints a committee to research and determine the boundaries.
4. **b** (70) A superior court appointed committee's boundary determination is final, unless it can be proved that the committee made an error of law in researching its conclusion.
5. **c** (70–71) The Connecticut Common Interest Ownership Act dictates what is required for a legally sufficient description of any common interest ownership unit, including a condominium unit. A recital of the boundaries is not required (because the boundaries will be set forth in the original declaration recorded in the land records, and recording declaration for that document is required).
6. **c** (68) For purposes of a contract, a simple street address can be used to identify property. However, for purposes of conveyance, a full legal description would be required.

CHAPTER 6

Real Estate Taxes and Other Liens

1. **b** (73) Municipal real property tax is based on the value of a parcel of real estate. *Ad valorem* is Latin for "according to value."
2. **d** (73) Connecticut property tax assessment is 70 percent of a property's market value.
3. **a** (74) At a minimum, towns must physically revaluate real estate located in the town for tax purposes every five years.

4. **d** (74) Reviewing the categories of real estate that are eligible for tax relief, the wetlands category is not included.

5. **b** (75) Connecticut's real property tax rate is quoted in mills.

6. **b** (75) Assessment value = $100,000 market value × 0.70 = $70,000.
Tax = ($70,000 × 20 mills) ÷ 1,000 = $1,400.

7. **c** (76) Connecticut property taxes become a lien as of the date of assessment.

8. **a** (77) ABC Construction company's priority is the date when they began work—May 1. Country Bank's priority is the date when the mortgage was recorded—July 2. City Bank's priority is date when the mortgage was recorded—July 1.

9. **a** (77) Conveyance tax is based on the selling price of real estate.

10. **c** (75) Assessment value = $200,000 market value × 0.70 = $140,000.
Tax = ($140,000 assessment × 25 mills) ÷ 1,000 = $3,500.

CHAPTER 7
Real Estate Contracts

1. **a** (81) The Connecticut Statute of Frauds requires that all contracts involving consideration in excess of $500 be in writing to be enforceable.

2. **d** (83) Connecticut law prohibits brokers and salespersons from engaging in the activities that require a license to practice law. Redrafting a contract provision would most likely amount to practicing law.

3. **b** (82) A person can legally contract at the age of 18. Before 18, a person is not legally bound by any contract entered into (with few exceptions).

4. **a** (83) Agency contracts are bilateral contracts because they consist of a promise for a promise: A client promises to pay compensation to a broker, and the broker promises to assist in the transaction.

5. **a** (84) A purchase and sale contract signed by both parties is legally binding on the parties. Therefore, all negotiation of the contract provisions should take place before the agreement is signed. Such an agreement does not need to be signed by an attorney or broker to be valid. The purchase and sale contract does not transfer title; it is the agreement to transfer title in the future.

6. **c** (86–87) The Property Condition Disclosure report must be given in all residential transactions containing one to four dwelling units, with a few exceptions. The report is not required when the property being sold is commercial property.

7. **a** (86) The law states that the report must be given to buyers before the buyer makes a written offer.

8. **b** (86–87) If a seller does not believe that there is a problem and has no knowledge of a problem, it is appropriate for the seller to check "no." If the seller did not have any belief one way or the other, than the appropriate answer would be "unknown."

9. **c** (84) The law requires money received on behalf of a client be deposited in an escrow account within three banking days of receipt.

10. **d** (85) The law requires that a lease must be in writing to be enforceable if it is for greater than one year.

CHAPTER 8
Transfer of Title

1. **b** (105) To be valid, a deed must be in writing and contain the signature of the grantor, two witnesses, and an acknowldgement. The signature of the grantee is not required.

2. **b** (105) Connecticut law requires that a deed be signed by two witnesses.

3. **d** (106) A warranty deed contains guarantees made by the grantor to the grantee, and a quitclaim deed does not. Both convey title, if the grantor has the title to convey, and both can convey fee simple title. Both deeds are valid ways to convey title. Neither deed cures title defects; however, if a warranty deed is given and there is an undisclosed title defect, the grantor would be able to sue the grantee on the guarantees.

4. c (107) If a residential property sells for $450,000, the total conveyance tax to be paid would be $2,745. The conveyance tax is calculated as follows: Municipal Conveyance Tax = Selling Price × 0.0011
   = $450,000 × 0.0011
   = $495
   State Conveyance Tax = (Selling Price up to $800,000 × 0.005) + (Selling Price over $800,000 × 0.01)
   = ($450,000 × 0.005) + ($0 × 0.01)
   = $2,250

5. a (108) By dividing the municipal property tax paid of $192.50 by the current town conveyance tax rate of 0.11 percent (165 ÷ 0.0011), you can calculate that the purchase price was $175,000.

6. b (108) Transfers to government agencies are exempted from the conveyance tax.

7. c (106) If the grantor has changed his or her name since acquiring the property to be conveyed, both names should be included on a deed.

8. b (109) The amount of the additional conveyance tax is based on a sliding scale of 0 to 10 percent of the total sales price. Given Farmer Jones conveyed in the sixth year, the penalty is 4 percent (10 − 6). $2,250,000 × 0.04 = 90,000.

9. c (109) The adverse possession time period in Connecticut is 15 years.

10. b (110) In Connecticut, a will may be prepared by anyone of sound mind who is at least 18 years of age.

11. b (111) Refer to Figure 8.1, Intestate Distribution.

12. d (111) In the event that no legal heirs or assigns can be identified within 20 years of a real estate owner's death, the owner's real estate would be transferred to the state by escheat.

CHAPTER 9
Title Records

1. b (115) Recording does not transfer title. Recording gives other people constructive notice that the transfer has occurred.

2. b (115) Title is transferred upon delivery of a deed; in this situation, the deed is delivered November 15.

3. c (115) All documents affecting the title to real estate are required to be recorded in the land records.

4. a (116) Documents required to be recorded must be done so within a reasonable time.

5. d (115) The town clerk of a municipality maintains the land records.

6. a (118) A certificate of title summarizes the status of the title found while conducting a title search and, generally, includes a brief opinion about the marketability of the title.

7. c (120) An unbroken chain must be established for a period of 40 years.

8. c (119) Title insurance does not insure that there are not title defects or encumbrances. It insures that the only title defects or encumbrances are those that were found during the title search.

9. b (117) The law requires that a change of name that would affect a document already in the land records be recorded in the land records within 60 days.

10. d (117) Land records documents are indexed through grantor/grantee indexes.

CHAPTER 10
Real Estate License Law

1. b (123) The Connecticut Real Estate Commission administers the Connecticut licensing laws.

2. c (123) The license laws require that a person "engaging in the business of real estate" for another and for a fee must be licensed. A person buying or selling a house for herself would not need to be licensed to do so. A person constructing a house does not need a real estate license.

3. a (125) The license laws list specific activities that are included under the definition of "engaging in the real estate business." These include buying, selling, and renting real estate, as well as reselling mobile homes. A real estate license is not needed to invest in real estate.

4. a (125) The license laws provide a list of persons who can engage in real estate activities without a license. An attorney, performing a real estate activity while serving as counsel for a client, is not required to have a license. None of the other answers falls under an exemption.

5. **d** (125) A clerical employee of a real estate broker who does not engage in real estate activities is not required to hold a real estate license.

6. **a** (126) A license candidate must submit an application to the Department of Consumer Protection. If the application is approved, the Department of Consumer Protection will notify the testing vendor of the applicant's eligibility to sit for the licensing examination, and the testing vendor will then notify the applicant. Answers b, c, and d are not required.

7. **c** (125) Regular employees of real estate owners or landlords are not required to have a license to perform real estate activities conducted in the regular course of their business as long as the employee works and lives at the site where he or she engages in licensed activities.

8. **d** (126) To apply for a real estate broker's license, a candidate must have 60 hours of principles and practice, 30 hours of real estate appraisal, and 30 hours of an elective real estate course.

9. **a** (128) The state testing vendor will inform applicants whether they have passed or failed the licensing exam after they complete the exam. Applicants who fail the examination will receive statistical information about their performance and can schedule to retake it.

10. **a** (127) Fees are set by state statute and are set out at Figure 10.1.

11. **a** (128) The Commission can refuse to issue a license to an applicant who has been refused a license in any state, for whatever reason, within the year preceding the current application. Therefore, Alan must wait one year from the refusal of his license in another state.

12. **b** (130) All nonresident applicants must file an irrevocable consent to suit with the Commission, which enables persons to sue them in Connecticut.

13. **d** (131) Salespersons' licenses expire annually on May 31; brokers' licenses expire annually on March 31.

14. **c** (131) Both salespersons and brokers are required to take 12 hours of approved real estate continuing education courses every two years.

15. **d** (135) An agency agreement must contain all terms and conditions including compensation to be paid, beginning and expiration dates, type of agency agreement, and signatures and addresses of all parties concerned.

16. **a** (131) A salesperson can change broker affiliation by registering the change with the Commission and paying a $25 transfer fee.

17. **b** (141) A real estate licensee cannot offer legal advice or counsel, unless the licensee is also an attorney.

18. **c** (134) The licensing laws require that licensees accurately represent the sales price of a property. A broker telling a lender that the sales price of a property is more than it actually is has violated the licensing laws (and possibly also committed bank fraud).

19. **d** (138–9) Salespersons must give their designated broker all deposits, and brokers must then place these deposits in an escrow account. Neither a salesperson nor a broker can commingle client funds with their own personal funds.

20. **a** (132) Licensees have a duty to disclose material facts in a transaction. While the licensee representing the seller owes a fiduciary duty to the seller, the licensee still must disclose material facts to potential buyers. Basement flooding would be considered a material fact because it could affect a potential buyer's decision to purchase the property.

21. **b** (132) Licensees have a duty to disclose material facts in a transaction. Theoretically, a murder would be considered a material fact because it could affect a potential buyer's decision to purchase the property. However, by state law, death or felony on the property, as well as a property occupant's disease, is not legally considered a material fact and is not required to be disclosed to potential purchasers.

22. **c** (135) All electronic communication, including e-mail and bulletin board postings, must contain the licensee's name and office address, the name of the real estate broker with whom the licensee is affiliated, and all states where the licensee is licensed.

23. **d** (135) Internet advertising, which includes Web sites, must include, on every page of the site, the licensee's name and office address, the name of the real estate broker with whom the licensee is affiliated, all states where the licensee is licensed, and the last date when the site property information has been updated.

24. **a** (135) To advertise the property of another broker on a Web site or elsewhere, Ben must get the permission of the other broker. Also, the listing information cannot be changed in any way without the permission of the other broker, and Ben must update the other broker's property information every 72 hours.

25. **a** (135) The licensing law requires that a broker who enters into an agency agreement with a seller make a diligent effort to sell the property listed.

26. **b** (135) A licensee who receives an offer on behalf of a client must submit the offer to the client as quickly as possible. In making a decision to hold offers without being instructed to do so by Sallie, Ben has violated the licensing law.

27. **d** (136) In a transaction where there are two brokerage firms involved, all compensation must be paid to the real estate broker of the cooperating agency; it cannot be paid directly to another broker's salesperson.

28. **a** (137) Connecticut law prohibits a licensee from interfering with the agency relationship of another licensee, and that includes advising a client of another licensee to break her agency agreement.

29. **b** (140) A person may recover compensation from the Guaranty Fund if they are aggrieved by the following actions of a licensed real estate broker, salesperson, or unlicensed employee of a broker: the embezzlement of money or property; obtaining money or property from persons by false pretenses, trickery, or forgery; or fraud, misrepresentation, or deceit by or on the part of the licensed broker, salesperson, or unlicensed employee of the broker. The person must first sue the licensee in court and obtain a money judgment; if the licensee does not pay the money judgment, the person can seek funds from the Fund.

30. **c** (140) The licensing law sets the maximum compensation to be paid in connection with any single claim or transaction at $25,000.

CHAPTER 11

Real Estate Financing: Principles/Practice

1. **a** (148) Mortgage priority in Connecticut is established as of the date of recording.

2. **d** (148) Given that mortgage priority is established at the date of recording, the first mortgage lender will have first priority because of an earlier recording date. The home equity lender will have second priority (assuming that no other mortgages have been recorded in the interim). That means if the first mortgage lender were to foreclose, the mortgage interest of the home equity lender would be extinguished.

3. **b** (135) Any person negotiating a mortgage loan must be licensed as a mortgage loan originator. There is no exemption for real estate brokers and salespersons if a mortgage lender or broker is providing the compensation.

4. **a** (148) Any document affecting the status of title must be recorded. The only document affecting the status of title in the answer list is the mortgage release, which extinguishes a lender's mortgage interest in the property. A mortgage commitment is a lender's agreement to lend and does not affect title. A listing contract and a sales contract are agreements to perform, and they do not affect title (a sales contract is the agreement to convey in the future, but it does not actually convey any interest).

5. **d** (154) Connecticut allows a lender to collect a deficiency judgment when a foreclosure does not pay off the outstanding loan amount.

6. **a** (151–2) Under a strict foreclosure of a first mortgage, the interest of junior creditors or lenders will be extinguished. So those other creditors are given an opportunity to redeem the foreclosing mortgage.

7. **b** (153) Any party to a foreclosure suit may request that the court order a foreclosure by sale. If the court proceeds with this method, the court will appoint a committee to actually conduct the sale.

8. **b** (152) A judgment of strict foreclosure can only be reopened prior to the time that the title passes from the borrower to the lender.

9. **d** (152) A lender acquiring property through strict foreclosure must record a foreclosure certificate in the land records in order to show others that title had been conveyed to the lender.

10. **a** (154) Strict foreclosure does not involve a sale, so answers b and d are incorrect. The only time a borrower can redeem property being foreclosed on is before title passes.

CHAPTER 12
Leases

1. **d** (160) Connecticut allows for the recording of a notice of lease.

2. **b** (161) Leases without a specific term or expiration date are deemed to be month-to-month.

3. **b** (162) A provision in a lease waiving the tenant's right to interest on his or her security deposit is unenforceable; however, such a provision will not make the lease unenforceable.

4. **d** (163) Tenants must be informed of rules and regulations at the time of the lease agreement or at the time such rules and regulations are adopted.

5. **b** (167) Heat is an essential service. If a landlord has agreed to supply heat and does not, a tenant can procure substitute housing and sue the landlord for costs above the regular rent that would have had to have been paid.

6. **b** (165) A landlord can terminate a lease after a tenant is nine days late on the payment of rent (because nine days is considered the grace period).

7. **c** (166) A landlord cannot take retaliatory action against a tenant by raising rents within six months of a tenant making a reasonable request for repairs (unless the property operating expenses have increased, in which case the time frame is four months).

8. **d** (162) The current law stipulates that landlords must pay tenants interest on their security deposits only in residential units. The rate of interest payable is a floating rate tied to the average savings deposit rate.

9. **a** (162) If any rental payment is received later than ten days after the scheduled due date, the tenant forfeits the interest for the month he or she is late in paying the rent.

10. **b** (166) A landlord can sue a tenant for unpaid rent. If there is any time remaining on the lease, however, a landlord must make reasonable efforts to re-rent the property to mitigate damages.

11. **c** (168) At the end of an eviction process, if the tenant does not move out of the leased property, a court can instruct a marshal to remove the tenant's belongings from the property and place them on the street.

12. **c** (169) If an evicted tenant's possessions are removed from the property, after so many days they will be taken off the street and stored; if the tenant does not claim them, they will then be sold with unclaimed proceeds reverting to the town.

13. **a** (162) Security deposits for residential leases are regulated but not required.

14. **a** (165) Intentional damage of leased property is a criminal offense.

CHAPTER 13
Real Estate Appraisal

1. **a** (179) Connecticut requires a real estate appraiser license for a person to value real estate for a fee or other compensation.

2. **b** (180) A certified residential appraiser is only allowed to appraise residential real estate.

3. **d** (179) In general, real estate salespersons and brokers are not exempt from the appraisal licensing requirement, meaning that they cannot value real estate for a fee without holding an appraisal license. The one exception to this is that real estate salespersons and brokers can estimate the value of real estate for a real estate client as part of a market study, as long as the estimate of value is not referred to as an appraisal.

4. **a** (180) A person can act under a provisional appraisal license for four years.

5. **b** (180) A supervising appraiser can only sponsor up to three provisional appraisers, without obtaining a limitation waiver from the Appraisal Commission.

6. **c** (180) *USPAP* stands for *Uniform Standards of Professional Appraisal Practice*.

7. **a** (184) A person is required to meet 3,000 hours of appraisal experience for certified general appraisals, in addition to the extensive education requirements.

8. **c** (180) To qualify as a provisional appraiser, 75 hours of appraisal education and a sponsor are required.

9. **d** (183) All Connecticut licensed appraisers must take 28 hours of continuing education every two years.

10. **d** (183) A temporary license allows appraisers licensed in another state to conduct appraisal work on a temporary basis within the state.

CHAPTER **14**
Land-Use Controls and Property Development

1. **b** (188–9) Under Connecticut law, the local planning and zoning authorities can either be separate or combined commissions.

2. **d** (189) Local zoning law controls the use of land within a city or town.

3. **a** (190) The local planning commission has authority to regulate and approve subdivisions of land.

4. **b** (190) The state authorizes municipalities to incorporate planned unit development regulations as part of the municipal zoning regulations.

5. **d** (189) A homeowner seeking a use that is not permitted by the zoning regulations would need to obtain a variance. A variance will only be granted if the owner can show unusual hardship in the application of the zoning regulations. Special permit is not the correct answer to this question because special permit and special exception are for uses that are allowed under the zoning regulations but that are only permitted if specific standards are met.

6. **d** (191) Subdivision plans must be drawn up by a licensed surveyor.

7. **b** (191) Approved subdivision plans must be filed in the town clerk's office within 90 days from the expiration of the appeal period.

8. **c** (195) The new home implied warranty that the home is constructed in a workmanlike manner lasts for one year. There is also a three-year implied warranty that the home was built in compliance with the building code.

9. **c** (196) A homeowner is not prohibited from hiring an unregistered home improvement contractor; however, the contract between an unregistered contractor and homeowner is not enforceable by the contractor.

10. **d** (198) Shares in a real estate investment trust are exempt from the Connecticut interstate land sales laws. Subdivisions of less than five parcels are also exempt.

11. **b** (198) Under the Connecticut Interstate Land Sales Act, a seller must give a potential buyer a prospectus within 72 hours before the purchase contract is signed.

12. **d** (194) The Affordable Housing Land Use Appeals Act gives a developer the right to appeal the denial of a land use application for affordable housing. As part of the appeal, the burden of proof that the denial is justified is shifted to the town.

CHAPTER **15**
Fair Housing

1. (203–4) Yes, this would be discrimination under both the state and federal laws that cover two- to four-family houses that are not owner-occupied. The owner's mother living in the house does not make it owner-occupied when the owner lives elsewhere.

2. (204, 207) No, they cannot refuse to sell to your client with minor children unless they are claiming the complex qualifies as "housing for older persons," which means 80 percent occupied by those 55 and over or 100 percent occupied by those 62 and over. The fact that they have such a bylaw prohibiting minor children would not be relevant because there is no such exception recognized under either state or federal law. Unless they can prove they are "housing for older persons," their refusal to sell to your client would be a violation of both state and federal law.

3. (204) Yes, this is discrimination under the state law. It stipulates that the owner has to allow the tenant to modify the apartment to make it accessible if the tenant is willing to pay to have it done. Federal law does not apply because it exempts up to four-family, owner-occupied dwellings

4. (206) No, since it is four rooms or less and the owner lives in one of the four units, the federal law does not cover it. The state law does not apply because it is an owner-occupied rooming house.

5. (206) Yes, under the Civil Rights Act of 1866, there are no exceptions when race, color, or national origin is involved.

6. (204) Yes, the state law includes "source of income" as a protective class. Therefore, you cannot refuse to rent to someone simply because they receive public assistance. Needless to say, if the income that person receives is not sufficient to be able to afford the rental, the person can be denied for that reason. The federal law does not cover "source of income" and does not apply.

7. (207) Yes, this is discrimination under the state law because it indicates with regard to "age" that the only exceptions are minors and "housing for older persons." Unless the co-op can demonstrate that it falls in this category, it can't discriminate because of age. The federal law does not apply here because it does not cover age and the couple doesn't have minor children to make it a "familial status" complaint.

8. (204) Yes, now if a couple is denied because of age, they can complain under the federal law covering "familial status" because the policy of selling to only those 35 and over has a discriminatory impact on families with minor children. Unless the co-op complex qualifies as "housing for older persons," it will be discrimination under both the state and federal laws covering "familial status" and under the state law covering "age."

9. (204) Yes, this would be discrimination under the state law, which does cover single-family homes without exception. Federal law does not apply because the property is being sold without advertising or the use of an agent.

10. (206) Yes, it would be discrimination under Connecticut law because there is an exemption for owner-occupied rooming houses. However, it would be a violation of federal fair housing law. (See principles text.)

11. (205) No, if you abide by the owner's wishes, you will be guilty of discrimination under both the state and federal laws. The state law covers all single-family homes, and the federal law covers single-family homes that are either advertised or leased using an agent.

12. (206) Yes, it would be discrimination under Connecticut law because there is an exemption for owner-occupied rooming houses. However, it would be a violation of federal fair housing law, which only exempts up to four units or owner-occupied housing. (See principles text.)

13. (209) No, brokers, salespeople, and sellers are not liable for failing to disclose to a buyer that the property was previously occupied by a person with AIDS.

C H A P T E R 16
Closing the Real Estate Transaction

1. a (215) It is the responsibility of the closing attorney to calculate the prorations between buyer and seller, search the title, and prepare the mortgage note and deed.

2. d (215) Most residential real estate closings are held face-to-face, meaning that all of the parties involved in the transaction actually meet together to sign documents and exchange funds.

3. c (215) Real estate closings generally are held at the office of the closing attorney.

4. c (246 [Appendix D]) The seller has paid $180 for the month. The seller lived in the property for two-thirds of the month (20 days out of 30); therefore, the seller has prepaid for one-third of the month when the seller does not own the property. So the buyer must reimburse the seller for the one-third of $180, which is $60.

5. d (214) A licensee is prohibited from practicing law, which would include drafting a legal document such as a deed.

6. **d** (215) The purchase price and terms of a sale are considered private information—not to be shared with anyone—until recorded for public record. A licensee can disclose information about a transaction that is a matter of public record.

7. **d** (215) A licensee can never reveal a client's confidential information.

CHAPTER **17**
Environmental Issues and the Real Estate Transaction

1. **c** (218) Many Connecticut state agencies have a hand in environmental regulation in the state. However, the primary state agency is the Department of Environmental Protection.

2. **a** (219) Connecticut law requires that defective lead-based paint must be abated in properties where children under the age of six reside, regardless of whether a child has lead poisoning.

3. **b** (219) Connecticut law requires that defective lead-based paint must be abated in properties where children under the age of six reside, regardless of whether a child has lead poisoning.

4. **d** (220) Connecticut law does not require that private residential wells be tested; however, if such a test is conducted, the results must be reported to the municipality's public health authority.

5. **a** (222) Connecticut requires an assessment of any discharge, spillage, uncontrolled loss, seepage, or filtration of hazardous waste at an "establishment" prior to the transfer of ownership of the property.

6. **c** (221) Answers a, b, and d apply in this situation. What does not apply is keeping the information from potential purchasers; the presence of an underground storage tank is a material fact that must be disclosed.

7. **c** (222) An off-site hazardous waste facility may very well be considered a material fact requiring disclosure. However, disclosure of the availability of the Department of Environmental Protection information legally meets the seller's duty to disclose the presence of an off-site hazardous waste facility.

8. **a** (218) True, asbestos contractors must be licensed in Connecticut.

9. **a** (220) True, radon contractors must be registered in Connecticut.

10. **a** (219) True, lead-paint abatement contractors must be licensed in Connecticut.

APPENDIX **A**
Real Estate Securities

1. **c** (228) A real property securities dealer must be a licensed Connecticut broker and have his or her license endorsed by the Real Estate Commission.

2. **d** (230) The license law lists extensive information that must be disclosed but does not require information about adjoining properties.

3. **a** (230) If the Commission does not reply to a real property securities dealer within ten days after receipt of the marketing material submitted for approval, the dealer may consider them approved.

4. **b** (228) Real property security payments are guaranteed by the person selling the security (or by that person's principal).

5. **d** (229) Civil action involving real property securities must be initiated within three years from the date of the sale.

6. **c** (232) A permit and prospectus are both required; a real estate broker's license is not required.

7. **a** (233) The real estate syndicate license law does not regulate syndicates of less than 18 persons.

8. **a** (233) In marketing real estate syndicate securities, a syndicator must submit to the Commission for approval any advertising materials he or she wishes to use at least three business days before use.

9. **b** (232) A copy of the prospectus to be given to purchasers is required to be submitted.

10. **b** (230) The Connecticut license law requires that real property securities dealers furnish the Commission with a financial report within 60 days from the close of the dealer's usual business period.

PRACTICE EXAM

1. Connecticut licensing law recognizes the following listing agreements:
   a. exclusive right to sell, exclusive agency, open listing.
   b. exclusive right to sell, exclusive agency, open listing, MLS.
   c. exclusive right to sell, exclusive agency, open listing, net listing.
   d. exclusive right to sell, exclusive agency, open listing, MLS, net listing.

2. Sharon Buyer called Agent Michael to view his listing on Monroe Street. Sharon does not have an agent. Michael provides a written Agency Disclosure Notice to Sharon stating that he represents the seller.
   a. Before showing the house, Michael must have Sharon sign an agency agreement.
   b. Before Sharon views the property, she must sign a dual agency agreement.
   c. Sharon is not required to sign any agency agreement prior to viewing the property.
   d. Sharon must sign a purchase agreement prior to viewing the property.

3. A buyer purchases a for-sale-by-owner home. A broker states an entitlement to a brokerage fee. For this to be the case, the buyer would have entered into which type of buyer-broker agreement with the broker?
   a. Exclusive agency right to represent buyer
   b. Open right to represent the buyer
   c. Nonexclusive right to represent buyer
   d. Universal agency right to represent the buyer

4. A licensee can do the all of the following without entering into a written buyer agency agreement EXCEPT
   a. give the buyer information on the licensee's firm.
   b. provide the buyer with information on mortgage rates and lending institutions.
   c. physically show the buyer in-house listings.
   d. ask the buyer to disclose his or her confidential information.

5. Under Connecticut licensing law, brokers and agents have to disclose a present or contemplated interest in a property listed with them
   a. only when executing a buyer's broker agreement.
   b. if they are contemplating purchasing the property for their own account.
   c. only when a buyer decides to make an offer.
   d. in the listing agreement and in any advertisements.

6. Which statement is TRUE under Connecticut law?
   a. Net listings are recognized as listings.
   b. A broker can accept a net listing if all funds over the stated brokerage fee are received as a bonus instead of a commission.
   c. Connecticut license laws provide that licensed brokers may not accept a listing that is based on a "net" price.
   d. Net listings require the consent of the seller, buyer, and real estate licensee.

7. Under Connecticut law, real estate brokers are required to retain certain brokerage records such as offers and counteroffers drafted by the brokers office, contracts, leases, agency agreements and disclosures, escrow and trust account checks, and bank statements. These records must be kept
   a. ten years.
   b. indefinitely by the broker.
   c. five years.
   d. seven years.

8. The time required for acquisition of prescriptive easements is
   a. 10 years.
   b. 5 years.
   c. 15 years.
   d. 20 years.

9. An easement by prescription may be extinguished if the owner takes, obtains, or regains an open and continuous control and possession of the property for
   a. 15 years.
   b. 23 months.
   c. 10 years.
   d. 25 years.

10. A couple were married on July 4, 2007. Both individually owned a condominium prior to their marriage in their own name. They decided to keep the condominium units separate. Once they are married in Connecticut, their former properties will
    a. be owned as tenancy by the entirety.
    b. be owned with survivorship.
    c. become community property.
    d. remain as separate interests.

11. In an involuntary partition action, the following statements are true EXCEPT
    a. there is a physical division of the co-owned real estate.
    b. committees are appointed by the courts.
    c. courts can never provide equitable relief.
    d. partitions cannot always be fair and equitable.

12. The Common Interest Ownership Act regulates common interest properties. Which BEST describes the properties governed by this act?
    a. REITs, condominiums, cooperatives
    b. PUDs, condominiums, cooperatives
    c. Condominiums, cooperatives, REITs, PUDs
    d. Assisted living, condominiums, cooperatives

13. Resale documents must be furnished to the buyer or his or her attorney before the closing or transfer of possession. The buyer's right to cancel a purchase contract is how many days after the resale documents have been delivered?
    a. 10 business days
    b. 15 business days
    c. 5 business days
    d. 14 business days

14. When a unit owner requests a resale certificate from the association in writing, it must be provided within how many business days, and what can the association charge for the resale certificate?
    a. seven days, $100
    b. seven days, $125
    c. ten days, $75
    d. ten days, $125

15. Sellers can obtain condominium resale disclosure documents from the
    a. secretary of state's office.
    b. property manager.
    c. association.
    d. Connecticut Real Estate Commission.

16. In cases of involuntary partition, the owners are advised to
    a. attempt to resolve the matter since nothing can be done.
    b. sell his or her share to someone else.
    c. petition the superior court for equitable relief.
    d. petition the superior court for substantive relief.

17. Legal descriptions of property in Connecticut predominantly follow the
    a. metes-and-bounds method.
    b. street address.
    c. government survey system.
    d. rectangular survey.

18. The Connecticut Department of Consumer Protection requires that land surveyors
    a. be licensed by the Department of Consumer Protection, Division of Land Surveyors and Professional Engineers.
    b. have a broker's license.
    c. be licensed under the Department of Consumer Protection Division of Surveyors.
    d. do not have to be licensed but must have worked under another surveyor's license for five years.

19. Questions about boundaries in Connecticut are resolved by
    a. the superior court.
    b. the superior court with the appointment of a committee.
    c. the superior court, a committee, and possibly a land surveyor.
    d. a committee.

20. The Connecticut Common Interest Ownership Act dictates that a legally sufficient description of a common interest ownership unit must contain all of the following EXCEPT
    a. the recording date of the original declaration.
    b. the name of the common interest community.
    c. the identifying number of the unit.
    d. a list of the unit owners, their payment history, and telephone numbers.

21. Real property taxes are ad valorem (based on value) taxes levied by
    a. the federal government.
    b. the state.
    c. local municipalities.
    d. the assessor.

22. The state requires the values placed on all properties be based on their
    a. assessed value.
    b. intrinsic value.
    c. ad valorem value.
    d. market value.

23. Connecticut law requires towns to revalue properties every ___ years by physical observation or statistical analysis. Physical inspection is required every ___ years.
    a. 10; 5
    b. 5; 12
    c. 5; 10
    d. 7; 10

24. Monica owns a property with an appraised value of $700,000. The tax rate is 25 mills (or $25 per $1,000 of assessed value). Compute her taxes.
    a. $12,250
    b. $17,500
    c. $14,500
    d. Need more information

25. Taxes are a lien on the property
    a. from the date of revaluation.
    b. generally from October 1.
    c. from the date of assessment.
    d. once federal taxes are unpaid for six months.

26. Connecticut statutes generally hold tax liens to a _____-year maximum. To be valid, tax liens must be recorded by the agency levying the tax within two years from the due date.
    a. 2
    b. 4
    c. 10
    d. 15

27. Liens have been recorded in Waterbury for a property located on Woodchuck Road. These liens are in addition to the tax and municipal liens. They were recorded in the town clerk's office in this order: February 11, 2000 (Lien 1), March 23, 2004 (Lien 2), April 18, 2003 (Lien 3), and May 22, 2005 (Lien 4). All liens were executed on the dates noted; however, Lien 3 was recorded after Lien 2. Which lien would have priority as third in line based on the date of recording?
    a. February 11, 2000 (Lien 1)
    b. May 22, 2005 (Lien 4)
    c. April 18, 2003 (Lien 3)
    d. March 23, 2004 (Lien 2)

28. State conveyance taxes and municipal conveyance taxes are
    a. based on a phase-in formula.
    b. paid by the buyer.
    c. based on a percentage of the selling price.
    d. based on a formula determined by each local municipality according to the sales price.

29. The Connecticut Statute of Frauds requires that all contracts affecting real estate must be in writing to be enforceable. All contracts over ____ must be in writing.
    a. $1,500
    b. $500
    c. $2,500
    d. $5,000

30. Real estate contracts must contain the basic legal elements to be enforceable. These include legally competent parties, offer and acceptance, legality of object, and
    a. no consideration.
    b. a minimum of 5 percent down.
    c. equal consideration.
    d. valid consideration.

31. In Connecticut, minors are generally permitted to void their contracts. In Connecticut, an individual may enter into a legally enforceable contract at the age of
    a. 21.
    b. 18.
    c. 16.
    d. 25.

32. Listing and buyer agency contracts are bilateral contracts. To be enforceable, agency agreements must be in writing and contain certain minimal provisions, EXCEPT
    a. identification of property involved in the transaction.
    b. compensation to be paid.
    c. beginning and expiration dates of the contract.
    d. statement of adherence to fair housing statutes.

33. Licensees receiving money from a client or customer MUST deposit the money in escrow
    a. within five banking days.
    b. within 48 hours.
    c. within three banking days.
    d. as soon as possible.

34. If the buyer or seller breaches a real estate contract ending in a dispute, the broker holding the escrow funds has the option to
    a. deposit the funds with superior court.
    b. deposit the funds with the Real Estate Commission.
    c. distribute funds to the person not breaching the contract.
    d. hold the funds until he or she is told how to disburse them.

35. Residential property condition disclosure notices must be given to a property buyer by the seller in all residential transactions, EXCEPT in the case of
    a. condominiums and cooperatives.
    b. newly constructed residential real estate.
    c. residential units of one to four families.
    d. leases with an option to buy.

36. Which is TRUE for property condition disclosure notices delivered by the seller to the buyer?
    a. Notices must be delivered any time prior to the purchaser signing a written offer to purchase.
    b. A report with buyer and seller signatures must be attached to any written purchase agreement.
    c. Purchase options must also have property condition disclosure notices attached.
    d. If the seller fails to comply, the fine is $500 at closing.

37. Connecticut requires certain elements in a deed to convey title. Connecticut does NOT require
    a. deed signed by grantee.
    b. deed in writing.
    c. acknowledgment by the grantor to be his or her free act and deed.
    d. deed signed by two witnesses.

38. A couple sold their East Haven home to a buyer for $850,000. How much does the couple owe in municipal and state conveyance taxes?
    a. $5,185
    b. $4,000
    c. $4,500
    d. $5,435

39. A couple sold their home in East Haven for $650,000. How much do they owe in municipal and state conveyance taxes?
    a. $715
    b. $3,250
    c. $3,960
    d. $3,965

40. Farm, forest, and open space land is governed by a special conveyance tax in addition to the standard conveyance tax. If the grantor sells a property of this classification within the first year, the penalty on the sale is

a. nothing because it was paid as part of the initial transfer.
b. 5 percent.
c. 20 percent.
d. 10 percent of the sales price.

41. The prescriptive period to acquire adverse possession requires the adverse possessor to have had uninterrupted use for a period of

a. 25 years.
b. 10 years.
c. 15 years.
d. Not recognized in Connecticut

42. A man believes he has acquired title to a property by adverse possession. To make a legal claim, he MUST

a. bring a quiet title action in civil court.
b. bring a quiet title action in criminal court.
c. send a certified letter to the owner of the property.
d. record his right to adverse possession in the land records.

43. Connecticut requires anyone of sound mind who prepares a will to be of what age and to have how many witnesses?

a. 21, two
b. 18, two
c. 25, four
d. 16, two

44. If an individual dies intestate with no known beneficiaries, the estate escheats to the state after

a. 5 years.
b. 15 years.
c. 10 years.
d. 20 years.

45. In Connecticut, the land records are indexed by

a. grantor/grantee.
b. volume and page.
c. record ledger.
d. grantor.

46. An accurate search of title is MOST important to a(an)

a. grantee.
b. grantor.
c. lender.
d. attorney.

47. Christine's attorney has advised her to have a more complete examination of the land records. She should request a(an)

a. title search.
b. certificate of title.
c. title insurance.
d. abstract of title.

48. A marketable record of title is unbroken for

a. 40 years.
b. 60 years.
c. 50 years.
d. as far back in time as it is possible to go.

49. In Connecticut, title passes on

a. delivery and acceptance.
b. recording.
c. indexing.
d. seller signing.

50. Recording the documents affecting the title to real estate gives

a. active notice.
b. actual notice.
c. permanent notice.
d. constructive notice.

51. Regulations regarding Connecticut licensing laws are enforced by the

a. Connecticut and National Association of REALTORS®.
b. Real Estate Commission.
c. Connecticut Department of Housing.
d. Banking Commission Division for Brokers and Salespersons.

52. The Commission is made up of eight members:
    a. governor, four persons in real estate (two licensed brokers, two licensed salespersons), three members of the public.
    b. Five real estate brokers and three licensed salespersons.
    c. Four real estate brokers and four licensed salespersons.
    d. Five in real estate (three licensed brokers, two licensed salespersons), and three members of the general public.

53. Greg, a licensed salesperson, does not renew his license. One month after the expiration of his license, Greg's last listing with ABC Realty closes. He had worked on this transaction for three months. Greg
    a. is entitled to the commission as procuring cause.
    b. is not entitled to anything.
    c. can designate who in the office receives the commission.
    d. is entitled to a referral fee since he was unlicensed at the time of the closing.

54. Sarah works as an on-site property residential superintendent for House and Home Realty. She is unlicensed, is a regular employee, is employed on-site as a custodian, resides where she works, and engages in licensed activities. Sarah
    a. needs a salesperson's license.
    b. needs a property manager's license.
    c. does not need a license.
    d. can only do clerical work.

55. Connecticut licensing law requires that in order to sit for the state exam and obtain a real estate broker's license, the candidate must successfully complete from an approved school
    a. 30 hours of principles and practices, 6 hours of appraisal, and 30 hours of other real estate coursework.
    b. 60 hours of principles and practices, 12 hours of appraisal, and 30 hours of other real estate coursework.
    c. 45 hours of principles and practices, 30 hours of appraisal, and 30 hours of other real estate coursework.
    d. 60 hours of principles and practices, 30 hours of appraisal, and 30 hours of other real estate coursework.

56. In order to sit for the Connecticut broker's exam, the candidate must be a minimum of _____ years of age and pay an initial fee of _____ .
    a. 18, $375
    b. 21, $375
    c. 18, $565
    d. 21, $565

57. A salesperson's license fee is _____, and he or she must pay _____ to the Guaranty Fund.
    a. $285 annually; $20 one time
    b. $285 annually; $20 annually
    c. $285 every two years; $20 one time
    d. $285 every two years; $25 annually

58. Crystal, a convicted felon, has made application for a real estate license. The licensing body will decide
    a. convicted felons cannot be issued a Connecticut license.
    b. since Crystal was refused a Rhode Island license six months ago she cannot obtain a Connecticut license.
    c. Crystal has served her time for the felony and can be issued a Connecticut license.
    d. only the Commission can determine if Crystal is suitable for a license.

59. Business entities such as LLCs, corporations, and partnerships

    a. have the option of obtaining a real estate license in the name of the legal entity.
    b. do not hold licenses; only individuals do.
    c. must have 51 percent or more of the individuals who own or control the business entity as licensed brokers.
    d. can have more than one designated broker.

60. Nonresident applicants for a real estate license *MUST*

    a. file proof of licensure.
    b. file irrevocable consent to suit.
    c. be from a state with a reciprocal agreement.
    d. provide proof of experience but do not need to pass exam requirements.

61. House Bargain Realty LLC does not maintain a definite place of business or display a license or sign indicating the licensee is a broker. This

    a. is allowed under the Connecticut statutes.
    b. violates Connecticut licensing law.
    c. requires the Commission to notify the firm it has 60 days to comply with state licensing laws.
    d. requires a hearing to be held before the Commission as to the firm's legality of operation.

62. A broker candidate *MUST*

    a. have had a license for two years and sold 12 houses.
    b. have been licensed two years and passed the exam with a grade of 70.
    c. have been licensed two years and passed the exam with a grade of 75.
    d. have been licensed two years, passed with a grade of 75, and sold at least one house.

63. Salespersons and brokers are required to take ___ hours of continuing education every ___ years.

    a. 12, two
    b. 15, two
    c. 9, four
    d. 12, four

64. Change of broker affiliation requires all of the following *EXCEPT*

    a. payment of a $25 transfer fee.
    b. the salesperson return all records and information to the designated broker.
    c. the original designated broker give an accounting to the salesperson within ten days of the return of the information.
    d. the accounting include the amount of commission the broker is entitled to and when those monies will be paid.

65. In their conduct as a licensee, a broker and salesperson must disclose all of the following *EXCEPT*

    a. their present or contemplated interest in real estate.
    b. their fiduciary duties to the client of care, obedience, accounting, loyalty, and disclosure.
    c. even if the licensee represents a seller, he or she must disclose any known material facts to the buyer.
    d. confidential information obtained under an expired agency agreement.

66. Which can a licensee do when advertising?

    a. Advertise another broker's property if it is on the MLS
    b. Run blind ads because they are legal in a few cases
    c. Fully disclose the broker's name in all advertising
    d. Update properties listed with another broker every 72 hours

67. Robert, a licensed real estate salesperson, does advertising on the Internet. The advertisement must include all of the following *EXCEPT*

    a. the licensee's name and office address on every page of the Web site.
    b. the name of the broker the licensee is affiliated with.
    c. the first date the property was updated.
    d. a listing of all the states where the licensee is licensed.

68. When Charles, a licensed real estate salesperson, advertises on the Internet, he *MUST*
    a. place his name and office address on the first page of his Web site.
    b. list the states where his broker is licensed.
    c. include the name of his broker on the site.
    d. indicate the dates the site has been updated.

69. Amber is concerned about disclosing off-site conditions. She can *BEST* protect herself and her agency by
    a. written disclosure to contact the local health department.
    b. written disclosure to contact the Connecticut Department of Public Health.
    c. doing nothing unless she is the selling agent.
    d. providing a written notice from the seller to the purchaser of the availability of Connecticut Department of Environmental Protection lists.

70. A house is for sale. The salesperson sent an e-mail regarding the sale of the house. On the e-mail, the salesperson must
    a. include the broker's name and office address.
    b. include her name, the name of her designated broker, and office address.
    c. include her state license number.
    d. list all states where she is licensed.

71. Connecticut licensing laws state that
    a. a licensee must obtain the verbal consent of an owner to place a sign on the property.
    b. offers must be submitted within 72 hours of the agent receiving the offer.
    c. without a prior agreement the listing agent is not obligated to market a property once an offer is accepted.
    d. net listings are legal with a written agreement.

72. A postal worker told a broker about several houses where the owners were elderly and considering a move. The broker can pay the postal worker
    a. nothing because he is unlicensed.
    b. with a gift card to thank him.
    c. by suggesting he become licensed and so able to collect referral fees from the broker.
    d. with a $100 gift card for each lead.

73. A man meets a broker at a social gathering. The broker gives the man a card in the event the man's listed home expires from the market. The broker also suggests how he might break the agreement. Which is *TRUE* for the broker in this situation?
    a. The broker has broken the licensing law.
    b. The broker lacked reasonable cause to interfere.
    c. The broker cannot solicit a property already listed.
    d. The broker was in her rights because she did not seek a property already listed.

74. Escrow funds must be deposited within ___ days or the broker will be fined up to _____.
    a. Three banking days, $2,000
    b. Three days, $2,500
    c. Five banking days, $500
    d. Five days, $2,000

75. The interest from real estate escrow/trust accounts is paid to the
    a. buyer.
    b. Connecticut Real Estate Commission.
    c. Connecticut Housing Finance Authority.
    d. CHIF.

76. A salesperson is concerned that she might have her license suspended or revoked. Which is the one item she should *NOT* worry about?
    a. Waiting two weeks to turn over the escrow funds in her possession to her broker
    b. Disclosing to the licensing authority she is a convicted felon
    c. Automatically extending a buyer broker contract
    d. Depositing monies into the escrow account

77. A salesperson is headed to a hearing before the Real Estate Commission to determine if her license should be revoked or suspended. Which activity is *NOT* a violation of the licensing laws?

    a. Commingling funds for 24 hours

    b. Giving agency disclosures to the parties as required by Connecticut statutes

    c. Receiving funds from another broker with the knowledge of her broker

    d. Disclosing her mother was purchasing the property she sold

78. The maximum compensation that can be paid from the Real Estate Guaranty Fund is _____, and the fund cannot exceed _____.

    a. $25,000, $500,000

    b. $50,000, $250,000

    c. $35,000, $250,000

    d. $35,000, $500,000

79. First and second mortgage lenders and brokers must hold an appropriate license from

    a. Connecticut mortgage lenders.

    b. the Department of Consumer Protection.

    c. the Connecticut Department of Banking.

    d. the Connecticut Real Estate Commission.

80. Which license *MUST* a real property securities dealer hold in Connecticut?

    a. Broker's or salesperson's license

    b. Broker's license

    c. Security dealer's license

    d. Insurance license

81. Jake, a licensed real estate salesperson, intends to have his clients come to him to obtain a first mortgage. Jake *MUST*

    a. receive a secondary license from the banking commission.

    b. obtain licenses for his whole office.

    c. hold a first mortgage broker's license.

    d. not sell mortgages.

82. A lender practices illegal, unfair, and abusive lending practices inducing buyers to purchase more than they can afford. The lender is guilty of

    a. prime lending.

    b. predatory lending.

    c. foreclosure-induced lending.

    d. all of the above.

83. A mortgagor, whose property is being foreclosed, can redeem the property by

    a. deficiency judgment.

    b. redemption.

    c. law day or bidding successfully at the auction.

    d. law day.

84. Connecticut Savings Bank has foreclosed on a property located at 2306 North Airline Road, East Haven, Connecticut. Connecticut Savings needs to record

    a. the deed in town hall.

    b. a satisfaction of foreclosure notice in town hall.

    c. a foreclosure certificate in town hall.

    d. an assignment of release in town.

85. Chris and Jim owe more on their mortgage than the value of the property. There is a deficiency after the strict foreclosure. Which is *TRUE* in this situation?

    a. They will owe the difference between the amount of the claim and the court appraisal.

    b. Deficiency judgments need not be recorded since they are part of the court documents.

    c. The strict foreclosure wipes away any deficiency.

    d. A lien for the deficiency cannot be ordered.

86. Juanita is eligible for a Connecticut Housing Finance Authority (CHFA) loan. CHFA offers loans providing

    a. foreclosure protections.

    b. a zero interest rate.

    c. below-market interest rates.

    d. market-based interest rates.

87. Refusing to lend in specific areas based on protected classifications is defined as
   a. DML.
   b. redlining.
   c. violating SMSA.
   d. blockbusting.

88. All of the following statements are true about security deposits *EXCEPT*
   a. they can be subtracted from the rent on the anniversary date of the lease.
   b. interest is paid on the anniversary of the lease.
   c. interest is only paid on residential units.
   d. interest rates float.

89. If the lessee intentionally damages leased property, he or she has committed a crime and can be prosecuted. If the damage exceeds $1,500
   a. it is a misdemeanor.
   b. it is a felony or misdemeanor.
   c. the lessor can be fined double the cost to repair.
   d. it is a class D felony.

90. The following are exempt from licensing requirements for appraisals *EXCEPT*
   a. persons hired by a municipality to perform revaluations.
   b. prospecting to list or sell real estate.
   c. agents doing a market analysis.
   d. agents doing a market analysis for a mortgage company.

91. A certified residential appraiser is only allowed to appraise
   a. 1–4-unit residential structures.
   b. 1–4 residential structures, vacant or unimproved land.
   c. 1–4 units and unimproved land being evaluated for a condominium.
   d. 1–4 residential units, unimproved or vacant land for 1–4 units.

92. A supervising appraiser can only supervise up to
   a. three certified appraisers.
   b. three provisional appraisers.
   c. three provisional appraisers or more with a waiver from the Real Estate Appraisal Commission.
   d. no limit.

93. *USPAP* requires all of the following from appraisers *EXCEPT* the
   a. appraiser's name typed or printed.
   b. category of license held and license number.
   c. state of issuance and expiration date of the license.
   d. name and license number of supervisory appraiser.

94. Which contractor does *NOT* need to be registered in Connecticut?
   a. Home improvement contractor
   b. New home contractor
   c. Residential construction contractor
   d. Property development contractor

95. The Connecticut General Statutes require all municipalities to have a(n)
   a. inland wetlands commission.
   b. town government-controlled zoning commission.
   c. planned unit development commission.
   d. state-run village district.

96. When a certificate of occupancy is issued for a new home from the town, the new home builder guarantees to the buyer that the home is in compliance with the building code. The implied warranty for building code violations is for
   a. three years.
   b. two years.
   c. three months.
   d. 18 months.

97. The Guaranty Fund for new home contractors is capped at _____ for a single claim.
   a. $20,000
   b. $25,000
   c. $30,000
   d. $50,000

98. Mike is advertising resort property in North Carolina for sale. He is advertising in the *Hartford Courant* and the *New Haven Register.* In compliance with the Connecticut Interstate Land Sales Act, he must register with the

a. Real Estate Commission.
b. Connecticut Department of Consumer Protection.
c. Connecticut secretary of state.
d. Real Estate Commission and the Connecticut secretary of state.

99. An individual purchasing property under the Connecticut Interstate Land Sales Act MUST be presented with a clear prospectus within

a. 24 hours.
b. 48 hours.
c. 72 hours.
d. five banking days.

100. Which class is NOT a protected class under the Connecticut fair housing laws?

a. Learning disability
b. Mental disability
c. Drug addicts
d. Sexual orientation

101. A licensed Connecticut broker has refused to rent an apartment to a bisexual couple. The broker has

a. violated the federal Fair Housing Act.
b. violated the Connecticut and federal Fair Housing acts.
c. violated the Connecticut Fair Housing Act.
d. not violated the federal Fair Housing Act.

102. Other than sexual orientation, which classification is only a protected class under Connecticut but not federal statutes?

a. Mental disability
b. Learning disability
c. Familial status
d. Lawful source of income

103. In Connecticut, prosecuting violations of federal fair housing laws can be handled by the

a. Commission on Discrimination.
b. Fair Housing Commission.
c. Connecticut Commission on Human Rights and Opportunities.
d. Connecticut Commission on Housing and Urban Development.

104. Bianca owns her own home and is not and has never been a real estate agent. She refuses to rent an apartment in her house to a homosexual couple. The homosexual couple files a complaint that she has discriminated again them. She has not used an agent and no advertising has occurred. Most likely, Bianca

a. has violated the law.
b. will be fined a minimum of $10,000.
c. has not violated the law.
d. knows they are homosexual but refuses to rent saying their orientation is not good for her young son, and so is guilty and ready to go to a hearing.

105. Persons claiming to be discriminated against have ___ days to file a complaint with the CHRO and can be awarded ____ in punitive damages.

a. one year, $50,000
b. six months, $100,000
c. one year, $100,000
d. six months, $50,000

106. Kyle has listed his cousin's three-family home in Middlebury. Kyle is aware that a prior tenant's child had a high level of lead after living there three months. The health department's order to abate the lead has been done, but the town wants it retested every year. The day before the one-year anniversary, the house is sold. The sellers do not disclose anything about the inspection. They were told of the abatement but not about the annual inspections.

a. Kyle is not guilty of anything.
b. The buyer's broker should have warned the buyers the house had contamination and needed reinspection.
c. The buyers have grounds for a lead-paint lawsuit against the seller.
d. The house closed and the buyers have no recourse.

107. Real estate property securities and real estate syndicate securities are regulated by the

a. Real Properties Security Commission.
b. Real Estate Syndicate for Securities.
c. state banking commission.
d. Connecticut Real Estate Commission.

108. A real estate property securities dealers must hold a(an)

a. salesperson's or broker's license.
b. insurance license.
c. broker's license.
d. security dealer's license.

109. What is the minimum number of investors a real estate syndicate MUST have?

a. 15
b. 12
c. 18
d. 10

110. Which is NOT true regarding real property securities?

a. They are regulated by real estate license law.
b. The fee of $300 to $1,500 is based on total value of interest issued in Connecticut.
c. Copies of the written statement containing required information given to the purchaser must be retained for four years.
d. They are administered by the Real Estate Commission.

PRACTICE EXAM ANSWERS

1. **a** (25–26) Connecticut licensing law recognizes exclusive right to sell, exclusive agency, and open listings. MLS is a service where agents pool their listings. Net listings are illegal in Connecticut.

2. **c** (10) Sharon is not required to enter into an agency agreement to see this listed property, because the property she is viewing is an in-house listing with Michael and his firm. Michael has provided her with a written agency disclosure notice. If Sharon proceeds and purchases this property, she will most likely be an unrepresented party.

3. **a** (25) The buyer has most likely signed an exclusive agency agreement where the buyer is obligated to pay the buyer's broker the commission agreed on in the buyer agency agreement, regardless of how the buyer found the property.

4. **d** (26) A licensee cannot ask about confidential information unless a written buyer agency is entered into, or the licensee is going to represent the seller and has presented the buyer with the required agency disclosure notice stating that the licensee represents the seller.

5. **b** (29) If the broker or agent has a present or contemplated interest in the property the broker has listed, the broker or agent must disclose that interest to the buyer.

6. **c** (28) Net listings are illegal under Connecticut license law.

7. **d** (31) Records must be kept for seven years. Records include transactions that did not close and buyer agency agreements where the buyer never purchased.

8. **c** (55) The time required for prescriptive easements is 15 years.

9. **a** (55) An easement by prescription may be extinguished if the owner of the property on which the easement has been takes, obtains, or regains open and continuous control and possession of the property for the prescriptive period of 15 years.

10. **d** (60) After their marriage, the couple's individual properties owned prior to their marriage would remain as separate interests.

11. **c** (60) Partition actions are involuntary actions that resolve disputes between the parties. The courts attempt to provide equitable relief to the parties.

12. **b** (62) Common interest communities are legally described as condominiums, cooperatives, or planned unit developments (PUDs).

13. **c** (65) Buyers have a rescission period of five business days after delivery of the documents or seven business days if sent by registered or certified mail to rescind the purchase under the Common Interest Ownership Act.

14. **d** (65) Associations must provide the resale certificate within ten business days with a maximum preparation fee of $125 and an additional $10 if the documents are delivered within three days.

15. **c** (65) Sellers of common interest communities can obtain resale documents by contacting the association. C is the best answer because the property manager or association must file with the town clerk in the town where the community is located. It is not always easy to find out who to contact at the association.

16. **c** (60) When a partition is involuntary, the owner must petition the superior court for equitable relief.

17. **a** (68) For legal descriptions, Connecticut predominantly follows the metes-and-bounds methods.

18. **a** (70) A person who measures and maps property boundary lines must be licensed as a land surveyor.

19. **c** (70) One of the adjoining property owners in the event of a lost or uncertain boundary would seek relief in superior court. The court would then appoint a three-person committee, which may in turn seek the assistance of a land surveyor.

20. **d** (70–71) The Connecticut Common Interest Ownership Act states that a legally sufficient description of a common interest ownership unit must contain the name of the common interest community, recording data for original declaration, the town in which the common interest community is located, and the identifying number of the unit.

21. **c** (73) The Connecticut General Statutes provide local municipalities with the exclusive right to levy a real property tax.

22. **d** (73) The state requires that the values placed on all properties reflect their market value.

23. **c** (74) Connecticut law requires five-year real estate valuation and a physical inspection every ten years.

24. **a** (75) Correct answer is $12,250.

25. **c** (76) Taxes are a lien on the property as of the date of assessment.

26. **d** (76) Statutes generally hold to a 15-year maximum.

27. **c** (77) After tax or municipal liens, the date of recording takes priority. March 23, 2004, was recorded prior to April 18, 2003. All liens were executed as stated, but Lien 3 was not executed until after Lien 2 was recorded.

28. **c** (77) State conveyance taxes are based on the selling price of a property.

29. **b** (81) Connecticut requires all contracts over $500 to be in writing.

30. **d** (82) Valid consideration is necessary for a real estate contract to be valid and enforceable.

31. **b** (82) In Connecticut, the majority age is 18. At 18, a person can enter into a legally enforceable contract.

32. **a** (83) In most instances, property is yet to be identified at the time an agency agreement is entered into. All other provisions are required by law.

33. **c** (84) These deposits must be made within three banking days from the date of obtaining all signatures from all parties to the transaction.

34. **b** (85) In the event of a dispute, deposit the funds with the Real Estate Commission.

35. **b** (86) Newly constructed real property carries an implied warranty, and the property disclosure requirement does not apply.

36. **d** (87) The fine for not completing the property condition disclosure notice is $300.

37. **a** (105) Deed must be signed by the grantor (seller). A deed is not signed by the grantee.

38. **d** (107) Municipal conveyance tax: $850,000 × 0.0011 = $935. State conveyance tax (sales price up to $800,000 × 0.005) (over $800,000 × 0.01) $4,000 + $500 = $4,500. Conveyance tax total: $5,435

39. **d** (108) Municipal conveyance tax $650,000 × 0.0011 = $715. State conveyance tax ($650,000 × 0.005 = $3,250) $715 + $3,250 = $3,965.

40. **d** (109) Connecticut statutes have instituted a penalty of 10 percent of the sales price.

41. **c** (109) The prescriptive period in Connecticut is 15 years.

42. **a** (109) Connecticut requires the adverse possessor to bring an action to quiet title in the civil courts.

43. **b** (110) The majority age for writing a valid will is 18. Two individuals must act as witnesses.

44. **d** (111) If no relatives or heirs are found after 20 years, the property will escheat to the state.

45. **a** (117) Land records are indexed in the grantor-grantee index.

46. **a** (117) A title search will help the grantee (buyer) determine the status of title and whether the grantor (seller) can give good title.

47. **d** (119) Abstract of title is more than a certificate of title. It includes an examination of encumbrances, liens, and prior owners.

48. **a** (120) A marketable record of title is one that is unbroken for a period of 40 years.

49. **a** (115) In Connecticut, title passes on delivery and acceptance of the deed.

50. **d** (115) Recording documents provides constructive notice.

51. **b** (123) Real estate licensing is regulated by the Department of Consumer Protection under the Real Estate Commission.

52. **d** (124) The Connecticut Real Estate Commission is made up of eight members: five members must be in real estate (three licensed brokers, two licensed salespersons) and three members of the general public.

53.　**b**　(124) Greg is not licensed at the time of the closing. Only licensed brokers and salespersons can bring a legal action to collect compensation owed.

54.　**c**　(125) Sarah's activities are an exemption under the licensing law.

55.　**d**　(127) In order to sit for the broker's exam in Connecticut, the salesperson must have successfully completed 60 hours of principles and practices, 30 hours of appraisal, and 30 hours of other real estate coursework.

56.　**c**　(127) Connecticut licensing law requires that broker candidates have obtained the age of 18. The initial licensing fee for brokers is $565.

57.　**a**　(127) The salesperson pays a license fee of $285 and a one-time fee to the Guaranty Fund of $20.

58.　**d**　(128) Convicted felons can apply for and obtain a license. The Commission can determine if they are suitable to be licensed.

59.　**c**　(130) Business entities must be licensed in Connecticut. All active owners, members, partners, and officers in the business entity must be licensed brokers or salespersons and 51 percent must be licensed brokers.

60.　**b**　(130) Nonresident applicants must file an irrevocable consent to suit. This enables lawsuits and legal actions to be brought against the nonresident licensee in Connecticut.

61.　**a**　(130) House Bargain Realty LLC does not need to display a license, have a place of business, or display a sign.

62.　**c**　(127) A broker candidate must have two years' experience and pass the test with a grade of 75. There are no requirements regarding sales success.

63.　**a**　(131) Twelve hours of continuing education must be completed every two years.

64.　**d**　(131–2) All of the options are true except d. The salesperson must be given a statement as to commissions earned, all active listing agreements, agency agreements, and commission and compensation due the salesperson.

65.　**d**　(215) Brokers and salespersons cannot disclose any confidential information they have obtained under their agency agreement even if it has expired.

66.　**d**　(134–5) A, b, and c are all illegal in Connecticut. Property listed with another broker can be advertised with permission and must be updated at least every 72 hours.

67.　**c**　(135) Internet advertising must include the last date when the Web site property information was updated.

68.　**c**　(135) Charles must include the name of his broker on the Web site. The site must have the licensee's name and office address, where the licensee is licensed, and the last date when the site information was updated.

69.　**d**　(134) Amber should make certain the seller provides written notice to purchasers of the availability of the Connecticut Department of Environmental Protection lists.

70.　**b**　(135) Both the broker and licensee must be on the first or last page of the electronic communication.

71.　**c**　(136) The listing agent is not obligated to market a property once a property has a written contract on it.

72.　**a**　(136) Unlicensed individuals cannot be compensated in any way for real estate leads. This includes commissions and referral fees.

73.　**a**　(137) The broker broke the licensing law. Licensees cannot solicit properties already listed nor suggest how to terminate the agreement.

74.　**a**　(138) Connecticut statutes state that all escrow funds must be deposited within three banking days into an escrow account. Fines can be up to $2,000 and six months in jail.

75.　**c**　(138) The interest is paid to the Connecticut Housing Finance Authority (CHFA) for mortgage assistance for first-time homebuyers and low- and moderate-income families.

76.　**d**　(139) The salesperson can deposit escrow funds into the escrow account, but she cannot take them out. Need more clarification as to whether Samantha is a broker or salesperson.

77.　**c**　(139) The salesperson can represent another broker in a transaction with the consent of her employing broker.

78.　**a**　(140) The Real Estate Guaranty Fund cannot exceed $500,000, and the maximum allowed per claim is $25,000.

79. **c** (141) The Connecticut Department of Banking regulates first and second mortgage lenders and brokers.

80. **b** (142) Real property securities dealers must hold a broker's license in Connecticut.

81. **c** (149) A mortgage broker is defined as a person who for a fee or other valuable consideration negotiates, solicits, arranges, places, or finds a first mortgage loan that is to be made by the mortgage lender. Salespersons and brokers cannot act as mortgage brokers without being licensed.

82. **b** (151) Predatory lending is when someone uses illegal, unfair, and/or abusive practices inducing borrowers to buy what they cannot afford.

83. **c** (154) The mortgagor has two ways to redeem the property by: bidding at the auction or redeeming the property on the law day.

84. **c** (152) Once the foreclosing party redeems the party, he or she must file a foreclosure notice in the town hall where the property is located.

85. **a** (153) In the event of strict foreclosure with a deficiency, the foreclosed party is responsible for the difference between the amount of the claim and the court appraisal.

86. **c** (156) CHFA provides an additional source of mortgage financing for low-income and moderate-income families throughout Connecticut by offering below-market interest rate loans to qualified applicants.

87. **b** (157) Redlining is a violation of the Home Mortgage Disclosure Act.

88. **a** (157) The interest on security deposits must be paid on the anniversary of the lease. It can be subtracted from the next monthly rent payment after the anniversary of the lease.

89. **d** (162) Damage caused by the lessee is a class D felony if it exceeds $1,500.

90. **d** (179) Agents doing a market analysis for a mortgage company are in violation of the Connecticut appraisal statutes. Agents must do a market analysis in the course of trying to obtain a listing.

91. **d** (180) Certified residential appraisers can only appraise 1–4 units, land and unimproved land with use for 1–4-unit structures.

92. **c** (182) The maximum a supervising appraiser can supervise is three provisional appraisers unless a waiver is issued by the Real Estate Appraisal Commission.

93. **d** (183) All of the options are required except d. Appraisers do not have anyone supervising them.

94. **d** (195–6) There is no category known as a property development contractor.

95. **a** (191) The Connecticut General Statutes require all municipalities to have an inland wetlands commission to establish the boundaries of inland wetlands and watercourses within the municipality.

96. **a** (195) The implied warranty lasts for three years per CGS Chapter 827.

97. **c** (196) The reimbursement for a single claim is $30,000.

98. **d** (198) Mike must register with both the secretary of state and the Real Estate Commission unless he registers with the Federal Interstate Land Sales Full Disclosure Act.

99. **c** (198) The prospectus must be delivered within 72 hours.

100. **c** (204) Drug addicts are not a protected class in Connecticut. Protected classes in Connecticut include race, religion, color, national origin, ancestry, sex, marital status, age, lawful source of income, familial status, physical disability, mental disability, learning disability, and sexual orientation.

101. **c** (204) The licensed broker has only violated the Connecticut Fair Housing Act because sexual orientation is not a protected class under the federal law. It is a protected class under the Connecticut laws.

102. **b** (204) Learning disability is only a protected class in Connecticut and not under the federal fair housing laws.

103. **c** (207) The Connecticut Commission on Human Rights and Opportunities has the authority to prosecute violation of federal fair housing laws.

104. **c** (206) Bianca is not guilty and she is covered under an exception. The exception is that she did not use an agent, she lives on the premises, and she did not advertise.

105. **d** (207) The complaint must be filed within 180 days with punitive damages being awarded for $50,000.

106. **c** (29, 219) Kyle and sellers concealed a material fact and violated the lead-paint laws.

107. **d** (227) The Connecticut Real Estate Commission regulates securities and syndicates.

108. **c** (228) Real estate property securities dealers must hold a broker's license in Connecticut.

109. **c** (233) To be considered a real estate syndicate, there must be a minimum of 18 investors to invest in real estate.

110. **b** (228–30) Fees based on the total value of real estate are for real estate syndicate securities and not real properties securities.

Index

A

Abandonment, 55
Abatement, 219
Absentee landlord, 170
Abstract of title, 119
Accessibility requirements, 209
Actual eviction, 168–170
Addendum for Use of Electronic Signature and Record, 253
Adjustments, 216
Administrative complaint, 207
Administrator deed, 106
Adverse possession, 109, 112
Advertising, 30–31, 134–135, 205, 230, 233
Affordable housing appeals procedure, 194
Age, 206
    of majority, 82
Agency/agent, 1, 5
    agreements, 25–27, 135–136
    disclosure, 10, 30, 134
    documents, 12
    property condition disclosure, 87
    representation agreements, 12
    umbrella, 6
Agency Disclosure Notice, 12
Agency relationship, 1, 5
    creation of, 6–7
    fiduciary responsibilities under, 7–8
    in practice, 11, 13
    interference in, 137
    types of, 8–11
Aggregate value, 233
Agreements, 28
Alternative mortgage loans, 157
Americans with Disabilities Act (ADA), 209
Apartment Owners Association of Connecticut, 171
Appeals, 169
Appraisal, 214
    certification, 184–185
    management companies, 185
    review, 184
Appraisal Foundation, 183, 186
Appraisal Standards, 183
Appraiser
    certification, 141
    license, 179
    license categories, 179–180
    licensed in another state, 183–184
    license renewal, 183
    obtaining license for, 180–182
Architecture
    information sources for, 240
Asbestos, 218
Assessment, 73–74
    appeals, 74
    dates, 76

lien, 63
ratio, 75
Assignment, 149

B

Benchmarks, 69
Bilateral contracts, 83, 84
Binder of Sale (Offer to Purchase), 84, 99
Blind ads, 31, 134
Blockbusting, 205
Boards of Realtors, 82
Boundary
    locations, 55
    lost, 70
Broker, 1, 3, 125
    affiliation change by, 131–132
    assisting in mortgage transaction, 150
    authority to prepare documents, 81–82
    compensation/commission, 11, 13
    fair housing and, 210
    requirements for, 127
Brokerage, 1
    compensation/commission, 242–243
    information sources for, 237
Broker-salesperson relationship, 3
Broker's lien
    notice and filing of, 21
Broker's lien, 14–15, 77
Building accessibility, 197
Building inspection contingency, 84
Burden of proof, 55
Business ownership, 61–62
Buyer
    information for, 87
    property condition disclosure, 87
Buyer Agency Agreement, 12
Buyer agency/brokerage agreements, 25, 26–27, 83
    content of, 26–27

C

Cancellation right, 65
Capital gains tax, 76–77
Cease and desist orders, 234
Certificate
    of Licensure, 128
    of occupancy, 164, 195
    of Public Safety and Necessity, 222
    of Registration, 63
    of satisfaction, 152
    of title, 118, 119
Certified general appraiser, 179, 181, 182, 184–185
Certified residential appraiser, 180, 181–182, 184–185
Chain of title, 119

City and Town Development Act (CTDA), 194–195
Civil action, 208, 231, 234
Civil Rights Act of 1866, 206
Civil Rights Act of 1968
    Title VIII, 207
Cleanup costs, 221–222
Closing
    at, 215–216
    process, 213–215
    property taxes, 246
Cluster developments, 190
Co-brokerage, 10–11
Combined Contingency Addendum to Purchase and Sale Agreement, 84, 94–96
Commercial construction, 197
Commercial lease commission rights, 15
Commissioner of Economic and Community Development, 194
Commissions, 11, 136
Common Interest Ownership Act, 62–66, 70–71
Compensation, 11, 136
Condominiums, 62
    conversion to, 65–66
Conduct, 8
Confidential information, 7–8, 215
Connecticut, 2–5
    Adverse Possession Law, 112
    Appeals Board for Property Valuation, 74
    Appraisal Commission, 183
    Banking Department, 157
    Building Code, 199
    Commissioner of Consumer Protection, 220
    Commissioner of Environmental Protection, 221
    Commissioner of Public Health, 220
    Commission of Revenue Services, 106
    Commission on Human Rights and Opportunities, 206, 207, 210
    Contaminated Property Transfer Program, 223
    Department of Banking, 141, 149, 171
    Department of Economic and Community Development, 155
    Department of Environmental Protection, 30, 192, 218, 220, 221, 222, 223
    Department of Health Services, 218, 220
    Department of Public Health, 219
    Department of Revenue Services, 78
    Fair Housing Center, 210
    Fire Safety Code, 199
    Foreclosure Law/Mediation Program, 158
    Hazardous Materials and Waste Management Information, 223
    Housing Finance Authority, 85, 138, 156, 158

Judicial Department, 154
Landlord/Tenant Law, 171
Lead Poisoning Prevention and Control
    Program, 223
Licensing Info Center/Database, 142, 186
Mold Information and Guidelines for
    Mold Remediation, 223
Office of Legislative Research, 151
Office of Policy and Management, 193
Probate Court, 57, 112
Radon Program, 223
Real Estate Appraisal Commission, 178
Regional Planning Organizations, 199
Rental Assistance Program, 155
River Watershed Council, 223
Secretary of State, 198
securities and, 227, 228
Siting Council, 222, 223
taxation, 76, 78, 106, 107, 108
Trust for Historic Preservation, 57
Underground Storage Tank Information,
    223
Water Diversion Policy Act, 221
web site for, 236
Connecticut Association of Land Surveyors
    Standards, 71
Connecticut Association of Realtors, Inc., 16,
    84
    buyer/seller information, 87
    electronic records, 252–253
    environmental hazards, 223
Connecticut Department of Consumer
    Protection, 16, 63, 66, 87, 123, 128, 185
    appraisers, 186
    contractor registration, 195–196
    e-mail list, 179
    land surveys, maps, 70
    licensing, 142
    municipalities, 121
    notification registry, 132
    registration application as Community
        Association Manager, 66
    security deposits, 171
Connecticut General Statues
    mortgages and liens, 158
Connecticut General Statutes, 16, 29, 57, 61,
    62
    affordable housing, 194, 199
    appraisers, 186
    Chapter 392, 16, 32, 87, 123, 142
    Common Interest Partnership Act, 66
    Community Association Managers, 66
    corporations, 66
    fair housing, 202, 210
    inland wetlands, 191–192, 199
    intestate distribution, 111
    landlord, tenant rights, 171
    land use, 189
    leases, 160
    mortgage denial reasons, 157
    new home implied warranty, 199
    planning, 199
    real estate securities, 227
    real estate syndicates, 234
    real property securities, 234
    taxation, 73, 76, 78, 105, 112
    Title 20, 178
    Title 49, 147
    zoning, 199

Connecticut Real Estate Commission, 2, 4–5,
    9, 11, 123–124, 142
    buyer agency and, 26
    fair housing, 208–209
    interstate sales, 198
Conservation restriction, 54
Constructive notice, 115
Consumer
    credit licenses and, 150
    electronic signatures and, 250
    transactions of, 250–251
Contamination, 221–222
Contingency provisions, 84
Continuing education, 131, 183
Contractor registration, 195–196
Contracts
    listing and buyer brokerage, 83
    purchase and sale agreements, 83
    requirements of, 82–83
Conveyance taxes, 77, 105, 106–108
    for farm, forest and open-space lands, 109
    percentages of, 243–245
    purchase price based on, 108
Convicted felon, 128, 130
Cooperation, 137
    sale documents for, 12
Co-ownership, 59–60
Corporations, 61–62
Court action, 168
Crime conviction, 140
Criminal damage, 165
Curtesy, 53–54
Customer, 1, 6

D

Damages, 208
Day book, 117
Deceased person's property transfer, 110
Declaration, 63–64
Deed(s)
    delivery of, 213
    in lieu of foreclosure, 151, 154
    of conveyance, 59–60, 105–106
    restrictions/covenants for, 54, 197
    types of, 106
Defaults, 85
Deficiency judgment, 153, 154–155
Deposit money, 84
Designated agency/broker, 2, 3, 9
Development properties, 194–195
Diligent effort, 28, 135
Disclose, 2
    of material facts, 29
Disclosure
    licensee conduct and, 132–138
    of agency, 30
    of agency representation, 10
    of interest in property, 29
    of nonmaterial facts, 29–30
    of off-site conditions, 30, 87, 222
    of property condition, 30, 86–87
    of sales price, 30
Discriminatory housing practices, 204–205
Dispose, 198
Divorce, 60
Dower, 53–54
Drywall, 220
Dual agency, 2, 8

Dual Agency Consent Agreement, 8–9, 18
Dual Agency/ Designated Agency Disclosure
    Notice and Consent Agreement, 12
Dual Agency/Designated Agency Notice and
    Consent Agreement, 9, 19–20
Dwelling, 204–205

E

Easement
    acquisition of, 56
    by prescription, 53–55
Economic information sources, 239
Education
    information sources for, 236
    of appraiser, 180–182
    of broker/salesperson, 126
Ejection, 153, 169
Electronic communications, 135
Electronic contracts, 81
Electronic records, 249–250
Electronic Records and Signature in Commerce
    Act (E-sign), 249–250, 252
Electronic signatures, 248–253
E-mail notification registry, 179
Eminent domain, 199
Engaging in the real estate business, 125
Engineering
    information sources for, 240
Environmental issues information sources, 240
Escheat, 111
Escrow
    accounts for, 84, 138
    agreements for, 85
    closing in, 213, 215
Establishment, 222
Eviction of elderly, blind or disabled, 170
Examination
    content of, 129
    written, 127–128
Exclusive Agency Right to Represent Buyer or
    Tenant Authorization, 45–47
Exclusive-Agency Right to Sell, 36–38
Exclusive agreements
    agency right to represent buyer, 26
    obligations, 28
    right to represent buyer, 26
Exclusive Right to Represent Buyer or Tenant
    Authorization, 42–44
Exclusive-Right-to-Sell Listing Contract,
    33–35
Executor deed, 106
Exempted properties, 74
Experience, 127

F

Face-to-face closing, 213, 215
Fair housing, 29, 138, 202–203
    administrative enforcement of, 207–209
    exceptions to, 206–207
    information sources for, 238
Fair rent commission, 170
Fair Rent Commission Information, 171
Familial status/family, 54, 206
Farm land, 74, 109
Feasible alternative, 192
Federal Civil Rights Act, Title VIII, 202

Federal Financial Institutions Examination Council
  Appraisal Subcommittee, 182
Federal Interstate Land Sales Full Disclosure Act, 198
Federal Section 8 Housing Payment Assistance Program, 155
Felony, 165
FHA loans, 156
Fiduciary duties/responsibilities, 1–2, 7–8
Fiduciary Powers Act, 61
Financial report, 230
Financial services, 155
Financing, 214
Fines, 231
Floating rate, 162
Foam, 220
Foreclosure
  by sale, 153, 154
  certificates of, 152
  modification of, 152
  rescue services for, 150
Foreclosure Mediation Program, 153–154
Forests, 74, 109
Fraud, 151

G

Graduated payment mortgage, 157
Grand List, 73
Grantee/grantor, 106
  indexes, 117
Groundwater contamination, 220–221
Growing equity mortgage, 157

H

Hazardous waste, 221–222
Hazardous waste notice, 224
Homebuyer mortgage program, 156
Home improvement
  contract for, 196
  contractors for, 196–197
Home Improvement Guaranty Fund, 188, 197
Home Investment Partnerships Program, 155
Home Mortgage Disclosure Act, 157, 158
Homeownership program, 156
Homestead property, 54
Housing
  information sources for, 238
  programs for, 155
Housing and Urban Development
  Secretary of U.S. Department of, 207
Hubbard Clause Contract Addendum, 84, 97–98
Hunting properties, 134

I

Implied warranty, 195
Independent contractor, 4
Industrial construction, 197
In-house sale documents, 12
Inland wetlands, 191–192
Inspections, 214, 219
Interest in property, 29, 132
  disclosure of, 133
Interest on deposits, 138

Internet advertising, 31, 135
Interstate land sales, 198
Intestate distribution, 110–111
Irrevocable consent to suit, 130

J

Joint tenancy, 110
  with right of survivorship, 59, 60
Judgment liens, 77

L

Landlord
  abandonment by tenant and, 166
  absentee, 170
  action against to enforce responsibilities, 167–168
  actions by, 166
  obligations of, 164–165
  recourse for, 165–166
  right to enter, 163–164
  rules of, 163
  supplying essential services, 167
Landlord and Tenant Act, 161–168
Land records, 116
Land surveyors, 70
Land Trust Alliance, 57
Land use, 188
Lawful source of income, 206
Lead-based paint, 219
Leasehold estates, 161
Leases, 85, 160–161
  for common interest units, 62
  information sources for, 238
  provisions of, 161–162
Legal advice, 141
Legal information sources, 237
License, 56, 123
  activities requiring, 124–126
  application for, 126
  broker affiliation change and, 131–132
  continuing education and, 131
  exemptions from, 125–126
  fees for, 124
  grounds for refusal of, 128, 130
  information sources for, 236
  issuance of, 128
  of appraiser, 179
  of corporations, other entities, 130
  of mortgage broker, 149
  of nonresidents, 130
  procedure for, 126–130
  renewal of, 131
  requirements for, 127
  state law for, 2–5
  suspension, revocation of, 139–140, 141
Licensee
  conduct of, 132, 134–138
  fair housing and, 207
Light and air easement, 55
Limited liability company, 61–62
Limited partnerships, 61
Lis pendens, 151
Listing Agreement, 12
Listing agreements, 25–26, 83
  content of, 27–28
Local zoning officer, 189

M

Management services, 63
Marital status, 206
Marketable record title, 120
Marketable Record Title Act, 120
Market value, 73, 74, 75
Material facts, 29, 132
Mechanics' liens, 77
Metes-and-bounds description, 68–70
Mills, 75
Misdemeanor, 165
Modified title theory state, 147
Mold, 220
Money handling, 138
Monuments, 69
Mortage broker
  license for, 149
Mortgage, 147
  contingency for, 84
  deed/note for, 106, 147–149
  foreclosure and, 151–155
  fund sources for, 155–156
  information sources for, 239
  lenders/originators of, 141–142
  release of, 148–149
Mortgage broker, 141–142
Mortgage brokerage, 149–151
  service fees of, 16
Mortgage brokers
  license verification for, 158
Mortgage lenders, 141–142
Mortgage originators, 141–142
  license for, 149
Multiple listing service, 205
Municipalities, 112
  conveyance tax of, 77, 106, 107, 108
  information and records of, 237
  land records of, 115
  web sites of, 199

N

Name change, 117
National Appraisal Registry, 186
National Association of Realtors® (NAR), 10
Native American land claims, 120
Negotiable compensation, 11
Net listings, 28
New Haven Commission on Equal Opportunities, 207
New home construction, 195–196
New Home Construction Guaranty Fund, 188, 196
Nonmaterial facts, 29–30, 132, 134, 209
Nonresident
  appraiser as, 183–184
  broker agreements, 136
  landlord registration for, 170
  license of, 130
Nonresident licensing, 4–5
North v. Belden, 116
Note, 147
Notice of Commission Rights, 15, 22
Notice of lease, 160
Notice to Quit, 168
Notification registry, 132

O

Offer and acceptance, 83
Offers, 135–136
Off-site conditions, 30, 87, 134, 222
Older person housing, 207
Open Listing Agreement, 39–41
Open right to represent buyer, 26
Open Right to Represent Buyer Authorization, 48–50
Open-space land, 74, 109, 191
Order of descent, 110
Out-of-state broker agreements, 136

P

Parker v. Griswold, 56
Partitions, 60
Partnerships, 61
Party
    capacity of, 82–83
    signatures of, 84
Penalty conveyance tax, 109
Percentages, 242–245
Person, 125
Personal assistants, 126
Personal effects, 169
Personal property, 84
Planned community, 62
Planned unit developments (PUDs), 62, 190
Planning, 188, 190–191
Plan of development, 190
Plot/plan mortgage survey, 193
Pollutant discharge, 221
Possession, 153
Preapproved forms, 82
Predatory lending, 151, 158
Prelicensing educational requirement, 124
Premises
    destruction of, 85
Preservation restriction, 54
Principal, 1
Priority of liens, 77
Private land-use control, 197
Private lawsuit, 207
Probate court, 54
Property
    abandonment of, 166
    condition report for, 30, 81, 134
    damage, destruction of, 167
    identification of, 82
    possession of, 153
    specific information on, 237
    transfer of, 222
Property taxes, 73–76
    calculation of, 75
    liens of, 76
    payment for, 75–76, 216
    percentages for, 243
    prorations of, 246–247
Prorations, 216, 245–247
Prospectus, 232, 233
Protected classes, 203–204
Provisional licensed appraiser, 180, 182, 184–185
Prudent alternative, 192
PSI, 142
Public accommodations law, 209
Public Health Commissioner, 132

Public hearing, 208
Public Land Survey, 70
Public offering statement, 64
Punitive damages, 208
Purchase and Sale Agreement, 84, 88–93
Purchase and sale agreements/contracts, 81, 83–85
Purchase price
    based on conveyance tax, 108
    based on conveyance tax percentages, 245
Purchaser's lien, 77

Q

Question of fact, 55
Quiet title action, 109
Quitclaim deed, 106

R

Radon, 219–220
Real estate
    license for, 1
Real Estate Agency Disclosure Notice Given to Unrepresented Persons, 2, 10, 17
Real Estate Appraisal Commission, 180
Real estate broker, 125
Real Estate Guaranty Fund, 140–141
Real estate salesperson, 125
Real estate securities
    regulations on sale of, 228–229
    types of, 227–228
Real estate syndicate securities, 227, 228, 229, 232–234
Real property securities, 227, 228, 229
    dealers in, 142
Reasonable cause for payment, 11
Reasonable effort, 166
Reasonable time, 116
Reciprocal agreement, 4–5, 130
Recording, 116, 148
Record retention, 16, 31–32, 233
Rectangular surveys, 70
Redemption, 154
Referral fees, 15, 137
Regional planning Agencies, 193–194
Regulations, 2
Rehabilitation mortgage loan, 156
Rent receipt, 165
Resale
    certificate for, 64–65
    of units, 64–65
Research Guide to Connecticut Land Records, 121
Residential Lease, 172–175
Residential mortgage fraud, 151
Residential Property Condition Disclosure Form, 87
Residential Property Condition Disclosure Report, 84, 100–102
Residential real estate-related transactions, 205
Revaluation, 74
Reverse annuity mortgage, 157
Right to enter, 163–164
Riparian rights, 56

S

Sales agreement, 83
Salesperson, 1, 3, 125
    fair housing and, 210
    requirements for, 127
Sales price, 30
    disclosure of, 134
S corporations, 61–62
Security deposit, 162
    returning, 163
Security deposits
    interest on, 162–163
Seller
    information for, 87
    property condition disclosure by, 86–87
Seller Consent to Subagency, 12
Sex, 206
Sexual orientation, 206
Shooting properties, 134
Short sales, 150
Signature, 248–249
Signs, 31, 135
Single agency, 8
Sliding scale fees, 232–233
Sooperatives, 62
Special permits/exceptions, 190
Special taxes
    assessments, 75
Sponsoring broker, 3
Standard Metropolitan Statistical Area (SMSA), 157
Status change, 117
Statute of frauds, 249
Statutory year, 245–246
Stay of execution, 169
Strict foreclosure, 151–152, 154–155
Subagency, 10–11
Subdivision plan, 192
Subdivisions, 191
Summary process, 168–170
    by other than landlord, 169

T

Targeted investment communities, 107
Tax
    abatement of, 74
    bill issuance for, 76
    collector deed for, 106
    relief of, 74
Tenancy in common, 60
Tenant
    obligations of, 165
    protection against retaliatory action for, 166
    recourse for, 166–168
Tidal Wetlands Program, 192
Time Share Act, 66
Title
    evidence of, 117–120
    insurance for, 119
    records of, 115–117
    search for, 117–118
Torrens land registration system, 120
Town mill rates, 78
Transaction documentation, 241
Trust account, 84, 138
Trusts, 61

U

Underground Storage Tank Petroleum Fund, 221
Underground storage tanks, 221
Uniform Electronic Transactions Act (UETA), 250–252
Uniform Limited Partnership Act, 61
Uniform Partnership Act, 61
Uniform Standards of Professional Appraisal Practice (USPAP), 180, 182–183, 186
Unlawful occupancy, 164–165
Unlicensed personnel, 4
Unrepresented persons, 10
Urea-formaldehyde foam insulation (UFFI), 220
Use of Unlicensed Persons by Licensees, 4–5
Usury, 148

V

VA loans, 156
Variable-rate mortgage, 157
Variances, 189–190
Village districts, 190
Vision Appraisal, 121

W

Walk-through inspection, 214
Warranty deed, 106
Waste disposal sites, 222
Water
    diversion of, 221
    rights to, 56
    wells of, 220–221
Wills, 110

Written agreements
    contracts, 6
Written agreements/contracts, 2, 82

Z

Zoning, 188–190
    board of appeals for, 189–190
    commission for, 191

Notes

Notes